human resource management in libraries

THEORY AND PRACTICE

RICHARD E. RUBIN

NEAL-SCHUMAN PUBLISHERS, INC.
NEW YORK   LONDON

Z
682
·R83
1991

Published by Neal-Schuman Publishers, Inc.
23 Leonard Street
New York, NY 10013

Printed and bound in the United States of America

Library of Congress Cataloging-in-Publication Data
   Human resource management in libraries : theory and practice /
Richard E. Rubin.
     p.   cm.
   Includes index.
   ISBN 1-55570-087-X
   1. Library personnel management.   I. Title.
Z682.R83 1991
O23'.9--dc20   91-12670
                                                          CIP

Table of Contents

Preface

The library workplace is becoming increasingly complicated and so are the demands on the human resource manager. These demands come from many sources: library workers, who expect good salaries, benefits, and working conditions; library patrons, who want and expect competent, courteous, and efficient service; and library board members, who expect all personnel practices to be conducted in a legal and fiscally responsible manner. In addition, the development of new technologies is dramatically changing not only the library work environment but the organizational structure and skills needed by library workers.

Unfortunately there are no simple recipes for dealing with people, and no individual can possess all the necessary knowledge. *Human Resource Management in Libraries* is intended as a useful source of information and guidance on human resource management for library managers, administrators, other interested professionals, and students. It is written primarily for the manager from a management perspective; but it also accepts, as a fundamental principle, that the employee must be respected as a worker and as a person. This book is not a legal text, and although legal issues are discussed, readers are cautioned that whenever the potential for legal liabilities arises, the employer should seek competent legal counsel.

The term *human resource management* (HRM) is relatively new, even in business and industry; its popularity grew in the 1970s. As a term, it is rarely used in libraries or in the library literature. This is not to say that the activities involved in human resource management are new to libraries or other public employers; it has been part of American management since the turn of the century. The human resource manager must have a sound background in the development and administration of personnel policies and procedures; but managing people also entails an understanding of the psychological and sociological forces that affect worker attitudes and performance. The library work force is heterogeneous, containing individuals of varying ages, levels of education, career expectations, personalities, and needs. The human resource manager must understand how these factors interact in the workplace.

Of particular importance for library managers is recognizing the critical role of female professionals in librarianship. For this reason, this book focuses special attention on the factors that affect the performance and treatment of women.

The manager's knowledge of how to deal with employees must not be based solely on personal experience and anecdotal information. Such knowledge, although valuable, does not take advantage of a vast body of research on human resource management. A concerted effort has been made to integrate research findings that have been reported in the library, management, and psychosocial literature on the creation, administration, and effects of personnel practices.

Chapter 1 presents the context in which human resource management in libraries exists. It includes a discussion of the duties of the human resource manager, the characteristics of the library labor force, and the laws and regulations that affect human resource administration. The central section of the book—Chapters 2 through 6—is arranged by personnel processes: hiring, evaluating, dealing with problem employees, wage and salary administration, and collective bargaining. Following the discussion of these activities, Chapter 7 focuses on human factors in the workplace including a discussion of job satisfaction, worker motivation, and commitment. The final chapter deals with a subject that is seldom discussed in library literature—employee turnover. Particular attention is paid to the causes of turnover, its advantages and disadvantages, and how turnover can be measured and controlled.

The library manager is facing ever-increasing challenges, and the volume of knowledge required to perform effectively is overwhelming. Human resource management is only one aspect of management, but its importance cannot be overstated: done well, the health of an organization is substantially improved; done poorly, the essential functions of the library are seriously impaired.

Acknowledgments

I could not have completed *Human Resource Management in Libraries* without the assistance of several individuals. The efforts of graduate assistants Deanne Morgan, Daniel Mack, and Thomas Marlatt were especially helpful. I thank Norman Holman, who reviewed the chapter on collective bargaining, for his comments.

I am especially indebted to my wife, Marcia, whose editorial assistance proved invaluable, and to my daughter, Rachel, who accepted patiently her father's preoccupation with completing this book.

1
Human Resource Management in Libraries

There are few library functions that do not require people to execute them; there are few library goals that can be satisfied without the cooperation and support of the staff. The human resource manager has a special responsibility to direct the library work force so that the library can accomplish what it is meant to do. Discharging this responsibility requires the manager to understand two basic ideas: that people are different and that people make a difference.

PEOPLE ARE DIFFERENT

There are no simple formulas or recipes for dealing with people. It would be wonderful if behavioral scientists, psychologists, and geneticists could tell us exactly what to do in order to make our employees work harder and be happy. Certainly there are some generalizations that are helpful, but there remains a considerable residue of human unpredictability which the manager of people must accept.

It is easy to see human resource management as the creation of rules, regulations, and procedures. Certainly, these are necessary parts of any personnel program, but it can be deceiving if one thinks that once these rules have been created, people will manage themselves. People don't fit neatly into categories; rules don't always neatly apply, nor do they always have predictable effects on the people to whom they are applied. The appearance of order through regulation is not the same as managing people; it is only one aspect of the human resource manager's responsibility. Managing people always requires understanding them as individuals, and adapting to their particular wants and needs.

PEOPLE MAKE A DIFFERENCE

Employees have a profound effect on how the library operates and how it is perceived in the community. These effects occur on at least four different levels: the individual, the social, the organizational, and the environmental (Figure 1-1).

FIGURE 1-1.

THE EFFECTS OF THE INDIVIDUAL
ON FOUR LEVELS OF THE ORGANIZATION

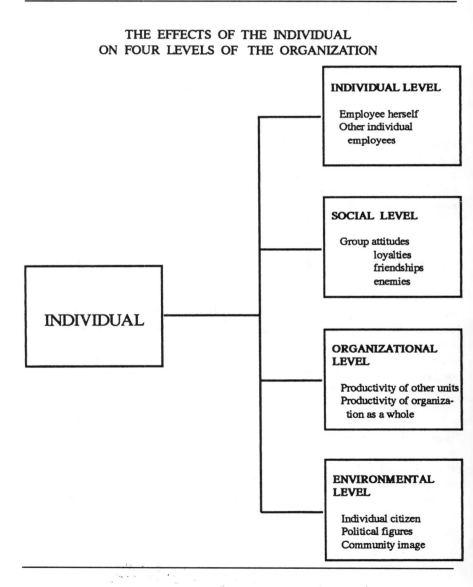

INDIVIDUAL LEVEL

Employee herself
Other individual
    employees

SOCIAL LEVEL

Group attitudes
    loyalties
    friendships
    enemies

INDIVIDUAL

ORGANIZATIONAL
LEVEL

Productivity of other units
Productivity of organiza-
    tion as a whole

ENVIRONMENTAL
LEVEL

Individual citizen
Political figures
Community image

Individual Level

On the individual level, employees perform particular tasks or sets of tasks. These sets of tasks play their own special role in the accomplishment of the organization's goals. If employees fail to play their part, then other parts of the organization will be affected. The ability or inability of individuals to perform successfully may affect both their attitudes toward themselves and toward the organization.

Individuals also affect other individuals. There can be little doubt, for example, that if an employee has a poor attitude, he or she can affect the attitude of other individuals. Similarly, it is quite common in libraries for the work of one individual to rely on the work of others. Therefore, the performance of one individual affects the performance of others. The implications are significant: single individuals can affect the attitude and performance of others, which can have a profound effect on organizational performance.

Social Level

In any organization that involves people, one quickly discovers that people are not simply separate cogs performing their jobs in social isolation. On the contrary, people in organizations develop social bonds: friendships are made, loyalties formed, enemies discovered. Organizations are composed of social clusters within which communication networks and social supports develop. The members of these groups can and often do act in a coordinated fashion with the potential for substantial impact both positive and negative.

Organizational Level

It goes without saying that employees' performance affects the accomplishment of organizational goals. For libraries, most employees are part of a complex network of interrelated functions. The failure of one or more people has a ripple effect that may damage not only the productivity but the morale of the organization as a whole.

Environmental Level

Employees also have influence outside the library. A library with outstanding employees may create in the public's perception a positive image which in turn can enhance the political and financial condition of the library. Poorly performing employees may have the opposite effect, producing angry patrons and unhappy politicians. Each library worker must be perceived as having the capacity to influence the sensitive environment in which the library must operate.

THE LIBRARY WORK FORCE

Libraries generally employ many different kinds of people performing widely different functions and requiring different levels of skill, education, and experience. Consequently, the library draws from a varied labor pool: from professional personnel to custodial, from administrators to student assistants. Sound personnel management requires understanding the characteristics of this work force.

Data on the library work force are sparse, and multiple sources must be consulted. The information here should be considered estimates, rather than definitive.

The general labor force of library workers has been estimated by the Office for Research (OFR) of the American Library Association (ALA) to be 341,108 as of 1985. Of this total, 137,695 are librarians (40%), 15,065 (5%) are other professionals; and 188,348 (55%) are support staff (Table 1-1).[1]

TABLE 1-1. Composition of the Total Library Work Force by Type of Library.

Category	(C%)*	All Staff N*	(R%)*	(C%)	Professional N	(R%)	(C%)	Other N	(R%)
Academic	(26)	88,568	(100)	(14)	21,919	(25)	(35)	66,649	(75)
Public	(27)	92,178	(100)	(24)	37,570	(41)	(29)	54,608	(59)
School									
Public	(28)	96,324	(100)	(39)	59,467	(61)	(20)	36,857	(39)
Private	(05)	16,628	(100)	(06)	8,924	(53)	(04)	7,704	(46)
Special	(14)	47,410	(100)	(16)	24,880	(52)	(12)	22,530	(48)
Total		341,108	(100)		152,760	(45)		188,348	(55)

*   C=Column; R=Row; N=Number.

Table compiled from data in: Mary Jo Lynch, Libraries in an Information Society: A Statistical Summary, *Chicago: ALA, 1987.*

Data from the National Center for Education Statistics (NCES), collected by King Research for 1982, report a slightly lower figure; total employment in libraries is slightly over 307,000, but this figure represents the number of library *positions* expressed as full-time equivalents. When the NCES data are broken down by type of position, the results are similar to OFR data: approximately 44% (136,120) of the work force being librarians, 5% other professionals, and 51% support staff.[2] Interestingly, the ALA data suggest that academic libraries rely more heavily on support staff than any other type; nearly 75% of the work force consisting of support staff.

In terms of the total work force, ALA estimates suggest that approximately the same number of people work in public and academic libraries; the school work force is somewhat larger, and the special library work force about half that of publics or academics. The NCES data on the relative representation of professionals by type of library are quite similar: 48% of the librarians work in school libraries, 23% in public, 15% in academic, and 14% in special.[3] It should be noted that although school libraries employ the most professionals, more than 40% of them do not have a master of library science degree, but rather a B.A. in library science or school library certification.[4]

Outlook for Growth

Data collected by the Bureau of Labor Statistics (BLS) (Table 1-2) also place the work force of librarians at 136,000, but this is a 1986 estimate.[5] There is little current indication of over or under supply; the BLS reports that unemployment rates for librarians are low compared to the general labor market and average when compared to professions requiring at least a four-year college degree.[6] The outlook for growth in the number of library positions is, however, not optimistic. The BLS projects growth of 13.4% in the library labor force by the year 2000. This rate is similar to the projected growth of secondary school teachers (13.4%), but when compared to other growth rates in professional occupations that require at least a four-year college degree, the library growth rate is considered very low.[7] For example, employment growth for social workers is projected as 32.7%.[8] This slow projected growth is consistent with NCES data; in 1978, the number of librarian positions expressed as full-time equivalents was 126,420; this figure rose to 136,120 in 1982, a growth of only 7.6% over a four-year period. In all but special libraries, the growth has averaged about 1% a year. Special libraries have grown faster, but only at a 4% rate per year.[9] Although strong growth is not anticipated, library unemployment rates remain quite low ranging from 3.7% to less than 1%.[10]

The library work force is one component in the broader category of information professionals: educators, researchers, computer analysts and programmers, and other providers of information services (Table 1-3). One estimate places the number of information professionals at 1.64 million; it is estimated that librarians comprise only 10% of this total population. Among information professionals, computer workers form the largest group with 42%.[11] Most of them are employed in industry (71%), while a much smaller percentage is employed in state and local (22%) and federal government (5%).[12] An examination of growth rates suggest that the field of information professionals is

TABLE 1-2. General Work Force of Librarians 1986 and Projected 2000 (in thousands)

	1986	2000	% Change	Sep.* Rate	% p.t*	Ages			% F*	% B*
						16-24	25-54	55+		
	136	155	13.5	13.2	25.2	8.1	71.4	20.5	85.9	7.5
Library Asst.s	102	114	11.8	27.4	59.4	43.4	43.5	13.2	76.0	13.1
Technical Asst.s	51	57	12.9	—	—	—	—	—	—	—
Secondary teachers	1128	1280	13.4	9.1	9.5	3.7	85.5	10.7	54.9	7.8
Teachers (all)	1702	2066	21.3	12.4	14.7	6.6	84.8	8.6	87.9	11.4
Social Workers	365	485	32.7	10.1	9.8	7.1	83.5	9.4	65.0	17.8

*Sep. Rate: Separation Rate; p.t.: part-time; F: Female; B: Black.

Source: Bureau of Labor Statistics, Occupational Projections and Training Data, *A Statistical and Research Supplement to the 1988-89* Occupational Outlook Handbook, *Bulletin 2301. Washington D.C.: U.S. GPO, April 1988.*

growing at a much faster rate than that of librarians (Table 1-3) with rates of more than 70% in some specialties.

The growth of the information profession coupled with a leveling off for librarians suggests that new forces for change, such as technological developments, will continue to influence how HRM is administered in libraries. Clearly, as change occurs at increasingly rapid rates, the need to monitor work force conditions will grow.

Demographic Composition

Age

Data on the age distribution of librarians (Table 1-2) reveal that few are under 25, and a large percentage are between 25 and 54. This is reasonable since approximately 70% of librarians earn a master's degree or school library certification, therefore few would graduate before the age of 23. This pattern is similar to that in other predominantly female professions, such as teaching and social work. Interestingly, librarians

TABLE 1-3. Work Force of Selected Information Professionals for 1986
Projected to the Year 2000

	1986	2000	% Change	Sep.* Rate	%* p.t.	Ages 16-24	25-54	55+	% F*	% B*
Computer programer	479	813	+69.9	11.4	6.7	20.9	76.4	2.7	34.0	5.9
Systems analysts	331	582	+75.6	8.2	4.4	9.6	86.7	3.7	34.4	6.6
Medical records technicians	40	70	+75.0	12.8	13.6	18.5	66.9	14.6	93.3	16.0
Computer operators	309	457	+47.7	15.4	11.8	26.8	67.1	6.1	68.5	14.0

*Sep. Rate: Separation Rate; p.t.: part-time; F:Female; B: Black.

Source: Bureau of Labor Statistics, Occupational Projections and Training Data, *A Statistical and Research Supplement to the 1988-89* Occupational Outlook Handbook, *Bulletin 2301, Washington, D.C.: U.S. G.P.O., April 1988.*

appear to have a somewhat larger percentage of workers who remain at work beyond the age of 55.

Gender and Race

It is, of course, no surprise to find that a large proportion of the library work force is female. The numerical predominance of women has been a characteristic of the profession for years. Schiller reports that the percentage of women has fluctuated between 75% and 91% since 1900.[13] The BLS (Table 1-2) reports an 85:15% ratio in favor of women among librarians. A 1985 estimate by the Office for Library Personnel Resources (OLPR) of ALA based on a survey of academic and public libraries, is somewhat lower: 75:25%.[14] According to the data, (Table 1-4) the public library work force has a substantially greater percentage of women (80%) than the academic library work force (66%).[15]

For black librarians, the BLS data (Table 1-2) suggest a pattern quite similar to other professions, with representation (7.5%) far below that in the general population. These data are confirmed by the OLPR (Table 1-4) which gives 6% as the figure for black librarians in public

TABLE 1-4. Distribution of Total Work Force by Racial/Ethnic/Sexual/Group for Librarians in Academic and Public Libraries

		ACADEMIC		PUBLIC		TOTAL	
		NUMBER	PERCENT	NUMBER	PERCENT	NUMBER	PERCENT
AMERICAN INDIAN/ ALASKAN NATIVE·	F	10	0.1	20	0.2	30	0.2
	M	5	0.1	7	0.1	12	0.1
	T	15	0.2	27	0.2	42	0.2
ASIAN/ PACIFIC ISLANDER	F	214	3.2	283	2.3	497	2.6
	M	91	1.3	51	0.4	142	0.8
	T	305	4.5	334	2.8	639	3.4
BLACK	F	218	3.2	756	6.2	974	5.2
	M	56	0.8	119	1.0	175	0.9
	T	274	4.1	875	7.2	1149	6.1
HISPANIC	F	61	0.9	162	1.3	223	1.2
	M	37	0.5	77	0.6	114	0.6
	T	98	1.5	239	2.0	337	1.8
WHITE	F	3943	58.4	8504	70.1	12447	65.9
	M	2115	31.3	2153	17.7	4268	22.6
	T	6058	89.7	10657	87.8	16715	88.5
TOTAL	F	4446	65.9	9725	80.2	14171	75.1
	M	2304	34.1	2407	19.8	4711	24.9
	T	6750	100.0	12132	100.0	18882	100.0

Reproduced with permission of the American Library Association, Academic and Public Librarians: Data by Race, Ethnicity, and Sex, *project director Jeniece Guy, p. 7; copyright © 1986 ALA.*

and academic libraries. Again, it is the public libraries that employ the most blacks (7.2% compared to 4.1% for academics).[16] The pattern of larger percentages of women and blacks working in public libraries may, in part, be accounted for by the fact that public libraries generally require less formal education.[17]

Of special interest when addressing affirmative action issues is the distribution of librarians analyzed by level of position. Both blacks and women are under-represented in administrative positions (Table 1-5). Women comprise 80% of the public library work force, but only 67% of administrators; in academic libraries, women comprise 66% of the total work force, but 48% of the administrators. Interestingly, OLPR data report that middle management positions are more evenly distributed between sexes, suggesting that the major impediments to mobility are related to gaining top administrative posts.[18] Overall, job segregation by race and sex is still significant in the library profession, and rapid improvement is not likely. Comparing the 1986 OLPR study with one conducted in 1980 led OLPR to conclude that a generally static condition persists in the library work force.[19]

Another interesting factor to examine is why women leave and reenter the library work force. BLS considers the rate at which librarians leave the profession to be "very high."[20] Studies suggest that a substantial majority of female librarians leave for family reasons including marriage, pregnancy and child care.[21] Disturbingly, only a small percentage of those who leave, return to the workplace. Dickson's study of reentrants found that only 16% returned or attempted to return to library work. Among the barriers to reentry were geographical constraints, lack of jobs, low salaries, lack of part-time work and lack of flexible scheduling.[22] About half of those who left would have stayed if they could have secured part-time positions.[23]

Part-time employment appears to be extremely important for the library labor force. BLS data reveal a comparatively high percentage of workers who are voluntarily employed part-time.[24] Because women often require part-time rather than full-time employment in order to fulfill family obligations, it is logical that part-time workers form a larger percentage of the library work force than that of other occupations. But it also appears that even more part-time work would increase the number of female reentrants.

Before leaving this topic, it is important to note that although most women who *leave the work force* leave for family related reasons, most women who leave their *positions* go to *other library positions*, just as their male counterparts do.[25] There is no evidence that turnover rates for women are higher than those for men among librarians, nor is there any evidence that they are less committed to library work.

HRM: DEFINITION AND DYNAMICS

The underlying purpose of human resource management is to encourage workers to accomplish the goals of the organization in the most effective way. Over the years HRM has grown in sophistication, technique, and purpose, but it retains its focus on the *human* aspect of organizations. HRM's importance is especially great in labor-intensive organizations like libraries where the essential functions of the organization are dependent on humans.

TABLE 1-5. Sexual Distribution of each Racial/Ethnic Group for Directors, Deputy, Associate and Assistant Directors in Academic and Public Libraries

		ACADEMIC NUMBER	ACADEMIC PERCENT	PUBLIC NUMBER	PUBLIC PERCENT	TOTAL NUMBER	TOTAL PERCENT
AMERICAN INDIAN/ ALASKAN NATIVE	F	2	66.7	5	71.4	7	70.0
	M	1	33.3	2	28.6	3	30.0
	T	3	100.0	7	100.0	10	100.0
ASIAN/ PACIFIC ISLANDER	F	6	42.9	10	83.3	16	61.5
	M	8	57.1	2	16.7	10	38.5
	T	14	100.0	12	100.0	26	100.0
BLACK	F	32	84.2	29	69.0	61	76.3
	M	6	15.8	13	31.0	19	23.8
	T	38	100.0	42	100.0	80	100.0
HISPANIC	F	4	80.0	9	47.4	13	54.2
	M	1	20.0	10	52.6	11	45.8
	T	5	100.0	19	100.0	24	100.0
WHITE	F	405	46.5	762	67.4	1167	58.3
	M	466	53.5	369	32.6	835	41.7
	T	871	100.0	1131	100.0	2002	100.0
TOTAL	F	449	48.2	815	67.3	1264	59.0
	M	482	51.8	396	32.7	878	41.0
	T	931	100.0	1211	100.0	2142	100.0

Personnel management in the public library sector has generally been unsystematic, perhaps because there are many libraries too small to justify appointing someone to deal solely with personnel issues. Few libraries have the money, staff, or facilities to develop sophisticated human resource programs. The result has been that HRM too often is dealt with as a secondary or tertiary function; its duties assigned to someone with other important responsibilities to fulfill.

The responsibilities of HRM in libraries are broad and various (Figure 1-2). Among the functions of HRM are:

1. Recruiting and Hiring Staff

A vital function of HRM is ensuring that there is an adequate pool of qualified applicants for library positions, and that the most qualified applicants are identified, interviewed and selected. The human resource manager must develop and maintain effective systems of recruitment, screening, and interviewing. This means making sure that interviewers conduct interviews in a lawful fashion, and that the decision-making processes focus on prospective workers' ability to perform a specific job, rather than on extraneous considerations. Similarly, the monitoring process includes controlling the formal offer to hire so that incorrect or inappropriate promises or statements are avoided.

2. Orienting, Training, and Developing Staff

The orientation and training period for a new employee is critical to developing employee commitment; failure to handle this early stage properly can significantly affect an employee's future attitude and performance. The human resource manager is responsible for creating a system that acquaints employees with their job tasks, the policies and procedures of the organization, information on future opportunities, and the larger goals of the organization. HRM also encompasses designing programs to identify and develop the skills of current employees. Rapid changes in the workplace, rising employee expectations, the need to identify and reward good performance and to improve marginal performance, all highlight the need for effective staff training and development programs.

3. Evaluating Staff

It is crucial to identify both good and poor performers. The human resource manager must develop, implement, and monitor the system used to evaluate employees. HRM helps ensure that employees understand the evaluation system, that job standards are job-related and realistic, that supervisors are adequately trained to conduct reviews, and that unlawful discrimination is avoided.

FIGURE 1-2. The Functions of Human Resource Management

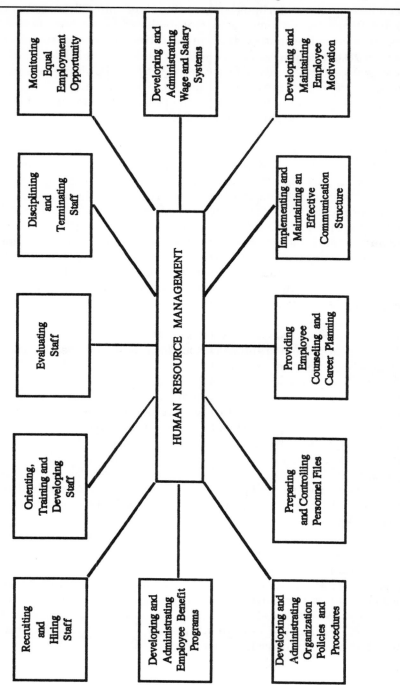

4. Disciplining and Terminating Staff

An especially delicate area of employee relations involves attempts to correct employee behavior or remove employees. The potential costs in time, legal expenses, and stress for all involved make this an important area of HRM. The manager must not only make sure that discipline and termination policies are lawful and clear, but that training and control are exercised over supervisors. Disciplinary meetings, grievance procedures, and related actions all must be carefully monitored and administered so employees are treated fairly.

5. Monitoring Equal Employment Opportunity and Other Labor Laws

Given the current litigious climate, the need to closely examine all personnel actions is mandatory. Hiring, job assignments, performance evaluation, disciplinary actions, employee benefits, and unionization, are just some of the areas an employer must watch for discrimination or unfair labor practices. The need to develop a monitoring system, as well as training programs for supervisors, is a primary responsibility of HRM.

6. Developing and Implementing Wage and Salary Systems

The system by which employees are compensated and the resultant wage levels have a substantial impact on the ability of the organization to recruit and retain employees. The system must equitably compensate workers based on the level of their work, their years of experience, and the quality of their performance. It must be based on a sound job analysis, with jobs ordered in proper relation to each other. Salaries must be competitive in the market place and allocated without discrimination.

7. Developing and Administering Employee Benefit Programs

Administering employee benefits has become increasingly complex. Changes in the work force (e.g., increases in the number of women in the workplace), the development of alternative medical plans (e.g., HMOs), deferred compensation and pension plans, plans in which the employees select from a menu of benefits, combine to make this a challenging area for HRM. Government regulations and laws such as those for workers' compensation and unemployment benefits add to the administrative complexities.

8. Developing and Administering Organizational Policies and Procedures

The manager of human resources must be sure that the policies and procedures established for the organization are followed by staff members at all levels. This means developing clearly written policies, communicating these policies effectively, and enforcing them in a uniform and fair manner. Creating and administering policies that affect employees can have serious repercussions on costs and practices if done improperly. Personnel managers must be especially sensitive to legal restrictions such as legislation regarding maternity leave. In addition, certain topical issues are complicating policy making, such as policies on smoking, drug-testing, and AIDS testing in the workplace.

9. Preparing and Controlling Personnel Files

Various state and federal laws deal directly with both the protection of an individual's right to see their own files, (i.e. privacy acts) and the right of the public to view files (i.e. public records acts). The manager of human resources must create and implement policies that assure employee access, control the types and accuracy of materials placed in files, and protect the privacy of employees.

10. Providing Employee Counseling and Career Planning

An important part of working with employees is dealing with their professional and personal needs. Opportunities to discuss future opportunities or aspects of work that satisfy or dissatisfy a person can be helpful to both the employee and the organization. Discussing an employee's needs and goals can assist in preparing a career plan, and demonstrates the organization's commitment to the employee as an individual. From time to time, employees experience emotional or physical problems and at these times, they often need to talk. A sound human resources program provides open channels for communication so that employees can discuss sensitive matters without fear and with the prospect of assistance in resolving their problems.

11. Implementing and Maintaining an Effective Communication Structure

Well-run organizations invariably have an effective structure for communication throughout. HRM involves developing both a structure and an atmosphere so that employees feel comfortable transmitting information to any part of the organization. This involves an understanding and use of both formal and informal channels.

12. Developing and Maintaining Employee Motivation

Over the last two decades, there has been considerable research into the psychosocial aspects of workers. It has become clear that human motivation is not a simple phenomenon and that there are no easy formulas for increasing workers' motivation. HRM attempts to analyze those characteristics of the workplace that affect motivation and to apply knowledge about motivation directly to the workplace. This includes understanding the relationship of motivation to wage and salary, performance review systems, and supervisory behavior.

FACTORS INFLUENCING HRM

Contemporary management theory tells us that organizations exist in a manner similar to that of living organisms. Instead of a static and self-sufficient entity, the organization is viewed as constantly interacting, adapting, and countering threats from both inside and outside. This viewpoint, sometimes called an *organismic* or *open systems* approach, is quite useful when attempting to understand HRM. It is useful to examine both the internal and external factors that are affecting the labor market as a whole as well as libraries in particular (Figure 1-3).

Internal Factors

1. Attitude of Management

The kinds of HRM programs implemented, the amount of money spent, and human resources used depend on the commitment of management. One can tell a great deal about management's philosophy by examining personnel practices in such areas as hiring, employee evaluation, wages and benefits, and training and development.

2. Function of the Organization

Different types of organizations may require different HRM strategies and techniques. Libraries oriented to research may develop different recruiting, training, and decision-making strategies than libraries devoted to serving the general public.

3. Unionization

HRM policies and practices are profoundly affected by unions. In general, unions wish to bargain over areas central to HRM such as wages and benefits, training, promotion, employee discipline, and termination.

FIGURE 1-3. Factors Affecting HRM

HUMAN RESOURCE MANAGEMENT

EXTERNAL FACTORS

Aging of the work force

Increasing levels of schooling

Increasing numbers of women in the work force

New technologies

Emphasis on worker health

Increasing demand for satisfying work

Increasing legal protection

Available supply of workers

Funding sources

Competitors

Consumers

Increasing legal restrictions

INTERNAL FACTORS

Attitude of management

Function of the organization

Unionization

Type and number of workers

Adequacy of internal communications

4. Type and Number of Workers
HRM is affected by the composition of the work force, including employees' levels of education, age, sex, and years of experience. Librarianship tends to have better educated and older workers. In addition, it is numerically dominated by women in both the professional and support staff ranks. These factors present special challenges to the human resource manager because such workers tend to have higher expectations than workers with less education and experience.

5. Adequacy of Internal Communication
Effective communication structures are essential for HRM to work effectively. HRM depends on being able to disseminate and receive information from all parts of the organization. If communication lines are ineffective, distortions and distrust will make managing people extremely difficult.

External Factors

1. Aging of the Work Force
With the aging of the population born between 1945 and 1965, and the much lower birthrate that followed, it is inevitable that the work force will continue to age. Some estimates suggest that by the year 2000 the average age will be 45, compared to 32 in 1960.[26]

2. Increased Schooling
Individuals entering the work force are better educated than those leaving it. The employment demands of the better educated are greater than those with less education.[27] Given the fact that library employees are often better educated than most, library employers should anticipate greater and greater pressure for job enhancements and improvements in the quality of work life.

3. Increased Number of Women in the Work Force
The number of women in the work force has increased dramatically since 1945, especially working mothers with young children. This may substantially affect the types of benefits sought (e.g. child care) and scheduling (e.g. job sharing). In addition, increased numbers of women highlight the special responsibilities of the human resource manager to ensure that sex discrimination and sexual harassment are prevented.

4. New Technologies
For many years the effects of automation both good and bad have been prophesied. Certainly, the technological developments of the last decade, especially the microcomputer, are changing the workplace. Not

only are the skills required shifting, but so is the location of the workplace. With microcomputers and modems, employees are performing many work functions at home rather than on site. The new technologies also bring challenges in terms of potential health hazards, and the alienation and fear that frequently arise when they are introduced and replace familiar procedures.

5. Increased Emphasis on Worker Health

Workers' health has become an important consideration for employers. Maintaining employee health is expensive, but also cost effective. It is essential that human resource managers keep up with improved information on workplace health and health issues. These issues include the health effects of technology, health maintenance programs such as smoking cessation and weight reduction, and intervention services such as employee assistance programs.

6. Increased Demands by Workers for Satisfying Work

The days when employees were submissive to the will of the employer are long gone. Employees expect their employers to provide not only fair remuneration for work, but also a work environment that is stimulating and satisfying. This may involve opportunities for further education and training as well as greater decision-making authority. HRM requires a deep understanding not only of job satisfaction, but of human motivation and job commitment as well.

7. Available Supply of Workers

If an organization cannot recruit qualified employees for its essential functions then its survival is threatened. Some factors may be out of the library's control; for example, there may be few training or educational institutions producing qualified individuals (e.g. no library schools nearby). The geographic region may not be attractive to individuals whose skills are desired by the library. Unions can also affect the supply of workers through conditions in the union contract. Other factors may be directly under the library's control. For example, pay, benefits, and working conditions may serve either to attract or diminish a potential employee's interest in the library. In any case, the organization must concern itself with maintaining a pool of qualified individuals from the outside environment.

8. Funding Sources

Most libraries depend primarily on governmental bodies and the taxpayer for support. A large percentage of most library budgets consists of salaries and related labor costs. Funding sources must therefore be of special interest to the human resource manager.

9. Competitors

As the information industry expands, libraries may find that there is considerable competition for both fiscal and human resources. Competition for professional librarians already exists and is likely to persist in such sectors as publishing, information technology vendors, and industries requiring researchers and information managers. Competitors for support staff include private businesses, and government-funded agencies such as police, fire, and recreation departments, and schools. It is important to note that government agencies not only compete for human resources but also money. Such agencies may preempt funds needed for the library, especially for salaries.

10. Consumers

HRM must concern itself with the relationship of support staff to the patrons of the library. The taxpayer expects good service from the library. Poorly trained and supervised staff can irritate citizens with damaging consequences for the library.

11. Increased Legal Restrictions

It is most important for HRM to ensure that lawful personnel practices are followed. Various agencies that influence HRM activities are regulators of equal employment opportunity, labor-management relations, and immigration; and labor lawyers representing individuals bringing actions for wrongful discharge or unemployment compensation.

HRM: THE LEGAL CONTEXT

Almost all personnel decisions are in some way influenced by laws, government regulations, or judicial decisions. Certainly, the human resource manager must be concerned for a variety of reasons. Violations of the law, even if inadvertent, can be costly to the library. These costs arise from many sources including the costs of legal counsel, the costs of supervisor's and administrator's time in preparing for legal action, and the costs incurred should the library be found liable. There is also a cost in terms of loss of public image or professional reputation, if a legal action becomes public. This loss can occur regardless of the outcome of the case.

Unfortunately new laws and regulations, and novel judicial decisions, are being formulated all the time, and it is impossible for most library human resource managers to keep up with this plethora of information. For this reason, whenever dealing with issues that involve legal liabilities, the library should consult competent legal counsel. The laws that affect personnel decisions appear at all levels of government: federal, state and local. What follows is a brief description of the types of laws that affect HRM; it is not intended as a complete or detailed review.

Provisions of the U.S. Constitution

Various provisions of the U.S. Constitution have been applied to labor-management relations. These include the following:

The First Amendment

This amendment deals with the right of free speech and expression. Historically, it was thought that public employees gave up most of their First Amendment rights when they entered public service. This has been modified in recent years, and employers must take care not to infringe on the right of free expression unnecessarily. This is not to say that employees can say anything they wish, especially if it has the effect of interfering with the employer's ability to function, but it does mean that the employer must be cautious in restricting or regulating the speech of its employees.

The Fourteenth Amendment

This amendment gives citizens the right to *due process*. In terms of the workplace, the right to due process has been especially important when disciplinary actions are taken against employees. In such circumstances, the employee has a right to an orderly process in which all concerned parties are heard, and there is a right to review evidence and appeal decisions.

Federal Legislation and Regulations Preventing Employment Discrimination

These laws were designed to ensure the rights of specific groups, called protected classes. Protected classes are groups of individuals who have been the victims of past discrimination. These classes are generally defined as:

- Blacks: Persons of African descent as well as those from Jamaica, Trinidad, and the West Indies.
- Hispanics: Persons of Mexican, Puerto Rican, Cuban, Latin American, or Spanish descent.
- Native Americans: Persons who identify themselves or are known as such by virtue of tribal association, and Eskimos, Aleuts, or Alaskan natives.

- Asian Americans and Pacific Islanders: Persons of Japanese, Chinese, Korean, or Filipino descent.
- Veterans: Including Vietnam-era and disabled veterans.
- Handicapped employees: Including individuals with mental and physical disabilities, including AIDS.
- Persons Over the Age of 40.

Any member of these groups can charge an employer with discrimination. Employers must keep in mind that employers may be found to have practiced discrimination even when discriminatory intent is not found. In addition, charges of "reverse" discrimination have been leveled by individuals who are not members of these groups claiming that members of protected groups have unfairly received special treatment.

The Civil Rights Acts of 1866 and 1871 (42 U.S.C. 1981, 1983, 1985)

Although the best known civil rights legislation appeared in the 1960s with the passage of the Civil Rights Act of 1964, several acts, sometimes referred to as the Reconstruction Civil Rights Acts, were established after the Civil War. These acts give nonwhite citizens the power to seek remedies in court if they are deprived of their civil rights. These rights include those to form contracts, to own property, and to sue. These laws are particularly important to employment discrimination for two reasons:

- they provide constitutional protections to nonwhite citizens, who form a major constituency in employment discrimination cases, and
- they can be used in legal actions against state and local governments.

Employers must be cognizant of these laws for a variety of reasons, not the least of which is that the statute of limitations on such laws is not explicitly stated. In general, the statute of limitations is based on whatever each state's limitation is for personal injury. This is usually much longer than the time limit permitted under Title VII of the Civil Rights Act of 1964.[28] Hence, the employer's liability for discriminatory acts is extended.

Equal Pay Act of 1963

This act, which is an amendment to the Fair Labor Standards Act, prohibits discrimination in the payment of wages on the basis of sex, as long as the jobs require equal skill, effort, and responsibility, and are performed under similar working conditions (Appendix A-1). Defining skill, effort, and responsibility for a job can be a difficult task. The *skills* for a job generally include such factors as experience, ability, training, and education. Skills not required for the job are not considered when comparing the skills of men and women in similar positions. *Effort* concerns itself with the amount of physical or mental exertion required. *Responsibility* involves the job's obligations, and the extent to which employees are accountable for their work. *Working conditions* are concerned with two factors: surroundings and hazards. Surroundings involve environmental factors such as the presence of toxic fumes; hazards involve the potential for injuries in the workplace and their likely severity.

Even when skill, effort, responsibility, and working conditions are the same, the employer may still discriminate in pay between men and women if the differential is based on one of four conditions:

- if the employer has a merit system
- if there is a bona fide seniority system
- if payment of wages is measured by quantity or quality of production, and
- if pay is based on any factor other than sex.

Violation of the equal pay act can be expensive to the employer. If willful discrimination is found, criminal penalties can be imposed; otherwise, individuals who are found to be victims of wage discrimination can receive not only back pay, but also damages. In addition, employers cannot "remedy" the situation by reducing the wages of males who have been paid more; rather, the employer must increase the wages of females.

It should be kept in mind that the Equal Pay Act deals only with differences in pay by sex, and with jobs that are similar; this is in contrast to "comparable worth" cases, which deal with jobs that are essentially dissimilar. (See Chapter 6.)

The Civil Rights Act of 1964 and the Equal Employment Opportunity Act of 1972

The Civil Rights Act of 1964 (Appendix A-2) was intended to eliminate the problem of discrimination on the basis of race, color, religion, sex, and national origin. It focuses on private employers and employees of the federal government. The pertinent section of the Act for employers is Title VII dealing specifically with employers. It states in part:

Sec. 703
(a) It shall be an unlawful employment practice for an employer—
(1) to fail or refuse to hire or to discharge any individual or otherwise to discriminate against any individual with respect to his compensation,

terms, conditions, or privileges of employment, because of such individual's race, color, religion, sex, or national origin; or

(2) limit, segregate, or classify his employees or applicants for employment in any way which would deprive or tend to deprive any individual of employment opportunities or otherwise adversely affect his status as an employee, because of such individual's race, color, religion, sex, or national origin.

It is important to remember that the original civil rights act passed in 1964 attempted to deal with intentional discrimination against individuals. It was only later that the courts and legislature focused on employment practices that seemed to be neutral in regard to individuals, but which, in fact, had a discriminatory impact on minorities as groups. Although the act also created the Equal Employment Opportunity Commission (EEOC), attempts to make it an "enforcement" arm failed. Rather, its original function was to formulate regulations, provide interpretations of the law, and make attempts at conciliation. It is also interesting to note that the addition of "sex" to the bill was not the result of considered debate but of a last-minute compromise.

Unfortunately, although the 1964 Act was intended to solve the problems of discrimination, it became apparent that more needed to be done. Although literally thousands of discrimination cases were filed, a significant number were not being resolved satisfactorily. In addition, analyses of the labor market suggested that the job situation, especially for blacks and women, had not improved. These problems were in part attributed to the fact that the EEOC had few powers to act on behalf of the victims of discrimination. As a consequence, the Equal Employment Opportunity Act of 1972 was passed. This Act amended the 1964 Civil Rights Act and added several significant features to the law. First, it extended protection of the law to state and local government employees. Second, it gave the EEOC much broader powers. Now it could represent a complainant and sue the employer if it believed that discrimination had occurred.

The Civil Rights Act of 1991

At this writing, the Civil Rights Act of 1991 has been introduced into the federal legislature but has not yet been passed. This bill makes substantial modifications to present civil rights acts, and if passed, it will likely have a major impact on the way employers deal with equal employment opportunity issues. Civil rights supporters have many reasons for creating this legislation. Of primary concern is that current civil rights laws appear not to have accomplished their intention, which was to prevent job discrimination and create a work force that is representative of the population in general. In addition there is concern that recent court cases have tended to make it more difficult for victims of discrimination to bring and win discrimination suits. Ironically, these court decisions have concomitantly made it easier for whites to challenge affirmative action plans.

The current provisions of the new law could have a significant impact on public employers. It would place a greater burden on the employer to prove that it has not discriminated by requiring the employer to demonstrate that each consideration in the employment process is not only job related but also essential or indispensable. In addition it would permit the awarding of punitive and compensatory damages for acts of intentional discrimination especially against women, permit jury trials in discrimination cases, and restrict those who feel they have been adversely affected by affirmative action plans to challenge such plans.

Some believe that the law would produce at least two undesired consequences. First, there would be a significant increase in the number of court cases because attorneys would be more willing to take cases where monetary damages can be assessed. Second, because the burden of proof would be much greater for employers, employers would turn to quotas for minorities and women. This latter point is disputed by civil rights advocates. Nonetheless, because of the importance of this legislation, employers must follow its progress closely and consult with legal counsel concerning its implications.

Executive Order No. 11,246 (1965)

This order, issued by President Lyndon Johnson in 1965, was intended to prevent discrimination by federal contractors involving contracts of $10,000 or more. Both contractors and subcontractors are included. Among the obligations set forth in the law are:

1. that federal contractors may not discriminate on the basis of race, color, national origin, religion, or sex; and
2. that federal contractors are obligated to take *affirmative action* to ensure that employees and applicants are treated without regard to these factors.

This obligates employers to analyze their work force to determine whether its composition matches that of the general work force. If the contractor's work force is not representative, then it must establish numerical goals and timetables to correct the problem, and make an effort to meet these goals.[29]

Enforcement of this executive order is through the Office of Federal Contract Compliance (OFCC) which is part of the Department of Labor. Failure to comply with the Executive Order can lead to cancellation of the contract, the debarment of the contractor from future contracts, and the awarding of back pay to those who were discriminated against.[30]

The OFCC also is the enforcing agency for The Vietnam Era Veterans Readjustment Assistance Act of 1974. The purpose of this act is to prevent discrimination by contractors against Vietnam-era or other disabled veterans. The Act also encourages the promotion and advancement of such individuals.

Age Discrimination in Employment Acts (AEDA) of 1967 and 1975

The age discrimination in employment acts were passed to encourage the employment of older workers and to prevent discrimination in hiring, discharging, or establishing conditions of employment (Appendix A-3). Congress had found that older workers were being discriminated against especially in regard to obtaining new employment or in being laid off. In addition, the creation of arbitrary retirement ages worked to the distinct disadvantage of older workers.

Originally, the acts were designed to protect workers between the ages of 40 and 70. However, the upper age limit is no longer in effect; an amendment to the AEDA in 1986 extended age discrimination protection to individuals over the age of 70.

Enforcement of the Act is by the EEOC. However, there are special aspects of the law that make the employer's vulnerability even greater. For example, in contrast to most other types of discrimination, jury trials are permitted in age discrimination cases. Given the fact that older people tend to get sympathy from juries, employers are more likely to lose. In addition, the law permits the assessment of damages, i.e. the awarding of money above and beyond back pay, against an employer. Such awards can be substantial when discriminatory intent is shown. Employers should also keep in mind that although the act generally applies when the individual discriminated against is within the 40 to 70 category, it is possible to file a charge even when both individuals are within the category.[31] For example, a 65-year-old individual may file an age discrimination charge claiming that a 45-year-old worker received a promotion which the 65-year-old should have received.

Federal Pregnancy Discrimination Act of 1978

This act is an amendment to the 1964 Civil Rights Act and was meant to clarify what was meant when the Congress included "sex" as one of the classes that receive protection under the Civil Rights Act. The amendment was created because of a Supreme Court ruling, *General Electric Co.* v *Gilbert* (429 U.S. 125) that to discriminate against a pregnant individual did not constitute "sex" discrimination per se, but only discrimination against those who are pregnant in favor of those who are not. The Congress passed this amendment clarifying its intent that discrimination against women due to pregnancy, childbirth, and recovery, constituted sex discrimination. The amendment reads, in part, as follows:

> The terms 'because of sex' or 'on the basis of sex' include, but are not limited to, because of or on the basis of pregnancy, childbirth, or related medical conditions; and women affected by pregnancy, childbirth, or related medical conditions shall be treated the same for all employment-related purposes, including receipt of benefits under fringe benefit programs, as other person not so affected but similar in their ability or inability to work... (Section 701 (k))

Pregnancy is treated as an illness or disability. This suggests that insofar as the employer treats a pregnant employee in the same manner as a sick or disabled employee, the employer is acting in accordance with the law. Of course, this is a complicated legal area, and library employers should seek good legal counsel when designing and implementing any policies related to pregnant workers.

Rehabilitation Act of 1973

This Act was designed to protect handicapped workers from discrimination in federally assisted programs and in federal agencies (Appendix A-4). This Act is an amendment to the Vocational Rehabilitation Act and was created because handicapped individuals were not receiving adequate services and programs, and urgently needed help to become fruitful members of society. Among the barriers that contributed to this lack of integration was employment discrimination.

Employers should be aware that the concept of a handicap is often broadly construed. The definition used by the EEOC is as follows:

> (a) "Handicapped person" is defined for this subpart as one who: (1) Has a physical or mental impairment which substantially limits one or more of such person's major life activities, (2) has a record of such an impairment, or (3) is regarded as having such an impairment."[32]

Such a definition could include a large number of infirmities. What does it mean to have a condition that limits a "major life activity?" The EEOC has defined such activities as those involving such things as walking, seeing, hearing, speaking, breathing, and working. Does this mean that a near-sighted individual is handicapped under the law? Similarly, the EEOC defines a "physical or mental impairment" in an extremely broad manner:

(1) any physiological disorder or condition, cosmetic disfigurement, or anatomical loss affecting one of more of the following body systems: Neurological, musculoskeletal; special sense organs, cardiovascular; reproductive; digestive; genito-urinary; hemic and lymphatic, skin; and endocrine; or (2) any mental or psychological disorder, such as mental retardation, organic brain syndrome, emotional or mental illness, and specific learning disabilities.[33]

In fact, courts have granted handicapped status to many types of employees including those with nervous conditions, heart problems, dyslexia, sensitivity to tobacco smoke, depressions, and joint problems. Recently the Court noted in the case *Arline* v *School Bd. of Nassau County* that even individuals with contagious diseases, in this case tuberculosis, can be considered handicapped. The implications of this decision could be far-reaching, especially as it relates to employees with AIDS or AIDS-related conditions. Library employers should consider the distinct possibility that employees diagnosed as having AIDS are protected under this Act; great care should be taken in the treatment of such individuals in the workplace.

Another important aspect of the law covering handicapped individuals is that the employer is required to "accommodate" a handicapped applicant or worker; that is, an employer, when identifying a handicapped applicant or worker, must be willing to make a reasonable accommodation to the employee's handicap. To what extent must an employer make adjustments in the workplace in order to hire or retain a handicapped employee? Among the types of activities the EEOC considers as accommodation are the following:

(1) Making facilities readily accessible to and usable by handicapped persons, and (2) job restructuring, part-time or modified work schedules, acquisitions or modification of equipment or devices, appropriate adjustment or modification of examinations, the provision of readers and interpreters, and other similar actions.[34]

Library employers may wonder how costly such accommodations would be, and whether they could create administrative or staff problems. Each situation must be assessed individually. An employer who believes that the necessary accommodations would be extremely costly or disruptive may argue under the law that the accommodation would create an "undue hardship." It would then be necessary to demonstrate this to the satisfaction of the EEOC or court. If there is any question concerning the need to make an accommodation, legal counsel should be sought.

Americans with Disabilities Act (ADA)

This act, passed in July 1990, was created to eliminate discrimination against the handicapped. Previously, the Vocational Rehabilitation Act of 1973 provided the major federal protection but this covered only employers who received federal funds. The ADA, in contrast, is a broad-ranging bill covering not only job related issues but those related to public accommodations, transportation, and telecommunications. From the employment perspective the bill is designed to prevent employers from using an individual's disability as a reason for refusing to hire so long as the individual can perform the "essential functions" of the job. The employer is responsible for making a "reasonable accommodation" to the employee's disability insofar as the accommodation does not create an "undue hardship" on the employer. Of course, the questions as to what accommodation is "reasonable," what is an "undue hardship" on the employer, and who determines which job functions are "essential" remain open. What is clear is that the definition of handicap is extremely broad and it is estimated that 43 million individuals would be covered by the act. The potential for increases in the number of discrimination charges is considerable. The Equal Employment Opportunity Commission estimates that there could be as much as a 20% increase in EEOC filings with the passage of the act. For this reason, a careful review of the act by legal counsel is vital.

The Equal Employment Opportunity Guidelines for Sex Discrimination

Along with the actual laws protecting the rights of employees, the EEOC (the enforcing agency for most of these laws) develops specific guidelines for employers (Appendix B). These guidelines provide critical information to the library employer. They include definitions of important concepts, such as "reasonable accommodation," and instruct the employer in appropriate and inappropriate actions. There are guidelines for avoiding religious discrimination, discrimination by national origin, age discrimination, sex discrimination, and discrimination on the basis of handicap.

Given the fact that the library work force is numerically dominated by women, it is especially important to understand how these guidelines set the context for sex discrimination. The most important aspects of the guidelines focus on the more insidious aspects of sex discrimination, that is, the negative assumptions and stereotypes associated with women as workers. Among the actions that the EEOC finds anathema are the following:

(1) The refusal to hire a woman because of her sex based on assumptions of the comparative employment characteristics of women in general. For example, the assumption that the turnover rate among women is higher than among men.

(2) The refusal to hire an individual based on stereotyped characterizations of the sexes. Such stereotypes include, for example, that men are less capable of assembling intricate equipment; that women are less capable of aggressive salesmanship. The principle of nondiscrimination requires that individuals be considered on the basis of individual capacities and not on the basis of any characteristics generally attributed to the group.

(3) The refusal to hire an individual because of the preferences of co-workers, the employer, clients or customers...[35]

Library employers should ensure that those who hire employees do not impose such stereotypes when hiring. In addition, the employer should review any organizational rules or practices that:

- restrict women from certain positions or job activities such as lifting or working at night;
- provide women with extra rest periods, physical facilities, or benefits, or discriminate against women in the provision of benefits;
- permit different seniority systems for males and females;
- permit advertising of positions as "male" or "female";
- restrict employment of *married* women, if married men are not similarly restricted;
- restrict employment of pregnant women.[36]

The EEOC guidelines related to gender also deal with the area of sexual harassment. Harassment involves *unwelcome* sexual advances or requests for sexual favors, verbal abuse, or physical contact. In general, for the conduct to be considered harassing it must meet at least one of three conditions.

(1) [When] submission to such conduct is made either explicitly or implicitly a term or condition of employment, (2) submission to or rejection of such conduct by an individual is used as the basis for employment decisions affecting such individual, or (3) such conduct has the purpose or effect of unreasonably interfering with an individual's work performance or creating an intimidating, hostile, or offensive environment.[37]

It is the third criteron that is especially problematical for employers because it relies almost entirely on the perspective of the individual who claims to be harassed. What is intimidating or offensive to one individual may not be to another. Employers must therefore be extremely cautious in allowing any form of potentially offensive speech, such as sexual jokes or language, in the workplace. In addition, this criterion suggests that sexual harassment can occur even when the individual performing the harassing conduct is *not* a supervisor, and does not control the employee's employment. The EEOC has noted that if the employer knew or *should have known* about the conduct, then the employer may be held responsible for the acts of a fellow worker. Indeed, the employer may also be responsible for the sexually harassing conduct of any individual who is *not* employed by the library, for example, a library patron. Finally, the employer may be held liable if, in granting a promotion or other favors to an individual who has submitted to sexual harassment, it has subsequently discriminated against individuals who have not succumbed to this harassment.

Employers may reduce their liability for sexual harassment claims by taking several steps:

- Establish a written policy that makes it very clear that sexual harassment will not be tolerated.
- Establish serious penalties for violation of the sexual harassment policy, and punish those who violate it.
- Develop training programs to sensitize supervisors and other employees to what constitutes sexual harassment, and how to prevent it.
- Communicate clearly to all employees that sexual harassment will not be tolerated.
- Ensure that all employees know how to file a complaint of sexual harassment with the library management.
- Take immediate and effective action to protect employees from further sexual harassment if it has occurred.

OTHER FEDERAL LAWS

Fair Labor Standards Act

The Fair Labor Standards Act (FLSA) was first passed in 1938. Originally it applied to organizations involved in interstate commerce and dealt with such areas as minimum wage and overtime provisions, as well as child labor. In 1966, the scope of the law was widened to include public institutions such as schools, universities and hospitals. Despite this expansion of coverage, there has been serious question whether the provisions of this law extend to governmental bodies including public libraries. Recent decisions, most notably *Garcia v San Antonio Metropolitan Transit Authority*, suggest that the provisions of FLSA concerning minimum wage and overtime provisions do apply.[38] Library employers should therefore take heed of its requirements, and consult with legal counsel regarding how to implement the law.

Immigration Reform and Control Act of 1986

This act is intended to prohibit the hiring of unauthorized aliens. What makes this law different is that it places the burden of proving an employee is able to work on the shoulders of the employer. The law makes it illegal to hire employees without obtaining evidence such as: passports, certificates of naturalization, birth certificates, and social security cards. It also makes it unlawful to discriminate against an individual due to citizenship status except an unauthorized alien.

STATE AND LOCAL LAWS

There are various state laws that affect the practice of HRM. The most common are those involving wage and hour laws, worker's compensation, unemployment compensation, child labor laws, employment discrimination, contract law, and state collective bargaining bills. The library employer should keep in mind that discrimination laws within the state may vary from the federal law. For example, the state law for employment discrimination may apply to organizations with fewer employees than those covered under federal law. The employer must therefore be conversant with both the state and federal law. Similarly, state collective bargaining laws may be at variance with the National Labor Relations Act, which covers collective bargaining in the private sector. In general, there are few local laws that directly affect personnel management. The most notable concern civil service. Some municipalities may require employees to be residents of the town to be eligible for hire. Such a law is designed to provide jobs for local people, but also can affect the quality of the labor pool from which the organization draws its staff.

PRINCIPLES OF HUMAN RESOURCE MANAGEMENT

HRM is really about managing people in all their complexity. It encompasses legal and ethical dimensions, as well as administrative. Managing people is quite simply a difficult job. Managers who are sensitive to people are apt to feel many stresses and misgivings as they try to respond to an individual's needs and still be fair to all employees. Such feelings of strain and misgiving are not without their rational foundation. Often managers try to satisfy incompatible interests when there are neither complete nor entirely satisfactory solutions. The best the manager can do is to recognize and follow some basic principles with the understanding that sometimes these principles come into conflict.

The Principle of Organizational Survival

HRM's most important purpose is to help accomplish organizational goals by managing people properly. It creates conditions in which human work is most effectively coordinated and directed to the organization's success.

At first glance this seems like a logical and laudable task, especially in organizations such as libraries which provide substantial societal and individual benefits. But underlying this important principle is the less recognized notion that people are the tools or means to an end. The principle of organizational survival requires that personnel policies and practices be designed to promote the survival of the organization. From time to time, personnel policies and procedures may confound the legitimate needs of individuals in order to benefit the organization as a whole. That can be disconcerting to the thoughtful human resource manager who believes that each person is important. After all shouldn't we treat all people as ends in themselves, and never as means to an end? This dilemma is addressed in a second principle of personnel management, the 'Principle of Individuality.'

The Principle of Individuality

Although the primary responsibility of HRM is to design and administer the regulations and procedures that maximize human work (i.e. productivity) for the good of the organization, there is a second principle of nearly equal importance. This principle recognizes that people are important *as individuals*, and must be afforded attention and respect even when organizational ends may be affected. This principle manifests itself in generous benefit programs for health, education, or counselling. Such programs may be quite expensive, and one may be hard-pressed to prove that they actually increase productivity sufficiently to offset the costs of their administration. Nonetheless, it is an important aspect of HRM to recognize that people *deserve* such benefits as people. The principle of individuality also recognizes that workers should be able to exercise their rights of free speech and expression, to have their privacy respected, and insofar as possible be free to express themselves in their manner of dress and behavior. A sound personnel system does not require that all people believe the same thing, and behave the same way.

The Principle of Consistency

The responsiveness of a personnel system to individual needs is severely limited by the need for policies and procedures to be administered consistently. Administrators who are perceived to apply rules in an arbitrary or capricious fashion quickly lose the confidence and respect of employees, and subject themselves and the organization to legal liabilities. Yet a personnel manager may rightfully feel both compassion and frustration at being "tied" to a rule which seems unfair in a particular circumstance. The fact that the rule is designed for the "greater good" often seems an anemic, albeit necessary, justification. It is a dilemma for the personnel manager: being consistent often interferes with being fair.

The Principle of Fairness

Where consistency demands uniform application of rules and regulations, fairness demands that the rules themselves be just, and justly applied. An employee, for example, may not question the fact that a particular rule is applied to everyone in the same way; nevertheless he or she may argue that the rule itself is unfair. The concept of "fairness" may vary from person to person, but the principle requires that personnel policies and practices be reasonable, and be sufficiently flexible to allow for extenuating or unusual circumstances.

The Principle of Legal Responsibility

In today's litigious climate, it is essential that personnel policies and practices remain firmly within the bounds of the law. No personnel system should be constructed in a manner that violates legal codes, nor should such a system permit any employee to commit unlawful acts in the workplace without severe sanctions. Similarly, no individual in authority should be permitted to order or encourage an employee to commit an unlawful act.

The Principle of Happiness

A personnel system should promote the greatest happiness for the greatest number. This means that personnel policies and practices should be designed to maximize job satisfaction within a context that allows the organization to accomplish its goals. Such a view is not as radical as it may appear. For many years, management theorists and social scientists have recognized that meeting the physical, emotional, and social needs of employees can have many benefits for the organization. People spend much of their waking life in the workplace, and it is only right that employers try to make work life as pleasant as possible.

The Principle of Ethical Action

It should be troubling to us that the American citizenry is skeptical about the ethics of public administrators and institutions. Too many times people have read in the newspapers about improprieties or the appearance of improprieties in high offices or important public institutions. These have weakened the citizenry's confidence in the trustworthiness of public officials.

Recently, many organizations have become more cognizant of ethical issues, leading them to create and publish a code of ethics for all employees. In a recent survey in the private sector, 72% of the organizations surveyed had a published code of ethics.[39] The only counterpart in librarianship is the Code of Ethics of the American Library Association. This code is particularly useful in regard to the provision of library service, and could serve a useful personnel function if officially adopted as an ethical standard for libraries.

Human resource managers have a three-fold responsibility in regard to ethics: first, to create an HRM system that treats staff ethically; second, to ensure that they themselves do not commit breaches of ethical conduct; and third, to ensure that the job-related actions of all staff, including managers and administrators, are ethical.

It is clearly a breach of law to discriminate against employees, to knowingly commit unlawful acts, or encourage others to commit them. In addition, there are some actions that are clearly unethical as well as unlawful. Below are some examples of ethical breaches that can occur within the context of personnel management:

Violations of Privacy
- Revealing information about employees to individuals who do not need to know such information, or which may unnecessarily damage the individual's personal or professional reputation.
- Misuse of personnel records or files including inappropriate access to computer files.
- Collecting any personal information about employees that is not related to the necessary functions of the organization.
- Conducting inappropriate investigations of an individual's personal history, or using nonrelevant personal information to make a personnel decision, e.g., for hiring purposes.
- Conducting drug, alcohol, AIDS, or other testing unless it is essential to the safe operation of the job, or is directly related to the safety of others.
- Monitoring employees with video cameras or tape recorders without their knowledge or consent, unless significant and specific job related reasons make such monitoring necessary.
- Use of the polygraph unless there is clear and substantial reason for its use, e.g., in cases of suspected theft.

- Attempting to censor the writing or speech of employees unless such speech or writing would significantly damage the institution's ability to perform its essential function.

Misuses of Authority

- Showing favoritism to friends or relatives.
- Making personnel decisions out of anger or spite.
- Writing inaccurate job references for employees to prevent them from gaining other employment, or to encourage their departure.
- Collecting job related information from employees, for example, for disciplinary action, without informing them of the potential consequences.
- Retaliating against employees who are outspoken or who have merely exercised their legal rights.
- Withholding information from an individual to ensure or promote job failure.

Organizational Inadequacies

- Designing a system of rewards that fosters cheating, sabotaging the work of others, or withholding important information; or that places emphasis only on quantity rather than quality (e.g. providing substantial financial rewards for higher library circulation).
- Paying wages and benefits that do not give minimal protection and security to employees.
- Creating a personnel system that discriminates, or is unfair in administering essential personnel functions.
- Permitting the hiring and placement of individuals with a Master of Library Science degree in support staff positions.
- Misusing behavior modification techniques to manipulate employees.
- Knowingly allowing employees to work in unsafe or unhealthy working conditions, especially without their knowledge or consent.

THE CHALLENGE OF HRM

HRM is one of the most complex activities in any library. The manager of personnel must balance many competing forces: legal, humanistic, ethical, fiscal, political, and organizational. There is no magic formula to determine which of these forces should weigh most heavily in a given circumstance. Each situation brings with it unique circumstances as well as common ones.

The challenge of HRM is to be clear and objective: to clarify which issues are important and should be considered before making a decision; to place each consideration in its proper perspective, and to come to a balanced, unbiased judgment that serves the organization in the long run. This is not a task for the weak of mind or the weak of heart, but for the fine mind and the generous heart.

FACTORS RELATED TO HRM

1. Each individual is different and there are no simple formulas for managing employees effectively.

2. Each employee has the capacity to affect the organization on many levels and can affect the public's perception of the entire library.

3. It is crucial to understand the composition of the library work force which is comprised of a substantial number of female and part-time workers.

4. The library labor force will grow slowly increasing by only 13.4% by the year 2000.

5. Blacks and women are under-represented in management positions.

6. HRM involves many different responsibilities including hiring, evaluating, disciplining, administering wages, salaries and benefits, and developing and enforcing organizational policies and procedures.

7. Among the factors influencing HRM is the aging work force, increased levels of schooling, new technologies, increased legal protections and greater demands for satisfying work.

8. There are many laws currently protecting the civil rights of employees, not just the Civil Rights Act of 1964. This includes the Civil Rights Acts of 1866 and 1871, the Equal Pay Act, and the American's with Disabilities Act.

9. HRM requires attention not only to the law but also to ethical practices. Although the organization's survival is of primary importance, individuals must be treated with respect and dignity.

Endnotes

1. Mary Jo Lynch, *Libraries in an Information Society: A Statistical Summary*, Chicago: American Library Association, 1987: 19.
2. King Research, Inc. and National Center for Education Statistics, *Library Human Resources: A Study of Supply and Demand*, Chicago: American Library Asociation, 1983: 39.
3. King Research Inc.: 34.
4. King Research Inc.: 44.
5. Bureau of Labor Statistics, *Occupational Projections and Training Data*, Bulletin 2301, Washington, D.C.: U.S. G.P.O, April 1988: 28.
6. Bureau of Labor Statistics: 13.
7. Bureau of Labor Statistics: 13.
8. Bureau of Labor Statistics: 27.
9. King Research Inc.: 34.
10. King Research Inc.: 30.
11. Anthony Debons, "The Information Professional: A Survey in *The Information Professional*, Proceedings of a Conference Held in Melbourne, Australia, edited by James Henri and Roy Sanders, November 26-28, 1984, Melbourne: Riverina-Murray Institute of Higher Education, 1985: 24-25.
12. Debons: 25.
13. Anita R. Schiller, "Women in Librarianship" in *The Role of Women in Librarianship 1876-1976: The Entry, Advancement and Struggle for Equalization in One Profession*, edited by Kathleen Weibel and Kathleen M. Heim, Phoenix, Oryx, 1979: 238.
14. Office for Library Personnel Resources, ALA, *Academic and Public Librarians: Data by Race, Ethnicity and Sex*, Chicago: ALA, 1986: 3.
15. Office for Library Personnel Resources: 5.
16. Office for Library Personnel Resources: 3, 7.
17. American Library Association: 7.
18. Office for Library Personnel Resources: 15.
19. American Library Association: 5.
20. Bureau of Labor Statistics: 13.
21. Katherine Murphy Dickson, *Women Librarians Re-Entering the Work Force*, Chicago: ALA, 1985: 5.
22. Dickson: 9.
23. Dickson: 25.
24. Bureau of Labor Statistics, *Occupational Projections and Training Data*, 1986 edition, Bulletin 2251, Washington, D.C.: U.S. G.P.O., April 1986: 49.
25. Richard E. Rubin, "Employee Turnover Among Full Time Public Librarians," *Library Quarterly* 59 (January 1989): 27-46.
26. Roy W. Walters, "HRM in Perspective," in *Human Resources Management and Development Handbook* edited by William R. Tracey, New York: AMACOM, 1985: 19.
27. Walters: 20.
28. G. Rutherglen, *Major Issues in the Federal Law of Employment Discrimination*, 2nd Edition, Washington, D.C.: Federal Judicial Center, 1987: 71.

29. Mack A. Player, *Employment Discrimination Law*, St. Paul: West, 1984: 37.
30. Steven C. Kahn, Barbara A. Brown, and Brent E. Zepke, *Personnel Director's Legal Guide, 1988 Cumulative Supplement*, Boston: Warren, Gorham, and Lamont, 1988: 6.01.
31. Kahn, Brown, and Zepke: 1-7.
32. *Code of Federal Regulations*, "Prohibition Against Discrimination Because of a Physical or Mental Handicap," Washington, D.C.: GPO: 303.
33. "Prohibition Against Discrimination Because of a Physical or Mental Handicap": 303.
34. "Prohibition Against Discrimination Because of a Physical or Mental Handicap": 303-304.
35. *Code of Federal Regulations*, "Guidelines on Discrimination Because of Sex," Washington, D.C.: GPO, 1989: 193.
36. *Code of Federal Regulations*, "Part 1604—Guidelines on Discrimination Because of Sex," Washington, D.C.: GPO, 1989: 193-202.
37. Code of Federal Regulations, "Part 1604—Guidelines on Discrimination Because of Sex": 197.
38. *Garcia* v *San Antonio Metropolitan Transit Authority*, 105 S. Ct. 1005 (1985).
39. James Court, "A Question of Corporate Ethics," *Personnel Journal* 67 (September 1988): 37.

2

The Hiring Process

Hiring is an expensive process, and because a mistake can prove even more expensive, the employer must regard this process as one of its most important functions. Before an organization begins hiring, certain structural features should already be in place: written policies, application forms, equal employment opportunity (EEO) monitoring systems, and interview training programs.

Written Personnel Policies
Libraries should have written statements of hiring policies, practices, and procedures. These include:

- A statement clearly affirming the library's intent to conform to all equal employment opportunity laws and regulations. This commits the organization to hiring without regard to race, creed, color, national origin, sex, handicap, or religion. In addition, the policy should make clear that hiring is based solely on the candidate's qualifications.
- A statement defining who is eligible to apply, the policy for receiving applications, and the length of time applications are considered active in the personnel files.
- A statement regarding the probationary status of newly hired employees, including the means by which they may be terminated from employment and their rights to appeal their termination through grievance procedures.

Application Forms
The institution should have application blanks. The forms should be neatly printed, easy to complete, use language that is understood by those with a minimal education, and should be organized to provide the maximum information. Libraries should not rely solely on resumes because the type of information provided varies from applicant to applicant and the library should try to collect similar information from each applicant.

FIGURE 2-1. Model of the Hiring Process

MODEL OF THE HIRING PROCESS

EEOC Monitoring System
Each library should have in place a system for monitoring all hiring decisions to ensure that there are no unlawful discriminatory practices. One person should be appointed as the EEO officer, who reviews hiring decisions and collects data on overall hiring practices.

Training Programs
All individuals involved in the hiring process should receive training on interviewing techniques and on the laws and regulations governing hiring. These programs should include written materials which the interviewer can review before conducting a job interview.

THE RECRUITMENT PROCESS

The need for a consistent and substantial pool of applicants is basic to the survival of any organization. For this reason, the library establishes processes and policies for recruiting and hiring new staff. Such policies and procedures should embody the recognition that the labor force is not static; that its composition, needs, and level of skill may change depending on a variety of conditions. The process of securing an adequate pool of qualified applicants is called *recruitment.*

Because employee selection is such an important activity, it is best that recruitment be done in a systematic fashion that is consistent with the organization's goals. Serious recruiting takes time and money. The strategy used and the time and fiscal resources devoted to recruitment should reflect an objective assessment of the library's needs. In the final analysis, the library must try to match the wants and needs of employees with those of the organization. It is useless to recruit individuals who are not "fitted" to library work, even if they are hard workers.

In terms of professional librarians, both the national and local data should be obtained. National data can be obtained from the Office of Library Personnel Resources of ALA. Its report, *Academic and Public Librarians: Data by Race, Ethnicity, and Sex,*[1] provides a national demographic breakdown of librarians with special attention to racial and sexual labor force patterns. Local data may be harder to come by. Some states maintain census data by region and occupation which can be helpful. The actual available pool of librarians for a given library may vary significantly and depend on such factors as the existence of a local library education program.

Labor force information for support staff classifications such as clerical or custodial workers should generally be obtained only on the local rather than national level. Data for such classifications may be available through state employment agencies, state data centers, or equal employment opportunity offices. In addition, local labor market surveys may have been conducted by voluntary business organizations such as the Chamber of Commerce.

A library is just one of many organizations that compete for human resources within a particular market. Depending on the economic conditions and available supply, the library may have a large or small pool of individuals from which to draw. Although librarians as an occupational group have relatively few alternatives for employment, which is advantageous to the library employer, there is also a relatively small pool of librarians from which to draw. A particular library must still compete with other libraries, bookstores, or related agencies. Indeed, the competition may be on a national scale when looking for librarians of exceptional skill or talent.

A substantial portion of the library work force is composed of support staff. Such individuals have skills which can be transferred to a variety of business and industries. Competition with other employers for these individuals may be intense.

Methods of recruitment vary widely and reflect factors such as many or few available workers, turnover rate of the library, and need to recruit for equal employment opportunity purposes. Among the various recruitment sources and techniques are the following:

External Sources

Consultants
For upper-level or special positions, the employer may use an outside consultant to locate qualified candidates. These individuals, sometimes called "headhunters," provide initial search and screening services for the employer. It is critical for the employer to make sure the consultant has a clear idea of the type of individual required. The use of a consultant will increase recruitment costs.

Professional Associations and Conferences
National associations such as ALA have services for employers to review job resumes and interview candidates at their conferences. At the very least, employers who review the number and type of applicants available for library positions can get a general idea of the quality of applicants in the job market.

Library Schools
The nearest library school is an obvious source, especially for beginning professional positions. It may also be a source of part-time support staff who are looking for library experience. Library schools are often willing to post job notices through their placement services, and may hold job

fairs for their upcoming or recent graduates in which prospective employers may participate.

Local Employment Agencies

Regular contact with agencies or organizations that perform job referral functions is a basic part of the recruiting process. For support staff positions, the local unemployment bureau may be a good source of contacts. Similarly, agencies for special groups such as the NAACP, the Urban League, and The American Association of Retired Persons may prove to be fruitful contacts. One must be very careful that the employment agency understands precisely what is desired. Inappropriate referrals waste both the employer's and applicant's time. Individuals unfamiliar with libraries may seriously underestimate the skills and knowledge required to perform basic library jobs.

Local High Schools and Colleges

Local colleges and schools are good places to find part- and full-time support staff. Secondary schools and colleges are often productive sources for shelvers, and colleges can provide other support staff as well. The opportunity to recruit in such institutions may come through job boards where the library can post a job notice or through job fairs where a library representative can talk to students. Similarly, some high schools permit librarians to talk to students in their classrooms about summer or part-time employment. In any case, library employers may locate not only prospective support staff, but also excellent candidates for future library school attendance.

The Library Personnel Office

The success of a library's recruiting effort also depends on the personnel office—its policies and the personality of its staff. For example, having convenient hours for potential employees to apply for positions and arrive for screening interviews serves as an effective recruiting tool. Personnel staff should make regular recruiting trips to library schools, library conferences, and libraries, regardless of the current availability of a position, in order to maintain a pool of applicants from which to draw when openings occur.

Other Libraries

An often overlooked source for recruitment is other libraries. Many libraries are willing to post job openings on staff bulletin boards as a professional courtesy.

Training and Vocational Schools
The need for employees with strong clerical backgrounds is still great in most libraries. Vocational schools that train individuals in basic word processing, filing, and writing correspondence are a rich source of employees with these skills. These programs may be independent, or associated with local schools, or social agencies such as the Urban League.

Internal Sources

Internal Promotion Programs
Some libraries give preference to applicants who are currently employed in the system. When recruiting for some jobs, this is an excellent way to obtain job-related information concerning the performance of the individual, while concomitantly increasing the morale of the staff.

Library Scholarships or Financial Aid
The library may develop internal recruitment mechanisms for professional employees. This is particularly helpful when, for various reasons, it is difficult to attract professionally trained librarians, or when it is necessary to increase minority recruitment. Offering scholarships, or other generous financial assistance, is a good way to attract individuals who show promise for the library profession.

Word of Mouth
One of the most common methods of recruitment is "word of mouth." Put simply, it occurs when an employee or former staff member persuades an acquaintance to apply for a position. This method is quite effective when, through personal persuasion, employees who are good workers bring other good workers into the organization. These employees know what the library is like and are able to refer individuals who are right for the organization.

Obviously, there can be negative aspects as well. There is no guarantee that all prospective candidates will be good workers. Interpersonal strains sometimes arise in the workplace between the new employee and the friend who made the referral. Even more troublesome are possible adverse effects on equal employment opportunity. In organizations that are composed primarily of white employees, using word of mouth techniques could perpetuate a racially homogeneous work force. This technique should therefore be used only in combination with other more systematic ones.

Media

Newspapers and Journals

An obvious tool for recruitment is the newspaper. It is important to assess which advertising sources have the appropriate mix of readers for the particular job. Circulation size, type of reader, and cost of ad, all play a role in advertising strategy. For support staff positions, the local or community papers may serve quite adequately. Even a neighborhood publication may be best when looking for a branch position. For professional positions, local and state publications and newsletters, and national journals such as *American Libraries*, *Library Journal*, or *LJ Hotline* provide good exposure. For specialized positions, journals catering to these narrower interests, such as the *Journal of the American Society of Information Science*, may be more appropriate.

Considerable attention must be given to the preparation of job advertisements for newspapers and journals. An ad should include some "promotion" as well as information. Mention might be made of the "progressiveness" of the organization and the "challenge" of the position, as well as describing the knowledge, skill, and abilities needed for the job. Guard against any statements in the ad which could be construed as discriminatory, such as requiring the applicant to be of a certain race, sex, age group, or religion. Indeed, a statement about the anti-discrimination policy of the library is advisable if not mandatory. The ad should also include the name and address to which to respond, information about what to include in the application (e.g. letter of references), a deadline date for application, and a salary range. The language and format of the ad should contribute to its overall clarity.

The limitations of advertising include the expense. Ads in major journals or newspapers can be expensive, especially if the ad is lengthy and is reprinted several times. In addition, journals do not reach everyone, and the audience reached may depend on the number of times the ad is run. Finally, the number of applications that will be received is unforeseeable. An ad may get no response or the response may be in the hundreds. In the latter case especially, the time and expense required to analyze and respond to applications may be considerable.

Recruitment Letters

For important positions, directors or board members may solicit the names of qualified candidates from other knowledgeable individuals. The named individuals are contacted to determine if they are interested in the position. Care must always be taken not to make commitments or promises to the prospective candidate to attract their application.

THE APPLICATION PROCESS

Organizations vary as to the manner in which applications are made. In some cases, only a resume is requested from the candidate. Certainly, much information can be obtained this way. When using just the resume, however, the employee, rather than the employer, exercises control over the content and order of the information provided. The employer may have questions that the candidate has not answered in the resume, or information may not be clearly presented. For this reason, an application blank should be used to organize information in the proper order.

The Application Form

The application form serves many purposes. Foremost, it helps the employer determine the suitability of the candidate. But it also serves other purposes, most notably it constitutes a written record of the applicant's job-related background. This record may be necessary for a variety of reasons including monitoring the hiring process for equal employment opportunity; in rare cases, it may be used as proof of falsification or misrepresentation of credentials. Another purpose is as public relations. The hiring process is a delicate matter, and for public institutions the need to treat taxpayers well is particularly important. A well designed application form can suggest to the applicant that the library is a professional and objective organization.

Applications *give* information as well as receive it. Notably, the application forms should begin with a strong statement of nondiscrimination in employment. This assures the applicant that the organization recognizes its responsibility under the law to objectively assess the candidate's qualifications. The form should be designed to obtain the most information in the least space. The format of the application is important (Figure 2-1): it should be readable by individuals with a basic education, and should provide sufficient room to respond to the questions. Aside from personal data such as name, address, and phone number, the application should also ask for the applicant's educational and work background. Questions concerning race, sex, religion, and marital status should be avoided. However, it may be necessary to broach the subject of age to ensure conforming with the law. For example, if the state child labor laws have strict hours and times that young people may work, it may be necessary to ask on your application: "Are you under the age of 18?" Otherwise, specific questions regarding an applicant's age should be avoided. Questions about physical and mental handicaps should be phrased so that they are job related. For example: "Do you have any physical or mental impairments that would affect your ability to perform the job for which you are applying?" Failure

FIGURE 2-2. A Sample Employment Application

Akron-Summit County Public Library Employment Application

In compliance with Federal and State equal employment opportunity laws, qualified applicants are considered for positions without regard to race, color, religion, sex, national origin, age, marital status, or the presence of a non-job related medical condition or handicap.

Identification

Name: Last	First	Middle
Street Address		Telephone Number
City	State	Zip	Social Security No.

Under 18? Yes_____ No_____

General Information

Are you interested in full time work? _____ Part time work? _____

Can you work evenings and Saturdays?_____

List professional, business, civic or volunteer activities and offices held: (Omit any group which would indicate race, color, religion, sex, national origin or age).

_____

_____

Do you have a disability, a handicap, or medical condition that limits your job performance? Yes_____ No_____
If yes, please explain.

_____

_____

Have you served in the U.S. Military?_____ If so, give dates and branch of service._____

_____

Have you ever been convicted of a felony? _____ If so, give date of conviction and describe the nature of the offense.

_____

FIGURE 2-2B.

What types of jobs are you interested in?

☐ Professional librarian   ☐ Clerical/Secretarial   ☐ Library Assistant   ☐ Custodial
(requires M.L.S. or M.S.L.S. degree)

☐ Graphic Artist   ☐ Technical   ☐ Other Please specify _____

Education

Training	Circle Highest Year Completed	Name and City	Did you Graduate? circle	Major Subjects or Types of Courses	Grade Point Average
High School	Years 9 10 11 12		Yes No		
Business Correspondence or Vocational School	No. of Months		Yes No		
College or University	Years 1 2 3 4		Yes No	Degree Received	
Graduate School	Years 1 2 3 4		Yes No	Degree Received	
Other Courses or Special Training	No. of Months		Yes No		

SPECIAL SKILLS (Include knowledge of Audio Visual equipment, Word Processing etc.)	Shorthand Speed wpm
	Typing Speed wpm

Previous Employment Please start with most recent position first

Place of Employment	Duties
Address	Reason for Leaving
Supervisor's Name	Dates of employment: From _____ To _____
May we contact this employer? Yes ☐ No ☐	Rate of pay

complete form by continuing on back ▷

FIGURE 2-2C.

Previous Employment (continued)

Place of Employment	Duties
Address	Reason for Leaving
Supervisor's Name	Dates of employment. From _____ To _____
May we contact this employer? Yes ☐ No ☐	Rate of Pay
Place of Employment	Duties
Address	Reason for Leaving
Supervisor's Name	Dates of employment From _____ To _____
May we contact this employer? Yes ☐ No ☐	Rate of Pay
Place of Employment	Duties
Address	Reason for Leaving
Supervisor's Name	Dates of employment From _____ To _____
May we contact this employer? Yes ☐ No ☐	Rate of Pay

Agreement (please read before signing)

I certify that answers given herein are true and complete to the best of my knowledge.
I authorize you to make such investigations and inquiries of my personal, employment, financial or medical history and other related matters as may be necessary in arriving at an employment decision. I hereby release employers, schools or persons from liability in responding to inquiries in connection with my application.

In the event of employment, I understand that false or misleading information given on the application or in the interview(s) may result in discharge. I understand, also, that I am required to abide by all rules and regulations of the Akron-Summit County Public Library.

Date_____ Signature _____

to know about such handicaps before hire can create serious complications later.

Another question that is sensitive involves prior criminal conduct. It is *not* appropriate to ask about *arrest* records. It *is* appropriate to ask individuals if they have been *convicted* of a felony and what the felony involved. The last thing an employer wants to discover after the fact is that the children's librarian they hired is a convicted child molester, or that the new clerk-treasurer was convicted of embezzlement.

The education section of the application blank should allow room for the candidate to list not only secondary schools, colleges, and universities, but other types of educational and training programs. There should be available space to record training in vocational and technical schools, short-term training programs (e.g. an Urban League clerical training program), and job-related training in the armed services, and a place to indicate whether the programs were *completed*.

When asking questions concerning work experience, it is important to get complete addresses of previous employers, and the names of the applicant's former immediate supervisors. It is also essential to get specific dates of employment for each position. This information helps the employer determine whether the applicant is able to hold a steady job or switches jobs frequently. It also reveals job gaps. Similarly, the application should ask the reason for leaving each position. Because space on the application is at a premium, it is not possible to get a detailed explanation of why the employee left; that is a job for the interviewer. Nonetheless, one can sometimes determine whether the employee left voluntarily or was terminated. It is also important to get permission from the employee to contact each previous employer. In this way, the library's right to consult with previous employers about the applicant's work performance is assured.

The application form should also include a place for the applicant to identify individuals who would provide a reference. Work references are preferable to personal references who are more likely to discuss matters unrelated to work. Sufficient space is needed for complete names and addresses of referees.

The final part of an application blank should be an agreement to be signed by the employee. This agreement should, at the least, include a promise that the statements made by the applicant are true, and that the employer has a right to make whatever investigations are necessary to determine the suitability of the applicant for employment. The applicant should be warned that deliberate misrepresentation or falsification can result in dismissal. There should be a place for the employee to sign and date the application below the agreement.

The Pre-Employment Inquiry Form

Because of Equal Employment Opportunity laws, the application process may include an additional form which asks questions regarding the race, sex, age, handicaps, and status as a veteran (Figure 2-3). This form is used to monitor the hiring process to ensure nondiscrimination. Such a form should state clearly that the purpose is solely to *prevent* discrimination. In addition, the form should be filed in a location separate from the completed application form to ensure that only authorized individuals are aware of the information on it.

The Application Procedure

In general, the library should create generous opportunities for individuals to apply for positions in the library. This means that applications should be taken whether a specific position is open or not. By taking applications throughout the year, a large applicant pool will be available when a position does open, and the chance of missing a good candidate is reduced. Similarly, there should be many channels through which an application can be made. Respond promptly to requests by phone, by letter, or in person. All individuals requesting applications should be informed of interviewing hours if general screening interviews are conducted.

Some employers conduct screening interviews as part of the application process. The qualifications of applicants and their suitability for employment are reviewed even when no position is open. The purpose of screening is to get as much information as possible about the applicant pool in advance of deciding whom to interview for a specific position. In some cases, employers conduct screening interviews only when an opening occurs. The purpose is essentially the same: to locate a group of candidates who are suitable for further interviews. As with all interview situations, the interviewer must concentrate on work-related factors.

The application process is also a public relations activity for most libraries. Many applicants are library users, or are members of the community that supports the library. For this reason, as well as many others, all applicants should be treated with courtesy and respect.

THE SELECTION PROCESS

The selection of employees is crucial in any organization and especially in labor-intensive ones. The detrimental consequences of hiring a poor performer are manifest. Poor hiring decisions:

FIGURE 2-3.

PRE-EMPLOYMENT INFORMATION FORM

In compliance with Federal and State equal employment opportunity laws, qualified applicants are considered for all positions without regard to race, color, religion, sex, national origin, age, marital status, or the presence of a non-job—related medical condition or handicap.

To help us comply with Federal/State equal employment opportunity record keeping, reporting, and other legal requirements, please answer questions below.

This Pre-Employment Information Form will be kept in Confidential File separate from the Application for Employment. This information is to be utilized for Affirmative Action use only.

Answer all questions. Please print.   Date _____

NAME _____   TELEPHONE _____
    Last   First   Middle

ADDRESS _____
                    City   State   Zip

Please check the appropriate items:

1. SEX: _____ Male   2. AGE: _____ Under 18
        _____ Female   _____ 18 to 70
                          _____ Over 70 years of age

3. RACE/ETHNIC GROUP: 4. VETERANS INFORMATION:
    _____ White _____ American Indian/ Are you a Vietnam Era veteran?
    _____ Black   Alaskan Native _____ Yes   _____ No
    _____ Hispanic _____ Asian/Pacific Islander Are you a Disabled veteran?
                              _____ Yes   _____ No

5. Do you have a Disability, a Handicap, or a Medical Condition that limits your job performance? [answer to this question is voluntary]
    _____ Yes   _____ No
    If yes, please explain _____

Reprinted with permission from the Akron-Summit County Public Library, Akron, Ohio.

- Waste the resources of the organization. The time spent on recruiting, interviewing, and processing a new employee is considerable. Roos and Shelton estimate the cost of hiring an academic librarian is between $10,000 and $12,000;[2]
- Reduce staff morale when the new employee fails to perform up to expectations;
- Waste the time and energy of the supervisor who must devote unnecessary attention to evaluate, correct, or limit unproductive behavior;
- Waste the time taken to train the employee;
- May lead to increased absenteeism and accidents which increase organizational costs;
- Expend the time of administrators who must deal with deteriorating performance; and
- Decrease the quality of service delivered to the public.

The opportunity to hire staff, especially professional librarians, is limited compared to hiring options in other types of organizations. Studies of employee turnover in libraries reveal that the rate of leaving is relatively low in both public and academic libraries.[3] These limited opportunities to bring in new people underscore the need for deliberate hiring policies and practices.

Generally, a selection process includes five activities:

1. interviewers must be selected;
2. candidates must be selected from a pool of applicants using the application form, resume, and references;
3. individuals must be interviewed;
4. selection decisions must be made; and
5. the candidates must be informed as to their selection or rejection.

Identifying the Interviewers

The interview process can be conducted by an individual, or a hiring committee, depending on the procedures of the institution. It is usually best to involve more than one person in the interview process. This tends to reduce bias by broadening the perspective. Of course, cost is an issue; interviewing is expensive, so only individuals who need to be involved should be included. The type of job to be filled may determine the number and level of individuals involved.

In some systems, the candidate is interviewed separately by various individuals, by combinations of individuals, and by committees. It is common in academic institutions for the interview process to last two days or more. Although this gives each person a "one-on-one" opportunity to meet the candidate it has several drawbacks. First, it tends to be time-consuming, hence expensive, for both the organization and the candidate; it is inefficient in that questions tend to be repeated, and responses to unique questions by interviewers are not heard by others involved in the selection process. For this reason, "panel" or group interviews may often be the desired course of action. Interviews using panel approaches have been shown to have strong validity.[4]

The number of candidates to be invited to interview varies, and unless there is established policy, common sense should prevail. The cost of the time required for interviewing is considerable, but the cost of hiring the wrong person is even greater. Therefore, every effort should be made to interview all candidates who appear qualified.

Determining Appropriate Candidates

Reviewing job applications and resumes is the most common method for identifying suitable candidates. But before doing this, it is essential to have an idea of what qualities are desired. A written job description should form the basis for evaluating candidates. It should include at least a basic description of the tasks and responsibilities to be performed, and the knowledge, skill, and ability needed to meet the minimum requirements of the job. Of course, each job is different and some characteristics may be more important in one than another. It is useful for those involved in the interview process to discuss what characteristics play the most important role so that the appropriate emphasis can be placed while screening the applications. For particularly important positions, it might be useful for the selectors to rank in order of importance those job characteristics that they wish the successful applicant to possess.

Questions to Ask When Reviewing Applications

When examining application forms, there are some questions the selector might ask:

- Is the resume or application form readable and well-written? Are there signs of carelessness such as misspellings or poorly constructed sentences?
- Did the applicant provide complete information? Are all the questions answered? Are full names, addresses, and dates of employment provided?
- Are there job gaps? Are there long periods of time which remain unexplained? Is there any indication of what the individual was doing between jobs?
- Has the applicant held many jobs over a short period of time?
- Are the reasons for leaving jobs missing, or do the explanations for leaving seem unclear or evasive?
- Does the person's education and work background conform to the job requirements?

It is important to remember that just because an application reveals job gaps, or has a spelling error, does not mean that the candidate should be excluded. Rather, it may highlight an area that needs to explored further in an interview. Generally, the selector should be looking for reasons to *select* individuals for an interview, rather than to eliminate them.

THE JOB INTERVIEW

The job interview is the most common technique for the selection of employees in libraries and other organizations, and plays an important role in the final determination. Some research has suggested that resumes and letters of reference have little effect on the final decision whether to employ an individual; rather, evaluation in face to face settings is used to sort the successful from the unsuccessful candidates.[5]

Characteristics of Good Employees

Libraries like any other organization want good employees. But what is a good employee? Certainly, employers should seek out people with appropriate knowledge, skill, and ability. But some of the characteristics desired are less tangible and more difficult to measure than others, yet they are important. What are some of these characteristics? Most employers look for:

- Ability to communicate: people who can speak and write well; who want to share ideas and listen to the ideas of others;
- Ambition: individuals who do not wish to stagnate; who want to progress either organizationally or intellectually;
- Attention to personal appearance: individuals who do not wish to offend others by careless personal hygiene, and who are able to determine what is appropriate dress;
- Commitment to the organization: individuals who will develop a sense of membership and belonging in the organization;
- Conscientiousness: individuals who will exhibit responsibility and dedication to their work;
- Cooperativeness: employees who can get along well with others; who can deal constructively and positively with coworkers;
- Creativity: individuals who can solve problems even when new solutions must be devised;
- Empathy: individuals who can put themselves in another's place; who can see things from different points of view;
- Good attitude: a desire to work, and a positive approach to the work of the organization;

- Health: individuals who will not become an absentee problem or whose performance will not be affected by emotional or physical illness;
- Honesty: individuals who will not steal property or money and who will not deceive the employer;
- Intelligence: employees who have the intellectual skills to accomplish tasks, and who can understand and adapt to changes in the work environment;
- Maturity: individuals who have relevant experiences which they can apply in a judicious manner; similarly, it needs employees who can learn from new experiences.
- Motivation: people who want to work hard, who persist until their tasks are completed;
- Patience: employees who are deliberative in thought and action; who do not act until they have all necessary information;
- Reliability: an employee who is consistent in attendance and in performance;
- Respect for authority: individuals who understand that decisions ultimately have to be made, and that such decisions require reasonable, although not blind, obedience.

Of course, there are few employees who possesses all these characteristics; nonetheless, it is important to realize that employment decisions are formed by many factors, not all of which can be easily quantified or even identified by examining resumes and letters of reference. Many of the candidate's qualities are revealed during the job interview.

Interview Effectiveness and Bias

Because the interview is so important, it is useful to examine some of the human factors that affect accuracy and success. The job interview has one primary purpose: to obtain sufficient information to select the candidate who will perform best on the job. While moving toward this goal, many other things are happening: the candidate is providing information about work background, knowledge, skill and ability; the interviewers are providing information about the goals and objectives of the organization; and, good public relations is being built as the organization conveys an image to a likely patron and taxpayer.

The interview is a highly complex activity. Most of all, one must recognize that it is a distinctly human process. Both the interviewer and the interviewee bring to the interview their unique attitudes, biases, beliefs, morals, gestures, facial expression, manner of dress, behavior, and way of speaking. Although interviews can and should be structured to try to reduce extraneous considerations, it is both impossible and undesirable to ignore these human considerations. By recognizing that these factors exist, there is a greater likelihood that the interviewer will be aware when these factors play an inappropriate role.

Research has not yielded convincing evidence that the job interview is a particularly effective technique for predicting job success. Early reviews suggested that the reliability and validity of interviews is low; that is, interviewers seldom obtained consistent amounts of information in the interviews, did not rate interviewees consistently, and could not, in fact, predict the candidates that were to succeed.[6] It is clear that the interview has many pitfalls. The interviewer must be constantly vigilant to prevent errors that could prejudice a hiring decision.

A recent review of the research on interviewing by Arvey and Campion provided numerous important insights that are important to the library interviewer.[7] Among these are the following:

Interviewer Decisions:

- Interviewers make decisions about candidates very early in the interviewing process. Some studies showed that interviewers made decisions in the first four minutes of the interview.
- Interviewers weigh negative information more heavily than positive information. Interviewers must therefore be careful not to focus only on negative information but to ensure that the candidate's good points are fairly evaluated.
- Interviewers who know more about the job to be filled are more likely to rate interviewees reliably. Such a finding is important because it suggests that library interviewers should possess a good knowledge of library practice. Similarly, it highlights the need to have more than one interviewer, especially if the position requires a wide variety of skills.
- Generally, there are considerable differences in how interviewers rate the same individual. Because of this, libraries must be scrupulous in their training of interviewers to ensure that they know clearly on what criteria they are basing their judgments. This may not entirely eliminate variations in ratings, but it will limit it.
- The interviewer's personal feelings (e.g. liking or disliking) toward the candidate weigh heavily in the interview decision and tend to overcome other pertinent considerations. Because interviewing is a distinctly human process, it is impossible for interviewers to set aside totally their subjective feelings. The fact that liking or disliking a candidate plays such a strong role emphasizes the importance of interviewers being sensitive to the potential for distorting their evaluations for subjective reasons. Libraries must be especially sensitive if this "liking" or "disliking" is based on the race, sex, age, handicap, religion, or national origin of a candidate.
- The interviewer's nonverbal behavior affects interviewee response; positive nonverbal behavior is perceived to relax the interviewee and leads to a better impression. The central purpose of the interview is to get as much information as possible from the interviewee. The interviewer can foreclose this process by behavior which indicates lack of interest, hostility, distraction, or frustration. It is a doubly difficult problem because inter-

viewers may not know that they are sending this message by body language.

- The interviewee's perceptions of the interviewer's personality, manner of delivery, and adequacy of information provided influences his or her attitude toward the organization and the likelihood of accepting the position. Because the interview is both a screening and recruiting tool, the library wants to put its best foot forward, especially to candidates that it desires. Interviewers should therefore strive to project a positive image to ensure that good candidates are not given a poor impression.

Interviewee Behavior and Characteristics

- Nonverbal behaviors such as eye contact, smiling, and low energy play an important role in influencing the evaluation of the interviewer. It appears that the body language of the interviewee is as important as the body language of the interviewer. Interviewers must avoid inappropriately weighing these factors in the decision-making process. A study by Forbes and Jackson involving more than 100 interviews revealed that rejections were often associated with the interviewee's poor eye contact, neutral facial expressions, and holding their heads still instead of nodding during conversation.[8] Although these factors should not be ignored, interviewers must focus on the knowledge, skill, and ability of the candidate, rather than personal mannerisms.
- Women are generally given lower ratings than men with the same knowledge and qualifications, especially when applying for jobs perceived as "masculine." Prejudices concerning the capacities of women may be particularly insidious in librarianship. Although women dominate numerically, they do not dominate in administrative positions, especially in the larger libraries. Interviewers must be very careful not to make false assumptions such as "women can not lead men"; or "women can not make hard or logical choices."
- Attractive candidates of either sex receive higher evaluations than unattractive candidates. As with nonverbal behavior, interviewers, like most other human beings, respond positively to what is socially deemed to be "beautiful," and negatively to what is deemed to be "ugly." Unfortunately, interviewers infer from this attractiveness a sense of competency on the part of the candidate. Interviewers must judge the candidate on abilities, not on physical attractiveness.
- Handicapped individuals are evaluated less favorably than nonhandicapped individuals. People who are different from us are often seen in a negative light. Unfortunately, many people react to individuals with obvious handicaps with discomfort. The interviewer must try to limit this reaction. This is important not just for legal reasons, but because it is ethically wrong to judge a person by their handicap. The interviewer must focus on what the individual can do and its relation to the essential functions of the job, not on what the interviewee can not do, or whether the candidate looks different.

- Applicants with definite foreign accents were given lower evaluations for high status jobs, and *higher* evaluations for low status jobs. As with other prejudices, foreign accents denote a "difference" which may wrongly suggest lack of knowledge, intelligence, or competence.
- Blacks are generally given *higher* evaluations than whites. This finding may be both surprising and curious to some. One would presume that in a world where racial prejudice is common, blacks would receive lower ratings. This is not the case. Possibly it is a result of the fact that interviewers are now highly sensitive to the principles of equal employment opportunity so they "bend over backwards" to give black candidates a fair break. It is certainly a promising finding, but whether actual hires increase is uncertain.

Interview Structure and Procedures

- Structured interviews are more reliable and valid than unstructured. It is easy for interviews to begin to wander and become unfocused. When this occurs, interviewers may find they have failed to collect all the relevant information so that candidates can be compared. Structured interviews require that the same basic questions be asked of all candidates, reducing the possibility of missing relevant information.
- Group or panel interviews increase the reliability and validity of interviews. When there is only one interviewer it is more likely that subjective likes and dislikes will influence the decision-making process. Because people vary in their likes and dislikes, multiple interviewers supply checks and balances against individual prejudices. In addition, slightly different questions and emphasis enrich the amount and type of information obtained.
- Interview evaluations are more accurate when based on specific job criteria. In general, interviewers should try to match the specific knowledge, skill, and ability of the candidate to specific job tasks. This is easiest for jobs with clearly defined tasks, rather than generalized criteria.
- Training improves the performance of interviewers. Library employers should make every effort to provide regular and intense training to all individuals who conduct interviews. Because of the many pitfalls in the interviewing process and the liabilities and expense of selecting the wrong individual, considerable fiscal and human resources should be devoted to honing interviewers' skills.

Suffice it to say that the research on interviewing tells us that the process is complex, difficult, and susceptible to many problems. Even extraneous things such as perfume scents, masculinity or femininity of dress, articulation, pauses in speech patterns, handshakes, physical distances, and seating arrangements have been known to affect interview outcomes. The interviewer should also be aware of two other psychological factors: contrast effect and confirmatory judgments.

Contrast Effect

There is some reason to believe that the order in which candidates are interviewed can affect interviewer ratings. For example, when two candidates are being interviewed back-to-back, if the first candidate exhibits excellent qualities for the job, the candidate following will be rated lower than would otherwise have been the case. Conversely, if the first candidate performs poorly during the interview, the subsequent candidate will be rated higher. In any case, the interviewer must be aware of this potential effect in order to compensate for distortions in the rating process.

Confirmatory Judgments

There is also evidence that interviewers construct or ask their questions in such as way as to confirm prejudgments of the suitability of the candidate formed before the interview was conducted. For example, a candidate's resume or letters of reference may have created a positive or negative impression in the mind of the interviewer. The interviewer then asks questions in such a way as to confirm this impression, which does not give an equal opportunity to prospective candidates. If the interviewer has a negative impression of the candidate, questions are more apt to be phrased in a negative manner or elicit negative responses.[9]

Gender and Interviewing

As noted earlier, the relationship of gender to employee selection is especially pertinent in librarianship where women dominate numerically. Because a disproportionately small number of women have managerial and administrative positions, there is reason to believe that selection procedures for higher-level positions may be faulty. Although it is tempting to believe that individuals intentionally apply discriminatory criteria, the problem is considerably more complex.

There is no research specific to libraries concerning gender bias in the interview process itself, but the general social science literature is suggestive. In general, women tend to receive lower ratings when applying for managerial, scientific, and semiskilled positions. This is echoed in academic institutions for professorships. When women are offered positions, they tend to be at a lower rank and for less salary.[10] It appears that the influence of sex bias is mediated by the type of job for which the individual is applying. When the applicant is applying for a job which is considered "appropriate" for a woman, for example teaching children, gender bias diminishes. This is called "sex-role congruence." In general, women were considered more desirable as employees when they exhibited less assertive, nonsuccess oriented (nonmasculine) traits. It is also important to note, however, that men suffer from similar problems. Men who apply for jobs that conflict with their sex-role stereotypes (e.g. librarians?) receive lower ratings than their female counterparts.[11]

Especially important for the interview and selection process, bias was found to diminish as the amount of job-related information about the candidate increased. It is vital, therefore, that the hiring process collect as much job-related information as possible to keep biases to an absolute minimum.

Interview Preparation

Interview preparation is critical for two reasons: first, a great deal of important information needs to be gathered in an organized fashion, and second, good preparation tends to limit the biases and prejudices that can unconsciously skew the interview process. A structured interview process means asking each candidate the same basic questions. This does not mean that other follow-up questions based on the candidates responses are prohibited. On the contrary, follow-up questions are essential to elicit the necessary information. Some of the steps that should be followed prior to an interview are the following:

Steps to Follow Prior to an Interview
- Examine the current job description for the position. Make sure the information is accurate and identify the most important tasks, knowledge, skills, and abilities required.
- Prepare a list of questions that will elicit essential information from the candidate related to the important areas identified from the job description.
- Examine the candidate's resume to suggest special questions that might be asked related to the candidate's particular knowledge, skill, and ability.
- Review the questions that can *not* be asked because of equal employment opportunity regulations, and make sure no such questions are being asked in the interview.
- Make sure that the interviewing area is private and that the interview will not be disturbed. Remember that the candidate who must suffer interruptions from telephone calls or staff members coming in and out of the

room may feel that his or her candidacy is not being treated seriously and with respect. This is not good public relations and it also makes it difficult to assess the candidate when the train of thought of either the interviewer or interviewee is interrupted.

Question Formulation

Interviewer Obligations

Asking questions is a difficult task and a special responsibility. The interview setting is one in which the interviewer has considerable power, and the range of questioning can be broad and deep. Some interviewers may wander into personal areas that are not job related, and the interviewee may feel obligated to answer such questions, even though they are inappropriate. The ethical and professional obligations of interviewing must always be observed; nonjob-related questions must be avoided, and the interviewee's privacy must be respected. In a good interview, the interviewer asks not only for descriptive details of an individual's past, but also explores the attitudes, beliefs, and values related to the interviewee's work and education. This can often mean exploring areas that are sensitive. Most interviewers, like most interviewees, are uncomfortable about such explorations. For example, it is usually difficult and uncomfortable when the interviewer must examine the reasons why an individual was involuntarily terminated from a previous position. The interviewer must, nonetheless, explore this information in detail, especially if the reasons for termination might relate to the individual's ability to perform in the new position. Probing sensitive areas requires questioning skill, diplomacy, a nonjudgmental attitude, and patience. But it is an obligation of the interviewer to obtain any information that may help predict the success or failure of the employee. Many times, the interviewee, if given a chance, will provide ample and acceptable explanations for difficulties in previous work situations, which might not otherwise have been available to the interviewer.

Inappropriate Questions

Perhaps the most difficult part of preparing and conducting the interview is preparing and asking the right questions. Some believe that current antidiscrimination laws make it difficult to ask important questions. This is not true. All the important job-related questions can be asked. Nonetheless, it is important to identify those questions which are inadvisable in that they suggest underlying discrimination. Figure 2-4 lists questions that should *not* be asked. Some of the more important concern:

- **Age**: Generally, questions about age are inappropriate. There may, however, be job-related circumstances in which age is needed. For example, if the organization employs young people and they are required to work at night, various child labor laws might restrict work based on age. For such positions, the candidate's age may be asked.
- **Handicap**: General questions concerning a candidate's physical or mental impairments are not appropriate. However, it is permissible to ask if the candidate suffers any physical or mental disabilities that would limit his or her performance in a specific job.
- **Marital and Family Status**: It is inappropriate to ask questions concerning marital status, number of children, child-care arrangements, or pregnancy. If the interviewer is concerned about ability to meet a schedule due to family responsibilities, it is appropriate to ask if the individual would have any trouble meeting the work schedule as presented by the employer. Also, the interviewer may explore attendance records at previous jobs.
- **Race/Color**: Any inquiry concerning race or color, or any questions indirectly related to race or color, are inappropriate.
- **Religion**: Questions concerning religion are inappropriate, including questions about religious holidays that are observed. This is not to say that the issue of religious accommodation is irrelevant, but it must be related to meeting a regular work schedule rather than to the religious beliefs themselves.

Anchoring

A common problem when developing interview questions is vagueness. Too often they are formulated without direct reference to the candidate's educational or work record. For example, the interviewer can ask the candidate: "Describe what you want in a supervisor." But this question does not reveal anything about the attitude of the interviewee toward actual supervision. In contrast, one could ask questions that "anchor" general inquiries to specific work or educational experiences. For example: "Describe your last supervisor." "What did you like about his or her supervisory approach?" "What did you dislike?" or "Describe your favorite supervisor." "Why did you like this supervisor?"

This type of information gathering—anchoring general information to specific experience—gives the interviewer specific information about the interviewee's previous work experience and simultaneously explores general attitudes toward supervision. Underlying the technique of anchoring is the premise that performance in previous jobs is a stronger indicator of future performance than the interviewee's general remarks. Question formulation should focus on actual work and educational experience. This may also circumvent any tendency the interviewee has to "snow" the interviewer with glittering generalities.

A second sense of "anchoring" involves a common problem; interviewers sometimes express frustration because they have a "subjective" impression of a candidate, but have nothing "solid" on which to base it.

FIGURE 2-4.

AREA OF INQUIRY	LEGAL
1. Name	a) For access purposes, inquiry into whether the applicant's work records are under another name.
2. Address/Housing	a) To request place and length of current and previous addresses. b) To ask for applicant's phone number or how he or she can be reached.
3. Age	a) Require proof of age by birth certificate, *after hiring*.
4. Birthplace/National Origin	
5. Race/Color	a) To indicate that the institution is an equal opportunity employer. b) To ask race for affirmative action plan statistics, *after hiring*.
6. Sex	a) To indicate that the institution is an equal opportunity employer. b) To ask sex for affirmative action plan statistics, *after hiring*.
7. Religion/Creed	
8. Citizenship	a) Whether a U.S. citizen. b) If not, whether intends to become one. c) If U.S. residence is legal. d) If spouse is a citizen. e) Require proof of citizenship, *after hiring*.
9. Marital/Parental Status	a) Status (only married or single) *after hiring* for insurance and tax purposes. b) Number and ages of dependents and age of spouse *after hiring* for insurance and tax purposes.
10. Relatives	a) To ask name, relationship and address of person to be notified in case of emergency, *after hiring*.
11. Military Service	a) Inquiry into service in the U.S. armed forces. b) Branch of service and rank attained. c) Any job-related experience. d) Require military discharge certificate *after hiring*.
12. Education	a) To ask what academic, professional or vocational schools attended. b) To ask about language skills, such as reading and writing foreign languages.
13. Criminal Record	a) To request listing of convictions other than misdemeanors.
14. References	a) To request general and work references not relating to race, color, religion, sex, national origin or ancestry.
15. Organizations	a) To ask organizational membership — professional, social, etc. — so long as affiliation is not used to discriminate on the basis of race, sex, national origin or ancestry. b) Offices held, if any.
16. Photographs	a) May be required *after hiring* for identification purposes.
17. Work Schedule	a) To ask willingness to work required work schedule. b) To ask if applicant has military reservist obligations.
18. Physical Data	a) To require applicant to prove ability to do manual labor, lifting and other physical requirements of the job, if any. b) Require a physical examination.
19. Handicap	a) To inquire for the purpose of determining applicant's capability to perform the job. (Burden of proof for non-discrimination lies with the employer.)
20. Other qualifications	a) To inquire about any area that has a direct reflection on the job applied for.

ILLEGAL	LEGISLATION*
	Title VII of the Civil Rights Act of 1964 as amended by the Equal Employment Opportunity Act of 1972. (Title VII) Title IX of the Education Amendments of 1972. (Title IX)
a) To ask if a woman is a Miss, Mrs. or Ms. b) To request applicant to give maiden name, or any other previous name he or she has used.	
	Title VII
a) To ask age or age group of applicant. b) To request birth certificate or baptismal record before hiring.	Age Discrimination Act of 1967
a) To ask birthplace of applicant or that of his or her parents, grandparents or spouse. b) Any other inquiry into national origin.	Title VII
a) Any inquiry that would indicate race or color.	Title VII
a) To ask applicant any inquiry which would indicate sex, unless job-related. (Only such jobs in education would be a full-time locker room or restroom attendant.)	Title VII Title IX
a) To ask an applicant's religion or religious customs and holidays. b) To request recommendations from church officials.	Title VII
a) If native-born or naturalized. b) Proof of citizenship before hiring. c) Whether parents or spouse is native-born or naturalized. d) Date of citizenship.	Title VII
a) To ask marital status before hiring. b) To ask the number and age of children, who cares for them and if applicant plans to have more children.	Title VII Title IX
a) Names of relatives working for the institution or in a district (nepotism policies which impact disparately on one sex are illegal under Title IX.)	
a) To request military service records. b) To ask about military service in armed service of any country other than the U.S. c) Type of discharge.**	Title VII Title IX **EEOC interpretation on Title VII
a) Specifically ask the nationality, racial or religious affiliation of schools attended. b) To ask how foreign language ability was acquired.	Title VII
a) To inquire about arrests.	Title VII
a) To request references specifically from clergy or any other persons who might reflect race, color, religion, sex, national origin or ancestry.	Title VII Title IX
a) To request listing of all clubs applicant belongs to or has belonged to.	Title VII Title IX
a) Request photographs before hiring. b) To take pictures of applicants during interviews.	Title VII Title IX
a) To ask willingness to work any particular religious holiday.	Title VII
a) To ask height and weight, impairment or other non-specified job-related physical data	
a) To exclude handicapped applicants as a class on the basis of their type of handicap. (Each case must be determined on an individual basis by law).	Title IX (sight provisions)
a) Any non-job-related inquiry that may present information permitting unlawful discrimination.	

*The designated legislation is the primary statutory authority. However, the interpretive regulations of this legislation is the basis for determining the finer points and these regulations should be reviewed to determine

This is often caused by failure to "anchor" a subjective impression to a specific behavior or statement on the part of the interviewee. Whenever an interviewer begins to get a "feeling" about a candidate, it is incumbent that he or she try to anchor this feeling to a specific fact. For example, suppose the interviewer begins to feel that the candidate would not get along well with other people. The interviewer might employ such questions as: "What types of activities did you like best in your previous jobs?" (Looking for whether the candidate prefers to work alone or as part of a team.) "What was your most successful project in your previous position? What was your least successful project and why?" (The interviewer may discover communication problems or problems of coordination with others.) Similarly, the interviewer could ask for the interviewee's perception of his or her co-workers in previous position(s). In any case, subjective impressions should be anchored to "objective" statements by the candidate whenever possible.

Interview Questions

The type and content of interview questions vary considerably depending on the level of position that is open. Some questions are formulated to gather specific information, while others are devised to encourage expansiveness on the part of the candidate. Questions that can be answered very briefly or with a yes or no are referred to as "closed-ended" questions; those that are meant to encourage the candidate to talk are "open-ended questions." Both have a purpose. Closed-ended questions can often be used to verify information that is unclear or incomplete on an application, such as an address or name of a reference. Open-ended questions are meant to elicit information about the candidate's experience, education, abilities, and values. Open-ended questions play a vital role in the interview and should be used liberally. The following section gives some examples that could be used with appropriate modification.

Questions Probing Knowledge
Training and Education: The purpose of asking questions concerning training is to gather relevant information on the knowledge and skills acquired by the candidate while in school. Questions should be focused on the knowledge and skills required for the particular job itself.

Sample Questions
1. What courses did you take in school that would help you perform the job for which you are applying? How would you apply this knowledge to your job?

2. Did you receive special vocational or technical training that would help you perform this job? (Are you taking continuing education courses? What courses, and how do you think they will aid you in your work?)
3. Did you receive special training while you were in military service that would help you perform this job? What type of training did you receive and how would you apply it to this position?
4. Do you possess any other training which would help you perform your job? (For example, did the individual work in the school library?)

Self assessment of educational experience: It is important to determine the applicants' assessment of their own abilities. In addition, it is useful to find out to what they attribute their own successes or failures. Always keep in mind that an admission of failure is not in and of itself a negative; individuals who are thoughtful about their failures and indicate they have learned from them are demonstrating a valuable characteristic of an employee.

Sample Questions
1. Which courses did you like the best? The least? Why?
2. In which courses did you perform the best? Were there courses that gave you difficulty?
3. Are you particularly proud of any particular project or activity in which you were involved while you were in school? Tell me about it.

Questions Probing Work Experience

Reviewing the duties of the candidate's previous work can be very important. The interviewer can carefully probe the candidate's job values and attitudes, ability to communicate, plan, organize, budget, supervise, and work with others. The interviewer must carefully review the resume to determine if the candidate has substantial job gaps, or moves from job to job in short periods of time. These factors can often be examined while discussing the individual's reasons for leaving jobs. For *each* position held by the candidate, especially positions held in the last five years, the following general areas should be probed:

Job Tasks: Resumes provide a listing of the duties performed by the candidate. However, they seldom reveal the actual *amount* of experience the candidate has with the duties identified. For this reason, questions must be formulated to get a quantitative assessment.

Sample Questions
1. What were the specific tasks of your job?
2. On which tasks did you spend the greatest amount of time? What percent of the time did you spend on each task?
3. Which tasks did you enjoy the most? Which tasks did you enjoy least? Why? (This should help give information on the individual's desire to

work with the public, ability to get along with, and communicate with, others, etc.)

4. Describe the project or achievement in your last job of which you are proudest.
5. Was the position full- or part-time?
6. Describe your work schedule. Was this type of scheduling satisfactory to you? Would you prefer to have a different schedule? What is it?
7. Were you left in charge when the supervisor was gone? Why do you think you were given this responsibility? How did you feel about being left in charge?
8. What were your strongest points in working with the public? Were there areas where you thought you needed improvements? What were they?
9. Did you have to fill in for absent employees, or for employees who went on vacation? How did you feel about this?

Supervisory Relationships: It is important to get some impression of the individuals' attitude toward supervision. Do they work well under close or loose supervision? Do they have trouble getting along with supervisors? Some idea may be obtained with the following questions:

Sample Questions
1. Describe your work relationship with your immediate supervisor.
2. What did you like about your supervisor? What did you dislike? (This should assist in determining the supervisory style that the employee wants.)
3. If we contacted your immediate supervisor, what would they say about your performance?

Supervisory Responsibilities: If the position to be filled involves employee supervision, it is vital to probe an individual's experience with and attitude toward supervisory duties, especially the ones that involve potential legal liabilities such as discrimination.

Sample Questions
1. Did the position involve supervision? If the answer to this is yes, and the position for which the individual applying is supervisory in nature, then the following questions should be considered:
2. How many people did you supervise?
3. Were they full- or part-time?
4. Were they clerical or professional positions?
5. Did you hire, evaluate, discipline, or terminate employees?
6. How did you feel about disciplining or firing an employee?
7. How did you prepare for a disciplinary or termination interview?
8. What would you do differently as a supervisor today?
9. What was the most difficult aspect of supervision?
10. What characteristics do you look for in an employee?
11. How do you prepare for a performance evaluation of an employee?

12. Have you had to evaluate a poor performer?
13. How did you handle the situation?
14. Did the employee's performance improve? Why? Why not?
15. What could you have done differently?

If the candidates have not previously supervised, it is still important to ask questions concerning their knowledge and attitudes. A question such as: "How would you prepare for an interview with a poorly performing employee and why?" can provide revealing information.

Reasons for Leaving: There is, perhaps, no more delicate subject in the employment interview than probes of reasons for leaving a previous place of employment. The interviewer may, of course, make a direct query—"Why did you leave that position?" If, however, this seems threatening, the interviewer might, after discussing the job, say "...and then you left this position?" This approach invites discussion of the reasons for leaving in a less threatening way.

The reasons for leaving are important to the new employer. They may reveal aspects of the work environment that the employee likes or dislikes; information on supervisory preferences, salary requirements, and personal qualities. If, for example, the employee left because there was lack of variety in the job, the interviewer must assess whether the new job will provide ample variety.

It is also essential to know whether the separation was voluntary or involuntary. Keep in mind that "resigned" does not tell you whether the termination was voluntary or involuntary. Perhaps the employee was given the opportunity to resign, but failure to resign would have resulted in termination. Therefore, resignation should not be considered an adequate response to queries concerning reasons for leaving.

Sample Questions
1. Can you discuss with me your reasons for leaving this position?
2. Did you leave on your own accord or did your employer ask that you leave?
3. Can you discuss with me the reasons why your employer asked that you leave?
4. Can you describe your relationship with your supervisor when you left?
5. Can you describe the relationship with your co-workers or subordinates when you left?

From time to time an interviewee may refuse to discuss the reasons for leaving a position. It may be useful, however, for the interviewer to attempt to get minimal information such as whether the reasons were work-related or personal. It may then be necessary for the library to contact the previous employer for more information.

Work Environment: Working conditions can be a major source of employee discontent. It is critical that the interviewer determine what the future employee wants and needs in terms of the work atmosphere and environment.

Sample Questions
1. Describe your previous work environment. What did you like about it? What did you dislike about it?
2. How did you handle any dissatisfactions you had with the work environment?
3. Describe your ideal work environment.

General Questions

For most positions, there are some general questions that need to be asked. These may range from broad philosophical issues to specifics regarding ability to get to work and meet a work schedule. They can and often do deal with important considerations regarding the candidate's suitability for work in the library.

Sample Questions
1. Why have you applied for this position?
2. Given this position's work schedule, would you have any difficulty meeting a regular schedule?
3. Would you have any difficulty getting to work?
4. If you had your preference would you work full- or part-time?
5. Do you have a specific salary requirement?
6. Given the responsibilities of this job, would you have any difficulty performing the essential functions?
7. If you were offered the position, when could you start working?
8. Do you have any questions concerning this position or the organization?
9. Do you have any additional information that you would like to tell us that would help us make a decision?

Conducting the Interview

When conducting the interview, there are issues that the interviewer should keep in mind. Most important, interviewers must remember that this is a stressful time for the candidate. Many candidates listen very carefully to every word and study every nuance of the interviewer; often they interpret trivial or offhand remarks as having much greater meaning than they actually have. Candidates must always be treated with respect, sensitivity, and diplomacy.

Maintain a Positive Attitude
Research has found that the attitude of the interviewer affects interview responses.[12] The interviewer should be positive and professional in

approach and demeanor. Such an attitude puts the interviewee at ease and increases the chance that the interviewee will provide the most information. Similarly, the interviewer should not exhibit disapproval when negative information is supplied by the candidate. If a candidate indicates, for example, that he or she was terminated from a previous position, the interviewer should show a serious demeanor, rather than one of disapproval. The interview is neither a casual conversation nor an interrogation. It is a business activity designed to gather business-related information. In general, this can be accomplished with a friendly but business-like approach.

Make the Candidate Comfortable
If the candidate is meeting the interviewer for the first time, the greeting should be friendly and enthusiastic. A minimum amount of small-talk may help put the candidate at ease, but it should be limited. If there is going to be a group or panel interview, all members of the panel should be introduced and their positions in the organization identified. The interviewer should review for the candidate how the interview will proceed, and the interviewee should be allowed to ask any questions about the process before beginning.

Take notes: Maintaining records throughout the hiring process is essential. Written notes have three advantages:

- They are a valuable support for the memory of the interviewer. Often, interviews are lengthy, numerous, and conducted over a period of weeks. The interviewer is not likely to remember all the important points raised in a given interview.
- Written notes allow the interviewer to go back over the candidate's responses so that they can be analyzed, compared, contrasted;
- Written notes provide important documentation of a hiring decision if that decision is subsequently challenged by an unsuccessful candidate.

Notes should be made while the interview is being conducted. Sometimes this means that the interviewer loses eye contact with the interviewee. The interviewer must be sensitive to this, and make a significant effort to re-establish eye contact frequently. The interviewer should make an effort to *delay* recording negative information until after it has been given. If, for example, an applicant is discussing involuntary termination for misconduct, it is best to listen carefully, and record the information later.

From time to time, an applicant volunteers information that the interviewer does not want, such as religious beliefs, marital status, or number of children in the household. The interviewer must keep in mind that notes could be used as evidence in a subsequent challenge. When inappropriate information is given in the interview it should be ignored and should not be recorded in the notes.

Ask only job-related questions: The focus of the interview should be information that helps the interviewer predict the future success of the candidate. The interview should not wander into private or personal areas that bear little or no relation to the job. On the other hand, the range and variety of questions can be considerable so long as they are job related. The interviewer should emphasize open-ended questions which invite the candidate to talk, rather than closed-ended questions that can be answered with a simple yes or no.

Closing the interview: As the interview ends, the candidate should be allowed to ask questions, and to add any additional information that seems relevant. The candidate should be informed as to when a job decision will be made, and how the candidate will be notified. Because the job interview is also a public relations activity, it is important to thank the interviewee for taking the time to participate in the interview process.

Following the interview, it is useful to review your notes with particular attention to those responses related to the individual's knowledge, skill, and ability. Also, any responses which revealed potential problems with the candidate should be tagged for future review.

Showing the candidate around: It is the practice of some organizations to take the candidate on a tour of the facility. This gives the candidate a better idea of the organization and allows other employees to meet and talk to the candidate. Sometimes this may involve taking the candidate to lunch or dinner with other staff members. Although this may be a valuable practice, the interviewer must keep in mind that there is no such thing as an informal part of the hiring process. Staff members should be cautioned not to ask inappropriate questions. For example, staff members should refrain from asking questions about a person's race, religion, national origin, marital status, or family situation.

Potential Interviewing Errors

Because of the complexity of the interview process, it is useful to summarize potential interviewing errors. Here are some of the common failures in the interview process and their consequences:

- Failure to have a clear idea of the job to be filled, and to have a written description of the job. This results in an unfocused interview and will confuse the selection decision because the qualifications of the candidates cannot be compared against a set of job tasks.
- Failure to focus questions on the knowledge, skill, and abilities required for the job. This will also make it impossible to compare candidates' skills

with the job tasks. It may also open the library to charges of discrimination.

- Failure to prepare for the interview—to review carefully the application form and resume. This may waste library resources because unqualified or otherwise inappropriate candidates are invited for interview. Similarly, poor preparation can lead to a poorly focused interview and an impression on the candidate's part of an unprofessional organization.
- Failure to filter out preconceived notions about the candidate. This adversely affects the interviewer's ability to pick the best qualified candidate thus damaging the library's productivity. Similarly, it could lead to charges of discrimination if the preconceptions deal with race, religion, or other characteristics protected by law.
- Failure to make the candidate comfortable so that free expression is encouraged. This results in inaccurate or insufficient information in the interview, and gives the interviewee a poor impression of the library.
- Failure to conduct a structured interview in which the same basic information is gathered from all candidates. This severely limits the ability to compare candidates and gives the impression of confusion to the interviewee.
- Failure to ask questions of each candidate in a positive way and in a similar manner. This gives an unneccesarily negative cast to interviewee responses, and gives the interviewee an impression that a prejudgment has been made. It also reduces the candidate's communicativeness.
- Failure to probe sensitive but job-related areas. This leads to loss of vital information, and possibly hiring a person who may be inappropriate and harmful to the library.
- Failure to evaluate responses in a consistent fashion. This leads to the unfair elimination of qualified candidates and the hire of lesser qualified ones.
- Failure to listen carefully to the candidate and to take detailed notes in the interview. Candidates cannot be adequately compared unless the information is absorbed by the interviewer; similarly, without written notes, it is hard to document a job selection if the decision is challenged.
- Failure to abide by Equal Employment Opportunity laws and regulations. This subjects the organization to unnecessary and considerable liabilities. It is also unethical and unprofessional conduct.
- Failure to provide privacy and a comfortable setting for the candidate. This seriously restricts the chance that the candidate will be expansive, and interferes with the interviewer's ability to question and absorb important information.
- Failure to give the applicant an opportunity to ask questions. This affects the applicant's ability to assess the suitability of the job. Consequently, candidates may mistakenly decide that they do not want a position with the library. Similarly, the types of questions a candidate asks may provide additional information to the interviewer concerning what the candidate thinks is important.
- Failure to wait until the interview is over before drawing conclusions about the candidate. This leads to incorrect judgments and fails to give candidates an equal chance to convince the interviewer of their suitability.

USING TESTS AND TRYOUTS

The selection interview is the most common method of hiring in business, industry, and librarianship. Its ubiquity despite evidence that it is problematical suggests that the interview may serve other functions than just prediction of knowledge, skill, and ability on the job. Research suggests that such characteristics as motivation and ability to work with people are also being assessed.[13] Other techniques, notably tests, have also been used, particularly by industry, to determine job suitability. There is no available information on exactly how many libraries use such tests in their hiring process, although anecdotal information suggests that few do.

No matter what test is used, the employer must be aware that testing is subject to close scrutiny by the Equal Employment Opportunity Commission. To the Commission, a test is very broadly construed and includes "measures of general intelligence, mental ability, and learning ability; specific intellectual abilities, mechanical, clerical, and other aptitudes; dexterity and coordination; knowledge and proficiency of occupational and other interests; and attitudes, personality, or temperament."[14] It also includes less obvious parts of the selection process such as interviewer ratings. For this reason it is crucial that each test be carefully developed. Employers should be particularly sensitive to the possibility of interviewers or supervisors administering a self-styled test without the knowledge of the administration. Interviewers must be cautioned that informal quizzing of the candidate could be construed as a test and subject to challenge.

There are many aspects of a given test that the employer must consider. Of critical concern is the fact that many job tests have been shown to have differential results along racial lines; blacks tend to score lower than whites on employment tests, and such conditions can lead to charges of "adverse impact." If differential results are occurring, it becomes necessary for the employer to validate the test; that is, establish that the test is a valid measure of future performance on the job. In other words, the employer must demonstrate that the test measures what it is supposed to measure. Because this usually requires statistical analysis, the employer should have an expert validate the test. In smaller organizations, however, this may be prohibitively expensive. Consequently, the employer should monitor test results very closely. If more blacks, or other minorities, are failing the tests than whites, the organization must consider either eliminating the test or spending money to validate it. Validation standards are issued by the government in the *Uniform Guidelines on Employee Selection*, and *Questions and Answers on the Uniform Guidelines on Employee Selection Procedures* (Appendix C).

When a test is proposed or developed it should at least possess what is called *face validity*. This means that there is an obvious relationship between the knowledge or skill being tested, and the activities of the job itself. For example, if a typist is being hired, then a typing test would likely have face validity, as long as the minimum standard set for the test is reasonably related to the job to be performed. This minimum standard should be met even in the absence of adverse impact. Similarly, libraries should be hesitant to borrow tests even from other libraries. The tests must be related to the specific job to be done, not to some other job in another library.

It is also important for the employer to have a realistic view of tests and a clear idea of how they fit into the hiring process. Employers must be especially scrupulous if test scores, in and of themselves, are used to *eliminate* a candidate for consideration. Such a test plays a vital role and great care must be exercised not only in its preparation, but also in its administration and evaluation. In general, a single test should not be used to exclude an individual from consideration. As any former student is aware, test taking is as much an art as it is a measure of knowledge or skill. A good employee may be lost by the employer if the applicant is the type of person who is extremely nervous or anxious in the test-taking situation. A test should be considered as part, not all, of the hiring process.

Paper Tests

There are many different types of paper and pencil tests. The most common is the intelligence test. It seems unlikely that intelligence tests would be necessary in the library setting. In the past, some libraries have used paper and pencil tests to assess a librarian's knowledge of titles. For example, some tests asked the candidate to identify works of a certain period, or of a certain genre. It is important that the employer using such tests ensure that this type of knowledge is essential to the performance of the job and that a primary responsibility of the job entails this type of title recognition. Other paper and pencil tests for support staff may be appropriate. For example, the Minnesota Clerical Test might prove useful for clerical staff and shelvers. Of course, the library should attempt to validate the use of such a test before using it to make job decisions.

Work Simulation

In a work simulation test, the actual tasks of the job are simulated. For hiring library support staff, such activities as typing and filing tests are common; for shelvers some libraries ask the applicant to shelve some books so that their accuracy can be evaluated. These tests are fairly straightforward. Careful attention must be paid to the activity simulated to be sure it is similar to the actual tasks to be performed on the job.

Job openings for librarians, managers, and administrators may require more complex tests, which, in turn, makes them somewhat more difficult to evaluate. Simulations may include exercises for interviewing, problem-solving, scheduling, and planning. One technique that can test several skills at once is the *in-basket* test. In this test, the candidate is given a variety of documents—correspondence, memoranda, letters— and asked to deal with the issues raised in the documents. Because the tasks are complex, so is the evaluation. Before administering such a test, the evaluators should have a clear idea what types of responses receive the most points, and which the least.

CHECKING REFERENCES

Although checking references is a common activity among employers, there is substantial reason to believe that they are not especially useful in helping interviewers judge prospective employees.[15][16] Generally, references are positive, or sufficiently circumspect so that little concrete assistance is given. Nonetheless, the employer would be remiss to ignore this source of knowledge of employee performance. Emphasis should be on work rather than personal references, and on factual information rather than on personal opinions about the candidate's suitability.[17] This should help ensure that the information obtained is work related.

It is important that the employer get consent *in writing* from the prospective employee to check references. This can be accomplished with a statement at the end of the application form which must be signed and dated by the candidate. It should say that the potential employer may contact any or all former employers as well as any and all references given by the candidate. The agreement should note that the information obtained may be favorable or unfavorable. It is useful to have legal counsel review this agreement for correct wording. In the work experience section of the application form, it is useful to have a space for each position which the candidate may check if the employer may be contacted. This assures that the employee assents to a reference check for each previous job.

When candidates are currently employed, they usually do not wish their employers to be contacted. They may rightfully worry about jeopardizing their jobs if it became known that they were applying for another position. In such cases, the employer can hire the candidate contingent on obtaining a reference from the current employer.

Written references are generally preferable. Although some people may be more forthright over the telephone or in person, it is best for the future employer to secure information that can be documented if the decision is challenged. If a previous employer does not have the courage to put information down in writing, the future employer should be wary of using it to make an employment decision. In any case, the employer should ask similar questions for all referees, and the questions should be job related.

This places in relief two of the problems with reference checking: unwillingness of past or current employers to write references, and the possibility that employers will not answer truthfully. Former employers fear liability for statements that may damage a person's future employability, and consequently may only be willing to provide such information as dates of employment. Under these circumstances, the prospective employer can do little. If, on the other hand, seriously damaging information is conveyed, it is necessary to discuss the issue with the candidate to get his or her side of the story before making a decision. The employer must make a concerted effort not to listen to libelous or slanderous information from a former employer.

The employer must also be aware that reference checking is subject to the same scrutiny in regard to employment discrimination as all other aspects of the hiring process. If the employer checks references of one candidate, it is wise to check references of all candidates. Similarly, the employer should try to check the same *number* of references for each candidate.

MAKING THE DECISION AND JOB OFFER

The Decision to Hire

The decision to hire has many factors. In some instances the choice is easy—one candidate is clearly superior. In other instances, it is a question of balancing the strengths and weaknesses of one candidate with those of others. Although it is desirable to narrow down the number of candidates in the final pool as quickly as possible, it is only fair to review each one's credentials carefully to identify all important strengths. Interview notes, resumes, letters of reference, and the application form should all be consulted. Emphasis should be placed on the candidate with the most suitable combination of knowledge, skill, and ability. When the selection is narrowed to a small number of qualified candidates, it is important to review any formal affirmative action policies to determine whether an affirmative action hire is appropriate. When selecting the successful candidate, a list of job-related reasons for the selection should be identified and written. This list forms the basis for documenting a hire in case of a challenge by an unsuccessful applicant.

Unless time is pressing, it is advisable to wait perhaps a day, before making the job offer. This gives everyone who made the selection an opportunity to think about their decision. It also gives the personnel officer or director a chance to review the decision, and make sure that the reasons for hire are reasonable and lawful.

Making the Job Offer

Job offers are usually done by phone or in person. It is important that the offer for employment be controlled so that incorrect expectations are not created. If one person is assigned to make all, or most, of the job offers, it is easier to establish exactly what information is to be provided. The greatest danger is that the individual offering the job may make promises implying conditions of a contract. For example, the person offering the job may imply that the employee is guaranteed at least one year of employment when in fact there is a 90-day probationary period. The basic information provided should include salary, starting date and time, name of the supervisor, and any important conditions of employment. This information should be followed by a letter restating all these points and a statement of the probationary period if any.

Informing Unsuccessful Candidates

It is regrettable that many organizations seem to forget the individuals who were unsuccessful in obtaining the job. A letter with a personalized salutation should be promptly sent to each individual indicating that another candidate was selected and thanking them for their willingness to participate in the interview process. It may be appropriate to wish the candidate good fortune in their job search. If the organization has a policy regarding retention of their application, then this should also be part of the letter. Generally, it is not necessary to go into lengthy discussions as to why the candidate was not selected, although it may be appropriate to mention the high quality of the applicant pool. The tone of the letter should be that of appreciation that the candidate considered working for the organization.

PAPERWORK

The selection procedure generates a considerable body of paper which the employer must organize and control. Some of this material is retained in the successful applicant's personnel file: applications, letters of reference, copies of the official offer of employment, and the employee's written acceptance. Interviewers should retain interview notes and ratings, and their reasons for making the decision in case of a subsequent challenge.

In addition to individual records, it is important to make a record of the hiring process as it is occurring. This is sometimes done with what is called an applicant flow log. It lists the names of individuals considered for the position, their race and sex, the referral source, and the disposition of the candidate (e.g. interviewed but not selected, selected, not interviewed). Some logs may ask for reasons regarding selection and nonselection. Such logs are important for monitoring the hiring process to determine if minorities are being disproportionately screened out of the selection process. It is important to remember that each part of the hiring process is subject to scrutiny, not just the final decision.

For the successful applicant, there is a need to create new records. These include the completion of federal and state withholding forms for income taxes, and the collection of personal information such as age, marital status, and family size for insurance purposes. In addition, an I-9 form must now be completed to ensure that the employee is legally able to work in the United States.

THE HIRING PROCESS: LEGAL CONSIDERATIONS

The process of selecting individuals must be conducted within the confines of a variety of laws, regulations, and court decisions. The most prominent ones are those related to employment discrimination. Two basic types of discrimination must be considered by the library administrator: "disparate treatment" and "disparate impact."

Disparate Treatment

The original intent of the 1964 Civil Rights Act was to eliminate intentional discrimination against individuals. This is referred to as "disparate treatment." An individual who believes he or she has been discriminated against must establish what is referred to as a "prima facie" case. The court case frequently cited as defining what is involved in establishing a prima facie case is *McDonnell Douglas Corporation* v *Green*.[18] The court noted that the individual had to show:

> (1) that he belonged to a racial minority, (2) that he applied and was qualified for a job for which the employer was seeking applicants; (3) that, despite his qualifications, he was rejected; and (4) that, after his rejection, the position remained open and the employer continued to seek applicants of complainant's qualifications.

Establishing a prima facie case may not be very difficult. Note that the individual, at this stage, does not have to prove that anyone acted intentionally to discriminate. Once an individual is able to make a prima facie case, the employer is obligated to "articulate some legitimate, nondiscriminatory reason for the employee's rejection."[19] This responsibility highlights the importance of a nondiscriminatory hiring process which focuses on the knowledge, skill, and abilities of the candidate. This helps ensure that unlawful considerations, such as race, are not a factor in the selection process.

If the employer can provide a legitimate business reason for its hiring decision, then it becomes the responsibility of the individual making the charge of discrimination to show that the reason given is merely a "pretext" for actual discrimination.[20] Although this responsibility falls on the shoulders of the individual, it is an important warning to the employer—the reasons for hire, as with any other job decision, should, in fact, have nothing to do with race, sex, age, or any other unlawful consideration. The reasons for selection should be strictly job related.

Although disparate treatment has been reviewed in terms of the hiring process, similar criteria can be applied to other job-related decisions, for example, promotions. One commentator on job discrimination cases has noted that in many instances, individuals will be able to make a prima facie case, and employers will be able to state a legitimate business reasons for their actions. Therefore, the issue will focus on whether the employer's reason was a pretext for discrimination.[21] This means that any actions or statements that the employer has made that may suggest discriminatory intent could be damaging. Scrupulous attention to each aspect of the hiring process is essential and includes explorations of attitudes and actions of individuals involved in the hiring process; even actions that are not directly a part of the hiring process. For example, supervisors who tell racial, ethnic, or sexual jokes may find that their comments, if revealed, play a role in establishing discriminatory intent.

Disparate or Adverse Impact

In addition to disparate treatment, the EEOC has identified disparate adverse impact as a fundamental concern in the prevention of employment discrimination, and has provided a detailed discussion of its definition and measurement in its *Uniform Guidelines on Employee Selection Procedures* (Appendix C).[22] The terms "adverse impact" or "disparate impact" are used to characterize discriminatory *effects* of employment practices rather that intentional acts against individuals (disparate treatment). The *Guidelines* state that:

...a selection process which has an adverse impact on the employment opportunities of members of a race, color, religion, sex, or national origin group...and thus disproportionately screens them out is unlawfully discriminatory unless the process or its component procedures have been validated in accord with the Guidelines...[23]

It is important to note that these guidelines apply to a broad spectrum of employer actions of which hiring is only one. All employment related actions such as decisions to retain, promote, dismiss, and transfer can be subject to the guidelines. Any tests used to make hiring or promotion decisions should conform to the requirements of these guidelines.

A frequently cited example of the legal ramifications of disparate impact is the Supreme Court case, *Griggs* v *Duke Power Co.*[24] In this case, several black employees challenged the requirement that only individuals with a high school diploma, and who took specific intelligence tests could transfer to other departments. The employees were able to demonstrate that this had the effect of disproportionately eliminating blacks from consideration. The court stated that:

...if an employment practice which operates to exclude cannot be shown to be related to job performance the practice is prohibited...practices, procedures, tests...neutral on their face and even neutral in terms of intent cannot be maintained if they operate to freeze the status quo of prior discriminatory practices...[25]

In order to retain practices that have the effect of disproportionately screening out individuals, the court noted that the employer must show that the practice was a "business necessity." For such requirements or tests to meet the definition of a business necessity they must have, at the least, a clear relationship to successful performance on the job. If the employer cannot demonstrate this, then the practice is discriminatory, even though it is not intentional or conscious.

The *Guidelines on Employee Selection Procedures* provide a four-step process to determine "adverse impact" in the hiring process using what is sometimes called the "four-fifths rule." The process involves the following:

(1) Calculate the rate of selection for each group (divide the number of persons selected from a group by the number of applicants from that group). A "group" can be defined as any member of an "affected class" such as blacks, individuals of Hispanic origin, handicapped people, or females.

(2) Observe which group has the highest selection rate;

(3) Calculate the impact ratios, by comparing the selection rate for each group with that of the highest group (divide the selection rate for a group by the selection rate for the highest group).

(4) Observe whether the selection rate for any group is substantially less (i.e. usually less than 4/5ths or 80%) than the selection rate for the highest group. If it is, adverse impact is indicated in most circumstances.[26]

The example provided by the EEOC is instructive. In the case below, an organization is assessing its overall hiring practices by comparing the rate of hire for blacks and those for whites:

Applicants	Hires	Selection rate/percent
80 White	48	48/80 or 60%
40 Black	12	12/50 or 30%

If one compares the black selection rate with the white, one sees that the black selection rate (30%) is one-half or 50% (30/60 = 50%) of the rate for whites. The 4/5ths rule dictates that the selection rate for blacks should be no less than 80% of the white one, therefore an adverse impact has been demonstrated. Note that the reasons *why* such a difference exists is not the issue, nor is discriminatory intent. If such a disparate impact is found, the employer needs to assess the factors producing the disproportionate hiring of whites.

It is important that employers try to ensure that the end result of their hiring practices conforms to the four-fifths rule established by the *Guidelines*. It should be noted however, that employers should also try to apply these guidelines to each part of the hiring process, not just to the final hiring decision. When employers only monitor the hiring decisions themselves, they are using what is called the "bottom line" criteron. It assumes that if, in the end, the work force selected meets the four-fifths rule, then the various procedures leading to the selection decisions were nondiscriminatory. This assumption, however, has been successfully challenged in the Supreme Court in *Teal* v *Connecticut*.[27] The Court noted that all the procedures leading up to the selection can be challenged for adverse impact, and the "bottom line" criterion does not relieve employers of the responsibility to scrutinize the individual steps in the selection process. Employers must therefore be careful that discrimination is eliminated throughout the process of hiring.

Nonetheless, the legal climate may be changing. Recent Supreme Court decisions appear to place less emphasis on statistical procedures that demonstrate adverse impact. The Court appears to be leaning more toward the need for individuals to show that an employer intentionally discriminated. Only careful attention to current court decisions and consultation with competent legal counsel can keep the human resource manager adequately informed of the changing legal situation.

Among the individual factors that employers should examine are the following:

- The recruitment process: Are ads placed only in periodicals that would be read by whites? Do recruiters only visit schools where white students receive training?
- Application process: Are the hours for making applications likely to be more convenient for whites? Are the applications of minorities more likely to be considered for low paying positions?
- Interview process: Are whites more likely to be selected for interview than minorities?
- Selection process: Are whites more likely to be hired?

Affirmative Action

The concept of affirmative action is a controversial one inspiring much litigation and debate concerning its fairness. Underlying the need for affirmative action is that fact that minorities and other groups have, for generations, been subject to discrimination. This discrimination has resulted in a work force in which whites, especially white males, enjoy a privileged position. They occupy the highest paying and best positions and have greater access to superior education, training, and promotions.

Affirmative action is an attempt to remedy this situation. The EEOC defines "affirmative action" as those actions "appropriate to overcome the effects of past or present practices, policies, or other barriers to equal employment opportunity."[28] This is usually accomplished by singling out members of minorities and other protected classes for special consideration. Of course, by singling out members of protected classes for special treatment, affirmative action is criticized for merely changing the victims of discrimination from minorities and women, to white males—hence the term "reverse discrimination." The situation is fraught with opposing social values and beliefs, and the issues will not be resolved here. Nonetheless, reviewing some of the characteristics of affirmative action provides some perspective on this important aspect of human resource management.

Affirmative action may arise from several sources. First, it may be dictated by law if, for example, the library contracts with the federal government. In addition, state or local laws may require that public institutions have affirmative action plans. Second, affirmative action may be ordered by a court if it determines that the employer has discriminated. Finally, affirmative action may arise as a voluntary action on the part of the employer. This is especially true if the library determines that its current work force does not reflect the work force at large in regard to minorities or other protected classes. Voluntary affirmative action is a vital aspect of society's attempt to provide equal opportunity to all workers. Library employers, like other employers, have a positive duty to provide this opportunity, even when there is no threat of legal action.

Voluntary Affirmative Action

It should be emphasized that affirmative action is not needed if the composition of the library work force reflects the work force at large. Indeed, library employers should generally avoid instituting any affirmative action programs until they have compared their work force to the surrounding community. In order to determine if affirmative action is needed, the library should conduct what the EEOC refers to as "reasonable self-analysis." There is no one method of analysis required by the EEOC, but generally it involves a "utilization" study, which compares the local labor force with the library's labor force. For example, if 22% of the library clerical staff is black, but 35% of the clerical work force of the city in which the library is located is black, then there is reason to believe that the library is not hiring enough black clerical workers. When disproportionately small numbers of individuals from a protected class, such as blacks, are represented, this is referred to as "underutilization." In some cases, the "local" work force with which comparisons are made may be geographically larger than the city or town in which the library is located. For example, if the work force of librarians is being studied, the labor force from which librarians are drawn may be statewide, or national. In this case, comparison of the internal work force would be to the state or national work force. Utilization studies are not the only method of analysis possible. An inequality may be obvious. For example, there may be no women or blacks in administrative positions. This is sometimes referred to as a "manifest imbalance." When the discriminatory effect is obvious, there is little need for a utilization study to prompt an affirmative action plan.

If a library has a reasonable basis to conclude that its current work force of minorities and other protected classes, for whatever reason, does not reflect the work force at large, it may consider taking affirmative action. Although some aspects of affirmative action plans deal with promotional and training opportunities, a major focus is often the hiring process. This is the most effective, rational, and nonpunitive way to make changes in the composition of the work force. However, an employer should never discharge current employees in order to make room for minorities or other protected groups.

Usually, the strategies for affirmative action are recorded in a written plan which is formally adopted by the library. This plan includes an analysis of the library work force and sets short-term hiring targets and long-term hiring goals. For example, a library may determine that in order to create a representative work force of black clerical workers, it will need to hire ten black workers. An affirmative action plan may set a short-term (one-year) target to hire two such workers. The long-term goal (five years) would be to hire ten such workers. Some may object that such goals mean that the employer is becoming "race conscious," which is prohibited by the Civil Rights laws. Although this is a very complex legal area, it appears that setting such targets when the employer has identified an underutilized category of workers is not, in itself, unlawful. Of course, any affirmative action plan should be reviewed by legal counsel before being adopted.

Among the strategies that the EEOC has recommended to procure minorities in accordance with affirmative action targets are (a) the establishment of a recruitment program to attract qualified candidates; (b) changing job selection tests or procedures which have the effect of eliminating members of protected classes; (c) developing procedures to ensure that all qualified applicants from protected classes are actively considered when positions open, and (d) developing monitoring programs to measure the effectiveness of the affirmative action program, and the development of efficient means to change the program as needed.[29]

There have been many challenges to affirmative action, but employers should try to develop a plan which is fair to all while attempting to remedy past inequalities. The library should be careful that nonminorities do not suffer unduly under the plan. Among the characteristics that a good affirmative action plan should have is (a) the plan should be tailored directly to the problems identified in the self-analysis; (b) the plan should not unnecessarily restrict opportunities for advancement or promotion for the work force as a whole. That is, nonminorities should not be prohibited from advancing in the organization; (c) the plan should not dictate the discharge of nonminorities in order to hire members of protected groups; and (d) the provisions of the plan should only be in place so long as the imbalance exists and should be discontinued when the affirmative action goals have been achieved.[30, 31]

Affirmative action plans are an important expression of the library's intent to provide equal employment opportunity to all workers. A written plan not only makes clear how the library will remedy inequities, it also serves as a staff-education and training tool. It provides important information especially to those involved in the hiring process. Employers must be careful that supervisors are guided only by affirmative action that has been formally agreed upon; individual supervisors applying their own "personal" affirmative action plans when hiring could create serious problems for the library.

ORIENTATION AND TRAINING

The hiring process does not end when the job offer is made and the paperwork completed. The hiring process must also include preparing the employee as a full and productive member of the organization—this involves orientation and training. To some extent orientation can be distinguished from training. Through orientation employees are able to "get their bearings," to find out how they fit into the total organizational structure. In training, employees receive instruction on how to complete the specific tasks of their jobs.

The orientation process is important for establishing and maintaining a positive and enthusiastic attitude on the part of the employee. The commitment of new employees to the organization is usually very high at this time they are excited about coming to work, they have high expectations, and usually they know few negatives about the job and organization. For this reason, orientation should reinforce the impression of enthusiasm and competence.

Levels of Orientation

Written Materials

Part of the orientation process includes giving various written materials to the new employee, such as a staff manual indicating the rules and regulations of the organization; materials on employee benefit plans, staff organizations or unions; an organization chart; and staff directory of employees' names and addresses. Optimally, a new employee should receive all written materials before meeting with library management so it can be reviewed in advance.

Meetings with Administrators

As part of the orientation process, the new employee should meet with the individual in charge of personnel (in small libraries this would be the director). During this meeting, the administrator should review the materials provided to the employee, including the basic rules and regulations of the organization and the benefits available, and answer any questions. It is also an important opportunity to talk further about the philosophy of the organization and the importance of the new employee in fulfilling the mission of the library.

The administrator's role in the orientation proces also helps protect the library from subsequent charges by employees that they did not know about certain rules and regulations. Some libraries use a written checklist during the orientation process checking off each subject identified on the checklist as it is covered with the new employee. When all the subjects have been discussed, the employee is asked to sign and date the checklist, thus providing documentation for the employee's personnel file.

Meetings with the Supervisor and Staff
Employees may also be oriented by the immediate supervisor and staff. This process may include a review of departmental rules and regulations, and a tour of the library, and/or the department in which the employee will be working. At this time, the employee may be introduced to various staff members; these members may be asked to describe their work and how their work is related to that of the new employee.

Training

The ultimate purpose of training is to improve the overall performance of the organization. The more direct purpose is to provide the employee with the knowledge and skills to perform the job. Reflecting one of the central themes of this book—that each individual is different—one must keep in mind that individuals react differently to the same training. In part, individual responses to training depend on personality, expectations, motivation, intelligence, motor skills, and degree of effort exerted. Consequently, although it may be necessary to impart standardized information, training programs that adapt to individual learning styles and abilities will be most effective.

In the case of a new employee, training accomplishes two important purposes. First, training usually helps make the employee more comfortable because the work process becomes less alien; the employee is allowed to develop mastery over the job. This is likely to reduce insecurity. Second, the training period also provides managers with an opportunity to discover whether an employee is right for the job. An employee who is unable to learn or who resists learning will require close monitoring and evaluation. Because new employees are usually in a probationary period, employees who fail to learn may be removed more easily. Of course, the concept of training applies to a broader range of employees than just new entrants, but the issues that affect training are usually the same.

Employers must pay particular attention to the training process. Inadequate training produces unfortunate side effects. Creth identifies five costs due to poor training: poor performance, low productivity, the need for increased supervision, higher employee turnover, and discipline and motivation problems in the workplace.[32] All of these factors are expensive and disruptive to the organization. Remember that the employee has little real knowledge about your library before training. Poor training can convey a lazy or uncaring impression. Such a negative first impression can have lasting effects that may take much time to overcome.

Before Training Begins

For the reasons noted above, it is crucial that the library make detailed preparations for training. Good preparation will substantially improve the chance that the training will work.

Selecting Trainers

Library managers must carefully select the right individual to conduct the training. A good trainer must have certain characteristics:

- Trainers must be good models. Employees tend to model their behavior after those who train them, especially if the trainer is perceived as competent.[33] If a new librarian is trained by a professional who is rude, or has a bad attitude toward patrons, it may reinforce poor attitudes and behavior on the part of the trainee.
- Trainers must be committed to the activity. If supervisors responsible for training feel that training is unimportant, they can convey this attitude to the new employee, or avoid training altogether.
- Trainers must be good communicators. They must put the employee at ease and be able to express themselves clearly. Similarly, they should be able to provide meaningful examples and be able to correct performance in a courteous and supportive fashion.

Job Clarity

It is crucial that the trainer have a clear understanding of the job for which training is offered. The trainer must be able to analyze the knowledge and skills that need to be taught. Similarly, the trainer must know at what level the trainee is expected to perform following the training. Only in this way can a program be designed in sufficient breadth and depth, and with the appropriate learning materials and techniques.

Materials Preparation

A training program in part depends on training materials provided by the organization. These materials should be designed in advance, and should be specifically tailored to the tasks to be learned. The trainer should also have an outline identifying various components and the times at which different types of training are offered.

Evaluation

Some method should be developed to determine if the training has been successful. Different approaches include having the new employee evaluate the training, having the supervisor evaluate the employee's performance, and administering written or performance tests to determine if the individual has mastered the knowledge required.

Factors Affecting Training Effectiveness

For training to be truly effective, "training transfer" must occur. Training transfer is the degree to which trainees actually apply the knowledge and skills obtained.[34] Too often training is given, but the actual transfer does not occur. One estimate is that American industry spends more than $100 billion on training, but less than 10% of these expenditures result in actual training transfer.[35] In assessing training, library managers should look at the employee's ability to apply training to specific tasks on the job, and to generalize their knowledge to new situations.

There are three basic components underlying successful training transfer:

* Characteristics of the trainee: ability, personality, and motivation
* Training design: the content, sequence, and teaching principles used
* Work environment: the support of trainers and administrators and the opportunity to use training.[36]

Certainly, there are many factors that influence the effectiveness of training, and numerous authors have investigated the conditions under which training is best absorbed.[37, 38, 39] Among the factors that should be considered are the following:

Trainee Characteristics

Expectations: Generally individuals will react to training according to the result they expect. An employee who has little faith that the training will provide a desired reward is not likely to absorb much information. Of course, the reward expected may vary: it may be just to improve in the job, but it also may be a pay increase or a promotion. The new entrants' expectations are most likely that the information will help them perform at an acceptable level.

Locus of Control: The term "locus of control" comes from the social learning theory literature and deals with the extent to which individuals believe that they personally control what happens to them. Individuals with an "internal" locus of control believe that they control events, that they are personally responsible for what happens to them. Those with an "external" locus of control believe that things happen to them; they are most likely to attribute their condition to luck or fate.[40] Generally, new employees with an internal locus of control are more suited to training because they believe that the information will help them control their environment; in contrast, training is likely to have little or no impact on employees who feel that external circumstances control their fate.

Motivation: Individuals must feel that the training is important and meaningful to them, that they want to be trained. In general, this is less of a problem with new employees who are excited about joining the library and want to demonstrate that they will do well. It could be more of a problem for people whose jobs are being changed. For example, when an employer automates, there may be employees who do not want to learn.

Maintaining high motivation throughout the training period is sometimes difficult. The greatest training transfer appears to occur when:

- employees believe they had a choice in the training,
- employees have a high level of job commitment,
- they believe that they will be applying the training directly in their job.[41]

The latter two characteristics are common among new employees. Maintaining motivation is also aided if the trainer rewards employees throughout the process. After the training process, it is possible to sustain motivation to apply the skills learned by setting challenging goals and providing continuous feedback.[42]

Training Design
Trainees should be taught not just particular skills but general rules and principles which they can use to deal with novel situations. For example, reference librarians need more than a knowledge of reference tools, they also need some psychology and communications background, especially as it applies to using interpersonal skills with patrons.[43]

Feedback: Employees need to know how they are doing. Such feedback can be accomplished in many ways including test scores, performance measurements, or comments by the trainer, supervisor, or coworkers. Two features of feedback appear to be especially important: timing and specificity.[44] Corrections by the supervisor should be made immediately so that employees do not "practice their mistakes." In addition, when employees are working correctly, the supervisor should offer praise as reinforcement and encouragement. Trainers should also be aware that they can overdo it, can give too much feedback to the trainee.[45] New employees must not feel that every move is being evaluated, or that they are under surveillance rather than supervision. Trainers should keep in mind that new employees are especially susceptible to criticism during this period because they are often on probation. The communication style established by the trainer must be one in which employees feel comfortable asking questions, and are able to admit that they do not understand what is being taught.

Practice: A critical aspect of training is the opportunity to practice often. Several characteristics of practicing are recommended:

- *Active practice*: Employees should be given clear instruction and then allowed to practice what they have been taught. The instruction/practice cycle (sometimes called "cumulative rotation") should be repeated to allow for variation in the learning process until the entire task is learned.[46] Preferably practice should be "real," that is, the actual activity is being performed. If this is impossible, the practice should be as close to the real task as possible. Giving an employee a test in which they give back the information received is not practice and is not sufficient.

- *Overlearning*: Employees must be allowed to practice repeatedly even after they have completed the tasks successfully. By allowing extended repetition the knowledge becomes so deeply ingrained that performance of the task becomes automatic.

- *Distributed practice*: The employee should be permitted to practice over a lengthy period of time rather than at one time only. Break up practice sessions with other types of work.

- *Size of practice unit*: Many jobs require that employees learn various interrelated, smaller tasks. Generally, employees need to learn smaller tasks first which they subsequently combine. Of course, some tasks are not readily separated into single components. For example, it is difficult to train a reference librarian just to answer the telephone; rather, they need to be trained to answer the telephone, use the card catalog, and answer the question all in combination. Clerical tasks on the other hand are more easily separated into distinct tasks.

- *Relevance*: Employees must perceive that the training is directly related to their work, and that the information is valuable. For new employees, this relationship may be obvious. Nonetheless, managers should be aware that employees undergoing training need to see that the training is clearly tied to the work to be performed.

- *Use of Examples:* Sometimes referred to as "stimulus variability," training programs need instructional materials that include many different examples in order to get across the major points. Research indicates that using a wide variety of examples when providing instruction is superior to one example used repeatedly.[47]

Work Environment

Training needs to be conducted in a supportive climate in which employees feel comfortable about asking questions and making mistakes. The supervisor plays a critical role here. When an employee enters the workplace, the supervisor should respond in a warm and friendly manner. Similarly, the supervisor should express confidence that employees will succeed, and assure them that help will be provided as needed.[48] If new entrants fear punishment, or humiliation for errors during the training period, or suspect that they will not get help and cooperation, then they are not likely to learn well, or to develop positive work attitudes. This is certainly true for all employees, not just new ones.

Types of Training

On-the-Job Training

There are many ways to train new employees. The most common is on-the-job training. Employees are placed directly in the workplace where they are supervised closely by one or more individuals. As different circumstances arise, the individual is able to perform various tasks. Feedback is provided by direct observation. The advantage is that the training activities are the real activities of the job. The disadvantage is that it is not systematic; it depends, to some extent, on the serendipity of events. Under these circumstances, important information may be missed, unless the appropriate situation arises.

Job Rotation

This type of training presumes that employees learn best when they are familiar not only with their own jobs, but with the related jobs of others. New library employees may, for example, be moved from one department to another for specified periods of time. This exposure is meant to deepen their understanding of library processes and relationships, which in turn should improve their performance on the job.

Classroom or Workshop Instruction

Groups of new employees may receive training in classrooms or workshops conducted by library staff. For example, beginning reference assistants may receive elementary training in basic reference materials. Such programs can provide important information. This type of instruction is useful for training numerous individuals at the same time, and the content can be controlled for quality and quantity. A disadvantage is that the trainer is not likely to be the immediate supervisor, and therefore employees don't get to know the individual who will supervise them.

Role Playing

Role playing allows participants to imitate real life situations by acting them out. For reference, some trainees may act out the role of reference librarian while others act out that of a patron. In essence, it is a form of practice, and should conform to the general rules for practice, i.e. the situations acted out should conform as closely as possible to real life situations in the workplace.

Types of Materials

Printed Materials
Some information is best imparted by giving the employees an opportunity to review written material. It may be instructions especially prepared for training purposes, or it may be pre-existing materials such as staff handbooks or procedure manuals designed for a variety of purposes, some unrelated to training. Training using written materials has the distinct advantage that employees can, within limits, pace themselves, reading and re-reading the material as needed. In addition, they can choose to learn the material in their own order, rather than in an order imposed by the trainer.[49]

Audiovisual Materials
Audiovisual materials have become an important training tool both in the classroom and one-on-one. They are particularly effective when used in combination with other training techniques. AV materials in libraries can show individuals how to deal with patrons or how to handle reference interviews. Of course, unless a trainer is present, the trainee is unable to ask questions for clarification. Also, it is more difficult to repeat parts of a film or tape, or to change the order of presentation, than with written materials.

Video especially is becoming a popular and effective training medium because of the relatively inexpensive video cameras and playback equipment that have been developed. Today, libraries can make their own training tapes at relatively low cost. Similarly, video taping can be used in conjunction with practice methods. For example, new reference librarians can be taped in actual or practice interviews. Later, the tapes are replayed for the employee and analyzed for strengths and weaknesses.

SUMMARY

Hiring could be considered the single most important function of human resource management. Organizations that can recruit and hire the best qualified and best suited individuals accrue a multitude of benefits. First, the organization functions most effectively, hence the library meets its ultimate goal of providing the best library service to its citizenry. Almost as important, good hiring significantly limits unnecessary expenditures for retraining, supervision, discipline, and termination of poor performers.

It is critical that clear hiring strategies be developed. These strategies must include a written hiring policy and procedures that conform to all equal employment opportunity laws, planning for recruitment of qualified candidates, and training interviewers so that the maximum amount of information can be obtained. Careful attention to the hiring process will not assure the perfect staff, but it can increase the chances that the organization will run well and serve the function for which it was designed.

FACTORS IN THE HIRING PROCESS

General

1. Have a printed hiring policy that guarantees equal employment opportunity.

2. Monitor the hiring process to ensure that all candidates receive an equal opportunity for hire without regard to race, color, national origin, religion, age, sex, or handicap.

3. Analyze the labor market to determine what positions will be most difficult to fill.

4. Develop recruitment strategies to maintain an adequate pool of qualified applicants.

The Application Process

1. Examine the application form for signs of carelessness, job gaps, jobs in which the employee stayed only briefly, or did not offer clear reasons for leaving.

2. Develop all necessary forms such as application, pre-employment inquiry forms, and post-hiring documents to ensure that a written record of the hiring process is available.

The Interview

1. Train interviewers in the art of interviewing.

2. Keep in mind that research has shown that:
   a. Decisions are often made very early in the interview;
   b. Interviewers are biased against women, handicapped individuals, or individuals with foreign accents
   c. Judgements are based on non-verbal behaviors and factors such as attractiveness, perfume scents, dress, and general likability of the candidate.

3. Conduct structured interviews in which questions are prepared in advance.

4. Have multiple interviewers to help filter out biases.

5. Ensure that interviewers are knowledgeable about the job to be performed.

6. Ensure that all interview questions are job related and are intended to elicit information about the relevant knowledge, skill, and ability of the candidate.

7. Attempt to anchor subjective impressions of the candidate to actual statements made by the interviewee.

8. While conducting the interview, maintain a friendly, positive attitude.

9. Always take notes during the interview.

10. Attempt to gather similar information from all candidates for comparison.

11. Use standardized or other employment tests only when they can be shown to be directly related to the actual job to be performed.

The Hiring Decision

1. Check references of all candidates interviewed.

2. The reasons for selection should be clearly understood before the job offer is made.

3. An oral job offer should be followed up by an offer in writing.

4. The offer to hire should be closely monitored to ensure that "implied contracts" are not made.

Orientation and Training

1. Ensure that the employee has a clear understanding of important organizational policies and procedures.

2. Ensure that the employee receives clear training regarding the responsibilities of the job and the expectations for performance.

3. Prepare all necessary orientation and training materials.

4. Ensure that trainers are good communicators, and are themselves good models.

5. Ensure that new employees are given an opportunity to practice what they have learned in a positive work environment that provides constructive feedback.

Endnotes

1. Office for Library Personnel Resources, *Academic and Public Librarians: Data by Race, Ethnicity and Sex*, Chicago: ALA, 1986.
2. Tedine J. Roos and Diana W. Shelton, "The Cost of Hiring an Academic Librarian," *Journal of Library Administration* 8 (Summer 1987): 89-90.
3. Richard Rubin, "A Study of Employee Turnover of Full Time Public Librarians in Moderately Large and Large Size Public Libraries in Seven Midwestern States," Ph.D. dissertation, University of Illinois at Urbana-Champaign, 1987.
4. David J. Weston and Dennis L. Warmke, "Dispelling the Myths About Panel Interviews," *Personnel Administrator* (May 1988): 109.
5. Richard D. Arvey and James E. Campion, "The Employment Interview: A Summary and Review of Recent Research," *Personnel Psychology* 35 (Summer 1982): 295.
6. E.C. Mayfield, "The Selection Interview: A Reevaluation of Published Research," *Personnel Psychology* 17 (1964): 239-260.
7. Arvey and Campion: 281-322.
8. Ray J. Forbes and Paul R. Jackson, "Non-Verbal Behavior and the Outcome of Selection Interviews," *Journal of Occupational Psychology* 53 (March 1980): 65-72.
9. John F. Binning, Mel A. Goldstein, Mario F. Carcia, and Julie H. Scattaregia, "Effects of Preinterview Impressions on Questioning Strategies in Same- and Opposite-Sex Employment Interviews," *Journal of Applied Psychology* 73 (February 1988): 34.
10. Veronica F. Nieva and Barbara A. Gutek, *Women and Work: A Psychological Perspective*, New York: Praeger, 1981: 70.
11. Nieva and Gutek: 76-78.
12. Arvey and Campion: 308.
13. Arvey and Campion: 314.
14. Uniform Guidelines on Employee Selection Procedures, Part 1607, Equal Employment Opportunity Commission, 1978.
15. Neil Anderson and Viv Shackleton, "Recruitment and Selection: A Review of Developments in the 1980s," *Personnel Review* 15 (1986): 22.
16. Arvey and Campion: 295.
17. Anderson and Shackleton: 23.
18. *McDonnell Douglas Corporation* v *Green*, 411 U.S. 792 (1973).
19. *McDonnell Douglas* v *Green*: 802.
20. *McDonnell Douglas* v *Green*: 804.
21. G. Ruthenglen, *Major Issues in the Federal Law of Employment Discrimination*, Washington, D.C.: Federal Judicial Center, 1987: 6-7.
22. *Uniform Guidelines on Employee Selection Procedures* (1978), Federal Register, Volume 44, No. 43—Friday, March 2, 1979: 11996.
23. *Uniform Guidelines*: 11997.
24. *Griggs* v *Duke Power Co.* 401 U.S. 424 (1971).
25. U.S. Equal Employment Opportunity Commission, *Eliminating Discrimination in Employment: A Compelling National Priority: A Handbook for State, County and Municipal Governments*, Washington, D.C.: U.S. EEOC, 1979: II-1.
26. *Uniform Guidelines*: 11998.

27. *Teal* v *Connecticut*, 457 U.S. 440 (1982).
28. *Code of Federal Regulations*, "Part 1608-Affirmative Action Appropriate Under Title VII of the Civil Rights Act of 1963, As Amended," 29 CFR Part 1608: 238.
29. *Code of Federal Regulations*, "Part 1607-Uniform Guidelines on Employee Selection Procedures," 29 CFR Ch. XIV: 235-236.
30. Steven C. Kahn, Barbara A. Brown, and Brent E. Zepke, *Personnel Director's Legal Guide: 1988 Cumulative Supplement*: S6-30.
31. *Code of Federal Regulations*, "Part 1608..." 29 CFR Part 1608: 241.
32. Sheila D. Creth, *Effective On-The-Job Training*, Chicago: American Library Association, 1986: 10.
33. Kenneth N. Wexley and Gary P. Latham, *Developing and Training Human Resources in Organizations*, Dallas: Scott, Foresman, 1981: 69.
34. Timothy T. Baldwin and J. Kevin Ford, "Transfer of Training: A Review and Directions for Future Research," *Personnel Psychology* 41 (Spring 1988): 63.
35. Baldwin and Ford: 63.
36. Baldwin and Ford: 65.
37. Felix and Lloyd Nigro, *The New Public Personnel Administrator*, Itasca, Ill.: F. E. Peacock, 1981: 360-363.
38. Kenneth N. Wexley and Gary P. Latham, *Developing and Training Human Resources in Organizations*, Dallas: Scott-Foresman, 1981.
39. Raymond A. Noe, "Trainees' Attributes and Attitudes: Neglected Influences on Training Effectiveness," *Academy of Management Review* 11 (October 1986): 736-749.
40. Noe: 739-740.
41. Baldwin and Ford: 69.
42. Baldwin and Ford: 69.
43. Baldwin and Ford: 66-67.
44. Baldwin and Ford: 67.
45. Kenneth N. Wexley and Gary P. Latham, *Developing and Training Human Resources in Organizations*, Dallas: Scott Foresman, 1981: 61-62.
46. Lyle M. Ehrenberg, "How to Ensure Better Transfer of Learning," *Training and Development Journal* (February 1983): 82.
47. Baldwin and Ford: 67.
48. Wexley and Latham: 69.
49. Jack Rabin, Thomas Vocino, W. Barley Hildreth, and Gerald J. Miller, eds. *Handbook on Public Personnel Administration and Labor Relations*, New York: Marcel Dekker, 1983: 213.

3

Performance Evaluation

Although in some books the terms "performance evaluation," "performance appraisal," or "performance review" are distinguished, in this chapter they will be used interchangeably. In its formal sense, performance evaluation is a period of time set aside by supervisor and employee for the discussion and written assessment of the employee's work performance. In a broader sense, performance evaluation is any assessment of an employee's performance. Supervisors may often make informal remarks both positive and negative concerning employees' performance on a daily or weekly basis; they may comment on their work on a particular program, activity, or the way they handled patrons. Although most of this chapter is devoted to the conduct of formal performance evaluation, it is clear that performance evaluation is a day-to-day process; that employees deserve to know how they are doing more often than once a year or semi-annually when formal reviews are conducted.

Performance evaluation is part of an interdependent network of basic management functions; it imparts vital information, which, if properly used, can improve and sustain the library's health (Figure 3-1). Among the parts of the organization influenced directly by performance review are:

1. Recruitment and Hiring
Performance evaluations may reveal that the wrong type of individuals are being recruited and hired. It may reveal that interviews are not providing relevant predictive information, or that the judgment of those hiring is flawed.

2. Training and Development
Performance evaluation may reveal that employees are being poorly trained or that additional training is needed.

FIGURE 3-1.   The Context of Performance Evaluation

THE CONTEXT OF PERFORMANCE EVALUATION

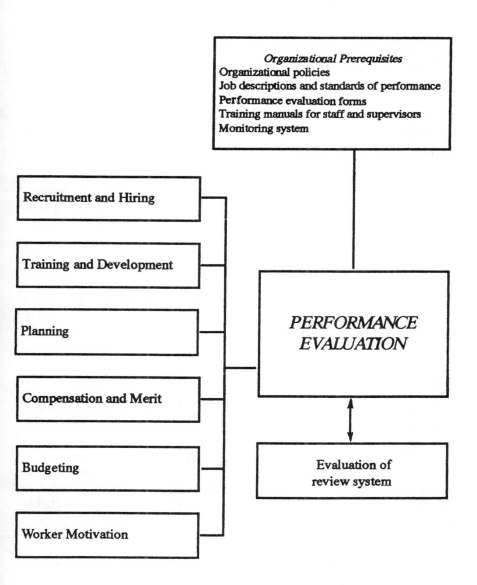

3. Planning
Performance reviews may reveal that certain areas of the library are understaffed while others may be overstaffed. In addition, reviews may help in assessing future personnel needs and the concomitant skills required to meet these needs. Similarly, reviews may indicate that new services may be needed and others eliminated or modified.

4. Creation, Modification, and Evaluation of the Review
Performance reviews may indicate that job duties have changed and that new standards must be created; or, that the system itself is defective and requires change.

5. Compensation and Merit Systems
Performance evaluation is often closely linked to decisions regarding whether an individual receives promotion or demotion, increases or decreases in pay.

6. Budgeting
Because performance review may affect all the vital areas mentioned above, it is closely linked with how the institution allocates its money for human resources and library services.

7. Motivational Factors
The type of review and manner in which a review is conducted has profound influence on a library employee's attitude toward the library and their specific job. There are few activities in a library that can have as strong an impact as the evaluation of a worker's performance.

WHY CONDUCT PERFORMANCE EVALUATIONS?

The performance evaluation is a curious mixture of reward, advice, discipline, self-evaluation, and organizational scrutiny. These complexities highlight one source of tension in the evaluation process: the evaluation is supposed to serve *both* the employee and the employer; it is supposed to perform both an evaluative *and* a developmental function. A review of the many aspects of performance evaluation from the employee's and employer's point of view reveals just how much tension exists in the process.

For the employee, performance evaluation:

- Ensures that the employee understands the level of performance necessary to meet the job requirements. Each employee deserves to know what is expected and what types of performance are considered satisfactory or unsatisfactory.

- Informs the employee of the quality of work currently being performed. Employees need and deserve to know "where they stand" in terms of the supervisor's and organization's attitude toward their work. In a good evaluation, an employee is given a clear idea of whether his or her work meets the standards that have been set.

- Helps the employee identify areas of performance that need improvement, and provides guidance on how to improve. The evaluation is an opportunity for the employee to acknowledge performance deficits and to discuss the means by which these deficits can become assets. When successfully handled, the evaluation develops employees so that their contribution to the organization increases.

- Provides the employee with a formal opportunity to communicate problems and issues of concern to the employer. Employees' attitudes and feelings are important to organizational health. The evaluation gives employees an opportunity to contribute to the library, albeit sometimes through sharp criticism, in a manner other than performing their job tasks.

- Provides recognition for outstanding performance. The employer can articulate recognition of employees' value and contribution to the library's goals.

For the employer, performance evaluation:

- Identifies excellent performers. This is most useful when promotion or expansion of duties is being considered. The identification of excellent performance is also useful for the allocation of pay increases. It is important for employees who perform well to know that their performance will be rewarded. Recognition of excellent performers strengthens motivation of the individuals who are contributing most to the organization. Failure to recognize high performance can have serious implications. When high performers see that others who perform poorly or less well receive the same rewards, the potential for demotivation and turnover is increased. The turnover of high performers not only hurts the library's productivity, but can ultimately produce a public relations problem: a reputation for "losing good workers" is hardly conducive to community support, or to maintaining a pool of high-quality applicants.

- Identifies poor performers. The need to identify poor performers is also great. Optimistically, these individuals are targets for additional training, or transfer to positions in which they can perform satisfactorily. Less optimistically, it identifies individuals who should be terminated. Unidentified poor performers can have long-term negative effects on the organization as a whole. They may not only be unable to perform assigned tasks and be frequently absent, but may also be responsible for sabotage, increased conflict, and the creation of poor morale among productive employees.

- Provides documentation in case of challenges to employment decisions. Performance evaluation is subject to the same legal scrutiny as hiring or other job actions. Consistent and fair evaluations that provide detailed information on the employee's performance protects from claims of discrimination, and other claims of wrongful action on the part of the employer. It may also provide support in subsequent administrative actions if the employee leaves, such as documentation in unemployment compensation hearings.

- Identifies institutional deficiencies. Although performance review focuses on the employee, other defects in the organization may be revealed. The employer must always keep in mind that poor performance may, at least in part, result from factors external to the employee's efforts.

Among the institutional problems that may become apparent are:

- *Poor hiring practices*: A poor review may suggest that an employee should never have been hired. The screening process may have been defective, there may have been favoritism, or the knowledge, skills, and ability for the job improperly assessed.
- *Poor supervision*: The supervisor may possess poor interpersonal skills, an inability to communicate the duties of the job, or might exhibit discriminatory behavior. Each of these areas indicate a need for organizational improvement.
- *Poor training*: The employee may have received insufficient or incorrect information on how to perform in the job. This information may have come from the supervisor, or may have been provided by other individuals or agencies within the organization.
- *Poor working conditions*: The employee may indicate that equipment is insufficient to perform the job, or that lighting or other environmental conditions affect performance.

The fact that performance evaluations serve so many purposes may threaten their effectiveness, especially if these purposes are incompatible. Incompatibility arises primarily when the review must serve as an evaluative tool while simultaneously serving as a coaching or counselling tool. Indeed, employees would naturally be reluctant to perform much self-criticism if it might affect their salary increase or opportunities for promotion, even if they also thought that such comments might lead to insight and personal development. To date, the evidence on whether to split evaluation interviews and counseling interviews is inconclusive.[1] In practical terms, for most libraries, supervisors do not have the time to conduct multiple employee performance interviews, and it seems likely that the single evaluation interview will persist.

PREREQUISITES FOR PERFORMANCE EVALUATION

Before performance review can be used most effectively, certain prerequisites must be established. Among them:

- *Written Policies and Procedures*: The review needs to be conducted in a consistent and fair fashion. A written policy stating the purpose of performance reviews, when they are conducted, who conducts them, and how they are used should be available to all staff. Such a policy should also make clear how an evaluation can be appealed. Written procedures should also be available to supervisors so that reviews are conducted consistently and competently. These written procedures can also be used for training evaluators.
- *Written Job Descriptions*: In order to evaluate employees, both the employee and the evaluator must have a clear idea what activities are pertinent to the rating process. This can only be accomplished with job descriptions that detail the responsibilities of each position.
- *Performance Evaluation Forms*: All staff should receive written reviews of their performance using standardized forms to assure consistency. The forms should include clear instructions and be easy to use and understand. (Different evaluation formats will be discussed later in this chapter.)
- *Training Programs*: Performance evaluation is a complex and difficult process. Supervisors should receive substantial training before conducting such reviews. Written instructions or manuals should be available for consultation. In addition, all staff should be oriented to the purposes of performance evaluation.

PSYCHOSOCIAL ASPECTS

Many supervisors are understandably reluctant to conduct performance evaluations. Often supervisors consider it a time-consuming and unfulfilling experience. Even reviews of excellent performers take time away from other duties. But it is the unpleasantness associated with reviews of poor performers that provides the greatest disincentives. The performance review process is a distinctly human one and the potential for conflict and distress gives people an uneasy feeling.

The stakes are high in performance review. Consider the issues that are inextricably linked to the review process:

- *Self-Worth*: For most people it is very difficult to separate work performance from a judgment of themselves as people. When employees are involved in performance evaluations their primary need is to be reassured that they are doing well.[2] To tell them that they work poorly may well be perceived as an attack on their character or intelligence. Criticism undermines their self-esteem. Although the purpose of a review is to apprise employees of their performance, any criticism actually has a negative effect on the outcome of the review and subsequent performance. The greater the criticism, the more negative the outcome.[3] This is not to say that criticism should not be part of the review process. There is some evidence that employees believe that reviews are more *useful* when criticism is part of the review, but it should be used with considerable discretion.[4]

- *Professional Worth*: Employees may perceive criticisms of their performance as reflecting on their professional knowledge, skills, and ability. Unlike the issue of self-worth, this perception may, *in fact,* be accurate, and the supervisor may be hard pressed to deny it.
- *Fiscal Security*: In most performance review situations, negative reviews may lead to demotion, lack of salary increases, even termination. Therefore, employees may perceive reviews as a threat to their well-being, financial security, and the well-being of their families.
- *Status*: Despite the fact that performance reviews should be confidential, it is not uncommon for other employees to know who received poor evaluations and who received excellent ones. Employees may believe that reviews affect the attitude of others, that others may believe their work is not comparable to that of co-workers. Such a potential threat to one's work status also increases the emotional potential of the review.

FACTORS AFFECTING THE REVIEW

It is little wonder that both employees and evaluators approach the performance evaluation with trepidation. The success of a performance evaluation depends on a delicate interaction of evaluator, evaluated, and the evaluation technique employed. Experienced library supervisors can attest that using the same style or approach for all employees is not likely to meet with equal success. *People are different.* These differences, of course, lie not only in the employee being evaluated, but in the evaluator. It is disconcerting to realize, that given these complexities, many supervisors receive little or no training for this daunting responsibility.

A variety of factors have been identified that influence the success or failure of the review process:

- *Credibility of the Supervisor*: For an effective performance evaluation, the employee must be confident that the supervisor understands the job being evaluated.[5] A supervisor who is not familiar with the job, or cannot communicate this familiarity, cannot be a credible evaluator. To some extent, this favors supervisors who "come through the ranks," because they are likely to be quite knowledgeable concerning the tasks being supervised. In any case, individuals selected for supervisory positions should always be able to demonstrate their they understanding of the jobs they supervise. Moreover, the issue of credibility is a strong argument for assigning the *immediate* supervisor to conduct a major part of the performance review.
- *Ability of the Employee to Participate*: Performance evaluation involves an exchange of views. Studies of employee attitudes toward evaluations reveal that when the supervisor welcomes employees' participation, there is greater satisfaction with the process, and, in some cases, better results.

This means that the supervisor should invite comments and observations from the employee; the supervisor should listen carefully without interrupting the employee's remarks, and should react in a way that demonstrates that the remarks are taken seriously.

Studies also suggest that interviews are most effective when employees develop a sense of "ownership." Employees need a sense that their thoughts are welcome and that they have responsibility for the review.[6] A useful practice is to let employees evaluate themselves in advance using the actual review forms developed by the organization. Under such circumstances, employees are able to have a measure of control through participation in the critical areas of the review process. The supervisor is then able to modify the form based on discussion with the employee. By allowing the employee to complete the evaluation form before the review, it also gives the employee time to think about and prepare for the evaluation. This has several positive benefits including a more positive outcome, more employee satisfaction concerning the review, and more job improvements stemming from the review.[7]

It should be noted, however, that the success of employee participation also depends on whether the employees perceive their participation as a threat. If previous evaluations were highly critical, or if there is distrust between employee and supervisor, then the employee may be reluctant, suspicious, even antagonistic toward participating in the evaluation. Under such circumstances it may be necessary for the evaluator to structure the interview so that little participation is required.

- *Mutual Setting of Performance Targets:* Consistent with the general view that participation is important, other studies reveal that evaluations are more effective when mutual goal setting is part of the process.[8, 9] Participation tends to increase satisfaction with the review, but goal setting and its related area of helping employees solve problems have been shown to improve subsequent performance.[10] Establishing job performance targets should be possible for all employees. Of course, all goals must be consistent with the goals of the library as a whole. The nature of job goals may vary substantially with the type of job being performed. Some studies suggest that different types of goals may be necessary for different types of jobs. Cederblom recommends that employees who perform routine tasks and who exhibit little need for independence should be reviewed with specific behavioral measures. This might apply to clerk-typists and library assistants performing routine circulation and other maintenance functions. These individuals have a right to an unambiguous set of statements describing the essential functions of and expectations for their jobs. On the other hand, individuals whose tasks are not routine and who need independence (e.g. jobs requiring the exercise of professional judgment) should have goal-based reviews or reviews that set general directions for activities rather than strictly quantitative behavioral measures.[11] All job goals need to be clearly written and well understood. Ambiguous goals can lead to lower employee satisfaction, and increase the possibility that the evaluator can impose personal biases on the review process.

- *Timeliness and Frequency*: The frequency of performance evaluation depends to some extent on its purpose. Evaluations serve many purposes and this complicates decisions concerning frequency. If the purpose of a review is only to record the overall performance of the individual, semi-annual or annual reviews may be all that is necessary for most employees. But if counselling for improved performance is a primary purpose, then reviews should be more frequent. Numerous studies support the notion that such reviews should be as frequent as is practical.[12] The more frequent the reviews, the more effective the evaluation process.[13, 14] This highlights the fact that performance evaluation should be considered both a formal and informal process. Information should be shared with employees as issues arise. The effect of information diminishes as the time between the performance and the information concerning the performance increases.[15] The absence of feedback may actually have an inhibiting effect on performance.[16]

- *Perceived Importance of the Review:* Libraries, like other organizations, communicate their priorities through actions. Simply telling employees that performance reviews are important is not enough. If the library does not demonstrate that performance evaluations are meaningful, then employees are less likely to treat the review seriously. Employees who perceive reviews as influencing the distribution of rewards—job assignment, raises, and promotions—are more likely to prepare for and participate in the activities of the review.[17] If libraries want employees to be willing to devote time and effort to the review process, they must establish a relationship between their effort and how the organization treats them.

EFFECTIVE EVALUATION TECHNIQUES

When assessing the effectiveness of evaluation techniques, consider such factors as validity, reliability, discrimination, freedom from bias, and relevance.[18]

Validity

The issue of validity is crucial to fair evaluation. Performance evaluation standards are valid when they measure what they are intended to measure. The responsibilities of each job must be clearly established so they can be measured. If an evaluation is supposed to measure the performance of a reference librarian, then the criteria must reflect accurately and completely that performance. High performing reference librarians should be getting high evaluations; low performers, low evaluations. Evaluation standards that are invalid can subject the employer to legal actions including charges of discrimination.

Reliability

Reliability of evaluations can be viewed as ensuring that evaluations are consistent. Three types of consistency are necessary. First, the same level of performance over one period should be evaluated similarly at another period. That is, the evaluation method should be consistent over time. Second, the same level of performance by two individuals should be measured similarly for each. An evaluation technique that does not rate two individuals performing at the same level in the same way is not reliable. The dangers of lack of reliability in this sense is considerable. Employees may feel that the supervisor is "easier" on one employee than another. This may lead to grievances or charges of discrimination. Third, different evaluators should rate similar performances in a similar way. Failure to ensure consistency among evaluators can lead to employees feeling that one department is "easier" than another; that employees in one department can "get away with" performance that is not tolerated in another. Such perceived inequities can create morale problems, turnover, and legal problems.

Discrimination

A performance review should be able to discriminate good performers from mediocre performers. The evaluation technique must be designed to identify essential functions of a job and measure the adequacy of performance. Of course, the ability of the evaluator to make discriminating judgments is also essential. A common defect in the rating process which can affect discrimination is called *central tendency*. This is the propensity of raters to select values on a rating scale near the center. This tends to group employees artificially near the average. A related defect is the tendency of some raters to give all employees artificially high scores. The reasons may be that the rater wishes to avoid conflict with the employees by giving them all good scores; or the evaluator may believe that lower scores would deprive employees of raises or other opportunities. The evaluator may feel that low scores reflect poorly on the evaluator's ability to motivate staff. In any case, the evaluation technique must be designed to encourage discrimination so the library can recognize and reward excellent performers, and identify and deal with poor performers.

Freedom from Bias

The issue of bias generally focuses on evaluators as a source of problems in the review process. Most prominent is the tendency of an antagonistic evaluator to rank individuals lower than deserved; that is, the criterion being used to lower the evaluation is not related to the performance standards established. This situation may manifest itself in regard to race or sex discrimination in the evaluation process and requires careful monitoring. The opposite case may also arise; the evaluator may give higher marks to employees than they deserve, perhaps because of a personal relationship. The employee may be a relative, spouse, friend, or dating partner. A more sinister possibility is that the high evaluation is being used as a form of sexual harassment in which the employee is asked for sexual favors in return for high performance ratings. The organization must monitor any type of evaluation bias. At the least, higher managerial levels should review performance evaluations, and in some cases, multiple evaluation from different parts of the organization may be necessary.

One way to help eliminate bias is to ensure that the job evaluated has clearly defined duties and tasks. The more general or vague the job, the greater the propensity of the evaluator to impose prejudicial beliefs on the evaluation.[19]

Relevance

A performance review should deal with the job in its entirety, and not just part of the job. Selectively reviewing only certain parts of a job may lead employees to believe that only their weak points are being considered. Or employees may feel that the evaluator has changed or limited their responsibilities without prior communication. A related problem is dragging in irrelevant factors such as responsibilities that were not assigned, or evaluating behaviors and attitudes that are unrelated to job performance. Finally, employees may feel that undue weight has been assigned to relatively minor issues, or that important issues are undervalued. Overemphasis on minor issues can seriously affect the employee's perception of equity.

Practicality

The performance evaluation system must be *practical*. Employees must be able to understand the purpose and procedures of the system. Systems that use complex formulas and points may be able to provide useful information, but they must also be intellectually accessible to the employee and the evaluator. The development of a complex system could breed suspicion that the system is being manipulated for devious purposes. Similarly, the system must be simple enough that supervisors and other raters can administer it correctly and fairly. All individuals who participate in the evaluation process need proper training. Recent court cases have suggested that clear instructions to raters in the use of performance evaluation is fundamental to establishing a system's fairness.[20]

GENDER BIAS

The numerical predominance of women in the library profession means it is important to focus on any possibility that gender itself affects performance review. There is ample evidence that female librarians receive lower salaries and that there is a disproportionately low number of females in upper level administrative and managerial positions. Although part of these gender differences can be accounted for by such factors as level of education and length of tenure, the findings of the existing library research suggest that these differences can not wholly be accounted for by factors other than gender. It would seem reasonable that part of this differential is caused by differential evaluation (formal or otherwise) related to gender, resulting in fewer promotions and smaller increases in pay. Unfortunately, there is little direct research on performance evaluation reported in the library literature.

There is cause for concern; women are evaluated differently, and generally, to their detriment.[21] For example, "attractiveness" appears to affect a female's evaluation and chances for promotion, while it has little or no effect for men. Interestingly, attractiveness appears to be advantageous for a woman when she is applying for nonmanagerial positions, but *disadvantageous* when applying for managerial ones.[22] This finding demonstrates that the relationship of gender to evaluation is complex; it is not always a disadvantage to be female. Indeed, evaluations of women in *professional* positions may be higher than they might otherwise be because evaluators are *surprised* that they perform so well on tasks traditionally thought to be the domain of males.[23]

Attribution theory

There is a growing body of evidence that female performance is undervalued. The issue is more complicated than just negative attitudes toward women. One theory is that evaluators may attribute the causes of job success and failure differently to men and women.

Called "attribution theory," it suggests that the success or failure of a given performance can be attributed to four possible reasons: luck, effort, ability, and task difficulty. For example, if a reference librarian is perceived to answer a reference question well, the evaluator might make one of four evaluations:

1. the librarian was just lucky to get the right answer (luck)
2. the librarian got the right answer because of the considerable work he or she put into answering the question (effort)
3. the librarian could answer the question because he or she is intelligent and very talented (ability)
4. the question was a very easy one to answer (task difficulty).

One can see that how the evaluator's perception of the performance could profoundly affect the evaluation. If job success is perceived as being a matter of luck or ease (external attribution), then the evaluation is not likely to be as high as if the success is perceived to be the result of effort and ability (internal attribution). In the former case, it is merely circumstances that lead to success; while in the latter case, it is the individual who is responsible for the success. Similarly, an individual who is perceived as talented, and possessing great ability (a "natural"), is likely to get a higher evaluation than a person who is perceived merely to "work hard." As might be expected, when this theory is tested, female performance is generally perceived to be a result of external factors such as luck and task difficulty, while male performance is seen as a product of skill or ability.[24,25]

When *unsuccessful* performance is viewed by evaluators, it is most often attributed to bad luck for the man, but lack of ability for the woman. However, the news is not always worse for women; men are evaluated more harshly for failure than women and receive more negative evaluations.[26] In essence, women are less likely to get credit for being successful, but also less likely to be blamed for failure. It appears that expectations for women are simply not as high as for men. Also of interest is the fact that the differences in attribution may be the same no matter whether the *evaluator* is male or female. This is consistent with research that indicates that females generally, although not in all circumstances, have a lower evaluation of their own abilities and skills than their male counterparts.[27, 28]

DEVELOPING A PERFORMANCE APPRAISAL SYSTEM

It is obvious, based on the previous discussion, that developing an equitable performance appraisal system for a library requires attention to many factors simultaneously. Of course, the degree of sophistication of a system depends to some extent on the size of the library: larger organizations will have to spend a good deal more time and money in training, developing, and testing the system. But even the smallest library must offer evaluations that are systematic and fair—good evaluation systems have common characteristics regardless of size. Keep in mind that developing a performance appraisal system is part of a continuous process of changes in goals, activities, and jobs in the organization. Standards, format, even purpose of the evaluation system may change as the organization changes. For this reason, it is necessary to build in a mechanism for review and modification. Ask these questions when developing an appraisal system:

- Who should conduct performance reviews?
- What standards and evaluation instruments should be used?
- What methods should be used?
- How should reviews be conducted?
- How should the library director be evaluated?
- How should the review process be monitored?

Who Should Conduct Reviews?

Employees find evaluations credible only if they believe that their evaluators are familiar with the tasks being evaluated. For this reason, the immediate supervisor is usually the logical choice to conduct most performance reviews. Although this is the most obvious, and probably the most practical approach, employers should realize studies show that the use of a single source for performance review is inadequate, because it provides only one perspective on the employee's performance.[29] Many jobs have many aspects, only some of which are best evaluated by the immediate supervisor. In addition, employees feel that unless they get information from other sources, they have not received an adequate or complete review.[30] Numerous sources such as self, supervisory, and peer evaluation are equally valid as sources of information on specific areas of performance.[31]

Consider the variety of sources from which useful information could be drawn besides the immediate supervisor:

Self-evaluation

Allowing employees to evaluate themselves satisfies several requirements for productive performance evaluation. It welcomes employee participation and helps establish "ownership" of the review process. It may cushion supervisory criticism because employees themselves are the source of the criticism. Self-criticism helps to validate the evaluations of the supervisor and others, however, the supervisor should not expect the employee to engage in much self-criticism. Contrary to popular opinion, employees are not more critical of their own performance than others, rather, they are *less* likely to criticize their performance than their supervisors.[32] Generally, employees think they are doing a better job than do their supervisors. In addition, employees may feel that self-criticism could restrict their opportunities for organizational rewards such as pay increases and promotions. Finally, it is important to realize that there may be gender effects in self-evaluation. In some cases, women tend to express less confidence in their performance than men; this may affect their evaluations.

Peer Evaluation: General
Peer evaluation is the process by which individuals who are in the same or similar job classifications are permitted to evaluate each other. There are many reasons why administrators are uncomfortable with such a process. The evaluation process is removed, at least in part, from the manager's control. There may also be fears that such evaluations are too often tainted by friendships or personal animosities that would distort the evaluation process.

There are, however, reasons to believe that peer review can be a valuable tool. Peers for example may work much more closely with an employee than the supervisor, and be able to observe performance with greater regularity. These individuals therefore possess special knowledge from a unique perspective regarding the individual's performance. If the purpose of evaluation is to get a realistic, three-dimensional perspective of performance, then peers can provide much needed information. Some researchers have argued that peer evaluations have greater validity in predicting success than any other measure.[33] Employees may perceive comments or criticisms from co-workers in a different and more constructive way. This in turn may have considerable and beneficial influence over work performance. Although employees still place considerable value on supervisor comments, supervisors regularly underestimate the importance of peer comments.[34] There is little tradition of peer evaluation in most types of libraries (academic libraries excepted). Nonetheless, the fact that the comments of peers are important to employees suggests that immediate supervisors, at the very least, should gather information from co-workers on the performance of an employee prior to evaluation.

Some of the factors that increase the chances of effective peer evaluations are:

- There must be enough reviewers to be reliable. No fewer than ten peers should be used in the rating process.[35]
- The need for relevant interactions: The peers must have been able to observe the individual performing relevant job behaviors. The greater the opportunity for the raters to interact with the ratee, and the more information they have about the employee, the better the chance for accuracy in the ratings.[36]

- The length of acquaintance: The longer workers are acquainted with each other, the more reliable the rating will be. But this is only true if the individual has been able to observe relevant job behaviors over time.[37]

Even under the best of conditions, however, peer review should not be used alone; it must be just one perspective of individual performance. Peer review is undoubtably vulnerable to its own forms of distortion. For example, although friendships between coworkers appear to have relatively little effect on peer evaluations, there is disturbing evidence that racial prejudice can be a significant factor.[38]

If the conditions are not especially good for peer review, this does not mean that the process should be discarded. Such reviews might be used for purposes other than administrative. For example, it could be used solely as a coaching tool for the manager, rather than as part of the process of making decisions for promotion, merit increases, or other job actions.

Peer Evaluation: Academic Libraries

Peer evaluation is more common in the academic setting where faculty institutions share power with the administration. University librarians are often involved in this model because peer review is a common model used for the promotion and tenure of academic faculty. An Association of Research Libraries (ARL) survey of libraries indicates that approximately 67% of ARL libraries use some type of peer review as part of performance appraisal with emphasis on promotion and tenure. Typically, the process is accomplished by committee. The survey also revealed that peer reviews are conducted as only part of a much larger review process that includes many different administrative levels.[39]

There is some evidence that the peer review process in academic libraries affects the priorities for performance. For example, in ARL libraries with peer review, there is greater emphasis on scholarship, research, and publication.[40] From the management perspective, this finding may be troubling if service, rather than research or publication, is the primary goal of the library. The cause of this problem is not peer review itself, but the conflicting organizational goals of the university as a research institution, and the library as a service organization.

Although peer review for librarians appears to be a generally attractive concept that is consistent with the faculty model, there is some evidence that faculty do not like the peer review process. One study of 174 faculty members revealed that 59% favored *discontinuing* the peer review process, and 30% favored revisions. More than half the faculty felt that friendships distorted the reviews and classified them as "not at all useful."[41]

Subordinate Review

Allowing employees to evaluate their supervisor provides a special perspective. Employees can provide information on such factors as communication, leadership, decision-making, and interpersonal relations. There is little evidence that subordinate evaluation is practiced systematically in many organizations; nonetheless, there are some areas that could be probed:

Issues for Subordinate Evaluation

Communication:
- Does the supervisor keep the staff informed of developments in the library?
- Does the supervisor provide clear instruction and information regarding work responsibilities?
- Does the supervisor listen to employees' opinions?
- Does the supervisor talk to employees informally about how they are performing?
- Is the supervisor pleasant, tactful, and courteous when talking with employees?

Motivation and Leadership:
- Does the supervisor encourage employees to increase performance?
- Does the supervisor recognize employees when they have done a good job?
- Does the supervisor include staff in problem-solving or in the generation of new ideas?
- Does the supervisor have reasonable work expectations, and make clear what is expected in terms of performance?
- Does the supervisor lead employees with a clear sense of the goals of the organization?
- Is the supervisor punctual; does she possess good work habits?

Decision-making and Problem Solving:
- Is the supervisor fair and impartial when making decisions?
- Does the supervisor get all the essential information before making a decision?
- Is the supervisor well-organized in trying to solve problems or make decisions?
- Is the supervisor able to arbitrate disputes within the department?
- Is the supervisor able to identify future problems before they become serious?

Interpersonal Relations:
- Does the supervisor work in a cooperative fashion with employees?
- Is the supervisor available when employees need to talk with him or her?
- Is the supervisor patient and empathetic regarding employees' concerns?
- Does the supervisor convey a sense of enthusiasm for the function of the department and the library as a whole?

- Does the supervisor admit when she has made an error?
- Is the supervisor fair in the assignment of work loads, scheduling, discipline, and privileges?

Performance Evaluation and Discipline:
- Is the supervisor well-prepared for performance reviews?
- Is the supervisor fair when conducting the review?
- Does the supervisor listen to the employee during the review?
- Are the remarks made by the supervisor useful to the employee?
- Does the supervisor make clear why the employee has received a particular rating?
- Does the supervisor make clear what needs to be done to maintain or improve performance?
- Does the supervisor give the employee adequate time to prepare for a review?
- Are the standards established with the supervisor reasonable?

Training and Orientation:
- Does the supervisor provide adequate training and orientation to new employees?
- Does the supervisor demonstrate knowledge in the subject area of the training?
- Does the supervisor encourage the development of new and current skills among the employees?
- Does the supervisor provide written materials which would assist the employee in orientation and training?

The administration of subordinate evaluations is problematical because there may be factors that distort the ratings. Bad feelings may lead to unrealistically low evaluations; other distortions may occur if the employee believes that the supervisor can determine who is the source of critical comments. Similarly, an employee may give unduly high reviews if they believe that they will reap monetary or other rewards for such flattery. In general, anonymity must be assured, and the tabulation of subordinate reviews should be done by someone other than the supervisor if possible. Despite the potential for distortions, however, evaluations by subordinates, when administered and used in a constructive manner, may provide helpful information to both the administration and the supervisor.

Internal and External Clients
The idea of consulting individuals with whom an employee "does business" is foreign to performance review in libraries. This is understandable, in that the clientele changes and is often characterized by one-time-only contacts. In some types of library jobs, however, it may be practical to gather information from clients. For example, some employ-

ees such as department heads and administrators may have regular contacts with community agencies (external clients), or, in the case of the academic library, contacts with other departments or administrators (internal clients). These may be valuable sources of information regarding the individual's responsiveness to client needs and their ability to deal effectively with the client in a professional and business-like manner.

What Standards and Formats Should Be Used?

The standards of performance developed and the means by which they are created have important effects on the satisfaction and productivity of employees. If the standards are new, then employees need to have a role in identifying and establishing them. Participation in developing such standards should increase job commitment and employees' understanding of their role in the organization.

Performance standards must be based on a well-written job description. It is not possible to write standards for a job with duties or responsibilities that can not be clearly delineated. The standard depends on the job to be performed. More routine tasks may have a greater number of quantitative standards, while managerial or administrative tasks may require more general goals or directions. Standards should share at least three common characteristics:

Standards Should Be Realistic

Standards should accurately reflect the stated duties of the job. In addition, standards should realistically reflect the knowledge, skills, and ability required for the job. If employees do not believe that they can accomplish the standards set, their motivation will be diminished. However, standards cannot be set too low, or the library will not be getting the performance it requires or the greatest productivity from employees. Standards should be difficult, but not impossible to achieve because setting difficult goals increases motivation.[42]

Standards Should Be Clear and Specific

Standards must be clear so that both the employee and supervisor understand what is expected. The language of the standards must be clear, easily understandable by the employee, and concise. Failure to be clear about the employee's role has been found to increase interpersonal tensions and stress, and lower job satisfaction.[43] This is one reason why quantitative measures are often recommended: they provide a clear notion of what is expected and make it relatively easy to determine whether the standard has been met, not met, or exceeded. Not all library duties are susceptible to easy quantification, often qualitative issues are involved. At the least, standards should describe behavior that can be directly observed or inferred from written records.

Standards Should Be Consistent
Similar standards should be set for employees with similar jobs requiring similar knowledge, skill, and ability. Employers should be careful to ensure that this consistency exists not only within departments but *across* them. This does not mean that standards can not be altered especially to increase the challenge of a job, but such changes should be reasonably related to the individual's knowledge, skill, and ability.

Methods of Measuring Performance

There is no perfect system for the evaluation of performance. The size and sophistication of the library, the money and staff time available to develop, implement, and maintain a system, and the purpose of the system must all be considered. In addition, it is quite possible that different types of systems may be used for different types of jobs. The system used to evaluate a director will be different from that used to evaluate a clerk/typist. Three approaches will be discussed here: trait-based, goal-based, and behaviorially based systems.

Trait-Based Systems
In the past, the most common evaluation method was a trait-based review, in which the evaluator rates the employee on the basis of general characteristics. Such traits include quality of work, quantity of work, knowledge of the job, attendance and punctuality, dependability, adaptability, initiative, judgment, cooperativeness, and personal qualities such as leadership, honesty, and appearance. In some of the newer trait-based systems, weights are assigned to each of the factors so that more important traits score higher in the overall evaluation. In addition, some forms allow for narrative comments to be made so that specific examples and explanations regarding the ratings are included.

In order to give at least an impression of objectivity, each trait is usually measured with a *graphic rating system* which allows the evaluator to assign a numerical (Figure 3-2) or categorical (Figure 3-3) value to the level of performance. Categories may range from unacceptable performance to outstanding work. When using such a system it is absolutely vital that clear definitions of each of the factors be given so that supervisors can be as consistent as possible in rating their employees.

Although some traits may be applicable to all employees, it is also possible that some traits will be unique to professional or administrative staff. For such individuals, factors such as ability to supervise, planning skills, organizing and delegating, problem-solving skills, decision-making skills, analytical abilities, leadership ability, and ability to appraise and develop the performance of others should be included on the evaluation form.

Trait-based systems have some distinct advantages. Such systems have the advantage of trying to measure some of the intangibles of work performance; characteristics that are hard to quantify and therefore difficult to fit into other types of performance review systems. Interestingly, there is a difference in how effective and ineffective managers use trait based systems: more effective managers place higher values on traits such as initiative, persistence, and broad knowledge; less effective managers emphasize cooperation, loyalty to the company, teamwork, tact, and consideration.[44] Given these differences, it appears that assigning weights to the traits is clearly advisable. Trait-based systems are generally easy to use, and they usually take little time to complete.

Trait-based systems can be problematical, however, especially when used as the sole technique of evaluation. Among the most frequently cited criticisms are the following:

- The system allows great latitude for rater bias. Because concepts such as honesty, cooperativeness, and adaptability are difficult to specify, the rater is vulnerable to imposing biases either intentionally or unintentionally on the ratee. Administrators operating in such a system must be particularly scrupulous that race, gender, or other legally proscribed biases are eliminated.
- Trait-based systems are more likely to be challenged successfully in court than other types of systems.[45] Some improvements can be effected if the evaluation form also gives the rater the opportunity to provide specific examples of employee behavior to support each rating, and if weights are assigned to the factors so that the employee knows what traits are most important.
- There is no good standard for comparison when trying to assign a rating on the more abstract factors (e.g. what does it really mean to be rated four out of seven on the factor of honesty?)
- A trait-based system focuses more on characteristics of the employees, rather than characteristics of the job performance, hence, it does not encourage a concentrated discussion on the tasks of the jobs themselves or future goals for the employee. Such a system emphasizes judging the person rather than the performance and diminishes the opportunity for a fruitful exchange between supervisor and employee.

Goals or Effectiveness-Based Evaluation Systems

A goals or effectiveness-based system tries to overcome the limitations of a trait-based system by emphasizing agreed upon performance goals rather than inherent characteristics of the employee. Employees do seem to prefer this type of evaluation over trait-based systems.[46] This

FIGURE 3-2.   Trait-Anchored Form with Numerical Rating Scale

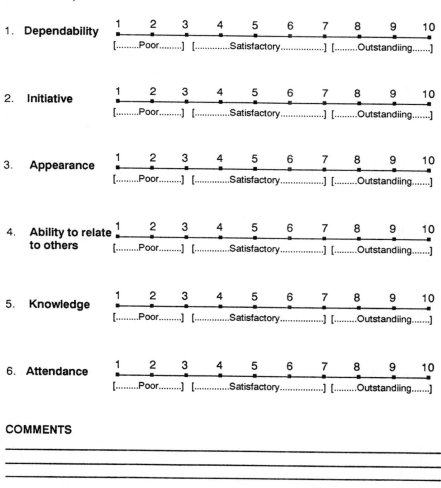

**Trait-Anchored Form
with Numerical Rating Scale**

Circle the appropriate number that best reflects the employee's performance over the review period.

1. **Dependability**   1   2   3   4   5   6   7   8   9   10
[.........Poor.........] [..............Satisfactory.................] [.........Outstandiing.......]

2. **Initiative**   1   2   3   4   5   6   7   8   9   10
[.........Poor.........] [..............Satisfactory.................] [.........Outstandiing.......]

3. **Appearance**   1   2   3   4   5   6   7   8   9   10
[.........Poor.........] [..............Satisfactory.................] [.........Outstandiing.......]

4. **Ability to relate to others**   1   2   3   4   5   6   7   8   9   10
[.........Poor.........] [..............Satisfactory.................] [.........Outstandiing.......]

5. **Knowledge**   1   2   3   4   5   6   7   8   9   10
[.........Poor.........] [..............Satisfactory.................] [.........Outstandiing.......]

6. **Attendance**   1   2   3   4   5   6   7   8   9   10
[.........Poor.........] [..............Satisfactory.................] [.........Outstandiing.......]

COMMENTS

FIGURE 3-3. Sample Graphic Rating Scales

SAMPLE GRAPHIC RATING SCALES

Characteristics	Unsatisfactory	Needs Improvement	Satisfactory	Excellent	Superior	Comments
Quality of Work						
Productivity						
Work Habits						
Knowledge of Job						
Initiative						
Relations with People						
Judgement						
Attendance & Punctuality						
Adaptability						
OVERALL RATING						

COMMENTS

approach was developed by Peter Drucker in a system called Management by Objectives (MBO), which has received considerable attention in the library press. Its primary target is middle-managers, although attempts have been made to apply it to other levels as well. The system is best administered only after the library as a whole has identified its goals, so that the goals of individuals are consistent with the goals of the organization.

Cohen has identified several steps in the goals oriented approach:

- Review the job description to make sure the responsibilities are those actually performed and are consistent with the goals of the organization
- Develop a performance plan in cooperation with the employee
- Get consensus between the employee and supervisor on the performance goals and means of measuring results
- Collect evaluative information during the evaluation period
- Give timely feedback to the employee at least quarterly.[47]

It is critical that the supervisor and the employee work together to set goals and means of measuring results for the coming review period. Generally, the results should be expressed quantitatively so that their attainment can more easily be determined. The overall performance plan may include areas of personal and professional development, exploring how employees can develop their own skills and professional expertise in order to accomplish the goals established.

The basic advantage to such a system is that employees formally participate in setting goals. Responsibility for evaluation is shared between supervisors and the employees, in contrast to a trait-based system in which the supervisor alone exercises total control. It is assumed that in most cases participation in goal setting should increase worker commitment and satisfaction. Certainly mutual goal setting should improve the employees' understanding of their actual jobs and the expectations of their supervisors. It also provides an opportunity for supervisors to develop employees' understanding of how their own goals fit into the broader goals of the whole library. In addition, the system improves supervisors' understanding of employees' tasks, and affords an opportunity to listen to employees' concerns and perceptions, and to offer advice and encouragement.

There are, however, some significant disadvantages:

- The system is time-consuming and costly when compared to a trait-based system. Time must be devoted to training and orientation of staff and supervisors as well as the time for developing and negotiating performance goals with employees.
- Goal setting may not work well in all situations: employees with little need for participation may resist mutual goal setting, wishing instead to have the goals set for them; jobs whose tasks are very structured and rou-

tine may find goal setting inappropriate; jobs which are very unstructured may have goals that are ambiguous. The library director's position may not be conducive to goal setting, especially if quantitative goals are required.

- The system requires strong communication skills, especially on the part of the supervisor. A supervisor who is really attempting to disguise an autocratic management style, or who is unable to deal with disagreement may find mutual goal setting to be stressful and unproductive. The same is true for an uncommunicative or arbitrary employee.
- The system may produce unethical conduct. When goals become the object of employee performance, the means by which the goal is accomplished may not be considered. There is always the possibility that employees might sabotage or delay the work of others in order to obtain their own goals.

Behaviorially Based Rating Systems

Another method of measuring performance is to focus on employees' behavior rather than on goals or on traits. One method, called the Critical Incident Technique, requires that the supervisor maintain a file of notable performances (negative or positive) of the employee. These incidents are then used as the foundation for discussion and evaluation at the time of performance review. There are several problems with this technique:

- Supervisors can't take the time required to record all the appropriate incidents
- Incidents tend to be described in narrative and qualitative terms which makes comparing incidents difficult
- Feedback on negative or positive performance is delayed
- Employees have little influence over the standards by which they are judged.[48]

In addition, negative events are likely to have a greater impact on the supervisor and therefore may be more likely to be recorded. Another behaviorial method is to identify a set of desired behaviors for the job to be evaluated. Employees are then rated on the degree to which they successfully mimic those behaviors. For example, on its simplest level, a behavioral standard for a clerical employee might involve a quantitative statement such as: "Files 40 cards per hour in the card catalog without error" or "Types 20 overdues per hour without error." The advantage to such an evaluation system is that the evaluation is clearly job related. As long as behaviors are easily quantified, and the tasks structured, behaviorially anchored ratings of this type might suffice.

A more sophisticated version of behaviorial evaluation involves using what are called Behaviorially Anchored Rating Scales (BARS). In this system, a job is broken down into its essential dimensions. For each dimension specific examples of performance behavior ranging from very poor performance to outstanding performance are identified based on the job description. These behaviors are given a specified number of points. A series of intermediate descriptions serve as the levels of evaluation between "very poor" and "outstanding." The evaluator selects the level of behavior which matches that of the employee and assigns the designated number of points. In addition, each dimension can be weighted to get a total performance score for each employee. Such a system can be refined and used for quite complex positions, including those of professional librarians.

A slightly modified example of behaviorally anchored descriptions for a reference librarian at the Downers Grove Public Library in Illinois is shown in Figure 3-4. The reference job has been divided into six distinct dimensions:

- Answering or referring reference questions
- Performing effective reference interviews
- Maintaining and developing special files, collections or equipment
- Preparing reports, statistics, and schedules, and planning and implementing new projects
- Selecting and evaluating collections
- Performing other duties as specified in the job description.

In principle, BARS appears to be a logical system; it is job related and focuses on actual behavior rather than on traits of the individual. This could be quite useful if the library has to defend its job decision in a court of law. Among its drawbacks is that it is quite expensive to develop and implement. Done properly, a considerable amount of time, analysis, and staff must be devoted to identifying job dimensions and appropriate behaviors, and ranking the behaviors. It must be noted as well that at least some studies report that BARS is no better or worse than other evaluation methods.[49]

A Contingency Approach to Evaluation Systems
The plethora of evaluation methods highlights the fact that there is no one way to conduct performance evaluations. It is natural for standards to vary considerably according to the many types of job responsibilities. The view that evaluation systems should vary according to the situation is called a "contingency approach." It may be that routine jobs such as clerical positions in libraries are more amenable to simple quantifiable standards, while professional and administrative positions may require combinations of goal-based and behavioral systems. Of course, it is not necessarily safe to assume that all clerical workers work best with quantifiable standards. *People are different.* Some clerical workers may

FIGURE 3-4.   Behavioral Anchors for a Reference Librarian

I. **Answering or referring questions**

POINTS   BEHAVIOR

1   Is not able to answer or refer reference questions.
2   Has difficulty answering and referring reference questions.
3   Is generally able to answer or refer most reference questions. Has knowledge of and ability to use sources. Chooses sources appropriate to the level of the patron. Learns about new sources as they are published.
4   Shows above average skill in answering questions. Makes proper use of local sources before referring. Continually works to improve knowledge of reference sources.
5   Has command of reference sources and is always able to answer or refer questions. Shows creativity and tenacity when answering questions. Questions are referred to this person by other staff because of her knowledge of sources.

II. **Performing effective reference interviews**

POINTS   BEHAVIOR

1   Does not perform an effective reference interview. Will not listen to patron or ask appropriate questions; is not approachable.
2   Occasionally does not perform a complete reference interview. May appear unapproachable to patrons. Occasionally will not be able to ascertain patron's real need.
3   Usually performs an effective reference interview. Suggests titles or strategies that are appropriate for patrons and asks open questions. Is approachable.
4   Almost always performs an effective reference interview. Asks follow-up questions. Almost always is approachable and suggests titles or strategies that are appropriate.
5   Demonstrates exceptional skill in interviewing techniques. Is always approachable to patrons.

III. **Developing and maintaining special files, collections or equipment**

POINTS   BEHAVIOR

1   Does not maintain the necessary files, collection, or equipment. Has no plan of service for the special collection, files or equipment.
2   Has difficulty maintaining special files, collections, or equipment. May not follow plan of service already developed.
3   Generally develops and maintains special files, collections, and equipment. Keeps files, collections, or equipment current and in working order. Has developed a workable plan for the future of the collection.
4   Changes and/or creates new files, collections, or equipment as need arises. Works to make the collections, files, or equipment accessible and understandable to staff and patrons.

5	Envisions and carries out practical and necessary improvements in area before need arises. Acts on own initiative and uses knowledge to improve the area and staff skills.

IV. Preparing reports, maintaining statistics, preparing schedules, planning and implementing new projects

POINTS   BEHAVIOR

1	Fails to prepare or is consistently late with reports, statistics, schedules. Does not plan or implement new projects.
2	Occasionally prepares incomplete and/or late reports, statistics, or schedules. Has difficulty planning and implementing new projects.
3	Generally prepares reports, statistics, schedules, and new projects in a thorough and timely manner.
4	Almost always hands in reports, statistics, and schedules on time and correctly done. Suggests improved ways of reporting. Volunteers to develop new projects.
5	Innovative in suggestions for projects which fit within overall department plan. Plans carefully, foreseeing possible difficulties and staff allocations. Reports, statistics and schedules are always filed within deadline and are professionally done.

V. Is competent in selecting and evaluating collections

POINTS   BEHAVIOR

1	Is unable to select and/or evaluate collection competently. Cannot stay within budget allotment for area. Oversights are frequent in providing material to the public. Cannot complete selection or weeding within reasonable time limits.
2	Has difficulty selecting and/or evaluating collection competently. Sometimes does not follow collection development or weeding guidelines. Has trouble completing selection or weeding within reasonable time limits.
3	Selects and evaluates collection competently. Consults standard sources when selecting or weeding. Materials are generally available promptly to the public. Stays within budget allotment for area. Applies library's guidelines when selecting or weeding.
4	Work with collection has brought recognizable improvements in quality and in patron and staff satisfaction. Uses weeding as an opportunity to develop a strategy for building a collection. Seeks out alternative sources of reviews or subject information when selecting.
5	Is particularly skilled in selection and evaluation. Innovative in developing and carrying out a plan to improve a collection and monitor the plan's results. Always consults both standard and special sources when selecting or weeding.

Reprinted with permission from the Downers Grove Public Library, Downers Grove, Illinois have a considerable need for participation and independence, thus, they might prefer goal-oriented approaches. Conversely, at least some reference processes performed by professional reference librarians may be amenable to quantifiable behaviors.[50] Unfortunately, it is not possible to tailor the evaluation to each person, some consistency is needed and would generally require that workers in the same or similar job categories be reviewed in a similar way.

Evaluating Library Directors

Evaluation systems are usually developed for several, even hundreds of employees. A special case involves how to evaluate the library director. The position of director is a pivotal role in any library and poor performance can have devastating consequences. Oddly enough, relatively little attention, and few published articles focus on evaluating this position.[51] There is reason to believe that few libraries actually conduct such reviews regularly. A survey of ARL libraries revealed that only half conduct reviews of their directors, and that in many of these libraries, reviews have been instituted only recently.[52] In many libraries, both public and academic, the review is informal, perfunctory, or nonexistent; in others the review may take place only once in three or five years.

Some differences in directorial evaluation in public and academic libraries may require different evaluative approaches. In academic libraries, for example, the library director may serve more as a middle-manager in terms of the entire university bureaucracy. Such directors usually would not be reviewed by a Board of Trustees, but by an administrative supervisor, peers in other academic departments or divisions, and by subordinates. In addition, an academic library director's position may be an academic appointment and governed by the rules and regulations covering the promotion and tenure of academic faculty. Public library directors, on the other hand, usually serve as the administrative head of the bureaucracy, and performance review is conducted by a Board of Trustees. Because there is less of a tradition of peer review or subordinate review in public libraries, the director is less likely to be evaluated by anyone other than the trustees.

Purposes of Directorial Evaluation

The formal evaluation of a director serves many important organizational purposes, some common to all performance evaluations, and some unique. The review of the director:

- Provides useful information to the director regarding his or her performance. Like all employees, directors have a right to know how they are performing and where improvement is needed.

- Provides the board, or in the case of the academic library, the university administration, with a means of enforcing accountability; it gives them an opportunity to assess how the director has fulfilled the mission of the library. Given the large amounts of public monies which are often administered by library directors, it is incumbent on trustees to review the practices of the individual most likely to allocate these resources.
- Reduces the chances that back-room politics or personal prejudices are involved in the evaluation process.
- Serves as an educational and review function for board members as they examine the goals and objectives of their own institution.
- Serves as a communication tool between the director and the board. A good performance evaluation should involve a give and take between trustees and the director regarding the direction of the institution and what needs to be done now and in the future.

Standards of Directorial Evaluation

The responsibilities of the director are broad and not easily defined or quantified. Because of this, it is more difficult to identify job standards precisely. Nonetheless, job standards should be segmented into basic categories reflecting general managerial responsibilities. These include the following:

Administration: The director should be evaluated in terms of the efficiency and effectiveness of the library operation in general. Policies and procedures established by the board should be implemented quickly, consistently, and fairly, with a minimum of conflict. The director should also be evaluated in terms of use of library services and materials, e.g. has circulation increased, has use of programs and reference services increased?

Leadership: Directors play a crucial role in setting the tone and direction of the organization. It is important to determine if the director has provided clarity of purpose for the staff. In terms of the board, the quality of the director's advice and guidance should be assessed as well as knowledge of new media and services. The director's ability to formulate and implement both short- and long-range plans should be evaluated.

Budget and Finance: The library budget is a central consideration in any evaluation. The director should be evaluated in terms of ability to develop a realistic budget, to administer the wage and salary system, to anticipate expenses, to obtain outside funding, and to communicate financial concerns to the board.

Communication: A key to any important administrative post is the ability to communicate. A director should be evaluated in terms of ability to communicate with staff, board members, and the public. Communication should be evaluated in terms of accuracy and diplomacy. The communication climate should be assessed in addition to the director's propensity to listen as well as communicate. The director should be held

FIGURE 3-5. Evaluating the Library Director

AKRON-SUMMIT COUNTY PUBLIC LIBRARY

QUESTIONNAIRE FOR PERFORMANCE APPRAISAL

OF THE

LIBRARIAN-DIRECTOR

FORM B

Use the following criteria by circling the appropriate
number following each answer:

5 = Superior

4 = Above Average

3 = Average

2 = Below Average

1 = Poor

0 = Not Applicable or
    Not Observed

A. Areas of Librarian-Director Functioning

I. Library Administration and Planning

1. Has provided leadership in developing an
    understanding of library goals and   5   4   3   2   1   0
    objectives

2. Has contributed to developing and enhancing
    the quality of the program and service of
    the library   5   4   3   2   1   0

3. Has promoted changes in operation and
    services in response to board policy
    recommendations, employees' suggestions
    and societal interests and needs   5   4   3   2   1   0

4. Has an awareness of latest library service
    ideas, trends and innovations   5   4   3   2   1   0

5. Supports the principles of intellectual
    freedom   5   4   3   2   1   0

6. Supports others in their efforts to
    accomplish procedures and/or library
    services   5   4   3   2   1   0

FIGURE 3-5.   Evaluating the Library Director

-2-

7. Takes initiative in program and staff
    development   5   4   3   2   1   0

8. Encourages and promotes long-range
    planning consistent with institutional
    needs   5   4   3   2   1   0

Budgetary and Fiscal Management

9. Provides sound fiscal management,
    including the ability to address
    budgetary matters in a way that
    achieves efficient and effective
    use of resources   5   4   3   2   1   0

10. Has ability to comprehend and
    evaluate fiscal and budgetary
    matters   5   4   3   2   1   0

11. Has a favorable record of attracting
    funds to the institution   5   4   3   2   1   0

12. Possesses a good understanding of the
    library's financial needs   5   4   3   2   1   0

13. Has promoted greater board/staff
    understanding of finances as they
    affect the institution   5   4   3   2   1   0

Communication

14. Communicates well his and/or the
    library's. position with (a) board   5   4   3   2   1   0
                            (b) staff   5   4   3   2   1   0
                            (c) public   5   4   3   2   1   0

15. Demonstrates accuracy and clarity in
    written and verbal communications   5   4   3   2   1   0

16. Has the ability to convince others of
    an idea, knowing how to be assertive
    without being offensive or antagonistic 5   4   3   2   1   0

17. Promotes esprit de corp and group
    identity within the library system   5   4   3   2   1   0

FIGURE 3-5. Evaluating the Library Director

-3-

18. Is accessible; promotes a feeling of openess in seeking the thinking of others	5	4	3	2	1	0
19. Is willing to discuss the rationale of administrative actions and decisions	5	4	3	2	1	0
20. Is credible and honest in face-to-face relationships with others	5	4	3	2	1	0
21. Has the ability to relate with persons as individuals or in groups both in and outside the library system	5	4	3	2	1	0

IV. Decision Making and Problem Solving

22. Possesses a clear vision of the goals and mission of the library	5	4	3	2	1	0
23. Is committed to the goals and welfare of the total library system	5	4	3	2	1	0
24. Delegates appropriate responsibility to subordinates and supports them in carrying out their responsibilities	5	4	3	2	1	0
25. Establishes standards of control, review and follow-up to insure efficient and effective task completion by himself and others	5	4	3	2	1	0
26. Has the ability to make sound, logical decisions, even under stress, is objective	5	4	3	2	1	0
27. Encourages participative decision making, seeking input from those most directly affected	5	4	3	2	1	0
28. Has competence to provide conflict resolution	5	4	3	2	1	0
29. Shows sensitivity for those affected by decisions	5	4	3	2	1	0
30. Has ability to identify and analyze problems and issues confronting the library	5	4	3	2	1	0

FIGURE 3-5.   Evaluating the Library Director

-4-

31.   Has ability to re-evaluate and if nec-
essary retract decisions   5   4   3   2   1   0

32.   Is well-organized and efficient in
accomplishment of his duties   5   4   3   2   1   0

External Relations

33.   Provides procedures for the public to
make their needs and interests known to
the library administrators   5   4   3   2   1   0

34.   Has the ability to relate to and communicate with the larger community external
to the library   5   4   3   2   1   0

35.   Represents the library in a positive
manner to its various publics   5   4   3   2   1   0

36.   Conveys a positive and progressive image
of the library   5   4   3   2   1   0

37.   Exemplifies high standards of citizenship
in both his personal and professional life 5   4   3   2   1   0

Personnel

38.   Seeks out those best qualified to fill
administrative and professional vacancies   5   4   3   2   1   0

39.   Maintains the confidence and trust of those
with whom he works   5   4   3   2   1   0

40.   Exercises good judgement in dealing with
sensitive issues regarding the administrative
professional and non-professional staff   5   4   3   2   1   0

41.   Gives due recognition to library staff's
individual or cooperative accomplishments   5   4   3   2   1   0

42.   Is effective in forming, developing, and
supervising an administrative network to
implement policy   5   4   3   2   1   0

FIGURE 3-5. Evaluating the Library Director

5

43. Shows evidence of the ability to select strong
    subordinates   5   4   3   2   1   0

44. Seeks and uses the counsel of immediate sub-
    ordinates   5   4   3   2   1   0

45. Provides an on-going procedure for evaluation
    of other members of the library management team   5   4   3   2   1   0

46. Displays an ability to motivate subordinates in
    positive ways   5   4   3   2   1   0

B. Administrative Effectiveness

    Please answer the final two questions as definitely as possible.
    Use additional paper if necessary.

    1. What makes this Librarian-Director an effective administrator?

    2. How do you feel the Librarian-Director could increase his effectiveness?

    _____
                Signature (optional)

When completed, please return sealed in the attached envelope addressed to the
Chairperson, Personnel Committee on or before _____.
                                                        (date)

accountable for creating a climate in which subordinates feel free to communicate new ideas and problems to the administration.

Decision-making and Problem Solving: It is important to review the important decisions made by the director to determine if they were logical, objectively made, and correct. In addition, evaluation should include the ability of the director to anticipate the effects of decisions and to limit harmful consequences of decisions. Similarly, the decision-making process should be assessed in regard to the director's appropriate or inappropriate use of delegation, and ability to design effective decision-making structures throughout the library system.

Public Relations: A critical aspect of the director's performance involves relating effectively with the public, or other agencies within a larger bureaucracy. The ability of the director to deal with friendly and unfriendly patrons, and his or her relations with political bodies and personalities, should be assessed. The overall image of the library should be evaluated and how the director promotes or fails to promote a positive image for the library.

Development of Human Resources: Ultimately, the director must be held accountable for the hire, evaluation, discipline, and termination of staff, as well as their general treatment and morale. The director should be accountable for designing a system of rewards that recognizes and promotes high performance while disciplining and eliminating employees who do not perform. The director's ability to promote a productive work environment which conforms to legal requirements should also play a central role in an evaluation.

Professional development: The director's own growth as a professional is a relevant concern of the board, because a director who does not keep up with the latest developments in librarianship is bound to make incorrect decisions. The director should be evaluated in terms of attendance at professional conferences and workshops, participation in statewide or regional library programs, and perhaps, authorship of publications.

An example of a public library director's rating form that covers most of these areas is shown in Figure 3-5. Keep in mind that this form is only part of the total evaluation process. In developing the form and standards of performance, joint consultation between the director and the board is important. Optimally, the director and the board should agree on each responsibility and standard. It would also be useful to have the director rate his or her own performance so that the board can assess the degree of agreement before the evaluation meeting.

How Should Performance Reviews Be Conducted?

The information presented here suggests that there is no simple recipe for conducting an effective performance evaluation. Certainly it is important that reviews be mandatory, consistently applied, and conducted regularly. Evaluation is an interaction between two or more individuals. Because *people are different*, the type of interaction depends in part on how the human differences between rater and ratee combine. Most managers are well aware that many factors influence the success of a review. Among them are:

- The attitude of the ratee and rater toward the review and towards each other. Obviously, if there is personal animosity or distrust, there is little likelihood that the review will be fruitful. The perceived importance of the review is also quite important. If the manager has given the impression that performance reviews are unimportant or just a nuisance, the employee is not likely to take the review seriously.
- The personal characteristics of the rater and ratee. Some personalities are harmonious, some clash. Each person brings to the review their own personal values, beliefs and prejudices, and interpersonal style. If the evaluator is a good communicator, is empathetic and diplomatic, and can use body language in a positive manner, the review is much more likely to end successfully.
- The degree to which the employee perceives the association of rewards to the evaluation. Employees must have incentives to perform. One could argue that the greatest incentive is fear of termination by the employer. But performance review should be perceived in a positive light. The employee should see a direct connection between improved performance and reward. Of course, rewards can take many forms: a raise, a promotion, or simple recognition by the manager of a job well done.
- The perceived commitment to the review process by top administration. No matter how excited the immediate supervisor may be about performance review, the attitude of the director and administration is critical. An employee is not likely to take the matter seriously, let alone the supervisor, if they believe that top management simply doesn't care.
- The type of review process and standards selected. Obviously, if the standards are perceived as inappropriate, or the review process is perceived as unfair, no constructive results can come about and there is great likelihood of increased worker dissatisfaction and grievances.

Only some of these variables can be controlled by the supervisor or manager. Nonetheless, the evaluator who lays the groundwork for an effective appraisal improves the chances of success.

Before the Review Period: Make sure employees understand what is expected of them. Go over the performance standards before the review period begins. These standards should be in writing. Indicate what areas are especially important and which areas are less important. It is critical that employees know what their job is. Finding out in a performance review that they have been working on irrelevant tasks, or devoting their energies to tasks considered trivial by the evaluator, will not result in a constructive appraisal. The review process should be discussed with new employees and they should be given a copy of the performance review forms used during evaluation.

During the Review Period: Let employees know throughout the evaluation period how they are doing on an informal basis. Formal performance appraisals should contain few surprises. An employee surprised by performance criticisms may react in an unpredictable and emotional fashion.

Before the Performance Review: Give employees plenty of time to prepare for the performance review. Make sure they know the date far in advance. As part of the preparation, employees should be given an opportunity to rate themselves on a form identical to the one used during the formal appraisal. This will give them an opportunity to think about their performance. However, as noted above, evaluators should not anticipate significant self-criticism.

Set aside sufficient time to conduct the review. Time considerations may vary depending on the type of evaluation system, complexity of the job tasks to be reviewed, and whether performance is good or poor. If the employee perceives that the review is treated as a cursory and superficial activity, the effectiveness of the review will be compromised.

Preparing for the Review: Before the appraisal, review the employee's performance in relation to the job standards. Preparation is vital. Assemble specific examples of performance for reference in the discussion. This is especially important if the rater anticipates an especially difficult review of a poor performer. It may be necessary to write down exactly what the rater wants to say to ensure completeness and accuracy. Be prepared to take some criticism. Some employees may have the courage to indicate problems in supervision. The supervisor should listen carefully and react with interest rather than animosity. Performance reviews can often provide valuable performance information for the supervisor as well as the ratee.

Make sure the review is not interrupted. This period is a rare opportunity for extensive and sometimes sensitive discussions. Concentration can be easily broken if phone calls or staff members are permitted to disrupt the review process. The employee should feel confident that the discussion will not be interrupted by phone calls or other employees.

During the Review: At the beginning of the review, make sure the employee understands the purpose of the review, and how reviews are used. If the employee has any questions on these matters answer them before the review continues. Because employees seek reassurance from performance appraisal, the supervisor should, at the earliest possible time, provide reassurance that they are doing well. This is more likely to set a relaxed atmosphere for the review. Of course, the supervisor should only provide this reassurance if it is an accurate reflection of performance.

Review the employee's self-appraisal first, or in conjunction with the supervisor's appraisal. This formalizes participation on the part of the employee. If the employee's perspective is left to last, it sends a signal that it's not important. Try to reach consensus on the evaluation for each standard of performance. This is often easier said than done. Evaluators have the unpopular responsibility of criticizing as well as praising. Success in reaching consensus depends on the seriousness of the disagreement, and the interpersonal skills of both the rater and ratee. The supervisor should be able to give specific examples that support the rating. However, supervisors must also keep in mind that they can be mistaken. The employee can offer new information that could change the rating. The rater must listen carefully so that the employee receives a fair hearing. A review should resemble more a conversation than a lecture. If poor performance has been established, the rater must ensure that the employee knows exactly what must be done to bring the performance up to standard. This may require putting in writing specific tasks which must be accomplished or training which must be obtained.

Near the end of the review, the evaluator should ask the employee if all concerns have been addressed. It is important that the employee feel that the review was complete; that her concerns as well as the concerns of the rater were discussed. Make sure that all review documents are signed and dated. If the employee has a specific form to respond to the review, the supervisor should remind the employee of this privilege and review the appropriate procedures. In addition, if there is any reason to believe that the employee wishes to appeal the evaluation, the procedure for appeal should be discussed.

After the Review: Following the review, consider how the review went. Significant comments made by the employee, such as complaints regarding possible discrimination, or problems in the system should be recorded in case further action is needed.

How Should the Review Process Be Monitored?

Procedures for Appeal

A good performance review system always permits employees to challenge the accuracy or fairness of a review. First, for legal reasons, providing a process of appeal ensures that the employee receives "due process." This is especially critical for public employers. Because most performance reviews become part of employees' official files, the right to challenge negative material may be assured by federal, state, or municipal laws. An appeal procedure may show defects in both the evaluation system and in the evaluator, that incorrect or inconsistent standards are being applied, or that the supervisor's rating is based on personal animosity rather than professional judgment. It is also an important safety valve for discontented employees. It is generally better that employees complain internally; if there is no internal route, employees are more likely to pursue their grievances in court. Generally, appeals should be handled by an individual on a higher managerial level than the rater.

Review by Administration
An appeals procedure should not be the only means by which the administration monitors the review process. As a general practice, each review should be examined by a higher-level supervisor. Reviews should be analyzed for completeness, clarity, use of specific examples, and evidence of bias. Any questions concerning reviews should be thoroughly discussed with the rater. It is better to identify problems early so that they can be remedied internally.

Statistical Analysis
Reviews of individual performance evaluations should be supplemented by an administrative analysis of evaluations overall. For example, evaluations can be broken down by race, age, and sex to determine if certain groups are receiving a disproportionate number of low or high evaluations. If a particular supervisor, or the system as a whole tends to down-grade particular groups of workers, then a total evaluation of standards and methods may be required to ensure that the system is fair, and that there is no alternative system that would eliminate the disparities in evaluation.

Training
A critical aspect of effective performance review programs is training for evaluators. Training requires an investment in time and money by the administration. A training program should include a performance review manual that is distributed to all individuals who conduct reviews. The manual should contain a discussion of the purposes of evaluation, common rater errors, who performs evaluations, how the review is to be conducted, how the form is to be completed, appeals procedures, and policies on nondiscrimination and the penalties for supervisors who discriminate. It should be noted that providing written instructions to raters significantly strengthens the legal position of employers if the reviews are challenged in court.[53]

The performance review manual should be supplemented with a training program. A specific time should be set aside for training raters. Topics include those covered in the manual, and raters are given an opportunity to ask questions.

LEGAL CONSIDERATIONS IN PERFORMANCE EVALUATION

Library employers must keep in mind that performance rating systems are subject to legal scrutiny, especially as they relate to equal employment opportunity. The *Guidelines* set forth by the Equal Employment Opportunity Commission have interpreted performance ratings as "tests" and treat them the same as tests for employment. The basic issues are the same as those for hiring tests: a performance rating system cannot adversely impact classes of people protected by law such as blacks, hispanics, and women. If an adverse impact is shown, then the organization must show that the performance ratings are valid and that there is no alternative evaluation system that works as well and eliminates the discrimination. This interpretation was confirmed by the U.S. Supreme Court in *Albemarle Paper Company* v *Moody*.[54]

Challenges to performance ratings have focused on two areas: how the system was developed, and how the system was administered. Successful challenges have been made in the following areas:

- The job standards were not based on a systematic job analysis.
- The job standards developed are too vague.
- The job standards were not clearly related to the job to be performed and were not validated.
- The standards of performance were not given weights so that the employee knew which standards were of greater importance.
- The standards were based on traits of the employees rather than on their actual performance.
- The evaluation depended too heavily on the supervisor's subjective judgments.
- The performance standards were not consistently applied.
- Racial or sexual bias was used in applying the standards.

In an analysis of actual employment discrimination cases involving performance appraisal systems, four factors appeared to affect legal outcomes. Verdicts in favor of the employer were more often found when:

- the employer had conducted a job analysis prior to implementing the system
- the appraisal system was behavioral rather than trait oriented
- the raters were given specific written instructions
- the appraisal results were reviewed with the employee.[55]

Given this information, the employer must concentrate on several important areas:

Well developed standards: Clearly written and quantifiable standards are best. Preferably these standards should be based on a previous analysis of the job so that they are relevant and realistic.

Well trained supervisors: The library must provide good training for supervisors so that their judgments are based on professional rather than personal evaluations.

Good communication with the employee: The supervisor should discuss performance issues directly with employees and be sure that they understand the responsibilities of the job.

A good monitoring system: The library must closely monitor supervisory ratings to ensure that employees are receiving similar evaluations for similar performance whether in the same department or in different departments. This should be accomplished by upper-level supervisors.

FACTORS TO KEEP IN MIND IN PERFORMANCE EVALUATION

1. Performance evaluation must be seen as closely related to other critical parts of the organization such as hiring, training, promotion, discipline, compensation systems and motivational forces.

2. Performance evaluation must be treated very seriously because it affects employees' feelings of personal and professional worth.

3. The effectiveness of performance evaluation depends on many factors. These include the credibility of the supervisor, the ability of the employee to participate in the evaluation, the extent to which the setting of goals is mutual, the timeliness and frequency of the review, the perceived importance of the review by supervisor and employee, the degree to which the employee perceives that rewards follow from the review, and the personal interaction of the rater and ratee.

4. Performance reviews must be relevant and practical.

5. At the minimum, a review should be conducted by the immediate supervisor.

6. It is best to get a variety of perspectives for evaluation including: self-evaluation, peer evaluation, evaluation by superiors, and subordinate evaluation.

7. Performance evaluation should be based on standards that are realistic, clear, specific, and consistently applied.

8. There are many types of performance evaluation systems:
   a. Trait based are quickest but allow the greatest subjectivity;
   b. Goal based systems focus on results rather than personalities but are more expensive and time consuming;
   c. Behavior based systems are also time consuming and expensive, but have the strength of being directly related to actual behaviors on the job.

9. It is essential that the director of the library also be evaluated based on criteria established by the Board.

10. Legal challenges to performance reviews have often resulted from vague standards, standards based on personal traits rather than job related criteria, and from inconsistently applied standards.

Endnotes

1. Douglas Cederblom, "The Performance Appraisal Interview: A Review, Implications, and Suggestions," *Academy of Management Review* 7 (1982): 220.
2. Wendell L. French, *The Personnel Management Process*, Boston: Houghton-Mifflin, 1982: 338.
3. Emanuel Kay and Herbert H. Meyer, "Effects of Threat in a Performance Appraisal Interview," *Journal of Applied Psychology* 49 (October 1965): 316.
4. Martin M. Greller, "The Nature of Subordinate Participation in the Appraisal Interview," *Academy of Management Journal* 21 (December 1978): 652.
5. Cederblom: 223.
6. Greller: 650.
7. Ronald J. Burke, William Weitzel, and Tamara Weir, "Characteristics of Effective Employee Performance Review and Development Interviews: Replication and Extension," *Personnel Psychology* 31 (Winter 1978): 916-917.
8. Cederblom: 223.
9. Burke et al.: 913.
10. Burke et al.: 915.
11. Cederblom: 226.
12. Frank J. Landy, Janet L. Barnes, and Kevin R. Murphy. "Correlates of Perceived Fairness and Accuracy of Performance Evaluation." *Journal of Applied Psychology* 63 (December 1978): 753.
13. Jeffrey S. Kane and Edward E. Lawler, III, "Performance Appraisal Effectiveness: Its Assessment and Determinants," *Research in Organizational Behavior* 1 (1979): 446.
14. William F. Gleuck, *Personnel Management: A Diagnostic Approach*, Dallas: Business Publications, 1974: 287.
15. Kay and Meyer: 317.
16. Paulette A. McCarty, "Effects of Feedback on the Self- Confidence of Men and Women," *Academy of Management Journal* 29 (December 1986): 854.
17. Burke et al.: 917.
18. Kane and Lawler: 427.
19. Kane and Lawler: 454.
20. Lawrence S. Kleiman, "The Implications of Professional and Legal Guidelines for Court Decisions Involving Criterion-Related Validity: A Review and Analysis." *Personnel Psychology* 38 (Winter 1985): 815.
21. See for example, Kay Deaux and Tim Emswiller, "Explanations of Successful Performance on Sex-Linked Tasks: What is Skill for the Male is Luck for the Female," *Journal of Personality and Social Psychology* 29 (January 1974): 80-85; Madeline E. Heilman and Richard A. Guzzo, "The Perceived Cause of Work Success as a Mediator of Sex Discrimination in Organizations," *Organizational Behavior and Human Performance* 21 (1978): 346-357; Bernice Lott, "The Devaluation of Women's Competence," *Journal of Social Issues* 41 (1985): 43-60.

22. Madeline E. Heilman and Melanie H. Stopeck, "Being Attractive, Advantage or Disadvantage? Performance-Based Evaluations and Recommended Personnel Actions as a Function of Appearance, Sex and Job Type," *Organizational Behavior and Human Decision Processes* 35 (April 1985): 212-213.

23. V.F. Nieva and B.A. Gutek, *Women and Work: A Psychological Perspective*, New York: Praeger, 1981: 72.

24. Deaux and Emswiller: 84.

25. Madeline E. Heilman and Richard A. Guzzo, "The Perceived Cause of Work Success as a Mediator of Sex Discrimination in Organizations," *Organizational Behavior and Human Performance* 21 (June 1978): 354-355.

26. Nieva and Gutek: 73.

27. McCarty: 841.

28. Madeline E. Heilman, Michael C. Simon, and David P. Repper, "Intentionally Favored, Unintentionally Harmed? Impact of Sex- Based Preferential Selection on Self-Perceptions and Self- Evaluations," *Journal of Applied Psychology* 72 (February 1987): 67.

29. Kane and Lawler: 446.

30. Martin M. Greller, "Evaluation of Feedback Sources as a Function of Role and Organizational Level," *Journal of Applied Psychology* (February 1980): 26.

31. Robert J. Vance, Robert C. MacCallum, Michael Coovert, and Jerry W. Hedge. "Construct Validity of Multiple Job Performance Measures Using Confirmatory Factor Analysis," *Journal of Applied Psychology* 73 (February 1988): 74.

32. Lynn McFarlane Shore, and George C. Thornton, III, "Effects of Gender on Self- and Supervisory Ratings," *Academy of Management Journal* 29 (1986): 116.

33. Arie Y. Lewin and Abram Zwany, "Peer Nominations: A Model, Literature Critique and a Paradigm for Research," *Personnel Psychology* 29 (Autumn 1976): 430.

34. Greller: 24.

35. Jeffrey S. Kane and Edward E. Lawler, III, "Methods of Peer Assessment," *Psychological Bulletin* 85 (May 1978): 564.

36. Lewin and Zwany: 435.

37. Lewin and Zwany: 435.

38. Lewis and Zwany: 434-435.

39. Judy Horn, "Peer Review for Librarians and Its Application in ARL Libraries," *Proceedings of the ACRL Third National Conference*, Seattle, April 4-7, 1984: 137-138.

40. Karen Smith and Gemma DeVinney, "Peer Review for Academic Librarians," *The Journal of Academic Librarianship* 10 (May 1984): 90.

41. Douglas Cederblom and John W. Lounsbury, "An Investigation of User Acceptance of Peer Evaluations," *Personnel Psychology* 33 (Autumn 1980): 572-573.

42. Edwin A. Locke, Karyll N. Shaw, Lise M. Saari, and Gary P. Latham, "Goal Setting and Task Performance," *Psychological Bulletin* 90 (July 1981): 127-129.

43. John E. Baird and Jerome C. Diebolt, "Role Congruence, Communication, Superior-Subordinate Relations, and Employee Satisfaction in Organizational Hierarchies," *Western Speech Communication* 40 (Fall 1976): 260-261.

44. Kane and Lawler: 453.

45. Hubert S. Feild and William H. Holley, "The Relationship of Performance Appraisal System Characteristics to Verdicts in Selected Employment Discrimination Cases," *Academy of Management Journal* 25 (June 1982): 400.

46. Cederblom: 222.

47. Lucy R. Cohen, "Conducting Performance Evaluations," in *Critical Issues in Library Personnel Management*, edited by Richard Rubin, Urbana, Ill: University of Illinois, 1989, pp. 42-44.

48. Henry M. Frenchette, Jr., "Performance Appraisal," in *Human Resources Management and Development Handbook*, William R. Tracey, ed., New York: AMACOM, 1985: 231.

49. Rick Jacobs, Ditsa Kafry and Sheldon Zedeck, "Expectations of Behaviorally Anchored Rating Scales," *Personnel Psychology* 33 (Autumn 1980): 635.

50. Tom Carter, "Performance Appraisal for Reference Librarians," *Reference Services Review* 13 (Fall 1985): 96.

51. See for example, Mike Simons and Anne Amaral, "Evaluating the Library Director," *C & R.L. News* (May 1989): 360-362; and Association of Research Libraries, *Executive Review: Spec Kit # 72*, Washington, D.C., March 1981; and Nancy M. Bolt, *Evaluating the Library Director*, Chicago: American Library Trustee Association, 1983.

52. *Executive Review*, Spec Kit #72, Washington, D.C., March 1981: 67-68.

53. Feild and Holley: 400.

54. *Albemarle Paper Co.* v *Moody*, 422 U.S. 405 (1975).

55. Feild and Holley: 397.

4
Coping with Marginal Performance

One of the primary concepts underlying human resource management in libraries is that people play a vital role in its operation; coordination and cooperation are essential. But if employees act in unpredictable or unreliable fashions, such synchronized activity is impossible. Libraries, like other organizations, cannot tolerate this situation for long before adopting practices to restore order and reduce unpredictability. These practices form the disciplinary structure of human resource management.

Individuals who do not perform well are sometimes referred to as "problem" or "marginal" employees. To some extent, it is a disservice to use the term "marginal employee." It implies that the individual is "marginal" rather than focusing on the performance itself. The reality is that most workers, at some time in their work life, have not performed to the best of their ability. The reasons are many and varied, but the employer must make performance the focus of attention, rather than the person. Nonetheless, poor performers can and do have serious detrimental effects on the library. They provide inadequate service to the public, waste the time and money of the library, often increase conflict and decrease morale. Employers must pay close attention to individuals who fail to meet the performance standards of the organization.

Dealing with marginal performance can be difficult and time-consuming. Supervisors and administrators are often reluctant to deal with it because of such factors as:

Unpleasantness of the task: It is seldom a pleasant experience dealing with problem employees. In most cases, dealing with a poor performer is stressful for both the employee and the supervisor; the employee may respond with anger, confrontation, tears, or stony silence. Anticipating such responses is high motivation to avoid the situations.

Belief that discipline doesn't work: The supervisor may feel that pointing out work deficiencies will exacerbate the problem; that the employee will become demoralized, angry, and disruptive to the work of others. If the supervisor is not confident that disciplinary techniques work, there is little motivation to correct poor performance. Some evidence does suggest, however, that supervisors who apply a combination of informal and formal warnings do increase the productivity of their departments.[1]

Fear of legal action: In today's litigious climate, supervisors are constantly reminded that their actions can result in lawsuits, charges of unfair labor practices, and equal employment opportunity complaints. These legal constraints have made the evaluation and disciplinary process more intimidating, formal, and fraught with pitfalls that even the most conscientious supervisor finds daunting. Consequently, the supervisor may overlook marginal performances in order to avoid the cumbersome and lengthy processes that many disciplinary processes require.

Feelings of lack of support: Supervisors may believe that they will be undercut by upper-level managers if employees complain, file grievances, or threaten to sue. If the administration is perceived as not supporting supervisors, the supervisors may feel that the stress and time required to deal with the poor performance is wasted and counterproductive.

Lack of Time: Dealing with poor performers is often a time-consuming task, which does not always produce the desired improvement. Indeed, it might make the work environment increasingly unpleasant. Supervisors must document poor performance and prepare carefully for discussion with the employee. Those who feel that they are already swamped with work may be hesitant to add another burdensome activity.

Lack of training and ability of the supervisor: Dealing with marginal employees requires knowledge of the tasks being evaluated, disciplinary policies and procedures, and good interpersonal skills. Supervisors may lack confidence in any or all of these areas and therefore be reluctant to face the problem.

Fear of the employee: The supervisor is often the target of the employee's displeasure when poor performance is identified. Employees vary in their ability to deal with emotional situations involving criticism. A supervisor may fear that the employee will become physically violent, abusive, or otherwise destructive.

Status of the employee: Some employees, although occupying a lower position in the organizational hierarchy, may have acquired considerable informal authority and influence by virtue of their reputation or by association with those who are powerful. A supervisor may be reluctant to anger or upset such individuals for fear of repercussions from friends of the staff member or from higher-level managers and administrators.

Sympathy and Guilt: Many supervisors have considerable compassion and empathy for their staff. Employees may elicit sympathy for a variety of reasons: they may be suffering severe personal or health problems, they may be putting out great effort but still failing, they may come from an economically or socially deprived environment. If a supervisor believes that the poor performance is a consequence of such external factors, the supervisor may feel guilty holding the employee responsible for his or her performance. Similarly, supervisors may feel guilty about damaging an individual's emotional and physical well-being by demoting, terminating, or otherwise disciplining the employee.

DEFINING MARGINAL OR PROBLEM PERFORMANCE

Although there are some instances of employee behavior that are clearly unacceptable (e.g. fighting or theft), some problems are not that clear-cut. Because of differences in attitudes and training, supervisors may differ as to what constitutes a performance problem and who is a marginal worker. Problem behaviors can generally be divided into two types: performance problems and misconduct. Performance problems relate to tasks that employees are supposed to perform; misconduct relates to more general behaviors which are inappropriate in the work setting. Among the more common examples of marginal or problematic behavior are the following:

Absenteeism or Tardiness: Two of the most common problem behaviors are workers who do not come to work, or who come to work late. This type of activity is called "withdrawal behavior" because individuals remove themselves from the workplace. The consequences of absenteeism and tardiness are detrimental because they tend to disrupt work schedules and increase work loads on those who attend work regularly. Three basic causes of absenteeism have been identified. Illness, both psychological and physical, is the first and primary cause of absenteeism. From a psychological perspective, worker attitudes toward the supervisor and coworkers appear to affect the disposition of the worker to come to work. The second cause involves environmental conditions such as heating and lighting. Interestingly, a third cause is the presence of a sick leave policy. Organizations that provide sick leave have considerably higher absentee records than those which do not.[2]

Substandard Work: Some workers simply cannot perform the tasks for which they were hired. Some are unable to perform them in a timely fashion. Unlike absenteeism or tardiness which can be easily quantified, the ability to assess poor performance in a library may be a difficult task.

Intoxication or Drug-Induced Behavior: It is a disturbing reality that many employees are addicted to drugs and alcohol. When influenced by such substances, the result may be inappropriate workplace behavior, chronic absenteeism or tardiness, and dishonesty. Dealing with this type of marginal worker has become especially sensitive in recent years with some employers using random drug testing for current employees, and mandatory tests for applicants.

Insubordination: A fundamental assumption of the workplace is that the supervisor has the authority to issue directives to subordinates. Insubordination usually involves the refusal of an employee to follow a directive from the supervisor. Dealing with insubordination can be an especially trying event for the supervisor and requires considerable patience and deliberateness. It is unclear to what extent such behavior occurs in the library setting, but unless the directive would involve illegal conduct, or place the employee in imminent physical danger, refusal to follow a directive should be considered a very serious problem.

Dishonesty: From time-to-time, employers discover that employees are dishonest. They may be stealing library property or money, or the property of staff or patrons. Employers must be especially careful in handling this problem. Not only must disciplinary procedures be scrupulously observed, but employers must be careful not to make false accusations. In addition, they must decide whether to file criminal charges. Despite the delicacy with which the problem must be handled, it is crucial to act as quickly as possible. Employees who steal are likely to repeat their actions until they are stopped.

Violence: In rare instances, employees act in a violent manner, often against other employees. Like dishonesty, the employer must act deliberately and with dispatch to prevent recurrences of the problem. In some settings, such as factories, violence is more common, but in public institutions like libraries it occurs rarely. Given the fact that libraries deal with many members of the public including children and the elderly, acts of violence by staff cannot be tolerated. It may also subject the library to liability if not handled with dispatch.

The Causes of Poor Performance

When employees are performing poorly, it is tempting to hold them personally responsible. Library managers must be cautious about such attitudes because there is evidence that different attributions for failure are assigned to men and women. When males fail to perform well, it is often attributed to bad luck; when females perform poorly it is attributed to lack of ability.[3]

Even when gender differences are ignored, supervisors may seek other simple explanations such as the employee is "lazy" or "slow." But it is important to recognize that there may be both internal and *external* causes of poor performance; that marginal work may be the result of organizational or social forces, rather than personal shortcomings. Some internal and external factors are summarized in Figure 4-1.

External Causes

Poor disciplinary and reward system: Employees do not work in isolation; rather, they work within the larger organizational environment. The system of compensation and discipline is an important part of that environment. Performance systems that do not accurately reflect employee performance or are too permissive regarding marginal performances, may provide no incentive for employees to perform well. Reward systems that are perceived as unfair or arbitrary will negatively affect job performance.

Poor supervision: The interpersonal and motivational skills of supervisors vary widely. If the supervisor fails to encourage workers by giving them appropriate recognition, autonomy, and responsibility, they may become demotivated and not perform up to standard. Similarly, poor performance may result from an inadequate number of supervisors. If a supervisor must try to oversee the work of too many individuals, poor performance may be missed.

Poor job assignment: Different jobs in a library require different knowledge, skill, and ability. An employee may fail in one position, but succeed in another. Poor performance may not reflect poorly on the talents of the employee, but on the ability of the organization to match these talents to the right job.

Poor equipment: Marginal performance may be the result of inadequate and poorly maintained equipment, or the lack of equipment. When employees are asked to meet standards that depend on well-maintained equipment, the employer must ensure that the equipment failure is not the cause of poor performance.

Lack of training: In order to perform well, an employee must be given the information necessary. Poor performance may result from an inadequate training program or trainers.

Unclear job responsibilities: In some cases, the employee may receive substandard performance assessments because the job duties were ambiguous, or because the supervisor did not properly emphasize which duties are most important. Consequently, the employee either performs the wrong duties, or devotes inappropriate amounts of time to duties considered unimportant by the supervisor.

Union contracts and governmental regulations: Although union contracts may quite rightly try to protect employees from unfair actions

FIGURE 4-1. Factors Affecting Organizational Performance

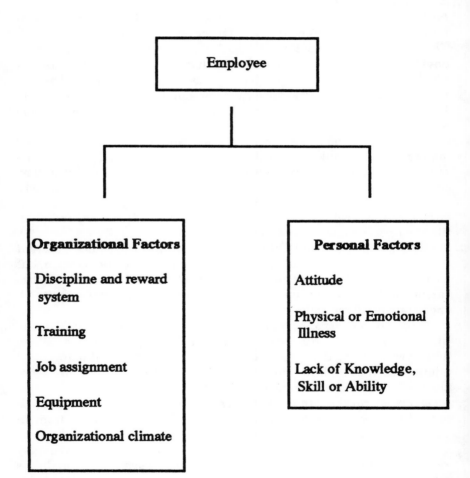

FACTORS AFFECTING ORGANIZATIONAL PERFORMANCE

Employee

Organizational Factors

Discipline and reward
 system

Training

Job assignment

Equipment

Organizational climate

Personal Factors

Attitude

Physical or Emotional
 Illness

Lack of Knowledge,
 Skill or Ability

by the employer, they may also protect workers whose performance is inadequate. Employees who believe the union will protect them even from inadequate performance may become marginal workers. Similarly, some labor laws such as equal employment opportunity and unfair labor practices laws may inadvertently protect employees who are not performing well; consequently, some employees may take advantage of the situation.

Inappropriately low standards: The standards of performance may not accurately reflect the library's needs. This may result from poor procedures when developing the standards. Supervisors, through friendship or empathy, may feel that more difficult standards would deprive their staff of opportunities for raises or promotion. The consequence is low levels of performance.

Tension with coworkers: Employee performance can be affected by tensions between coworkers. Other employees may harass a worker or refuse to assist or train her. In other cases, peer pressure can force a good worker to lower performance to conform with lower levels of performance of the group.

Cultural or ethical pressures: A worker's performance may be affected by cultural or moral perspective. For example, defense department employees may find working on armaments gives them moral qualms which reduces their effectiveness. Similarly, some cultures place different values on such factors as freedom and equity. If the work environment does not reflect these values, performance can deteriorate.

Internal Causes of Poor Performance

Of course, it is also possible that the employee is responsible for the marginal performance. Even so, it is important to distinguish between those characteristics that the employee can change and those that are either impossible or very difficult to correct. If the problem is simply that the employee does not have enough information about a job, then direct training may alleviate the problem. But if the employee lacks the mental ability (e.g. intelligence or memory), or the physical capacity to perform a task, then it may be unrealistic and unfair to expect satisfactory performance.

Poor work attitude: The attitude of employees toward work in general, and toward their library in particular, varies widely. Some employees consider their work as "just a job," or a "necessary evil"; these individuals may not have the motivation to work well. Such attitudes may develop during childhood, or result from factors entirely external to the library. (The issue of worker attitudes and motivation will be discussed in more detail in chapter 5.)

Physical illness: The employee may be performing poorly because of a physical infirmity. In many cases, deterioration in performance is temporary, but in the case of chronic illness or permanent injury, the situation becomes protracted. This is an especially complicated area for the employer because the employee may be covered under the civil rights acts protecting handicapped workers. Scrupulous attention to the responsibilities of the employer in accommodating employees who are ill is essential.

Emotional or mental illness: An employee may become distraught because of family, financial, or health problems. This form of stress can lead to "burnout." Performance deterioration can manifest itself in increased absences, tardiness, alcoholism, drug abuse, accidents, short-temper, and inefficiency in performing even simple tasks. Employer intervention for emotional distress is at best delicate and must be handled with discretion; but when job performance is being affected it is the responsibility of the employer to deal with it. Disciplinary action is one alternative; however, more progressive organizations are turning to employee assistance programs (EAP's) to aid the distressed worker.

Lack of Knowledge, Skill, and Ability: A major cause of poor performance rests with personal limitations including mental acuity, physical adeptness, and level of creativity, which can have substantial impact on the individual's ability to perform.

DEALING WITH POOR PERFORMANCE: EMPLOYEE DISCIPLINE

The best way to deal with poor performance is to prevent it. This can best be accomplished by a well-structured employee selection program including effective recruitment strategies, analysis of staffing needs, job placement, and interviewer training and techniques. The right hire goes a long way toward preventing future performance problems. In addition, once employees are hired, well-developed orientation and training programs, and skilled supervision can go a long way to prevent marginal performance. But organizations are not perfect; most contain at least some marginal performers. Dealing with these individuals requires good skills on the part of supervisors and a well-structured program of employee discipline.

How supervisors deal with poor performers can have serious consequences for the organization as a whole. If discipline is administered poorly, it can trigger decreases in productivity, feelings among workers that the organization is unfair, and decreases in job satisfaction overall. Conversely, if discipline is applied well, one can expect increases in productivity and job satisfaction.[4]

As with all aspects of human resource management, the issue of employee discipline involves a delicate interaction between supervisors, employees, and disciplinary policies and practices of the organization. Although it would be nice to develop a single formula for dealing with all employees, no effective system can disregard the unique character- istics of each disciplinary situation. The personal characteristics of the employee affect the efficacy of disciplinary action—intelligence, emo- tional and physical condition, values, verbal abilities, personal motiva- tion, and family situation—all affect how discipline is accepted.[5]

It is also clear that characteristics of the *supervisor* affect the disciplinary process. Although there is strong evidence that poor employee performance is a major determinant for supervisors' use of discipline, other, less relevant factors are sometimes at work. Supervi- sors who dislike an employee, or perceive the employee as a poor performer, are more likely to take punitive actions.[6]

Leadership style and the supervisor's job tenure also affect the use of discipline. Supervisors who identify more strongly with their workers have a tendency to give fewer informal warnings and more written warnings and more time to correct performance. The job tenure of a supervisor also affects the use of discipline. Supervisors who have been with an organization longer tend to use a more confrontatory style, and to be more concerned about obtaining adequate documentation.[7]

Library policies affect supervisory use of discipline. Supervisors who perceive that their own rewards are tied to the performance of their workers are more likely to strive in a positive way to correct poor performance.[8] Supervisors who have to deal with a greater number of employees are more likely to use formal discipline and to use counselling less than those working with fewer employees.[9] All of this suggests that the complex environment in which discipline is administered places a significant burden on the supervisor and the system to be fair and consistent.

As a side note, the relationship of gender to the use of discipline has been only superficially explored in the general management literature, and has received no attention from library researchers. Overall, there is no clear evidence that discipline is applied differently to female workers or applied differently by female supervisors.

The "Therapeutic Approach" to Discipline

Traditionally, when employees' performance is marginal, disciplin- ary measures are applied. This disciplinary approach is certainly nec- essary if the employer is to ensure the right to take subsequent action against an employee. Unfortunately, discipline is generally interpreted by the employee as a negative act. Such actions are not the best way to improve employee performance. Consequently, before discipline is applied, the employer should attempt to improve performance by less formal means. Sometimes called the "therapeutic approach," this method focuses on job counseling.[10]

An essential aspect of this process is good communication with the supervisor. Continuous dialogue is central to resolving the problem in advance of formal action. When performance problems begin, supervisors should deal with them immediately. Reasons for the problem performance should be discussed along with measures to prevent further problems. At this early stage, the supervisor needs to make sure that the employee has the essential information to perform the job. Questions that need to be explored include:

- Has the employee received the necessary training?
- Have adequate resources been put at his or her disposal to accomplish the tasks required?
- Are there extraneous factors (e.g. personal problems, conflicts with co-workers) that are inhibiting performance?
- Has the individual been incorrectly assigned and is nondisciplinary transfer a reasonable action?

Such discussions should be conducted in a nonthreatening fashion. The discussion should be conducted in a private area and should involve an exchange of opinions; it is not a time for assigning blame or making accusations. The supervisor should demonstrate genuine concern for the employee and should try to stimulate self-analysis and appraisal by asking the employee about the problem and how to resolve it. This, of course, requires considerable interpersonal skills. The supervisor must be able to elicit fruitful responses by skillful questions, and must listen carefully, providing feedback that encourages response from the employee.[11]

The outcome of informal discussions should be a plan of action that will overcome the problem performance. The purpose of such a meeting is wholly constructive. If further training is needed, then the supervisor should take responsibility for providing it. If personal problems are the cause, then referral to an Employee Assistance Program or counseling agency may be in order.

Personal problems are an especially delicate matter. The supervisor needs to be sympathetic and understanding. A demonstration of real concern may promote important communication between the employee and the supervisor. Of course, the supervisor should avoid trying to provide professional assistance, that is the job of an EAP or counselor, but offering support can be an effective technique for improving performance.[12] In any event, the supervisor must follow-up any discussion by monitoring the employee's performance to determine if it is improving.

Even in the informal or "therapeutic" approach to correcting marginal performance, some mention must be made of potential consequences, but it should comprise only a small portion of the discussion. The supervisor should make a note of such discussions so that if performance continues to be a problem, the informal attempts to resolve the problem can be documented. However, this material is not meant for the permanent file unless subsequent action merits its inclusion. Sometimes it may be necessary to talk with other staff members to get a full picture of the problem. Ideally, these discussions should occur in a group with the employee, or at least with the employee's knowledge and approval. Also, if the supervisor determines that the employee has made a successful effort to improve, the employee should receive verbal recognition.

The Application of Formal Discipline

Discipline is often perceived as a negative phenomenon; the concept is often confused with punishment. Punishment is, in fact, only one way to maintain or restore discipline. Examples of other techniques include informal discussion, job or task reassignments, and job counselling. Discipline is a normal and necessary part of our daily lives. In most situations, including those involving work, we impose discipline on ourselves: we get up at certain times, act in conformance with social conventions, and perform daily routines that have been repeated so many times that they become habit. Organizations, like people, require discipline in order to function.

Considering the many and various library activities that require coordination and communication among workers, it is obvious that the work process must be orderly. Library workers must be disciplined: they must conform to the needs, procedures, and policies of the library so that the goals of the library can be accomplished. In general, these needs are not inconsistent with the normal discipline with which most of us are familiar. Consequently, most libraries do not have to impose discipline on library workers in order for them to perform satisfactorily. In some cases, however, it is necessary for the supervisor to intervene when a marginal worker is unable to maintain the discipline necessary.

Because discipline can be unpleasant, supervisors often resist using it, but it is important for supervisors to consider the many factors that support its use. The primary reason to impose discipline is to correct poor performance, but there are other reasons that may have even greater impact on the organization as a whole.

Disciplinary actions may:

- *Prevent others from acting in a similar fashion*: When employees see that individuals who perform poorly are not disciplined, it may motivate them to imitate these acts. When employees are disciplined in a fair and timely fashion, it serves as a deterrent.

- *Assure others that inappropriate behavior will not be tolerated*: Even if employees do not intend to imitate improper behavior, they may become dissatisfied with the library if they see that no one acts to resolve performance problems. The consequences may be lower morale and higher turnover of productive employees.
- *Communicate administrative conviction*: Employees need to know how their employer feels about certain types of conduct. The employer is responsible for establishing an organizational tone, a standard of conduct to which employees should aspire. If the employer is perceived as fair, consistent, and intolerant of poor performance, employees are more likely to strive to meet the employer's expectations.

CHARACTERISTICS OF EFFECTIVE DISCIPLINE

The employer can take various approaches when applying discipline. Research, especially in the area of the application of punishment, reveals that there are some common factors that relate directly to the effectiveness of disciplinary actions. These include timing, intensity, relationship of the disciplinarian to the employee, schedule of discipline, provision of rationale, and availability of alternative behaviors.[13]

Timing

Disciplinary action is most effective when it is proximate to the undesired action(s) of the employee. Common sense tells us that waiting for weeks or months before applying discipline to an employee would likely lead to surprise and suspicion. In general, employees want to know immediately when they are acting in an unsatisfactory manner, if only to avoid repeating the behavior. Supervisors who save up incidents for later disciplinary action are not likely to gain the trust of their workers.

Intensity

One of the most difficult decisions is to determine what type of discipline should be used in a given instance. How employees perceive the appropriateness of a particular disciplinary action may influence not only their subsequent behavior, but also the attitudes of other workers. If employees believe that a disciplinary action is unnecessarily harsh, it may decrease morale or stimulate a search for collective action, such as unionization. Discipline must be moderately intense to create the desired result, but not so intense that it creates counterproductive anxieties. Unfortunately, there is no magic formula to determine how workers perceive the intensity of punishment. This requires knowledge of the type of employee in the specific workplace. It also highlights the need for employers to exercise great care when developing their overall disciplinary policies to reflect appropriate intensities.

Relationship with the Disciplinarian

What type of supervisory relationship is most effective if disciplinary action needs to be taken? Discipline appears to be most effective when there is a close and warm relationship between supervisor and employee. Of course, the use of discipline may well affect that relationship for the worse, but it appears that employees are more willing to change behavior when they respect the supervisor. This is logical; employees who are being disciplined by individuals they dislike or for whom they have little regard are not likely to be guided by their advice.

Schedule of Discipline

Many performance problems require more than one action in order to deter the undesired behavior. Discipline is most effective when three conditions are met:

- The discipline is administered consistently after every occurrence of the undesired behavior
- The same manager applies discipline in the same way to all employees
- All managers are consistent in disciplining employees in the same way.

This last condition is both difficult to obtain, and very important. Employees who are disciplined by one supervisor for actions that would receive no discipline from another may well find legal protection in equal employment opportunity laws. Unfortunately, this problem is widespread; supervisors perceive similar disciplinary situations in different ways and vary in their responses.[14]

Provision of a Rationale

Employees want and deserve to know *precisely* why they are being disciplined, and what will happen to them if their behavior continues. Providing a rationale also benefits the employer. It helps ensure that the employee receives due process if subsequent action such as dismissal is taken. In addition, if a rationale is provided, disciplinary action of lower intensity can be applied, thus reducing potential negative effects.

Availability of Alternative Behaviors

In order for discipline to be effective, employees must perceive that there are alternative actions which will satisfy the supervisor. Employees who feel that there is nothing practical they can do to satisfy the supervisor have no motivation to alter their behavior. In addition, the supervisor must provide encouragement to the employee who is making an effort to change; this support increases the effectiveness of the discipline.

THE DISCIPLINARY PROCESS

The previous discussion explored some of the many factors involved in marginal performance. Before the employer and supervisor can select the appropriate steps to restore discipline, it is essential that the causes of the problem are identified. Supervisors must examine all aspects in an analytical light, including their own possible contribution to the problem. Are there organizational, training, or communication problems? It is critical that supervisors characterize the problem in as specific terms as possible. Understanding specific issues involved should help supervisors in making a written record of the problem (an essential aspect of any good disciplinary process). Once the problem is understood, supervisors must judge how important it is. Applying discipline can be a time consuming and difficult task. In some cases, a problem first thought to be serious may be easily handled or trivial. In this case, disciplinary action may be unnecessary and counterproductive. If the problem is considered serious enough then the supervisor must act.

Similarly, even some serious problems may be handled by alternative actions other than discipline. Four such actions are giving an interim performance appraisal, referral to an employee assistance program, transfer to a more appropriate job, and retraining.[15]

Progressive Discipline

If alternative actions are inappropriate, then the employer must select the appropriate disciplinary action. This selection must take place in the broader context of what is known as "Progressive Discipline." Progressive implies that the problem employee is given several chances to improve before drastic action such as termination is taken. Under such a system, disciplinary action becomes progressively harsher if the poor performance persists.

To some extent, the type of discipline to be applied depends on the type of offense (Figure 4-2). Obviously, a harsher initial disciplinary action is necessary for theft or violence than for tardiness. Relatively

FIGURE 4-2.

DISCIPLINARY ACTIONS

INFRACTION OF RULES	1st Offense	2nd Offense	3rd Offense	4th Offense
1. Late reporting to work or returning from break (see definition, "Tardy")	Three times in one calendar quarter. First level warning. Time may not be made up, nor may benefit time be used to make up lost time.	Five times in six months. Second level warning. Time may not be made up nor may benefit time be used to make up lost time.	Six times in twelve months. Five working day suspension.	Seven times in one calendar year. Termination of employment.
2. Absent without proper notice or cause. (see definition, "Absent")	First level warning (time may be made up that work day, if schedule permits).	Second level warning (two times in a twelve-month period), time may not be made up, nor may benefit time be used.	Three times in twelve-month period. Three working day suspension without pay. Time may not be made up, nor may benefit time be used.	Four times in twelve-month period. Termination of employment.
3. Leaving job or regular work area during work hours for any reason without authorization from supervisor, except for lunch, rest periods, and going to the restroom.	First level warning.	Second level warning.	Three working day suspension without pay.	Termination of employment
4. Leaving work early without supervisor's approval.	First level warning. Time may be made up with use of accrued vacation or holiday time.	Second level warning. Benefit time may not be used to make up lost time.	Three working day suspension without pay. Benefit time may not be used to make up lost time.	Termination of employment
5. Smoking, eating and drinking in restricted areas.	First level warning.	Second level warning.	Three working day suspension without pay.	Termination of employment
6. Creating an unsafe condition or working in an unsafe manner.	Second level warning.	Three working day suspension.	Termination of employment.	
7. Abusive language or threats to fellow employees, or members of the public.	From second level warning to termination of employment, depending on the nature of the offense.			

minor offenses may require numerous disciplinary steps; while serious offenses may require only one or two steps. Some of the possible actions ranging from least severe to most severe include the following:

Informal Discussion

Some offenses, when taken singly, are best handled by an informal discussion. For example, an employee who is becoming an absentee problem may only require a "reminder" from the supervisor. This reminder should at least contain the following:

- Identification of the problem behavior
- Review of the present policy on such behavior
- What kind of problems can result if the behavior continues.

The supervisor should make a personal note regarding the date and time of the discussion.

Oral Warning

If the behavior persists, it may be necessary to hold a formal conference in which the employee is told that he or she is not performing properly. The warning should include the same information as for the informal discussion, however, the supervisor should also indicate that a record of the meeting will be retained by the supervisor and could be used as support for a subsequent disciplinary action if the employee's behavior persists. (An oral warning need not be placed in the personnel file, but the employee can be warned that further problems will result in a record being placed in the file.)

Written Warning

If the problem continues, or if the initial problem is serious enough, then a written warning should be issued (Figure 4-3). The structure of a written warning may vary from organization to organization, but it should at least include the following:

- Date of the meeting
- Purpose of the meeting
- Who was present at the meeting
- Statement of the facts
- Statement of the rules violated
- Indication as to when previous warnings or discussion took place
- A specific warning that the conduct is inappropriate
- Indication as to what the employee must do to improve
- Statement of consequences if improvement does not occur
- Date of next review
- Indication of whether the warning will go into the employee's personnel file

- Statement that the employee can write a written response
- Signatures of the employee and supervisor giving the warning.

It is important to be as specific as possible regarding the actual problem, the rules that are being violated, and the consequences of continued violations. This ensures that the employee fully understands the attitude of the employer toward the employee's actions.

Documentation

In order to protect the library from the possibility of successful grievances or legal action based on the improper application of discipline, it is essential that the employer have written evidence that the employee's actions required disciplinary action. This evidence is referred to as "documentation." Ruud and Woodford identify records that can serve as documentation:[16]

Business Records
These would include time cards and attendance records which could be used for absentee or tardiness problems; application forms may be used if falsification of credentials is involved; and performance evaluations and disciplinary warnings in the employees file may be used if marginal performance or misconduct is involved. Supervisors' notes regarding problems can also serve as support.

Written Complaints
These may include those from patrons or from staff. It is important to use complaints *only* if they are signed and dated. In addition, the employee must be able to read the complaint, and have the opportunity to provide a written response.

Examples of Poor Work
Errors can sometimes be documented by using samples. Copies of errors made on forms, letters, or on records such as overdue notices may serve as strong evidence of problems.

Recorded Testimony of Staff or Witnesses
Some types of problems, such as an employee who acts violently, or who is abusive or intoxicated, may be documented by taking the statements of employees or other witnesses to the conduct. These statements should be signed and dated, and the employee should have an opportunity to challenge statements made by others.

FIGURE 4-3.

WRITTEN WARNING

On March 15, 1989, Mary Phillips, Head Librarian of Oak Valley Branch, and Bill Young discussed Mr. Young's attendance. Mr. Young is a student assistant in Oak Valley who was hired as a student assistant on January 4, 1989. Mr. Young is a probationary employee in accordance with Section 2.04 of the *Employee Handbook.*

Upon reviewing Mr. Young's attendance record it was determined that he had failed to report for work ten times from January 20 to March 6. Mr. Young also changed his posted work schedule six times during the same period. When shown this information, Mr. Young agreed it was true.

After reviewing the above facts, Marilyn Halstead, Director of the library, has determined that Mr. Young is to receive a written warning. The warning is based on Section 4.3 of the *Employee Handbook* which reads in part: "Staff members should arrive to and depart from work according to scheduled hours," and "Staff members will be regular in their attendance." This rule is to ensure the smooth and efficient operation of the library.

Mr. Young is hereby warned that if, in the future, he fails to report for work as scheduled more than three times per calendar quarter or requests changes to the posted schedule more than three times per calendar quarter, he will be subject to further disciplinary action up to and including suspension or termination. Mr Young is to be reviewed no later than three months from the date of this warning or earlier if his absenteeism or tardiness continues.

Mr. Young is informed that this warning will be placed in his personnel file. Mr. Young may respond in writing to this warning within ten working days of the issuance of the warning. His response will be attached to this warning.

Mr. Young is requested to acknowledge by signing below that he has received a copy of this warning and has had an opportunity to discuss the warning with Mary Phillips in a meeting on this date _____. Mr. Young's signature does not indicate that he agrees with the substance of this warning.

This warning is in compliance with Section 2.1 of the *Employee Handbook.*

_____	_____
Bill Young, Student Asst.	Date
_____	_____
Mary Phillips, Head Librarian	Date

Photographs or Videotapes
In rare instances, such as in a case of theft, the library may have recorded the problem conduct on film or photographs. Such documentation may provide powerful evidence of misconduct.

Organizational Rules and Memos
In building a case concerning a problem employee, it is necessary to have written evidence that the employee should have known that the conduct was inappropriate. Consequently, the employer should be able to document in writing what the rules of the organization are, and that the individual could have been reasonably expected to know them. This is a particularly important reason to ensure that all employees receive a copy of the rules of the organization when they are hired, and that employees receive notification when rules are changed.

Preparation of Documentation

It is often the supervisor who must prepare the disciplinary documentation. When a supervisor must document a particular incident or set of incidents, it is important to follow some general rules. First, the writing should be clear, well organized, and objective. It may well come to pass that an outsider (e.g. a hearings examiner) will read the material. The documentation should be understandable and clear to such an individual. Expressions of anger, accusations, character slurs,. or other emotions have no place in documentation, and could support a charge of bias toward the employee. Second, the supervisor should focus on the facts. If the problem is tardiness, then the supervisor should indicate precisely how many times the employee was tardy over a given period, rather than simply say that the employee is a "tardiness problem." Third, the supervisor should deal only with the pertinent behavior. If the supervisor is documenting an absentee problem, then statements concerning other problems should be avoided.

It is especially useful if supervisors can give specific examples of problems. For example, if a librarian is having trouble dealing with the public, the supervisor's documentation should include specific incidents (including date of incident) which are described briefly. Some supervisors maintain a "Critical Incident File" which is used for the general purposes of performance evaluation. This file contains notable aspects (both positive and negative) of an employee's performance during the evaluation period. Such a file may provide considerable support if discipline is needed.

Conducting an Investigatory Hearing

From time to time, an employee's behavior may be so serious as to require a hearing to investigate the incident. Examples that may require such actions include fighting and suspected theft. Such hearings should conform strictly to the policies and procedures in the employer's personnel manual or union contract. The primary purpose of such hearings is to gather the relevant facts so that a determination can be made by the employer as to what disciplinary action, if any, is appropriate. It is *not* the purpose of a hearing to trick an employee into making damaging admissions.

Although hearings can be time-consuming and stressful, they can also be quite useful, especially in complicated and emotionally charged situations. Employers need to have as many facts as possible *before* making judgments; sometimes supervisors have acted improperly or contributed to a problem. It is better to find out what the problems are in an internal hearing than find out later in a court of law.

Procedures for conducting hearings should be carefully reviewed by the library attorney before adopting them. Generally, when conducting a hearing, the following guidelines should be observed:

- The employee should be given written notice of a hearing in advance. The employee should know the purpose of the hearing. Witnesses should also be given advance notice.
- Hearings should be held in a private place and should not be interrupted.
- The hearing should be conducted by an administrative employee (e.g. personnel director, assistant director, or director) rather than the immediate supervisor, who may be called upon to testify.
- Only individuals in a "need-to-know" position should be informed of, and present at, the hearing. Comments made to other staff should be scrupulously avoided since they may subsequently be construed as prejudicial or slanderous.
- The procedures should conform strictly to adopted policy of the employer or union contract.
- A record of the meeting should be maintained. If the hearing is being taped, approval for the taping should be obtained by all involved.
- Questions should be carefully prepared to elicit the facts and reasons for the employee's actions. The questioner should be neutral in the phrasing of questions, and should be *genuinely* interested in getting at the truth.
- All parties testifying should be given ample opportunity to express themselves completely.
- The employee should be informed when a decision will be made regarding possible disciplinary action.
- All testimony and information obtained in a hearing should be held strictly confidential.

Additional issues include the employee's right to have an attorney, a union representative, or a friend present at such a hearing, and the right of the employee to cross-examine those who testify. Procedures regarding these issues must be very carefully considered. The employer should seek advice from legal counsel to determine the best policy.

Informing the Employee About the Disciplinary Decision

If the decision has been made after proper deliberation then the supervisor must have confidence that the decision is a good one. Before the interview, the supervisor should review carefully the events leading up to the disciplinary action.

Of course, any disciplinary interview should take place in a private area. From the supervisor's perspective, the interview should be factual and oriented toward future behavior rather than past errors. The disciplinary interview has, by its nature, strong negative implications; harping on poor conduct will merely increase resentment and anger. The supervisor should indicate the type of discipline (written warning, suspension, etc.) and what will happen if there are reoccurrences. Emphasis, however, should be placed on the supervisor's confidence that the employee's performance will be fine in the future. The employee should also be informed of the right to appeal any disciplinary action taken and how to appeal. It is natural for an employee to be angry and upset. The supervisor must remain calm, and be prepared to take criticism from the employee.

Following the interview, the supervisor should make a written note concerning the interview. If the employee has made statements that concern the supervisor, such as charges of discrimination, these should be noted in as much detail as possible.

The Disciplinary Record

In most cases, a record of the disciplinary action should become part of the employee's personnel file. The employee should be so informed and should be given the right to attach a written response to the disciplinary record. The employee should subsequently be allowed to see the disciplinary record at reasonable times, and to make a copy. (Depending on your state's "Privacy Acts," the employee may be asked to pay for copies.)

Employees should not be asked to live with their mistakes forever. Some policy regarding the weeding of disciplinary actions in employees' files is advisable. This in itself may be an incentive for the employees to continue to act productively. Actually destroying employee records may not, however, be the best alternative. Legal actions by employees can be taken sometimes years later. One alternative might be to place the records in an envelope and seal them with an indication that they are not to be consulted for evaluative or promotional purposes.

Problems with the Disciplinary Approach

The use of progressive discipline is an improvement over the days when employers arbitrarily and capriciously applied discipline to their employees. It protects the employer if employees should challenge the disciplinary actions in court. Nonetheless, some have argued that the system is seriously flawed. Redeker identifies eight problems with progressive discipline:

- The purpose is to force an employee to obey company rules and regulations simply because of the rules themselves. This fails to instill in employees a feeling of responsibility for their actions
- Progressive discipline characterizes the employee as "bad" and hence destroys feelings of self-worth which in turn leads to anger and resentment
- The focus is on past conduct rather than on building strong employee-supervisor relationships
- Punishment is perceived as the primary motivator which seldom produces the desired change in attitude
- The fundamental relationship established in progressive discipline is adversarial rather than mutual cooperation toward organizational goals
- Progressive discipline encourages a parent-child role model in which the employee is scolded like a child and threatened with punishment
- Sole responsibility for improvement is placed on the employee rather than shared with the supervisor
- There is no positive reward system for stopping the undesired behavior, only the removal of punishment.[17]

For this reason, an alternative approach, often referred to as "positive discipline," is being used, primarily in the private sector. There are two fundamental differences between positive discipline and the traditional system. First, there is much less stress on punishment and greater emphasis on employees' sense of responsibility for their actions; and second, the process focuses attention on the future and employees' responsibility for deciding whether they can reach an appropriate level of behavior.[18] Emphasis is placed on the employees' decisions to commit themselves to the organization by accepting a job; the decision to remain with the organization falls squarely on the shoulders of the employee. Inappropriate behavior is viewed as *ipso facto* a deliberate decision on the part of the employee to sever ties with the organization and its goals.

This process begins at the time an individual is hired; the employee is asked to make a formal written commitment to the policies of the organization. If infractions occur, and informal discussions do not improve the situation, then the "first conference" is arranged. In this conference, discussion of problem behaviors is placed in the context that commitment to the organization requires conformity to organizational rules and regulations. Attention is only briefly focused on the problem behavior; the most time is spent in an effort to seek a mutually agreed upon solution to the problem. The attitude of the supervisor is centered on cooperation, joint responsibility, and problem resolution rather than punishment. The product of such a conference is a written memo, defining the problem and identifying agreed upon solutions including a timetable for solving the problem. The emphasis is not on punishment, but on actions to improve the situation. If the employee's performance improves in the time allotted, the supervisor is responsible for recognizing the employee's successful efforts and recording them in writing.

If infractions continue, a "second conference" is called. Again, the conference focuses on what to do to resolve the problem. The employee is given an additional opportunity to reaffirm his or her commitment to the organization, and to recognize that rules must be followed. This is recorded in a memo that is signed by the employee. This memo also includes a statement indicating that if the employee cannot resolve the problem, then employment will be terminated. In essence, the employer is telling the employee that further violations will be interpreted as a decision on the part of the employee that she is no longer committed to working for the organizations. Subsequent violations are interpreted as a voluntary resignation.[19, 20]

In some positive discipline systems, as a last resort, a *paid* one-day suspension is offered to employees. Employees are given the opportunity to think over if they really want to work for the organization under its rules. They are expected to return the next day, and meet in a "third conference" to give the employer a decision. If the employee wishes to remain, then a statement of commitment is made and signed by the employee with a recognition that any further violations would result in termination.[21] There is some evidence, although anecdotal, that the positive discipline approach is working better than the traditional progressive discipline. Some argue that supervisors have a stronger sense of community with employees, have a more positive experience in dealing with problems, and therefore are more likely to use the system.[22]

TERMINATING EMPLOYEES

The Bureau of Labor Statistics defines discharge as "termination of employment initiated by the employer for such reasons as incompetence, violation of rules, dishonesty, laziness, absenteeism, insubordination, and failure to pass the probationary period."[23] The key characteristics of a discharge are that it is involuntary, and that it is initiated by the employer. Sometimes, the notion of "involuntary" can be obscured. Employers who, for example, indicate to an employee that if they do not resign "voluntarily," they will be discharged, have, for all intents and purposes, discharged the employee. If the employer intentionally makes the work environment and job assignments so unpleasant and undesirable that the employee cannot remain, then a subsequent "resignation" by the employee can later be interpreted as a discharge. It should also be noted that in rare cases, an involuntary separation results from a source other than the employer. For example, an individual who is incarcerated or subject to a military draft is leaving involuntarily, but it is not a discharge.

Employers may decide to discharge employees for a variety of reasons. There is some evidence that discharge rates are higher for certain types of jobs and individuals. Employees with little tenure and few skills, as well as those in low level and low pay positions, are more likely to be discharged.[24] The reasons for discharge are generally the same as those that define marginal behavior: the inability of employees either to meet performance standards, or to conduct themselves in a fashion that is reasonable in the workplace. Employers, must of course, be especially careful with the decision to terminate. Termination results in direct loss of income and hence is a measurable damage if the employee seeks relief from an administrative or judicial body.

Terminating employees is an especially anxiety provoking situation. Many supervisors agonize over such decisions for months, even years. Decisions regarding termination can provoke feelings of guilt and sympathy or fear that the employee may not be able to obtain fruitful employment. They also have the greatest potential for emotional and physical conflict. Once employees believe that there is nothing left to lose, their antagonism and anger can magnify.

Termination is also a major decision because the organization incurs significant costs by failing to have selected the right employee. Aside from the possible legal costs if employees should appeal termination, there is loss of productivity during the period of the vacancy, disruptions in schedules, and possible decline in the morale of remaining employees. In addition, there are the subsequent costs of advertising, recruiting, interviewing, selecting, training, orienting, and evaluating a new employee.

The Employment-at-Will Doctrine

Traditionally, employers have exercised considerable power in their ability to terminate workers. This power resides in what is called the "employment-at-will" doctrine which has been part of our legal system for many years. This basic doctrine states that an employer, in the absence of a written contract, can terminate an employee for good cause, bad cause, or no cause at all. Underlying this view is the belief that employers have the right to run their businesses as they see fit. Even today, this basic right, or "management prerogative," has considerable weight, and defines the fundamental rationale on which employers rely in taking disciplinary actions against employees.

Wrongful Discharge

All employers, and especially public employers, must realize, however, that the employment-at-will doctrine has been seriously eroded over the years. The era in which employers can simply pick and choose which employees to fire and which to retain is long over. This erosion has occurred as courts have been willing to accept that some employees have been "wrongfully discharged" even when they were unprotected by a written agreement. Some laws, for example, prevent employers from making what is called "retaliatory" discharges. Employers cannot terminate employees for union activities, or for filing discrimination charges with the Equal Employment Opportunity Commission. Similar protections are extended to those who file Worker Compensation claims. Courts have also extended protections to workers who refuse to put themselves in "imminent danger," when ordered by an employer to do so.

Public Policy Exceptions

Another category of exception to the employment-at-will doctrine is called the "public policy exception." This exception deals with actions taken by employees that are in the public interest and therefore deserve protection. This would include preventing the termination of a "whistleblower." A whistleblower is an individual who exposes unlawful or otherwise unacceptable actions by an employer. Because termination of whistleblowers would have detrimental societal impact, they have been protected by the courts. The public policy exception has also been extended to employees who refuse to commit unlawful acts or commit perjury at the behest of their employer. Employers who ask employees to act unlawfully cannot terminate them if they refuse to comply. Similarly, employees cannot be terminated for giving truthful testimony that is damaging to the employer.

Implied Contracts

Some courts have been willing to extend protection to discharged workers when there appears to be an implied agreement for continued employment. Underlying this view is the belief that employers must act in good faith and deal fairly with employees even when no written contract is present.

An implied contract may arise from several sources. Employers are especially vulnerable if the organization's written personnel suggest that employees have rights to continued employment. The employee handbook may set a higher standard for termination than the at-will doctrine. For example, it may state that employees may be discharged only for "good cause." The at-will doctrine requires no cause. Similarly, the policy may state that once employees have passed a probationary period, then they may expect continued employment unless performance deteriorates. This promises much more than the at-will doctrine which raises no expectation of continued employment.

Another written policy that may restrict the at-will termination rights of the employer are the grievance and complaint procedures. Such procedures could be viewed by the courts as an assurance that these procedures will be strictly followed before the termination can proceed. Under the at-will doctrine termination could be immediate and without appeal.

Another vulnerable area involves oral agreements or promises. Employers who give oral assurances that satisfactory work leads to continued employment may be creating an implied contract even if these statements are not reflected in any written document. Employers must be very careful that supervisors and others involved in the hiring process make no promises regarding the employee's continued employment.

Implied contracts have also been found to exist for employees of long tenure who have been performing satisfactorily. In this case, the mere fact that the employer has retained the employee for years gives that employee a right to expect continued employment unless the employer can show good cause for the termination. Implied contracts have even been found for new employees when the employee has had to relocate and make fiscal sacrifices in order to take the job.[25]

It is important to note that the use of "wrongful discharge" challenges by employees have met with a mixed reception in the courts. It is vital that employers seek legal counsel to determine what the judicial climate is regarding these defenses against termination.

Intentional Infliction of Emotional Distress

Another approach to challenging terminations involves charging the employer with intentional infliction of emotional distress. Like the defense based on implied contracts, there is variation as to whether this approach is acceptable as a defense against termination. Generally speaking, the stress caused by the termination itself is not enough to satisfy the condition of emotional distress.[26] Rather the conduct of the employer must be "outrageous." For example, if the employer, in terminating an employee, were to handle an appeal in a trivial or humiliating manner, or if the employer subjected the employee to public abuse and excoriation, then the employer could be subject to a lawsuit. If the employee were threatened with violence or subjected to racial slurs in the process of discharge, then the employee may rightfully take legal action against the termination.[27] Evidence of intentional infliction of distress may also be found if the employer appears to be punishing the employee by withholding pay or other benefits following termination.[28] Kahn, Brown, and Zepke have identified four elements that seem to support claims of intentional infliction of emotional distress cases:

- The employer's action is "extreme and outrageous"
- The actions are "intentional or reckless"
- Real emotional distress occurs
- The effects of the distress are very serious.[29]

Common sense and proper supervision of the termination process are the keys to preventing this problem. The decision to terminate and the process of termination must be scrupulously objective. Employees should be regarded with the respect they deserve as human beings. Abusive conduct or actions taken that arise from personal animosity cannot be tolerated or condoned by the employer, and disciplinary action must be taken against any individuals who act in an irresponsible manner.

The Discharge Process

Generally speaking, a discharge should only occur after the process of "progressive discipline" has occurred. Similarly, by the time of discharge, a solid body of documentation should be available as evidence that the cause for discharge is just.

Because of the complexities of discharge, it might be useful for the library employer to apply a "test" used in the business world to determine if a discharge is correct. This test is based on the decision of a labor arbitrator, Carroll Daugherty, who identified seven questions that are pertinent to determine just cause.[30]

Daugherty's Seven Questions To Determine Just Cause

1. Did the company give to the employee forewarning or foreknowledge of the possible or probable disciplinary consequences of the employee's conduct?

2. Was the company's rule or managerial order reasonably related to (a) the orderly, efficient, safe operation of the company's business and (b) the performance that the company might properly expect of the employee?

3. Did the company, before administering discipline to an employee, make an effort to discover whether the employee did in fact violate or disobey a rule or order of management?

4. Was the company's investigation conducted fairly and objectively?

5. At the investigation did the company "judge" obtain substantial and compelling evidence or proof that the employee was guilty as charged?

6. Has the company applied its rules, order, and penalties evenhandedly and without discrimination to all employees?

7. Was the degree of discipline administered by the company in a particular case reasonably related to (a) the seriousness of the employee's proven offense and (b) the record of the employee in his service with the company?

The basic principles that apply to any disciplinary process apply to discharge. The employer should be able to state with confidence that employees knew or should have known that their actions would lead to discharge, and that the employer is able to provide substantial evidence that employees did, in fact, act in an undesirable manner that deserved termination. Objectivity and fairness are essential. The final decision to terminate should not be done by the immediate supervisor, but by an "objective" third party who, in practice, probably would be the director or personnel officer.

Despite the difficulties of the discharge process, it is absolutely critical that when an employer determines that a staff member should be discharged, constructive action must be taken. The costs in morale, money, and quality of service are too great to permit poor performers to remain. Of course, employers and supervisors are not perfect. Even a well-documented termination case can have its flaws. It is best to have legal counsel review the evidence and process when the decision to terminate is made. Barring protest from counsel, the unpleasant but necessary step of a termination interview should not be avoided.

The Termination Interview

Preparing for the Interview

As in any evaluation or disciplinary process, preparation is crucial. Errors at this stage may cause unnecessary and possibly costly problems. Termination should generally be the responsibility of the director or chief personnel officer. In this way, greater control can be exercised over what is said and done in the interview. It is also advisable to have more than one individual representing the employer present during the termination interview—perhaps the department or branch head, or immediate supervisor. The second person is a witness for statements made during the meeting, and may also afford some measure of support and security for the individual conducting the termination. Among the steps to be taken are:

- Review all the documentation that led up to the termination.
- Review the decision to terminate. Be prepared to state clearly the reason for the discharge, the events leading up to the discharge, and the organizational policies that support the termination.
- Prepare a notice of termination (Figure 4-4). This notice should be similar to a written warning. All such notices should be reviewed by legal counsel to ensure conformity with the laws of the state.
- Special preparation should be made if the employee is likely to become extremely upset or violent. This might include the stationing of a security officer nearby. Strategies for calming the individual should be considered. In cases where the employer anticipates that the employee could do harm to library property or to other staff, arrangements should be made with security to escort the individual out of the building.
- Arrange for a private area to conduct the interview. In some instances, it may be desirable that the interview be recorded. Make arrangements for such equipment in advance. (The advisability of taping such sessions should be reviewed with legal counsel.)

During the Termination Hearing

- Come directly to the point. Do not engage in unnecessary or lengthy small talk.
- Always conduct yourself in an objective and business-like fashion. Although the employee may become emotional or angry, you must remain calm and stay on the point. Do not engage in verbal accusations. Avoid any statements that might be construed as discriminatory or could otherwise give grounds for legal action.
- State the decision to terminate unambiguously. There should be no equivocation regarding the decision.
- Identify clearly and in a well organized fashion the reasons why the employee is being terminated. This should be done briefly, and not in an accusatory manner. Remember that the employee's ego is threatened in such a circumstance, and it is crucial that the meeting not be demeaning. However, do not attempt to "soften" the reasons for termination, or to misrepresent them. It is critical that the truth be told.
- Attempt to place the most positive light on the termination. This may be accomplished by discussing such issues as availability of continued benefits, payment of unused sick, vacation, and severance pay, job counseling and placement services. Sometimes, albeit rarely, a termination does not lead to anger or distress, but is understood by the employee. In this circumstance, it may be appropriate to express appreciation for the employee's efforts.
- Inform the employee of the right of appeal. This may include giving him or her a copy of the appeal or grievance procedure.
- Complete any paperwork or other procedural matters. This may include the signing of termination notices, and the return of library property such

FIGURE 4-4.

NOTICE OF TERMINATION

On June 1, 1988, a meeting was held with John Smilnor, Library Clerk in the Technical Services Department, Mary Smith, Head of Technical Services, and Barbara Wilson, Library Director. Mr. Smilnor was informed that he was being terminated because of poor attendance.

Mr. Smilnor had been warned orally about his attendance problem on January 18, 1988. He was subsequently given a written warning on March 22, 1988, and informed that he had two months to improve substantially his attendance record. Since March 22, 1988, Mr. Smilnor has been absent 14 work days. On seven of these days, he did not call in to report his absence. Mr. Smilnor has exceeded his sick time and all other available benefits.

Subject to provision 16.4 and 16.5 of the *Staff Policy Manual* which states in part: "Employees are expected to maintain regular attendance and to report to work on time. Employees may be terminated for poor attendance following the issuance of oral and written warnings," Mr. Smilnor is being terminated as of June 1, 1988.

Mr. Smilnor is informed that he may write a response to this notice of termination. The response will be attached to this notice and placed in the personnel file. Mr. Smilnor is also informed that he may appeal the decision under Section 4.3 of the *Staff Policy Manual*, "Staff Grievance Procedures."

This termination is in compliance with Section 2.4 of the *Staff Policy Manual*.

John Smilnor, Library Clerk	Date
Barbara Wilson, Director	Date
Mary Norton, Head, Technical Services	Date

as keys, identification badges, and staff library cards. If a written termination notice is given, the employee should receive a copy.

- *Do not change your mind.* The employee may become quite emotional and ask for "just one more chance." Although compassion is a worthy trait, this is not an instance in which to exercise it. Do not vacillate; remember why you decided to terminate and stick to these reasons.
- Indicate to the employee when the meeting is over and when he or she is expected to leave. Generally, the employee should be expected to collect his or her personal belongings and leave immediately. Of course, in many instances it may be reasonable to allow the employee an opportunity to say goodbye to some coworkers. However, if the employer believes that the employee may damage or remove library property, or otherwise act in a way destructive to property or staff, then the employee should be escorted to his or her desk, and then out of the building.

After the Termination Meeting

After a termination meeting, those involved are usually upset. Often the director or supervisor questions whether the decision was the right one. This loss of self-confidence may take a while to overcome. At these times, it is useful to review the reasons for termination, and to remember that it is the employer's *obligation* to remove poorly performing employees before they adversely affect service to patrons and staff morale. In general, the library will be much better off without the employee. Other steps to be taken include the following:

- Make or summarize any notes that may be pertinent regarding the employee's comments during the meeting. For example, if the employee makes charges of discrimination or abusive treatment, they should be noted. If necessary, they should be investigated.
- Inform affected individuals. Notify the departments or individuals that are directly affected by the termination. Do not discuss specific reasons for the termination. This is a matter between the employer and the employee. Do not make defamatory or critical statements about the employee even at social or informal occasions such as at meals.
- Do something for yourself. The strain of termination is considerable. Although you cannot talk to staff members about the termination, you can talk to fellow administrators. Sometimes simply talking about the issues can be comforting. Perhaps the best thing is to find a distraction that is not work-related. Whether it's movies, sports, museums, exercise, or visiting with friends, it is good to find an activity that takes your mind off the situation.

Miscellaneous Considerations

When to Terminate

Advice on when to terminate an employee is contradictory. Some recommend that termination be done at the end of the last day of the week.[31]

Others recommend that terminations *not* occur before a weekend; that termination should be done early in the week and at the beginning of the day.[32] There is no one right time to terminate. In effect, the day of termination may be based on the practical consideration of when the individuals concerned are available to meet. It is most important that the employer not appear to be insensitive. Terminating employees on their birthdays or when they have just returned from a vacation should be avoided if possible. Otherwise, the termination should occur as soon as possible after the employer has decided that termination is the proper course.

References

Giving work references for poor performers is a delicate area. To some extent, the employer may feel obligated to provide a truthful reference. It seems unfair to the prospective employer not to communicate a potential problem. Even if the employee was a poor performer, the employer may hesitate to provide the information because of fear of retaliation for alleged defamatory or false statements, or reluctance to damage the person's future job prospects. Certainly, there is reason to believe that employer liability has increased. Employers have been found liable for making false statements in a letter of reference, giving incomplete information, for deliberately interfering in the future job prospects of employees, or for writing a reference that is discriminatorily motivated.

Employers may defend their right to write a reference critical of employee performance in several ways. Employers may, for example, demonstrate that the information contained within the reference is *truthful*. It is incumbent upon employers to be able to prove whatever negative statements were made in the letter. Usually, employers cannot be held liable for giving accurate information.

Employers may demonstrate that there was *no malice* intended. Employers must control the writing of references so the administration may be confident that the writer is giving factual information, and not information based on personal animosities.

In some cases, employers have what is referred to as a "qualified privilege." This privilege is effected when "a duty (moral, social, legal) to speak and an interest to hear facts about another's performance are relatively more important than an individual's reputation."[33] It is logical that employers would feel a responsibility to respond honestly to a reference request in order to protect the future employer from a problem employee. It is important to emphasize that for such a communication to be privileged it should involve the communication of job-related information to those for whom the information is directly relevant. Such a privilege could be lost if the information were false, if it were disseminated with malice, if it were not job-related, or if it were volunteered rather than requested by the prospective employer.

As with most aspects of personnel administration, the legal complexities are many. It is best that the employer obtain written permission from the employee before writing the reference (Figure 4-5). This can often be obtained from prospective employers who have applicants sign a statement giving employers the right to collect references. In this case, a copy of the signed permission should be obtained before writing the reference. If an employer decides to write a negative reference, it is probably best that the library's attorney review the content before sending it. Employers should avoid giving a negative reference over the phone. There is no such thing as an "off-the-record" conversation.

Of course, the alternative is not to provide any information except dates of employment and job title. If this policy is adopted, it usually applies to all references, not only ones that would be negative. Although this appears to be a safer alternative, it may deprive future employers of useful and important information. One wonders about employers' liability in *not* providing a reference, especially for individuals whose performance involved dishonesty or violence. Could a former employer be held legally liable for subsequent actions with a future employer if pertinent information was withheld?

In summary, employers who consider writing a negative reference should consider the following points:

• Are the statements truthful?
• Are the writer's opinions identified as such, and not stated as facts?
• Are factual statements included to back up opinions?
• Is malice involved?
• Is discriminatory intent involved?
• Are all statements job related?
• Are statements factual and complete, and supportable if   challenged?
• Was consent for giving a reference obtained?

CONCLUSION

Poor performers can have devastating consequences for the organization; the most obvious is poor service to the library patron. But there are other important consequences as well, including affecting the morale of employees and wasting the time of supervisors and library administrators. The best way to deal with marginal performance is to hire only excellent workers. Unfortunately, the perfect employee selection procedure has yet to be developed.

Most library workers perform their jobs well, but when this is not the case, the employer is obligated to act either to improve the perfor-

FIGURE 4-5. Permission to Release a Reference

From time to time, the library receives request forms from employers, educational institutions or training programs for references about present and past employees. It is the practice of the library that such references are not completed until a release signed by the employee is provided. This release may have been signed by the employee when the employee completed a job application or application for admission to an educational or training program, or the employee may have signed a general release provided by our library. References involving evaluative statements will not be completed unless a signed release is provided.

There is certain information that the library will provide upon request without a signed release from the employee. This information is public information and generally consists of information that would be available in the minutes of the Board of Trustees such as dates of employment, job classification and salary.

When a request is made, the reference is forwarded to the employee's immediate supervisor, or other supervisor who has observed the performance of the employee. In general, references are written by supervisors who are currently employed by the library. If a supervisor is not available, the reference may be written by administrative personnel if adequate documentation is available from the personnel file of the employee. Documentation would include such items as performance appraisals, certificates indicating further education, attendance records and disciplinary actions. Nonsupervisory personnel are not authorized to provide references in the name of the library.

An employee may request that his or her supervisor write a general reference which would be included in the personnel file and released upon request for reference from an employer, educational institution or training program.

The reference release below permits the library to complete a reference and permits the employee to identify supervisors who may write a reference for the employee. Unless a reference request form specifically identifies the supervisor who is to write the reference, the library will select the individual to complete the reference form.

I hereby give permission to the Akron-Summit County Public Library, the Librarian-Director, Personnel Director or person hereinafter named, to provide a reference to prospective employers, educational institutions or training programs. I hereby release the Akron-Summit County Public Library, the Librarian-Director, Personnel Director or supervisor(s) hereinafter named from any liability or damages whatsoever which may result from providing such a reference.

Supervisor(s) hereinafter named:

_____

Date   Signature of Employee

mance or to discharge the employee. As with all other aspects of personnel management, it is critical to keep in mind that *people are different*. Although there should be a system for dealing with marginal employees, it is also necessary to understand each individual as an individual. Library administrators and supervisors should realize that there are a variety of ways to deal with the marginal performer—that they are not simply limited to punishment. First, they must consider whether the reason for the poor performance lies elsewhere than with the employee. Perhaps the training, supervision, or equipment is inadequate. Similarly, the causes of poor performance may lie outside the workplace. They may be related to personal or family problems.

If the cause of the poor performance is the employee's behavior, it is important that the supervisor provide opportunities for the employee to improve, and to inform the employee of the consequences of persistent substandard performance. This requires a well developed discipline system. The ultimate purpose of dealing with the poor performer is not to render judgments concerning the employee, but to correct performance. Whenever possible, punishment is best avoided, and substituted with encouragement and training. This latter context is more likely to produce the desired result for the employee and the organization as a whole.

FACTORS IN DEALING WITH THE MARGINAL EMPLOYEE

1. The cause of poor performance may reside not only in the employee, but in the organization including poor supervision, inadequate training and equipment, or poorly designed compensation, evaluation or disciplinary systems.

2. Before applying formal discipline, the manager should attempt to counsel the employee informally and in a supportive fashion.

3. Applying discipline fairly and firmly sends a necessary message to not only the marginal employee but other employees that the organization will not tolerate inappropriate behavior.

4. The effectiveness of employee discipline is affected by such factors as timing, intensity of the discipline, consistency of discipline, and the provision of a rationale for the disciplinary action.

5. The use of progressive discipline is an essential aspect of the disciplinary program. Such a program should include informal discussions, oral and written warnings, suspensions, and termination.

6. Supervisors must maintain excellent performance records to serve as documentation in disciplinary actions.

7. Employees must be given due process in the disciplinary process and treated with respect during all disciplinary activities.

8. Before training employees, review Daugherty's "Seven Questions" to determine just cause.

9. Careful preparation for a termination interview by the manager or administrator is essential.

10. Employers should be especially careful when writing reference for terminated employees to protect themselves from charges of libel or slander.

Endnotes

1. Charles A. O'Reilly, III, and Barton A. Weitz, "Managing Marginal Employees: The Use of Warnings and Dismissals," *Administrative Science Quarterly* 25 (1980): 477.
2. John B. Miner and J. Frank Brewer, "The Management of Ineffective Performance," in Bowman..: 1002-1003.
3. Veronica F. Nieva and Barbara A. Gutek, *Women and Work: A Psychological Perspective*, New York: Praeger, 1981:73.
4. Philip M. Podsakoff, "Determinants of a Supervisor's Use of Rewards and Punishments," *Organizational Behavior and Human Performance* 29 (February) 1982: 58.
5. John B. Miner and J. Frank Brewer, "The Management of Ineffective Performance," in Marvin Dunnette, ed., *Handbook of Industrial and Organizational Psychology*, Chicago: Rand-McNally, 1976: 997-998.
6. Gregory H. Dobbins and Jeanne M. Russell, "The Biasing Effects of Subordinate Likeableness on Leaders' Responses to Poor Performers: A Laboratory and a Field Study," *Personnel Psychology* (1986): 772-773.
7. O'Reilly and Weitz: 475-476.
8. Daniel R. Ilgen, Terence R. Mitchell, and James W. Frederickson, "Poor Performers: Supervisors' and Subordinates' Responses," *Organizational Behavior and Human Performance* 27 (June 1981): 405.
9. Podsakoff: 62.
10. Andrew E. Schwartz, "Counseling the Marginal Performer," *Management Solutions* 33 (March 1988): 30.
11. Schwartz: 31-33.
12. Clinton O. Longenecker and Patrick R. Liverpool, "An Action Plan for Helping Troubled Employees," *Management Solutions* (July 1988): 24-26.
13. Richard D. Arvey and John M. Ivancevich, "Punishment in Organizations: A Review, Propositions, and Research Suggestions," *Academy of Management Review* 5 (1980): 123-132.
14. O'Reilly and Weitz: 479.
15. Richard C. Grote, "Discipline," in *Human Resources Management and Development Handbook*, edited by William R. Tracey, New York: AMACOM, 1985: 775.
16. Ronald C. Ruud and Joseph J. Woodford, *Supervisor's Guide to Documentation and File Building for Employee Discipline*, Crestline, Calif: Advisory Publishing, 1984: 7-9.
17. Ruud and Woodford: 7-9.
18. Grote, "Discipline": 787.
19. James R. Redeker, *Discipline: Policies and Procedures*, Washington, D.C.: BNA, 1983: 35-39.
20. James R. Redeker, "Discipline, Part 2: The Nonpunitive Approach Works by Design," *Personnel* 62 (November 1985): 9-12.
21. Grote, "Discipline,": 788.
22. Redeker, "Discipline, Part 2...": 14.
23. U.S. Bureau of Labor Statistics, *Measurement of Labor Turnover, rev 1966*, cited in Robert C. Rodgers and Jack Stieber, "Employee Dis-

charge in the 20th Century: A Review of the Literature," *Monthly Labor Review* (September 1985): 35.
24. Rodgers and Stieber: 40.
25. Steven C. Kahn, Barbara A. Brown and Brent E. Zepke, *Personnel Director's Legal Guide*, Warren, Gorham and Lamont: 5-6 to 5-10.
26. Kahn, Brown and Zepke: S5-25.
27. Kahn, Brown and Zepke: S5-26.
28. Kahn, Brown and Zepke: S5-27.
29. Kahn, Brown and Zepke: S5-28.
30. Grief Bros. Cooperage Corp. and United Mine Workers of America, District 50, Local No. 15277, April 16, 1964, 42 LA 555, Arbitrator: Carroll R. Daugherty.
31. Paul M. Connollay, "Clearing the Deadwood," *Training and Development Journal* (January 1986): 59.
32. Cecil G. Howard, "Strategic Guidelines for Terminating Employees," *Personnel Administrator 33* (April 1988): 109.
33. James D. Bell, James Castagnera, and Jane Patterson Young, "Employment References: Do You Know the Law?" *Personnel Journal* (February 1984): 35.

5

Compensation, Classification, and Benefits

Libraries differ greatly in terms of their size and organizational complexity. For this reason, it is difficult to discuss job classification and compensation systems generally. Small libraries with few staff members have relatively little need to codify differences in job tasks, nor are subtleties usually required in the assignment of pay. In larger libraries there is often considerable sophistication in the specialization and departmentalization of tasks. Under these circumstances, refined job classification and compensation systems are needed and an outside expert may be required to design the system properly.

Job classification and compensation systems are very important because such systems identify the basic tasks for each job, establish specific levels of jobs, and assign monetary ranges to these levels. Employees' job tasks play a very important role in their overall satisfaction and commitment, but the pay they receive can also seriously affect their attitude toward work. Libraries must therefore devote considerable energy to ensuring that job classification and compensation systems are well designed and fair.

Equitable compensation and job classification systems are important to librarianship in particular because librarianship has traditionally been perceived as a women's profession with a resulting depression in salaries. It is an unfortunate reality that women's work has been undervalued in comparison to the work of men and that librarians have often been underpaid in relation to other workers. There is disturbing contemporary evidence that female librarians are paid less than their male counterparts, and that part of this disparity is attributable to sex discrimination.[1, 2] Sound classification and compensation systems can help diminish such inequities, although they can seldom prevent them entirely.

Although closely related, job classification and compensation are distinct. Job *classification* is concerned with:

- identifying and grouping like job tasks into classifications
- determining the relative position of each classification.

Compensation systems are involved in determining the actual monetary value of jobs within and among classifications, the related benefits to be provided, and the creation of rules and procedures for the distribution of monetary rewards and punishments. Compensation systems are "exchange relationships" between employee and employer: the employee exerts physical, mental, and emotional effort toward organizational goals in exchange for compensation from the employer. Although compensation is usually viewed as pay, this is not the only way that compensation can be understood. For example, when workers say that a job has its "compensations" they are often referring to much more than monetary rewards, including the opportunity for recognition, autonomy, achievement, and social intercourse. But this does not mean that pay and related compensations, such as benefits, are minor aspects of job motivation; pay is integrally related to these psychological motivators. Pay satisfies not only lower order physiological and security needs, but higher order needs such as recognition.[3]

The source of an employee's satisfaction or dissatisfaction with pay can be based on the many different ways in which pay can be perceived. Among these are:

- Pay *levels*, which consist of the actual rate of pay an individual receives. Generally speaking, the higher the rate of pay, the more satisfied an employee is.
- Pay *structure*, which consists of the hierarchy of pay levels in the organization. Employees may become dissatisfied if they believe that their position is underclassified or misclassified, hence receiving unduly low pay, or being deprived of appropriate authority and responsibility.
- Pay *system*, which involves the system of policies and procedures by which raises are computed and distributed. How a compensation system is administered has a direct relationship to the employee's satisfaction with pay. If employees perceive that the system is arbitrary, disorderly, or unjust, then satisfaction with pay is liable to decrease substantially.
- Pay *form*, which consists of the type of pay received, e.g. direct pay or fringe benefits. The extent to which benefits are provided with pay is strongly associated with satisfaction with pay. To have maximum effectiveness, the cost of the benefits should be considerable. Providing benefits which are perceived as trivial or minor is not likely to produce substantial satisfaction with pay.

An employee can be satisfied with one aspect of pay but not another. For example, an employee can be satisfied by the form of pay but not the pay level, or may be satisfied with pay level but not the pay structure.[4] The factors that are most strongly associated with pay satisfaction are pay level and pay form, especially benefits.[5] In addition, pay satisfaction is affected by the ability to make pay comparisons. That is, how employees see their own salaries in relation to others. The comparisons may not only be made with individuals within the organization, but also with those outside. If, for example, a reference librarian in one city knows that another reference librarian in a neighboring city is performing the same work but receiving substantially more money, then satisfaction with pay is likely to decrease.

Satisfaction with pay may be more important to one employee than another. One librarian may place little value on pay, so pay satisfaction does little to affect her overall satisfaction with the job; conversely, a librarian may feel that pay is very important. Pay is considered one of the two most important extrinsic rewards for the employee (the other being promotion), and the employer should consider it as a primary focus of concern for the library.[6]

HISTORICAL ASPECTS

Systematic efforts at wage and salary administration are primarily 20th century phenomena, growing from industrialization in the United States and Europe. Industrialization required large numbers of jobs, which in turn required specialization and division of labor. The inevitable result was large bureaucratic and hierarchical structures requiring defined tasks, and clear lines of authority and responsibility. The need was created for systematic job classification and compensation systems.

In addition to increasing organizational sophistication, political corruption contributed to the need for classification and compensation systems. Challenges to the arbitrary way in which government employees received jobs and were subsequently promoted led to the creation and expansion of the civil service in federal, state, and local governments. Job descriptions and salary classifications, as well as civil service exams were an early hallmark of such systems.

Librarianship was one of the first professions to embrace the job classification innovations of the civil service. In 1921, C.C. Williamson was actively recommending that job classifications be established in libraries.[7] At the same time, the American Library Association had established committees devoted to civil service issues. By 1926, 29 public libraries serving populations of 100,000 or more had wage and salary classification systems in place including Los Angeles, Boston, Minneapolis, Chicago, Philadelphia, and Brooklyn.[8]

Perhaps even more impressive was the fact that the library profession made one of the earliest efforts to develop a wage and salary classification system *for the entire profession*, based on civil service techniques. It was hoped that such a system would clearly define the various levels of jobs in academic and public libraries, suggest appropriate salary levels, increase the status of librarians, and provide libraries with tests for hire and promotion to various library positions.[9] Although the library classification system was never actually implemented, it is clear that libraries have been concerned with these issues either individually or collectively for many years.

THE IMPORTANCE OF CLASSIFICATION AND COMPENSATION SYSTEMS

In order to grasp the significance of a well-designed classification and compensation system, it is helpful to place it in the context of the broader organization and the labor market as a whole. Such systems often have profound implications for various other organizational functions. Among the effects of these systems are that they:

1. Increase the Chance that Employees Will See the System as Fair
Although no system can guarantee that employees will be satisfied, having written job descriptions, classifications, and salary scales decreases ambiguity and provides important information to the employee.

2. Assist in the Process of Hiring and Recruitment
Wages and jobs must be designed to attract valuable workers. These systems must be well designed from a labor market perspective as well as an internal point of view; that is, the pay for various jobs must be not only proper and fair in relationship to each other, but competitive with the labor market outside the library. Developing a good compensation system involves examining external conditions and setting competitive salaries so that the library can maintain a pool of qualified candidates for hire. Classification systems provide written guidelines to determine the qualifications required for various positions. They also describe job responsibilities to prospective candidates.

3. Assist in Training and Orientation
Good compensation and classification systems provide employees with information regarding the duties to be performed as well as the relation-

ship of their job to other jobs. They also provide information on the pay for a job and the potential for increased pay within that job category and other categories of interest to the employee.

4. Serve as a Motivator or Reward for Performance
The best classification and compensation systems are intimately related to performance evaluation systems. Employees who perform well receive increased compensation; those performing poorly receive less. The perceived relationship, or lack thereof, between pay and performance is an important factor in worker satisfaction and motivation.

5. Serve as a Critical Component in Budgeting
A major proportion of most library budgets is expended on personnel. A systematic compensation system helps the employer predict and plan for personnel expenses. It also allows the employer to adjust compensation equitably when increases or decreases in revenues occur.

6. Assist in Planning
As the library plans for the future, new or expanded positions are often needed. These may require workers with new knowledge, skills, and abilities. Classification and compensation systems provide techniques and a structure for defining new or modified positions in terms of job tasks and the relationship of the job to the organization and its pay scales.

7. Assist in Public Relations
Salary levels and raises are items often reported in newspapers or other media. Such items are particularly sensitive issues with the public. A fair and sound compensation system cannot prevent public dissent, but it can provide an intelligent foundation for discussing with the public how the library spends a considerable proportion of its revenues.

8. Assist in Management Decision Making
Managers must make decisions related to basic issues covered in a classification and compensation system. For example, if managers wish employees to perform certain duties, a classification system may indicate whether such duties are appropriate. Similarly, a manager may be able to determine if a particular employee is qualified for promotion to a new position, because he or she is able to identify what knowledge, skill, and ability is required.

9. Provides Legal Support
Good classification and compensation systems minimize the chances for arbitrary, capricious, or discriminatory assignments of jobs and wages. Both the Supreme Court, in *Albemarle Paper C.* v *Moody (1975)*, and the Equal Employment Opportunity Commission in its *Guidelines*, recognize the importance of job analysis when justifying employment decisions.[10] As such, well designed systems provide important support for the employer in case of legal challenges regarding job decisions.

THE LEGAL AND PUBLIC POLICY CONTEXT

Compensation and job classification systems, especially those in the public sector, operate within a broader legal context. Included among the elements of the legal environment are the following:

1. Civil Service Laws
Many libraries are part of municipalities or counties which have a civil service system. As a result, library job classifications and wages as well as merit systems are integrated into the larger civil service system. This can be especially troublesome for libraries because it places classification and compensation systems in the hands of individuals who have little knowledge of librarianship beyond its stereotypes. This has the potential of underclassifying library employees and hence underpaying them.

2. Fair Labor Standards Act
The 1938 Fair Labor Standards Act (FLSA) provides for the payment of a federally established minimum wage and overtime. Many states also have minimum wage provisions that affect library employers. Originally, the FLSA was not perceived as applying to most state or municipal employees. However, a 1985 Supreme Court decision, *Garcia* v *San Antonio Metropolitan Transit Authority,* strongly suggests otherwise and it appears that libraries should heed FLSA provisions at least for overtime and minimum wage.[11]

3. The Equal Pay Act of 1963 and Other Antidiscrimination Statutes
This act is an amendment to the Fair Labor Standards Act and requires that women and men performing similar tasks be paid equally. Job classifications and compensation systems must, therefore, conform to the provisions of this act. There are provisions in the act for the paying of dissimilar wages to men and women performing the same tasks, e.g., if a *bona fide* seniority or merit system is in place, but generally, library employers must conform to a wage system that does not differentiate

pay by sex within a particular job classification. Similarly, the basic provisions of the Civil Rights Act of 1964 and its amendments apply to any compensation and classification process conducted in a library setting.

4. "Prevailing Wage" Laws
These laws affect the payment of workers on public projects. Their purpose is to ensure that the wages paid on public projects reflect those of the local labor market.

5. Collective Bargaining Legislation
Many states now have collective bargaining bills that permit public employees to form unions, strike, and use compulsory arbitration. Generally speaking, unions have a tendency to increase the size of wage settlements and therefore affect compensation systems.

6. Retirement and Pension Laws and Regulations
Social security regulations and state pension plans affect employer compensation plans in many ways including setting the level of contribution which must be provided by the employer. It is therefore necessary for library employers to monitor such laws.

7. IRS Regulations
Recently, the IRS issued new rules based on amendments to Section 89 of the IRS Code. These rulings may affect the taxability of benefits as income, especially those provided to highly paid employees, and whether part-time employees must receive benefits as well as full-time workers. The impact on library budgets could be considerable, but the full implications of these rules are not yet clear.

8. Maximum Pay Laws and Regulations
These laws place a ceiling on certain salaries so that individuals in high administrative positions are not paid more than elected officials. Normally, these laws affect only the salaries of higher-level library administrators such as directors or deputy directors.

9. Payment Legislation
These laws regulate the manner and interval of wage payment. They may also deal with such issues as the collection of debt through the payroll and prohibit political kickbacks or other political influence on the payment of wages.

10. Pay Comparability Legislation
These laws attempt to provide adequate salaries to public employees by mandating the payment of salaries in line with those of the private sector. This ensures that public institutions will be competitive, especially for important positions.

Comparable Worth

In addition to the laws noted above, the last decade has seen the growth of a new doctrine, comparable worth, whose effect is yet to be determined. This doctrine has been used primarily to establish pay equity for predominately female occupations, although it is also being used to remedy racial discrimination in pay as well. The comparable worth doctrine demands that employers base pay levels strictly on the value of the job to the organization. Although, at first glance, this seems logical, there are many other factors that have traditionally affected rates of pay including the prevailing pay for jobs in the labor market and the supply of and demand for workers in various job classifications.

Many argue, however, that women have historically been underpaid for their work; that the stereotype of "women's work" has suppressed the salaries of jobs that are of equal value to those generally occupied by men. Jobs filled primarily by females (e.g. librarians, clerical workers) have been consequently underclassified and valued at disproportionately low rates of pay. In essence, different jobs of equal value to the organization have been compensated unequally because of the gender of the incumbents. A comparable worth approach requires that employers examine the value of the jobs to the organization as a whole without regard to the gender of the occupants, or the prevailing inequities in the labor market which have perpetuated unequal compensation of women.

Although its roots can be found in earlier antidiscrimination statutes, most notably the Equal Pay Act of 1963 and the Civil Rights Act of 1964, comparable worth cases attempt to broaden control over employers' wage and salary practices. For example, the Equal Pay Act deals with pay for *similar* jobs. Except under certain conditions, employers must pay men and women the same wage if they work in jobs that require the same skill, effort, and responsibilities. The comparable worth doctrine focuses on *dis*similar jobs; determining the value of dissimilar jobs is considerably more difficult.

The courts have been reluctant to endorse the comparable worth doctrine, and they have seldom accepted it as an independent legal theory. In one case, *County of Washington* v *Gunther* (1981), which involved the claim of unequal pay for male and female prison guards, the court did establish that pay equity for dissimilar jobs can be addressed under Title VII of the Civil Rights Act of 1964.[12] However, in a subsequent case, *American Federation of State, County, and Municipal Employees (AFSCME)* v. *State of Washington*, the court accepted the possibility that wages of particular positions might be dissimilar based on a *free-market* analysis of prevailing wages regardless of the fact that traditional social conditions may have suppressed wages for females. The court further suggested that a discriminatory motive would be needed in order to demonstrate sex discrimination in wages.[13]

Although the comparable worth doctrine appears to be weak from a judicial point of view, it would be irresponsible for the library employer to dismiss its significance. The fact that the work of females has been traditionally undervalued is not in doubt. Because the library work force is comprised primarily of women, it is critical that library employers attempt to overcome this undervaluation, and to reward library workers in just relation to their actual value. This requires overcoming stereotypes on the part of administrators, board members, and the public; the ethical duty to pay individuals what they are worth is not abrogated because the courts do not mandate it. To some extent, this has been recognized by states and municipalities which have passed legislation enforcing a comparable worth approach in public employment.

Interestingly, some have argued that insuring comparable worth through law or the courts may be counterproductive. Among the projected unintended consequences of enforcing the comparable worth approach are increased unemployment among the very people supposedly being protected, increased inflation, disruption of the wage structure, and disruption of labor market conditions.[14]

What is a Job Worth?

Determining the worth of a job is a fundamental aspect of any salary compensation system. Because classification and compensation decisions are important to both the employer and the employee, determining the worth of a job depends on from whose perspective worth is examined.

To the Employer
A job has a particular value to the employer to the extent that it contributes to organizational goals. Jobs in which the decisions made have major repercussions on the organization are likely to be of greater value than those in which decisions have only minor impact.

To the Employee
To the employee, the worth of a job has four main aspects:

* Worth in actual pay: that is, the pay in dollars one receives on a regular basis, (e.g. weekly, monthly)

- Worth in benefits such as hospitalization, vacation, sick leave, worker's compensation, pension or retirement systems
- Worth in personal status which arises from recognition and respect from friends, coworkers, and the community at large
- Worth in satisfaction which often arises from the ability to be creative, autonomous, to make a difference, to achieve and influence others for the benefit of the organization.

To the Society

A job also has worth to the community. Certain jobs are recognized by the society as having considerable worth, such as doctors. These jobs are likely to pay more and receive greater status. The worth of a job to society may be of special interest to librarians because how they are perceived by the society at large may have an impact on how much society is willing to pay for their services. If librarians are perceived as custodians of books and surrogates for child care, they are less likely to receive the money they deserve than if they are perceived as "information professionals."

Formal classification and compensation systems exist within this framework of worth. When employers evaluate the worth of a job, they see it from their own perspective; they assess the value in terms of what the position is worth to the organization. Although this is not incorrect, employers must also realize that this is not necessarily how the employees perceive the worth of jobs. To the extent that there is dissonance between employees' and employers' perception of worth, there is the possibility of significant job dissatisfaction and its encumbent negative results. Among the consequences of such dissatisfaction are higher turnover and absenteeism and greater susceptibility to unionization.[15]

JOB EVALUATION

The process that determines a classification and compensation system is called *job evaluation*. Glueck describes this process in the following way:

> Job evaluation is the formal process by which the relative worth of various jobs in the organization is determined for pay purposes. Essentially, it attempts to relate the amount of the employee's pay to the size of his job's contribution to organizational effectiveness.[16]

Four steps are necessary in order to conduct an appropriate job evaluation:

- job analysis and description

- determining the relative value of jobs
- determining the actual monetary value of jobs, and
- preparing a systematic set of job classifications.

Job Analysis and Description

Job analysis is the process by which the activities of each job are identified. The end product of the process is the job description. The term *job description* can be used broadly to encompass all aspects of the job including the tasks to be performed, the knowledge, skill, and abilities needed, and the relative position of the job in the organization. It can also be construed narrowly to mean just the basic tasks performed in the job.

From a purely theoretical perspective, job analysis is supposed to be conducted without reference to the particular individual performing the job. That is, jobs are perceived as distinct from the people performing in them; one defines the tasks of the job and then finds someone to fill it. In real life, we know that the activities of a job are often changed both qualitatively and quantitatively by the person performing them. Nonetheless, the overall function of the job analysis is to identify objectively the tasks required to perform specific jobs.

The first step in job analysis is to collect data on the job to be analyzed. Different individuals may perceive a particular job differently, therefore the information collected should be based on a variety of sources. These include:

- the employee performing the job currently
- the immediate supervisor, and
- other personnel who are familiar with the activities of the job.

Not only will gathering information from various perspectives increase the validity of the job analysis, it also increases involvement. Like other activities, participation by employees is more likely to increase commitment and satisfaction with the end product. Also, when gathering information, it is necessary to be sure it pertains to what is *actually* involved in the job, not what the person would like it to be.

Depending on the size of the organization and the amount of time and fiscal resources devoted to job analysis, a variety of techniques can be used, alone or in combination, to gather information. These techniques include:

- *Written questionnaires*: Forms are distributed to all employees asking them to describe their jobs in writing. One advantage to this technique is that it allows all staff to participate in the job analysis process.

- *Face-to-face interviews*: Interviews can be conducted with staff, gathering detailed information on specific job tasks. If interviewing all employees is impractical, a sample can be drawn to represent various perspectives.
- *Direct observation*: Individuals are observed, often by job analysts, who record their work activities.
- *Work sampling*: This technique applies random sampling of work activities over a defined period of time. At various times, the employee records what tasks are being performed. This requires a lengthy sampling period to ensure that all appropriate activities are recorded. This technique should only be used in combination with others.[17]
- *Diaries*: Job activities are recorded in a diary by the employee over an extended period of time. As with the previous method, it is unlikely that all vital information will be recorded, and the diarist may become bored or frustrated, so it should also be used in combination with other methods.[18]

Some of the many questions that should be raised during a job analysis are the following:

1. Job Responsibilities
- What are the specific tasks?
- What responsibilities are most demanding?
- Which responsibilities are most important?
- Which responsibilities take up most of the time or are performed most often?
- What decisions have to be made?
- What are the consequences if an error is committed?
- With what positions are communication and coordination required?
- With what outside contacts are communication and coordination required?
- What organizational purpose do these responsibilities serve?
- What special knowledge, skill, training, and abilities are required to perform these responsibilities?

2. Authority
- To what position does this job report?
- What other positions are equivalent to it?
- What positions report directly to this job (supervisory responsibilities)?

3. Demographics
- How many employees are supervised and at what levels?
- What is the budget for payroll and operations?

4. Job Environment
- What tools or special equipment are employed?
- What special difficulties or hazards are present?
- What physical activity is required to perform the tasks?

The purpose of gathering this information is not just to make a list of tasks performed but to get a broad perspective of the job. The records should include not only the specific responsibilities of the job, but the ranking of responsibilities in terms of importance, which are performed most often, how the job relates to other jobs in the organization, and what organizational purpose it serves. These broader questions have become more important over the years, because employers must validate their job descriptions in order to best defend legal challenges by employees. Supreme Court decisions have made it clear that minimum educational levels must have a valid relationship to the *actual* tasks to be performed. Tasks that are considered trivial, or infrequently performed, are not likely to be considered as good criteria for nonselection or discipline of an employee. Well written job descriptions and specifications which not only describe tasks but identify the important tasks, can help minimize misunderstandings of what the job entails.

Based on the information obtained in the job analysis, job descriptions are written, and jobs with similar tasks are grouped together under a given job classification. Generally, a single classification can be assigned when it can reasonably encompass the range of tasks identified and if the same basic knowledge, skill, and ability are needed to perform the tasks; otherwise a different classification is needed. Different classifications can also be broken down into subclassifications, sometimes referred to as *grades*. For example, there may be three grades under the general classification of Clerk-Typist, e.g. Clerk-Typist I, Clerk-Typist II, and Clerk-Typist III. Each grade reflects increasing job difficulty and the need for greater knowledge, skill, and ability. In larger libraries, the opportunity for growth within the sub-classifications can sometimes be used as a career ladder so that employees perceive opportunities for advancement within the organization. Such opportunities can limit employee dissatisfaction and turnover.

There are many ways to organize and write a job description. Sometimes the description is developed generically to cover all the jobs in a given classification; sometimes a separate job description is tailored to each particular position. The more generic version is called a *classification description* and attempts to describe the features of the classification that make it different from all other classifications. In such a description, all the major job tasks that fall within that classification would be identified. A given individual in that classification would not necessarily perform all these tasks, only some of them. If a description is written for a particular position, it is called a *position description*. Both classification descriptions and position descriptions contain similar if not identical information.

A position description (Figure 5-1) should include the following type of information:

- Position title
- Department in which the position is located
- Physical location if appropriate
- Date description was prepared
- Short description of the primary purpose of the position
- Description of the nature and scope of the position including the size of budget controlled and number of employees being supervised, to whom the employee reports, and who reports to the employee
- Identification of the primary responsibilities of the job
- Statement of the required knowledge, skill, and abilities for the position. (This might include a statement of "preferred" skills as well—skills that are desirable but are not necessary to perform the essential functions of the job.)

Obviously, more generalized descriptions encompassing a whole classification would be less specific but follow the same general pattern.

Determining the Relative Value of Jobs

Once classifications have been developed, it is necessary to establish their relative value in relation to all other classifications. Because of the legal climate in which organizations operate, establishing the relationship between job classifications has become very important. Most important for libraries is to ensure that positions in which women predominate are evaluated objectively so that jobs of comparable value are paid equally to those filled predominantly by men.

POINT FACTOR METHOD

There are several methods used in evaluating jobs. The most common is the point factor method. Although not new (its use was documented as early as 1926) this technique has become even more popular in recent times, because it is necessary for organizations to document the objectivity of their pay systems.[19] The use of points contributes to the image of neutrality and helps prevent comparable worth disputes. Essentially, the point factor system involves identifying the important elements of a job and assigning a certain number of points to each element. Jobs that receive the greatest number of total points are given higher classifications and higher salary levels. Those with fewer points receive lower classifications and lower salaries.

Several steps must be followed in order to reach a final determination of the relative position of jobs, including:

- determining what factors are important in evaluating jobs
- assigning weights to each factor so that more important factors are worth more points

FIGURE 5-1. Sample Job Description

I. *Title*: Reference Librarian I

II. *Department*: Science and Technology

III. *Location*: Main Library

IV. *Date Prepared*: August 7, 1989

V. *Job Summary*: This position provides reference and related services to members of the public.

VI. *Nature of the Position*: Incumbent reports to the Head of Science and Technology. Reporting to the incumbent are three student assistants. The incumbent's major concerns involve providing efficient, courteous, and accurate reference service to library patrons; and assisting patrons in the selection of library materials. Incumbent is also responsible for maintaining a well-organized and orderly collection by ensuring that materials are properly reshelved in the department.

VII. *Major Responsibilities*:
Answers reference questions from the public.

Provides assistance and instruction to patrons in locating and selecting library materials.

Supervises student assistants in the reshelving of materials.

Keeps abreast of professional issues affecting reference services.

Makes recommendations regarding the selection of reference materials.

VIII. *Required Knowledge, Skills, and Ability*
Strong interpersonal and human relations skills; ability to communicate well orally and in writing.

Possession of a Master's of Library Science from a library education program accredited by the American Library Association.

Ability to apply the principles and practices of library science effectively.

Any combination of education, experience or training that satisfies the requirements of the position.

- developing criteria so that the appropriate number of points can be assigned for each factor
- assigning monetary value to the job classifications.

Obviously, employing a point factor system is complicated and time consuming. The use of an outside consultant may be helpful. However, the institution should involve staff as much as possible in the process as well.

Determining What Factors Are Important

The point factor system relies on the identification of basic criteria. Among the common factors used to evaluate a job are the following:

1. Responsibility and Accountability
This factor measures the degree to which errors in the job have serious impact on the organization. For example, errors on the part of a shelver could cause difficulty in finding some library materials, but they would have limited impact on the budget, library personnel, or library policy. In contrast, errors by a library director have the potential to affect the well-being of the entire system. The library director would therefore receive more points for this factor than the shelver.

2. Job Complexity
This factor involves how difficult and varied the job is. It attempts to evaluate the extent to which mental and creative effort is needed to perform the job.

3. Supervision
This factor measures the amount and nature of supervisory responsibilities assigned to the job. Included are the number of employees and the variety of jobs supervised.

4. Contact with Others
This factor deals with the number and nature of contacts the employee has with the public and coworkers. It considers such factors as institutional meetings, amount of direct patron contact, and whether interpreting library policy is involved.

5. Working Conditions
This factor examines the amount of physical effort required in performing the job and the potential for hazard or danger in the work.

Determining the Weights for the Factors

All jobs in the library will be evaluated for the same factors; but clearly some of the factors are more important than others. For this reason, before the jobs can be evaluated, weights must be assigned to each factor indicating the relative importance of each in terms of the operation of the library. This is usually accomplished in two steps: first, each factor is assigned a specific percentage based on its importance. The greater the importance of the factor, the higher the percentage assigned. Second, points are assigned, usually up to 1000, that reflect the percentage assigned to the factor. The example in Figure 5-2 shows the factor weights used in one public library system. The most important factors in evaluating each job are complexity and responsibility.

FIGURE 5-2. Factor Weights for Library Positions

Factor	Weight	Total Points
Contact with Others	15%	150
Job Complexity	30%	300
Responsibility/Accountability	30%	300
Supervision	15%	150
Working Conditions	10%	100
Total	100%	1000

Developing Criteria for Assigning Points

The next step is to develop a means for assigning the appropriate number of points to each job in the library. To accomplish this, a series of behavioral descriptions are developed for each factor, and a specific number of points is assigned to each description. Each job is evaluated by locating the description for each factor that most accurately portrays the job being analyzed, and assigning the appropriate number of points for that description.

Figure 5-3 shows the series of descriptions and points for each of five factors for the Downers Grove Public Library. Note for example, the descriptions for the factor of responsibility/accountability. If, in the job being evaluated, errors have little or no impact, then zero points are assigned to this factor for this job. If, however, an error would affect all departments, resources, and staff, then the total number of possible points for this factor, 300, would be assigned. The value of an individual job is equal to the sum of the points assigned for each factor on that job.

If the classification process is done carefully, jobs in the same classification should have similar numbers of points. The weighted point system is especially useful in assessing dissimilar jobs that are often sex segregated. For example, bookmobile drivers are often male, and graphic artists, female. By evaluating the jobs on objective factors and points, the possibility of misclassifying the graphic artist position is reduced.

Benchmark Jobs

Before beginning the process of assigning points, it is necessary to provide some kind of structure to ensure that the process is producing a rational result. It is necessary to select certain jobs as points of reference for evaluating other positions. These reference points are called benchmark jobs; they are evaluated first and consensus obtained regarding the proper number of points assigned to each. When other jobs are evaluated, they are compared to the benchmark jobs to ensure that the system is progressing in a logical fashion. Benchmark jobs can be used subsequently to establish salary ranges; the ranges of other jobs are then compared to the benchmark ranges to assign compensation fairly.

Selecting the right jobs to serve as benchmarks is important. There are several important characteristics that benchmark jobs should have. First, they should be familiar to all or most of the workers. For example, a reference librarian's job is one with which most staff members are familiar; employees are able to compare their job to the reference librarian's position. Second, the jobs should be common ones in the organization. Again, a reference librarian is common throughout most library systems and would therefore meet the criteria; another example would be a clerk-typist position. Third, the jobs should represent the range of positions in the organization. Thus, the benchmark jobs should represent supervisory, public service, and clerical positions. Finally, the jobs should have clearly defined tasks, and clearly defined requirements in terms of the desired knowledge, skills, and ability.

The Assignment of Compensation

The final step in the process is to determine the appropriate wage ranges for various positions. Among the factors to be considered are:

1. Available Resources
A primary purpose of a compensation system is to control wages so that the survival of the institution is not threatened. If all the money is spent on personnel and none on library materials, there is no way that the goals of the library could be reached.

FIGURE 5-3. Descriptions of Five Factors and Point Values for the Downers Grove Public Library

---

CONTACT WITH OTHERS

This factor appraises the responsibility required for meeting, or influencing other persons. It considers the contacts an employee has with co-workers and the public.

Points	Description of Characteristics
0	No assigned duties requiring contact with the public, though may give occasional directional information.
30	Has intermittent contact with the public providing basic services of a narrow scope.
60	Has contact with the public at least 30% of the work day, providing basic services of a narrow scope OR Has no contact with public, but manages a department and represents library interests in professional groups.
90	Has contact with the public at least half the time, providing services of a diverse technical nature, or responding to questions from the public.
120	Has contact with the public and staff at irregular intervals, but contact often requires action in a critical situation, negotiating serious problems, and communicating and interpreting library policies.
150	Has contact with the public about 30% of the time. Negotiates with patrons to resolve problems. Has daily contact with department employees—resolving problems and making work assignments.

FIGURE 5-3. Descriptions of Five Factors and Point Values for the Downers Grove Public Library (Continued)

COMPLEXITY OF THE JOB

This factor assesses the mental effort required to perform the job. It considers the need to resolve problems, the difficulty and variety of assigned tasks, and the degree of creative or developmental work required.

Points	Description of characteristics
0	Activities are limited in scope and require basic skills. Clearly described routines and procedures are used to complete work. Activities do not include working with the public.
60	Requires a limited number of routine activities which almost always includes working with the public. Situations occasionally require use of independent judgement, but a resource person is available.
120	Performs technical activities that require strict adherence to rules to maintain quality control. OR Works with public to provide a variety of services requiring basic skills in librarianship.
180	Expected to use independent judgment and creativity in work. Responsible for a wide range of technical skills. Works with public to provide a variety of services requiring advanced skills in librarianship. Understanding of theory and general practice is important. Work is subject to general review.
(190-280)	Expected to use independent judgment and offer creative ideas to work. Develops the plan of services and sets objectives for staff work. Activities are divided between specialty skills and management responsibilities. Define at one of the following levels:
190	Is responsible for managing technical operations which require basic knowledge of librarianship
250	Is responsible for managing technical applications which require an advanced knowledge of librarianship; Is responsible for managing and developing services using specialized collections.
280	Is responsible for managing and developing services using diverse collections.
300	Work deals primarily with theory not technical detail. Makes broad managerial judgments which are rarely subject to review. Regularly exercises developmental and/or creative abilities. Makes decisions regarding policy.

FIGURE 5-3. Descriptions of Five Factors and Point Values for the Downers Grove Public Library (Continued)

RESPONSIBILITY/ACCOUNTABILITY

This factor indicates the impact that an employee's error may have on the organization. The error may be in judgment or in processing activities related to job assignments. The error may have financial or human impact, resulting in loss of materials or data, or cause damage to equipment or facilities.

Points	Description of Characteristics
0	Error in routine work results in minor inconvenience, but has no impact which is obvious to the public.
60	Error in routine work will result in inconvenience to co-workers and may cause passing annoyance to the public.
120	Technical errors could impair services in this and other libraries, or in other agencies in the community.
180	Error in work is generally confined in impact to a single public service department, and generally causes sharp criticism by the offended patron.
240	Technical or management errors may result in serious misdirection of departmental resources and staff. May cause major disruption in the library or in outside agencies.
300	Errors in planning or management may have serious impact on library resources and staff. Error likely to affect all departments. Serious error likely to affect public's perception of the library and affect their resulting level of support.

FIGURE 5-3. Descriptions of Five Factors and Point Values for the Downers Grove Public Library (Continued)

SUPERVISION

This factor examines the degree of supervision assigned to the job. Consideration is given to the amount of supervision provided, and the complexity and variety of jobs supervised.

Points	*Description of Characteristics*
0	Has no supervisory responsibility
30	Oversees the workflow during a shift of 1 or 2 employees who are responsible for a narrow scope of basic duties. Problems are referred to a superior.
60	Is expected to supervise work in the department when the department head is absent.
90	Regularly supervises a number of employees performing routine activities.
120	Oversees work of a number of employees performing diverse functions, although employees are not generally supervised directly. Has authority to resolve unusual operational questions and to interpret policy.
(130-150)	Plans and oversees work of an entire department. Define at one of the following levels:
130	Has general supervisory responsibility for seven or fewer workers.
140	Has general supervisory responsibility for eight to eleven workers.
150	Has general supervisory responsibility for twelve or more workers.

FIGURE 5-3. Descriptions of Five Factors and Point Values for the Downers Grove Public Library (Continued)

WORKING CONDITIONS

This factor examines the degree of physical effort required on the job, and the degree to which work may be uncomfortable or hazardous.

Points	Description of Characteristics
0	No significant effort generally required on the job beyond normal movement. Most work performed while seated, but little typing or keyboard terminal work required.
20	At least half the work day is spent in a combination of sitting and moving around the department. Some lifting or carrying required. May include moderate typing or keyboard work.
40	At least half the work time is spent moving around the library, and requires frequent lifting or carrying.
60	Much of work time is spent standing in one area.
80	At least half of work time is spent in typing or data entry at keyboard terminals.
100	Job requires frequent movement, climbing ladders, and frequent heavy lifting.

**Reprinted with permission of the Downers Grove Public Library, Downers Grove, Illinois

2. Prevailing Wage in the Labor Market

Useful information can be obtained by determining the average wage for a similar position in the local labor market. This information can sometimes be obtained from government documents, or salary surveys conducted by local organizations such as the Chamber of Commerce, or the library could conduct a salary survey of its own. However, libraries must be careful not to preserve inequities based on gender stereotyping. Because wage rates are often lower for jobs filled predominantly by women, libraries must not preserve these iniquitous conditions by using the prevailing wage as a justification for unduly low compensation.

3. Available Labor Pool

To some extent, wage rates will be affected by the number of individuals in the labor pool who can perform the tasks desired. A key function of compensation systems is to attract and retain workers. The ability to attract workers to some extent will be influenced by the available work force. If, for example, the library needs a children's librarian, but there are few such individuals in the labor market, the wage rate may have to be higher in order to attract a qualified candidate.

4. Competition

Competition can arise from many sources. In some communities, there are several libraries competing for the available supply of librarians. Competition may also arise from nonlibrary sources such as information brokers, vendors, schools, and publishers. Finally, competition may be great for positions requiring special skills such as computer programming. In so far as competition increases, it is likely that wage rates for such positions will be higher.

5. Importance of Positions

Positions that are critical to the library are more likely to have higher wages. If a library is finding it difficult to locate a qualified director, the wage rate may increase.

6. Historical Basis of the Pay Rate

A major consideration in setting pay rates is what the employees are currently being paid. However, this should be modified by the factors mentioned above; otherwise, historical inequities resulting in low pay for women will be preserved.

Sometimes the above considerations distort the relative value of jobs as determined by the point factor analysis. For example, the point factor analysis may assign a children's librarian and a general reference librarian the same salary ranges, but if there is a serious shortage of children's librarians, these wage ranges might be increased to attract the few available. However, altering a salary range, especially for short-term problems, is generally inadvisable. Changes may breed the perception of inequity within the organization, which can be costly in terms of lowered morale and employee dissatisfaction leading to turnover, lowered productivity, increased grievances, and unionization.

Pay Structure

The purpose of the job evaluation process is to establish an equitable pay structure. As in the process of determining the relative position of a job, it is best to establish the compensation range of the benchmark jobs first. Other jobs can be compensated in relation to these jobs. The pay structure is a graphic representation of the rate and range of pay for each classification in the organization (Figure 5-4).[20] Each job classification should have a salary range which establishes the highest and lowest amount of compensation that can be earned for the job. The salary ranges for a given classification may be broken down into increments. The number of steps varies. The first step is usually considered the entry-level or beginning wage for that classification, and the steps increase evenly at a fixed percentage. The means by which the employee moves up the steps is usually either by seniority or merit. As a general rule, the average pay separation between grades within a classification should be between 10 and 15%.[21]

When the classification and compensation system is complete, the library should have a hierarchical arrangement of job classifications based on systematic and objective measures. These classifications will have a corresponding hierarchy of salary ranges that reflect the relative value of these classifications. In addition, the specific job descriptions based on the classifications will help in the hiring, evaluation, and job assignment process.

SYSTEM OF REWARDS: MERIT OR SENIORITY?

A wage schedule forms the structure of a compensation program. Of equal importance are the policies and practices established to determine how the organizational rewards, especially pay, are distributed. The employees' perception of the administration of rewards has a significant impact on their satisfaction with the pay they receive.[22] In addition, the *system* of rewards affects employee motivation and job performance.[23]

The two usual approaches to the distribution of rewards are:

- The rewards are distributed "across the board". That is, everyone receives a pay increase at fixed time intervals
- The rewards are distributed based on performance (merit).

FIGURE 5-4.   Sample Salary Classification

CLASS TITLE	GRADE	A	B	C	D	E
PROFESSIONAL						
LIBRARIAN I	21	18240	19152	20118	21156	22200
LIBRARIAN II	24	21156	22200	23292	24438	25692
LIBRARIAN III	29	26994	28320	29730	31212	32778
ASST DIR	37	39840	41820	43908	46122	48414
PARA-PROFESSIONAL						
LIBRARY ASSIST I	12	11778	12378	13002	13626	14304
LIBRARY ASSIST II	15	13626	14304	15636	15792	16572
LIBRARY ASSIST III	19	16572	17376	18240	19152	20118
PERSONNEL						
PERSONNEL DIR	33	32778	34392	36108	37908	39840
PUBLIC INFORMATION						
PRINTER	13	12378	13002	13626	14304	15036
GRAPHIC ARTIST	16	14304	15356	15792	16572	17376
PR DIRECTOR	32	31212	32778	34392	36108	37908
CLERICAL & RELATED						
LIBRARY CLERK I	11	11232	11778	12378	13002	13626
LIBRARY CLERK II	13	12378	13002	13626	14304	15036
ACQUISITION SUPRVR	22	19152	20118	21156	22200	23292
CLERK-TYPIST I	12	11778	12378	13002	13626	14304
CLERK-TYPIST II	14	13002	13626	14304	15036	15792
SECRETARY I	16	14304	15036	15792	16572	17576
ADMINISTRATIVE SEC	20	17376	18240	19152	20118	21156
SWITCHBOARD OPER	14	13002	13626	14304	15036	15792
ACCOUNTING, DATA PROCESSING, AND RELATED						
ACCOUNT CLERK I	14	13002	13626	14304	15036	15792
ACCOUNT CLERK II	18	15792	16572	17376	18240	19152
DEPUTY CLERK-TREAS	24	21156	22200	23292	24438	25692
BUILDING OPERATION AND MAINTENANCE						
CUSTODIAN BLDG SUPTNDT	10	10680	11232	11778	12378	13002
ADMINISTRATION						
DIRECTOR	45	58836	61776	64884	69816	73308
CLERK-TREASURER	40	46122	48414	50838	53388	57438

These alternatives express a fundamental tension that exists in compensation systems. On the one hand, employees feel a sense of community by accepting the notion that they are "all in the same boat," when everyone receives similar wage increases. On the other hand, employees want to believe that they should be paid based on their level of performance; that excellent workers deserve more money than mediocre or poor performers. In part, this is why unions are less enthusiastic about merit than seniority systems; it tends to individualize the work environment, and to reinforce traditional bureaucratic powers by placing compensation decisions in the hands of supervisors.[24]

In deciding how to distribute compensation, there are other issues to be addressed by the employer as well. These include:

- What will various pay alternatives cost?
- What system will provide the greatest motivation and productivity?
- Which pay system provides the fairest way to distribute rewards?[25]

Pay for Years of Service

The first alternative is to pay individuals based on their years of service with the library. Individuals in a given classification, who have been with the library the longest, receive the highest pay. Such a system has many benefits including:

- Administration of wage increases is simplified. The only information that is required is the number of years of service for current employees. There is no need for spending administrative time differentiating between the performance of employees or reviewing decisions by lower level supervisors. At designated intervals, all employees receive their next increment of pay.
- Training time for supervisors is reduced. Although supervisors may need some performance review training, there is little need to train them to make subtle or elaborate distinctions concerning performance.
- The performance review system is simplified. Defining and documenting meritorious performance becomes unnecessary. The need to quantify or provide detailed reviews is lessened.
- Time is saved for other supervisory functions: If supervisors are relieved of the time required to conduct merit reviews, they are free to perform other supervisory tasks.
- Legal liabilities are reduced. Whenever supervisors are forced to make distinctions concerning work performance which have monetary consequences, the employer is liable to charges of arbitrary or discriminatory practices. If pay increments are awarded for time alone, this liability is reduced.
- Employee jealousy is reduced. A potential source of ill feeling among employees is the awarding of merit to some staff, while others do not

receive it. Many employees simply do not believe that their compensation is based on their actual performance.[26] This increases the potential for jealousy, feelings of inequity, and lowered morale. For many employees, the assignment of an increment to all employees is perceived as more fair than giving money to only a segment of the staff.

On the other hand, some employees, especially outstanding performers, may feel unjustly treated because they feel that they should receive more for superior performance. The result may be that good performers will leave the organization and poor performers will remain.[27] This leads to the second alternative—merit pay, otherwise known as "pay for performance."

Pay for Performance

In the merit pay system, high levels of performance receive higher pay. The reasoning behind this process is based on the behavioralist model: individuals who are rewarded for high performance will repeat the performance; individuals penalized for poor performance will not repeat their behavior. The logic seems simple and irresistible. There is evidence that organizations that attach pay to performance can and do experience increases in productivity.[28] Productivity increases can be as much as 29% to 63% using pay-for-performance systems.[29] The stronger the association with performance and reward, the higher the levels of *subsequent* performance.[30]

It is essential that employees understand what merit means to the organization. Merit pay can be considered as the total amount one receives in excess of the previous year's salary, or it can be perceived as the amount received in excess of the increase in the cost of living. This becomes an especially sensitive issue in times of high inflation. Telling an employee that he or she is getting a merit increase that is merely equal to the rate of inflation is not likely to be perceived as recognition or have the desired motivating effect. Employers should therefore realize that merit systems will be placed under greater stress in inflationary times.

Difficulties with Merit Systems

Merit pay provides substantial recognition which in turn can increase satisfaction and motivation. There are, however, noticeable problems in the administration of merit systems which may cause them to fail. Among these are the following:[31]

1. Poor Measures of Performance

One of the most difficult and complicated tasks that supervisors perform is performance evaluation. Often, the performance standards are neither precisely written nor sufficiently comprehensive to reflect overall performance on the job. In library work, as in other service occupations, this problem is magnified. Qualitative as well as quantitative measures must be used and it is difficult to determine exactly when an individual meets, does not meet, or exceeds such standards. In these circumstances, employees are bound to perceive that the supervisor is using subjective, rather than objective criteria to make performance judgments. This in turn can increase employees' suspicions that they are being treated in an unfair or discriminatory fashion.

2. Inadequate Communications

Often employees are not clear about how merit systems operate within their organization. This confusion is likely to breed suspicion. For example, what part of a wage increase should be considered "cost of living" and what part based on performance? If communication is not clear, then the perception of pay for performance will be clouded and lose its effectiveness. Similarly, some organizations keep the amount of merit increases and salaries given to employees secret. Although in public institutions, such information can usually be obtained, there are sufficient barriers—political, time, and complexity—to deter most employees. If the pay of others is secret, it is difficult for employees to know whether they are receiving the proper recognition for their work. Although there is little evidence that secrecy itself is directly related to pay satisfaction, the ability to make pay comparisons does affect it.[32]

3. Overly Complex Merit Systems

If the merit system is too difficult to understand, employees are not likely to see the direct relationship between their performance and their pay. The use of complicated forms, point systems, and formulas which are understood only by administrators, increases suspicion that the performance measures are being manipulated for subjective purposes.

4. Poor Managers

Merit systems will fail if managers do not conduct merit evaluations properly. Managers who have an egalitarian philosophy, or who merely wish to avoid conflict, may not be willing to recognize differences in employee performance. Similarly, managers with favorites who receive merit increases because of their friendship with the manager are bound to undermine employees' confidence in the merit system.

In addition to these problems, two others can cause significant problems. First, many employees believe that the size of the merit increment is simply too small to provide motivational effects. A *Wall Street Journal* survey noted that in order to be effective, annual pay increases should be between 20% and 30%.[33] Few libraries could provide such increases without heading swiftly into bankruptcy. Indeed, government organizations are often limited by fixed budgets which are not directly linked to increasing productivity on the part of the staff. Such limited budgets severely hamper pay-for-performance efforts because the manager is unable to provide proportional and substantial awards for increases in performance. Second, merit programs can cause "compression" of the salary schedules. That is, as high performers get merit increases, their salaries approach and sometimes exceed the salaries of individuals who are higher in the organizational hierarchy. This can cause conflict among staff.[34]

Instituting a Merit System

A variety of suggestions have been made to increase the chance that merit systems will work:

1. Communicate the Purpose, Policies, and Procedures Clearly
Information should be conveyed in written materials and orally by supervisors and administrators. A key purpose of communicating with staff is to build trust. Employees must believe that management genuinely supports the system of pay for performance and that the organization will devote substantial resources to rewarding employees and making the system fair.

2. Have a Good Performance Evaluation System
Emphasis should be on objective standards, and the evaluation should focus only on the performance for the time period under review. The evaluation system is the foundation of merit awards; if employees perceive inequity in evaluation they will perceive the system of rewards in the same way.

3. Differentiate Between Mediocre and Superior Performance
Employees will have little motivation to perform at higher levels if they see that the same rewards are given to average and superior performers. Although there are other factors besides money that motivate some employees, the merit system will not be able to serve a motivational purpose if it does not make these distinctions.[35]

4. Hire Individuals with a Strong Sense of Responsibility
Such individuals are more likely to perform well in a merit system because they believe that their own hard work will produce the desired result.

5. Train Supervisors to Conduct Effective Performance Evaluations
Supervisors who provide employees with information on their performance and conduct reviews in a fair and objective fashion increase confidence and decrease suspicion of the performance review and merit system.

6. Consider Awarding Merit to Work Groups or Departments
Such a system reduces the focus on individual competition which can often be as destructive as it is constructive and emphasizes the interdependence of individuals to meet the larger organizational goals. Substantial increases in group performance mean increases for all staff involved.

7. Provide a Broad Range of Merit Awards
When the range of merit is considerable, merit fosters higher levels of productivity.[36]

8. Provide an Adequate System for Record-Keeping and Monitoring
First, analyze the pattern of rewards comparing each merit award to the actual levels of performance, and to demographic factors such as age and race. Do white employees tend to get larger increments than black employees? Do women get less than men? Second, survey employees to determine their perceptions and concerns regarding the merit program. Is the merit program perceived as fair? Are performance standards clear and appropriate? Is the size of the merit increase sufficient? Do employees believe that pay and performance are linked? Third, examine the characteristics of the program. Are supervisors being trained? Is management communicating the purpose of the program? Are the performance criteria appropriate?[37]

9. Consider a Bonus System Rather Than a Merit Raise
The merit raise which is added to the salary of the employee remains with the employee year after year. In essence, this rewards the employee continuously even if subsequent years of performance are mediocre or poor. In contrast, a bonus is perceived as directly associated with the performance itself. Bonuses are most effective the sooner they are given in relation to the meritorious performance.[38] A fundamental principle

of successful merit systems is that the relationship between pay increases and high performance is crystal clear. A bonus system is more likely to reveal this relationship.

10. Consider Nonmonetary Rewards

This is a particularly important suggestion for libraries, and not altogether unrealistic. Although pay can serve as a motivator, other factors in the workplace can provide substantial motivation. There is no reason to exclude these factors as part of a reward program. For example, high performance could be rewarded with increasing responsibility and authority, i.e., job enrichment. In addition, recognition programs that provide material recognition by way of awards or commendations may also be successful.[39]

It is obvious that developing a merit system is a complex process with many potential pitfalls. It requires a carefully designed performance evaluation program, with strong communication lines, and well-trained managers and supervisors. Many different variations of a pay-for-performance system are possible. Perhaps a hybrid system is best. Winstanley, for example, suggests one alternative in which a fixed portion of a salary increase is guaranteed to all but the poorest performers, and the balance of the available money is distributed as bonuses to the outstanding performers.[40] This is not an unreasonable suggestion in public institutions whose fiscal resources are often limited and the need to provide some increase to everyone (to adjust for the cost of living) is important.

Incentives

In private industry, an increasingly popular approach to improving productivity is using incentive systems. These systems, referred to as "Spot Gain Sharing," are usually devised to deal with a particular need or problem, such as a backlog, or absentee problem.[41] Generally, spot gain sharing identifies a specific group of employees whose improved performance can resolve the problem. Productivity targets and rewards are established along with a fixed length of time for the program. If the employees resolve the problem, they receive appropriate monetary rewards. The benefits of spot gain programs are many: they increase productivity and resolve organizational problems, build teamwork, encourage problem solving, and increase morale.[42] Although not yet used in libraries, incentive programs could prove quite useful. For example, backlogs in technical processes might be eliminated using such incentives.

One special type of incentive technique is called the "lottery system." If, for example, an organization has an absentee problem, the employer contributes a certain amount of money into a fund monthly, e.g., $500. At the end of each month, the names of employees with perfect attendance for the month are placed in a pool, and one name is drawn. This person receives the $500. Of course, the intervals at which the lottery drawings occur could vary depending on the problem. Such a system could be used for other problems in libraries. In academic libraries where publication is important, the lottery might be available only to individuals who have published articles or books; in public libraries, the pool might be developed for individuals who attend conferences, or give speeches or presentations.

BENEFITS

An important complement to salary compensation is employee benefits. This often-overlooked aspect of human resource management can have a substantial impact on employees and the organization, both in terms of employee motivation, and in terms of fiscal health. Employee benefits can be a substantial drain on organizational resources. Estimates of a sound benefits program that includes paid time off account for as much as 50% of the money spent on payroll.[43]

Like other forms of human resource management, what benefits are offered and to what extent the employer contributes to them, grows out of the philosophy of the organization. Employers have profoundly different views of the purposes of benefits. Some consider them a necessary evil and provide the minimum range of benefits and the minimum contribution. Others perceive benefits as an integral part of the total compensation program. The program is seen as a way to motivate workers and maintain a competitive edge. High performers may become eligible for additional benefits, or be asked to contribute less to sustain them. Still other employers may perceive benefits as a social duty. Such organizations may provide a wide range of benefits including employee assistance programs and job counselling at little or no expense to the employees.

Employees also perceive benefits in different ways. Many see them as part of job security and as a right. Benefits are perceived as part of the employer-employee "exchange-relationship"; their purpose is to provide assistance in case of injury or illness, and to increase the quality of the employee's work life. A minority may perceive benefits as a way for the employer to avoid paying less money directly. This feeling of suspicion may increase if a significant number of such benefits cannot be used by the employee (e.g. dependent coverage when the employee has no children). Such individuals may prefer to receive wages in lieu of benefits.

The importance of benefits has changed over the years. The idea that employers should provide benefits to workers is a relatively new concept. During the nineteenth century, employee benefits were relatively unknown. Employees worked for wages. If employees were sick or injured, they were expected to fend for themselves. In the twentieth century, particularly with the growth of labor unions, benefits became a central aspect of labor negotiations. This had the effect of requiring increased sophistication regarding the management of benefits. Employers had to determine what benefits would be offered, who would receive them, and how much these benefits would ultimately cost the organization. Offering benefits was also seen as a way to attract and retain workers. Insofar as benefits provided high levels of security, an employee would be motivated to stay with an organization. Of course, however, the desire to stay does not necessarily mean the desire to work harder. In this sense, employers have had to become more expert at assessing the psychological effects of benefits; when they are motivators and when they are not.

TYPES OF BENEFITS

Benefits, when conceived in the broadest sense, are services, privileges, or monetary compensation provided in excess of wages. On first glance, we think of benefits as provided by the employer but in fact, they arise from both the employer and external sources, usually the government.

Government Sources

Retirement Benefits: The state and federal governments are common sources of retirement benefits for public employees. Generally, the pension plans provided for public sector employees are considered superior to those in private industry.[44]

Both private and public employees may be eligible for retirement income from social security (FICA). Based on a legislated formula, the employee and employer make contributions to the Social Security Administration. At age 65, or 62 if reduced benefits are accepted, individuals begin receiving a retirement income.

Some library employers need not participate in the social security system. These employers are often members of state retirement and pension systems. As with social security, both the employee and employer usually make contributions and retirement income is paid based on a predetermined formula. Such programs usually include additional benefits such as disability, death, and health insurance.

Other Government Benefits: Additional government benefits are available to most library workers, including worker compensation and unemployment compensation. Worker compensation is usually paid by the state when an employee is injured while performing work-related activities. Each state has its own laws and regulations governing who is eligible to receive compensation, and the amount of compensation. Unemployment compensation protects workers who have left employment. This is also regulated on a state by state basis. Eligibility for unemployment compensation is based on factors including the number of weeks worked and the reason for termination.

Employer Provided Benefits: Health and Quality of Life

Benefits provided by employers cover a vast area. Generally they fall into two classes: health benefits and quality of life benefits.

1. Hospitalization and Medical

The rising costs of medical care have made medical benefits an absolute essential. Plans for hospitalization and medical care vary widely from library to library. Either the library pays 100% of the monthly premium, or the employee and employer share the premium costs. Coverage is usually available not only for the employee but for the employee's spouse and dependents, although this usually increases the premium the employee pays. Given the rapid increases in medical costs, premiums are usually evaluated annually by the insurer and are based on general increases in medical costs and on the extent to which the insurance has been used by the staff over the period of coverage. It is therefore beneficial to minimize use.

Cost cutting can be accomplished in several ways. Most notably, the deductible can be raised, increasing employee liability for payment before the insurance coverage begins. A second method is to increase employee contributions toward the monthly premium. Employees, who know that their premium may rise due to unnecessary use, are less likely to abuse the benefit.

Two other alternative cost-cutting measures are Health Maintenance Organizations (HMOs) and self-insurance. HMOs are private medical corporations. These corporations contract with a group of physicians who agree to offer medical services to employees at specified fees. Financing for the HMO is based on monthly fees paid by the employer and employee. Employees who partake of such programs must use only the doctors who are part of the HMO unless given permission by the HMO to do otherwise. Often, these HMOs also have contracts with local hospitals, or are actually part of the hospitals themselves. HMOs must generally meet standards of medical care established by state and federal agencies. Proponents of HMOs argue that the increased control over the costs and medical services delivered increases the efficiency of the system and reduces health care costs. There is some argument as to whether HMOs actually save money, but they may also provide other benefits including excellent preventive medical care or employee assistance programs at little or no charge to HMO members.

A second cost-cutting alternative is self-insurance. The library sets aside an initial pool of funds to pay for anticipated medical costs of employees. This pool is replenished by regular payments usually made by both the employer and employee. Usually, self-insurance is possible only for large organizations, as it requires a staff of people to administer. This staff might be in the employ of the organization, or under contract. Also, such programs need contingency insurance in case medical costs for a given year exceed projections.

2. Sick Leave Benefits

There are basically two types of sick leave: paid and unpaid. Usually, paid sick time is accumulated based on a formula, e.g. one day per month for full-time employees, and prorated for part-time staff. Generally, the only requirement for employees to receive paid sick time is to notify the employer of illness, although, in some cases, employees may need to provide a doctor's certificate. For longer illnesses, employees may be required to take *unpaid* sick leave. Such leave is granted under certain conditions, e.g. doctor's certification. If the leave is extensive, the employer may set conditions for return to work including placing the employee in a new or equivalent position upon return.

3. Other Medical Benefits

There are many other types of medical benefits now available to employees. For example, dental plans have become popular over the last two decades. These plans became necessary because traditional health insurance programs did not include dental care. Often such programs emphasize preventive care or minor restorative procedures. They pay most of the costs of teeth cleaning and general examinations, but pay a smaller percentage for substantial restorative procedures such as crowns or orthodontia. Similar coverage is provided in some organizations for vision care.

Other health related benefits include life and disability insurance. Such programs are provided in case the employee dies or is seriously injured. Life insurance programs may pay a predetermined sum to the beneficiary in case the employee dies, or may be based on a percentage or multiple of the employee's annual income. Similarly, if the employee is permanently disabled, or disabled for a substantial period of time, disability insurance provides a percentage of the employee's earnings for a stipulated period of time.

4. Financial Services

Some employers provide programs that assist employees in financial planning. For example, employers may have a savings plan in cooperation with local banks or investment firms. The employer automatically deducts a specified amount from the employee's check each pay period and this money is invested as the employee desires. Depending on the type of investment program, the money saved might be sheltered from taxation.

Among the benefits that provide tax relief are tax sheltered annuities (TSAs) and individual retirement accounts (IRAs). These programs are offered by banks, investment firms, and insurance companies, and allow the employee to make deposits which are then reinvested in stocks, C.D's, or other instruments. When Internal Revenue Service (IRS) regulations are met, the money deposited is not taxed until it is withdrawn, which theoretically is when the employee retires and is therefore in a lower income bracket.

5. Quality of Life Benefits

Employees may receive benefits designed to help them live happier lives. The two primary benefits in this category are vacations and holidays. Vacation time varies from library to library, and also may differ according to whether the individual is a professional librarian or a support-staff worker. Normally, there is a formula for vacation time, e.g. 1.5 days per month for full-time employees. The amount of vacation time may also vary by years of service and whether the individual is a part- or full-time employee. Vacation for part-timers is usually prorated. Sometimes, the vacation benefit may cumulate from year to year up to a maximum. For example, an employee who gets four weeks of vacation a year, may forego vacation for a year and take eight weeks the following year. In addition, some institutions may allow the conversion of vacation time to cash, especially when the employee leaves or retires. In this case, the departing employee receives the balance, or proportion thereof, of their unused vacation time in cash.

Holiday benefits are usually on accepted legal holidays, such as Christmas Eve and Christmas Day, July 4th, Labor Day, New Year's Day, and Easter. Not all libraries recognize the same holidays. Some libraries, for example, close on Martin Luther King Day, others do not. For some holidays, such as Columbus Day, an institution might institute a policy of a "floating" holiday. In this case, the library remains open and some staff continue to work, but are given an opportunity to take another day off.

An especially difficult problem related to holidays is what to do about individuals whose religious holidays are important to them but are not recognized as legal holidays. Examples include Jewish employees who celebrate Yom Kippur. Employers should try to accommodate such individuals by giving them an opportunity to change their schedules so that they can take the time off. Employers should not, however, create a situation which produces an undue hardship on other employees. Because this area presents special legal problems related to the "religious accommodation" provisions of the Civil Rights Act of 1964, the employer should consult legal counsel before making a final decision.

Educational benefits are among those that affect the quality of life, and may offer time off, pay, and tuition reimbursement for employees who are seeking to improve their knowledge and skills. The provision of educational benefits may be affected by seniority, level of position, type of program to which the employee is applying, and the relevance of the education to the job worked by the employee. Benefits can be offered for a wide range of programs from half-day workshops to Master of Library Science programs. Educational benefits can be a most effective way of recruiting promising employees into the library profession by providing them with substantial financial assistance for library school. For libraries looking for minorities, this could be an especially good recruiting tool.

Public Versus Private Employee Benefits

Each institution tends to develop its own combination of benefits, but research suggests that there are patterns related to whether the library is in the public or private sector (Figure 5-5). For example, public libraries tend to provide more benefits, especially those related to worker security (e.g. retirement). Almost all public employers provide sick leave while only 70% provide such leave in the private sector. Generally, public employees with fewer years of service tend to receive more paid leave than those in the private sector.[45] In terms of health care, public employers are more likely to participate in HMOs than private employers.[46] Concerning retirement and pension plans, public employees again seem to have the advantage with more than 90% benefiting from such programs compared to 76% in the private sector.[47]

Although the length of the work week may not be, in itself, considered a benefit, the 40-hour, five-day work week is still common for the private sector while 40% of full-time public employees work fewer hours, often 35 to 37.5 hours a week.[48]

On the other hand, private employers do offer some superior benefits. For example, while nearly all full-time employees in medium and large firms in the private sector have vacation benefits, only 72% of those in state and local governments have them. In addition, private employers are much more likely to provide severance pay on separation from

FIGURE 5-5.   Comparing Benefits in the Public Sector with the Private Sector

Table 1.   Percent of full-time employees participating in selected benefits plans, medium and large firms in private industry and State and local governments

Benefit	Private Industry, 1986			State and local governments, 1987			
	All employees	White-collar employees	Blue-collar employees	All employees	Regular employees[1]	Teachers	Police and firefighters
Paid time off							
Lunch period	10	3	17	17	10	32	39
Rest time	72	63	82	58	74	16	48
Holidays	99	99	98	81	95	45	93
Vacations	100	99	100	72	93	13	100
Personal leave	25	34	15	38	32	56	36
Funeral leave	88	87	88	56	56	52	75
Military leave	66	73	58	80	85	65	86
Jury duty leave	93	96	90	98	99	97	92
Sick leave	70	93	45	97	97	95	97
Insurance							
Sickness and accident	49	31	69	14	18	5	14
Health	95	95	96	94	94	95	96
Life	96	97	95	85	85	82	91
Long-term disability	48	64	30	31	28	41	18
Retirement							
Defined benefit pension plans	76	78	74	93	92	95	93
Defined contribution plans	47	54	40	9	9	8	13

[1]Regular employees are all workers except teachers and police and firefighters.

Source: William J. Wiatrowski, "Comparing Employee Benefits in the Public and Private Sectors," Monthly Labor Review 111 (December 1988): 3.

employment, as well as free parking, accident insurance, recreational facilities, subsidized meals, in-house infirmaries, and long-term disability insurance.[49]

In a national survey of libraries with budgets of $500,000 or more, Laurie Hardaway found that libraries tend to spend less on benefits than private-sector companies, approximately 13% (range of 5%-21%). The primary costs of library benefits were absorbed by insurance such as health, life, dental, and disability.[50] All the responding libraries offered medical insurance; 90% offered life insurance, 80% death and dismemberment, 60% dental, and 50% disability insurance. Use of the medical plan was substantially greater than use of the dental plan.[51]

Benefits as Motivation

The numbers and varieties of benefits are great, but the question for the library employer is "Can benefits be structured to enhance productivity?" This is not to say that employees do not deserve basic health care, or paid time off, but benefits should be perceived as part of the total compensation program, and the ultimate purpose of such a program is to attract and maintain the most productive work force possible.[52]

Benefits are not generally designed as effective motivators, because they are considered system rewards rather than individual rewards. The same basic benefits are provided to all or most employees, rather than to individuals based on performance.[53] When everyone receives benefits, there is little motivational potential. When given to mediocre or poor performers, benefits only encourage them to stay with the organization. The consequence may be continued poor performance and low organizational productivity. Can library benefits be structured to improve motivation and productivity? The benefits currently offered in nonprofit organizations, including libraries, tend to have low motivational potential because they are focused on long-term, security benefits rather than short-term motivational ones.[54]

Motivation is a complex phenomenon which must take into account the interaction of employees' individual characteristics with those of the organization. If benefits are to be used as motivators, several factors must exist:

- The particular benefits must be seen as important and employees must value them. For example, employees without children simply will not find dependent health care insurance valuable and will therefore not be motivated by it.
- The benefits must be seen as having substantial monetary value. Benefits that appear to require trivial fiscal sacrifice by the employer are not likely to motivate employees to work harder.

- The benefits must be individualized. Benefits that are available to all without regard to performance are not likely to provide an individual with a reason to work harder. In this regard, employers must be aware of the changing demographic factors that will influence employees' perception of a benefit's value. Currently, benefits should reflect the aging of the baby boom population, and increasing numbers of women in the labor force, especially those with young children, as well as the increasing number of families with more than one wage earner.[55]

Cafeteria Approaches to Benefit Programs

Perhaps the best known alternative to traditional benefits administration, which offers the same benefits to all employees, is called the cafeteria approach, or "flexible benefits." Employers have turned to these programs to respond to employee needs and to control benefit costs.[56] Using a flexible benefit system, employers can add new benefits without having to provide that benefit to all employees whether they want it or not. Essentially, employees are given a certain number of credits to expend on a variety of benefit options. Some employees may choose to expend credits on health and dental insurance. Others, who may have health and dental insurance through their spouses, may choose more vacation time. Generally these credits are worth from 3% to 6% of employees' salary.[57]

The flexible benefit system, when properly administered, can meet the basic criteria for individual motivation. Employees can choose those benefits that are important to them, individualized to their needs. Because the number of benefit credits is associated with salary levels, employees are motivated to perform well to increase their salaries. If the library uses a merit system, then performance is linked to reward, a central aspect of motivating with pay.

Such a system does have some potential problems; perhaps the most important is the increased implementation and administrative cost. Although computerization is helpful, employers must monitor each selection made by each employee, and also future changes and additions. Libraries will spend considerable time preparing information on the various benefits and how the program operates. This involves increased training for administrative staff and supervisors. An even greater problem may be morale of employees who do not perceive benefits as rewards, but as rights. This attitude is common in a unionized environment and accurately reflects the social responsibility that library employers have to provide basic benefits to all. For this reason, a combination of a credit system in addition to a basic benefit package is advisable. The library provides a basic package of benefits available to all, additional benefits can be obtained through credits. This satisfies both motivational needs and the social obligations of the institution.

The difficulties of using benefits as motivators are manifest. Generally, it should be tried only by institutions that can offer a wide range of substantial benefits. In addition, because cafeteria programs rely at least in part on salary level, the library should have a well-developed performance review program so that benefit rewards are provided to the appropriate individuals.

Communicating Employee Benefits

Communication plays an important role in the system of benefits. Communicating employee benefits is more than just telling employees what benefits are available. It includes elucidating the organization's philosophy regarding benefits, who is eligible, how benefits are received, how to process claims, how to change benefits, and what to do if there are complaints about benefits.

The responsibility for communication permeates all levels of the organization, but the director and human resource manager are ultimately responsible for communicating information about the entire benefits package, and training managers and supervisors to interpret the program accurately to library staff.

Because cost containment is an important aspect of most benefit programs today, the administration should not shy away from telling employees directly that this is one of the goals. The responsible use of benefits is, in fact, vital to the fiscal health of the library. Clear, unambiguous explanations as to why containment is needed is the best way to get cooperation.

In larger libraries, a benefits administrator may be employed to implement, administer, and communicate employee benefits. The key responsibilities of such individuals are to make sure employees know what benefits are available, to ensure that claims are processed efficiently, and to monitor and evaluate the benefits system so that the fiscal health of the organization is protected and staff receive the appropriate benefits in a timely fashion.

Supervisors also play a vital role in the benefit communications process. Employees often rely heavily on supervisors because they are the source of a considerable amount of information about the organization. The role of supervisors is more than just communicating what benefits are available; they can also serve as informal counselors. For example, if a supervisor sees that an employee is having emotional difficulties, then it may be appropriate for the supervisor to remind the person of an employee assistance program that is available. For this reason, it is critical that supervisors have a solid understanding of the benefits provided.

There are many ways to communicate about benefits. Although written communications such as pamphlets and brochures dominate benefit communications, the use of audiovisual materials is increasing. More detailed information may be provided in staff handbooks or policy manuals. Written materials should have the following essential characteristics:

- The language should be appropriate for the audience: The tone should be neither too formal nor too informal. Because libraries employ individuals with a wide range of education and technical knowledge, the material should be written in an informal style so that individuals with a basic education can understand it. Martinez and Nally recommend the use of the 10-20-30 rule: limit paragraphs to an average of 10 sentences, sentences should be an average of 20 words long, and polysyllabic words should comprise no more than 30% of the entire document.[58]
- Examples should be used because many benefits are complex. If the pension plan is being explained, it is useful to provide an example of how much a typical employee with an annual salary of a specific sum will be paid following retirement.
- A "Question and Answer" format is also helpful for complex benefits; list the most important or commonly asked questions and give complete answers.
- Use simple language devoid of jargon. Many communications use unnecessarily repetitive and technical language. Sessions recommends that in place of such words as "compensation," "physician," "annual," and "accrued," use the terms "pay," "doctor," "yearly," and "earned."[59]

An especially useful time to impart employee benefit information is during orientation. At the time of hire, employees should receive a packet of written materials describing the available benefits. It is also important to review these benefits orally during an orientation session. In this way, employees have an opportunity for two-way communication, and the employer can be confident that they understand the program. It is also an opportunity for the administration to convey its philosophy of benefits and to reinforce positive aspects of the organization.

Benefit information can also be communicated effectively in group meetings. For example, insurers or pension administrators may be willing to come to the library and give presentations to the entire staff on the many aspects of their benefit programs. Such meetings may also provide an opportunity for questions of common interest to be answered. On a smaller scale, meetings concerning benefits may be held in departmental units.

Communication can also occur during a "one-on-one" counselling session if an employee has a particular problem or question about pension benefits, hospitalization, or policies for leaves-of-absence. The library administration should make sure that there is at least one individual who is identified as being able to answer specific questions regarding benefits. This may be the benefits administrator, personnel officer, or library director. If the library is unionized, union representatives may also serve as a source of benefit information.

CONCLUSION

There is little doubt that with the proliferating costs of employee benefits, employers must pay special attention to the type and extent of benefits offered. Where there was only hospitalization and medical coverage twenty years ago, now there are health promotion and maintenance programs to consider. Where twenty years ago, health insurance meant coverage for illness and injury, now there are wellness and employee assistance programs.

The purpose of benefits can be seen from at least two perspectives: to protect the employee, and to improve library productivity. This dilemma is particularly acute for the library manager with a humanistic philosophy, whose propensity is to maximize those benefits that would improve the quality of life for employees. The challenge, at the same time, for library managers is to create a strong benefit package that motivates workers and poses no threat to the fiscal well-being of the library. It is a formidable task, and one that is not likely to get easier in the foreseeable future.

FACTORS AFFECTING WAGE AND SALARY ADMINISTRATION

1. The relationship between pay and job satisfaction is related to pay level, pay policies and procedures, how the salary compares with others, and benefits.

2. Pay levels are of special concern to library administrators because of the historical discrimination against women which has depressed their pay.
   Employers must monitor the pay system to insure that women performing jobs of equal value to the organization are provided equal pay. In addition, all "comparable worth" court decisions and state laws should be monitored.

3. Systematic classification and compensation systems improve hiring and recruitment practices, increase the perception of fairness by employees, serve as a motivator of performance, and assist in planning, budgeting and decision making.

4. Good classification systems are based on systematic job analysis and objective techniques for determining the monetary value of a job. The point factor method is most common.

5. Wage ranges are affected by available financial resources, prevailing wages in the labor market, the available labor pool, the existence of competitors, and the historical basis of the pay level.

6. Monetary rewards are generally distributed in two ways: "across-the-board" and through merit. Across-the-board increases have the advantage of being simpler to administer; merit increases are more directly related to increases in performance.

7. For merit increases to have the desired effect, they must be large enough to be perceived by the employee as substantial.

8. The use of merit requires accurate and valid performance evaluation systems that distinguish between mediocre and strong performers.

9. The employer should think of benefits as part of the total compensation package. Benefits can be used not only to provide security, but also to motivate.

10. In order for benefits to be motivators, they must be perceived as important, have substantial monetary value, and must be individualized to the employee's needs.

Endnotes

1. Leigh S. Estabrook and Kathleen Heim, *Career Profiles and Sex Discrimination in the Library Profession*, Chicago: American Library Association: 38-39.
2. American Library Association, Office for Library Personnel Resources, *The Racial, Ethnic, and Sexual Composition of Library Staff in Academic and Public Libraries*. Chicago: American Library Association, 1981: 38.
3. Edward E. Lawler, III, "The Mythology of Management Compensation," *California Management Review* 9 (Fall 1966): 12.
4. Herbert G. Heneman, III, "Pay Satisfaction," in *Research in Personnel and Human Resources*, edited by Kendruth M. Rowland and Gerald R. Ferris, Greenwich, CT.: JAI, 1985: 119.
5. Heneman: 130-134.
6. Lyman W. Porter, Edward E. Lawler, III, and J. Richard Hackman, *Behavior in Organizations*, New York: McGraw Hill, 1975: 353.
7. C.C. Williamson, "Personnel Specification for Library Work," *Public Libraries* 26 (June 1921): 297-301.
8. Richard Rubin, "A Critical Examination of the *1927 Proposed Classifications and Compensation Plan for Library Positions* by the American Library Association," *Library Quarterly* 57 (October 1987): 404.
9. Rubin: 400-425.
10. Wayne Cascio, *Applied Psychology in Personnel Management*, Reston, Va.: Reston Publishing, 1978: 132.
11. *Garcia v San Antonio Metropolitan Transit Authority*, 105 S.Ct. 1005 (1985).
12. *County of Washington v Gunther*, 452 U.S. 161 (1981).
13. *American Federation of State, County, and Municipal Employees (AFSCME) v State of Washington*, 770 f. 2d 1401 (9th Cir. 1985).
14. Robert E. Williams and Lorence L. Kessler, *A Closer Look at Comparable Worth*, Washington, D.C.: National Foundation for the Study of Equal Employment Policy, 1984: 63-68.
15. Heneman: 136-137.
16. William F. Glueck, *Personnel: A Diagnostic Approach*, Dallas: Business Publications, 1974: 408.
17. Bryan Livy, *Job Evaluation: A Critical Review*, New York: Wiley and Sons, 1975: 50.
18. Livy: 51-52.
19. Livy: 72.
20. Samir A. Haddad, "Compensation and Benefits," *Human Resources Management and Development Handbook*, New York: Amacom, 1985: 645.
21. Haddad: 646.
22. Heneman: 131-132.
23. Richard E. Kopelman, "Linking Pay to Performance Is a Proven Management Tool," *Personnel Administrator 28* (October 1983): 61.
24. Rosabeth Moss Kanter, "From Status to Contribution: Some Organizational Implications of the Changing Basis of Pay," *Personnel* 64 (January 1987): 14.
25. Kanter: 12-13.

26. Kanter: 14.
27. Kopelman: 61.
28. Kopelman: 62-63.
29. A.N. Nash and S.J. Carroll, Jr., *The Management of Compensation*, Monterrey, CA: Brooks-Cole, 1975: 199-202. (As cited in Richard E. Kopelman, "Linking Pay to Performance Is a Proven Management Tool," *Personnel Administrator* 28 (October 1983): 62.
30. Richard E. Kopelman and Leon Reinharth, "Research Results: The Effect of Merit-Pay Practices on White Collar Performance," *Compensation Review* 14 (Fourth Quarter, 1982): 34.
31. Edward E. Lawler, "Merit Pay: Fact or Fiction?" *Management Review* 70 (April 1981): 50-53.
32. Heneman: 132.
33. A. Arthur Geis, "Making Merit Pay Work," *Personnel* 64 (January 1987): 53.
34. Kanter: 18-19.
35. Edward E. Lawler, "Merit Pay: Fact or Fiction," *Management Review* (April 1981): 50.
36. Kopelman and Reinharth: 40.
37. Frederick S. Hills, Robert M. Madigan, K. Dow Scott, and Steven E. Markham, "Tracking the Merit of Merit Pay," *Personnel Administrator* 32 (March 1987): 50-57.
38. Nathan B. Winstanley, "Are Merit Increases Really Effective?" *Personnel Administrator* 27 (April 1982): 38.
39. Winstanley: 40.
40. Winstanley: 40-41.
41. Kathryn A. DCamp and Robin A. Ferracone, "Compensation: Spot Gain Sharing Provides High-Impact Incentives," *Personnel Journal* (September 1989): 85-88.
42. DCamp and Ferracone: 86.
43. Haddad: 646.
44. Dallas L. Salisbury, "Regulatory Environment of Employee Benefit Plans," (39-51) in *The Handbook of Employee Benefits*, edited by Jerry S. Rosenbloom, Homewood, Ill.: Dow Jones-Irwin, 1984: 48.
45. William J. Wiatrowski, "Comparing Employee Benefits in the Public and Private Sectors," *Monthly Labor Review* 111 (December 1988): 6.
46. Wiatrowski: 3.
47. Wiatrowski: 4.
48. Wiatrowski: 7.
49. Wiatrowski: 4-5.
50. Laurie Hardaway, "Public Library Work Benefits Survey," *Public Library Quarterly* 6 (Fall 1985): 5.
51. Hardaway: 5.
52. Stephen C. Bushardt and Aubrey R. Fowler, "Compensation and Benefits: Today's Dilemma in Motivation," *Personnel Administration* 27 (April 1982): 24.
53. Bushardt and Fowler: 23.
54. Everett T. Allen Jr., "Designing Employee Benefit Plans," in *The Handbook of Employee Benefits* edited by Jerry S. Rosenbloom, Homewood, IL.: Dow Jones-Irwin, 1984: 24.

55. Mitchell Meyer, *Flexible Employee Benefit Plans: Companies' Experience*, Conference Board Report No. 831, New York: The Conference Board, 1983: 1.
56. Meyer: 3.
57. Robert W. Cooper and Burton T. Beam, Jr., "Cafeteria Approaches to Benefit Planning," in *The Handbook of Employee Benefits*, edited by Jerry S. Rosenbloom, Homewood, IL.: Dow Jones-Irwin, 1984: 371.
58. Thomas Martinez and Robert V. Nally, "Communication and Disclosure of Employee Benefit Plans," (829 to 851) in *The Handbook of Employee Benefits*, edited by Jerry S. Rosenbloom, Homewood, IL.: Dow Jones-Irwin, 1984.
59. Barbara Sessions, "Taking Aim at Jargon—Complying With the Plain Language Requirements of ERISA," 57-61, in *Communicating Employee Benefits*, edited by Catherine C. Hayne, Brookfield, WI.: International Foundation of Employee Benefit Plans, 1984.

6
Collective Bargaining

Collective bargaining is a vast and complicated area, and public sector bargaining presents its own special problems. In a private organization it is easy to identify the managers who control negotiations and who make the final decisions. In the public sector, however, there are often many levels of decision-makers: a city manager, a board of trustees, a city or county council, even a state legislature that must be dealt with before a bargaining agreement is ultimately ratified. In addition, collective bargaining in the public sector is closely circumscribed by state and local laws and regulations which define who can be represented by the union, what are the subjects of bargaining, and what are the rights of workers if bargaining fails. Finally, political considerations may influence the public bargaining process. Tensions between elected officials and vocal political action groups may influence how bargaining proceeds. Public employees or management may attempt to exploit these external political forces.

No single chapter can provide all the necessary information to conduct successful negotiations. This chapter is a general discussion of collective bargaining reviewing the factors that influence unionization, the effects of unionization, the characteristics of state collective bargaining law, the process of negotiation, characteristics of a labor contract, and some suggestions on how unionization can be avoided. Any library involved in unionization should obtain competent legal counsel. Failure to do so can and often does lead to well-meaning attempts that result in disaster.

FORCES AFFECTING UNIONIZATION

Some of the contemporary social forces that encourage or inhibit the development of library unionization are:

234

- The proliferation of state collective bargaining bills that permit public employees to form employee organizations, and in some cases to strike[1]
- The increasing concern over unequal and undervalued wages paid to women, which has stimulated unionization in professions dominated by women
- The increasing acceptance of unions among some professional workers such as teachers and nurses
- Increased fear of invasions of privacy especially in regard to drug and other types of testing
- The proximity of librarians to other unionized workers.

In addition, there is evidence that public employees actually have a stronger desire to unionize than private-sector workers, and that this is true for both men and women.[2,3] The strong support by public employees is attributed in part to the belief that collective action is a preferred strategy in the highly political arena of public employment. In addition, female public employees believe, even more than males, that collective bargaining will improve their wages and benefits.[4]

Counteracting the forces for unionization are:

- A general disinclination among white collar workers to involve themselves in unions traditionally associated with blue collar jobs
- A general disillusionment with the power of unions which has been highlighted by union contracts in which benefits and even wages have sometimes been reduced
- Declining employment in areas with heavily unionized industries
- The growth of "right to work" laws, especially in the southern states, which adversely affect union membership
- An increasingly strong union decertification movement in which employers are convincing workers to give up their union affiliations
- The increasing sophistication of employers who use a variety of legal and other means to deter unionization
- A traditional disinclination of unions to try to organize clerical or professional groups or groups dominated by females.

These inhibiting forces have had a strong impact in the private sector. Since the mid-1950s, union membership has steadily declined. In 1956, for example, the Bureau of Labor statistics reported that more than 38% of the labor force was unionized, by 1978 the percentage was less than 25%. By 1986, union membership in the private sector had declined to 14%.[5] Interestingly, this trend is *not* seen for blacks, women, or better-educated employees, whose proportion of the unionized labor force is actually growing.[6]

Despite the general trend in the private sector, the recent decades have shown gains in the unionization of government employees, including those who work in libraries. The Bureau of Labor Statistics reported that only 12% of the government work force was unionized in 1956. By 1978 this figure increased to more than 23%. By 1986, this number grew to 36% of the public work force.[7] Mitchell reports that the percentage may be as high as 43%.[8] The most recent estimate for state and local government (1983) indicates that approximately 32% of the public work force is represented by unions.[9] It appears however, that the peak period of unionization was between 1976 and 1978; since that time, union membership has remained stable, possibly declining slightly.[10]

Specific union information on libraries and librarians is limited. Kokkelenberg and Sockell, using Current Population Survey (CPS) data, report that by 1974, only 12.6% of all librarians were unionized, this percentage grew steadily to 30.6% in 1980.[11] This figure is still low compared to other local government workers whose union membership ranges from 35% (highway workers) to 67% (fire fighters). The only classification of local government worker with less than 30% union membership is public hospital workers (16%).[12] Some estimates of librarians' participation in unions are even lower. O'Reilly and O'Reilly estimated that approximately 25,000 librarians (20%) were represented by collective bargaining units in 1981.[13]

Despite the relatively low overall percentage of librarians who are union members, there is still a substantial number who are participating in the collective bargaining process. A study of Association of Research Libraries (ARL) members, for example, indicates that unionization is fairly widespread among such libraries: at least some level of library staff is represented in approximately 50% of the ARL libraries; professionals are represented in slightly under half of those with some type of union, some support staff are represented in almost all ARL libraries that have unions.[14] Among the larger group of Association of College and Research Libraries (ACRL), the percentage of representation is somewhat lower. Carmack and Olsgaard, in a survey of 298 ACRL libraries, estimate that aproximately 25% of these libraries were involved in collective bargaining, with the highest percentage located in the Northeast.[15]

Why Librarians Join Unions

Mika and Guyton have summarized the reasons why most librarians join unions as:[16, 17]

- Low salaries and poor working conditions
- Dissatisfaction with methods of library administration
- Concern over the economic health of the institution
- Lack of job security and fear of job loss
- The desire to increase involvement in decision-making.

One of the factors that makes collective bargaining more complex among librarians is that they are concerned with professional issues, such as institutional goals and directions, as well as with wages and working conditions. Professional issues are clearly of interest to support staff as well. Support staff in academic libraries are often well educated, and managers must pay considerable attention not only to wages but to opportunities for them to have a voice in planning and decision making.[18]

Despite the increasing unionization of libraries, efforts at unionization have come slowly to the library profession with public libraries leading the way and academics unionizing later. Three periods of library unionization have been identified. The first began just prior to 1920. The end of World War I provided considerable economic stimulation which in turn promoted the development of employee organizations. The development of library unions was consistent with these broader economic forces.[19] As early as 1919, an entire session was devoted to unionization at the ALA conference, and by 1922 an ALA committee on salaries had been created.[20][21] This period marked the development of library unions among major public libraries including New York, Boston, the District of Columbia, and Philadelphia.[22]

The second period of unionization occurred during the Great Depression, which saw particular growth of union membership among professional workers.[23] As might be predicted, much of the incentive for unionization grew out of the poor financial conditions of the country as a whole. Primary stimulants included low salaries, poor working conditions, and inadequate library funding. In general, when libraries did unionize, they affiliated with other national labor organizations.[24] Not only library professionals were involved in these unionization activities. Several library unions included all levels of staff, and some nonprofessionals (janitors) actually had their own unions.[25]

Unionization in academic libraries was even slower. Howard and Yale attempted to unionize in the 1930s and 1940s, but both attempts were subsequently abandoned.[26] Several explanations have been advanced for the generally lethargic character of library unionization. Two prominent proposals were that librarians believed (perhaps still do) that unions are not appropriate for professionals, and that collective bargaining is an inappropriate intrusion into administrative prerogatives. In addition, it must be remembered that the focus of union activity remained in the private sector; public employees, including librarians, were not an especially fruitful source of membership because it was often unlawful for public employees to unionize or to strike.

The third period of unionization began in the late 1960s and continued into the 1970s. In this period both academic and public libraries were prominent in collective bargaining. Representation was achieved for both professional and support staff, often as a single group in public libraries. In academic institutions, librarians were often grouped with faculty; support staff were left to unionize separately.[27] Three factors stimulated union activity during this period:

- A significant increase in the number of librarians
- The social activism of the 1960s
- The general push to unionize public employees throughout the United States.[28]

The latter reason must be coupled with the fact that many states began to pass laws permitting public employees to unionize and strike. In addition, labor market conditions provided the stimulus for unions to develop membership among public employees. The growth of public employment in state and local government was much faster than non-public employment, swelling the potential pool of union members.[29] Similarly, declining union membership among traditional blue-collar workers made librarians and other public employees appealing targets for recruitment.

This period also saw attempts at official recognition of collective bargaining by the American Library Association. By 1970, the Library Administration Division Board of Directors of the American Library Association felt it necessary to develop a position statement on collective bargaining.[30] This statement encouraged the education of librarians and administrators regarding collective bargaining and supported laws that permit librarians to organize. However, it also explicitly rejected the concept of ALA becoming a union itself, partly because the ALA included institutional and administrative members as well as librarians. The initial statement was first rejected by the ALA Council.[31] Some time later a similar statement was adopted affirming the right to organize without fear of reprisal and establishing an educational responsibility of ALA to inform and train librarians, administrators, and trustees concerning collective bargaining.[32]

THE EFFECTS OF UNIONIZATION

Are unions beneficial to organizations, or do they simply create problems? From the employer's point of view, there is a tendency to emphasize the potential negative aspects of unions: loss of managerial flexibility, lower productivity, work stoppages, increased labor conflict, and increased labor costs. From the employee's perspective, the positive aspects are emphasized: opportunity for a greater voice in the workplace, better salaries, benefits, and working conditions, and better communications on how and why management decisions are being made, with reductions in arbitrary and capricious behavior on the part of management.

Freeman and Medoff have provided substantial support for the view that unions are a positive force in most circumstances.[33] Following a review of the research and an extensive data analysis of thousands of employees primarily in the private sector, covering the decade of the 1970s, they concluded:

1. Unions Increase Wages and Benefits

Employees' wages and benefits are better than they would have been if there were no union. This is especially true for less educated workers, and younger workers with less job tenure. The standard wage effect of unions in the 1970s in private industry was between 20% and 30%. The wage effect for service workers (the analysis category most analogous to librarians) was 12%. It should be noted, however, that the power of unions to affect wages depends in large part on their ability to maintain a monopoly over the labor force. If a union can organize a large portion of the available labor force, then it will have a much greater impact than if a large percentage of the labor force is not unionized.

Unions also have a substantial effect on employee benefits, increasing them an average of 30%. Generally, the increases benefit older rather than younger workers by improving pensions, health, life, and accident insurance.[34]

Interestingly, Freeman and Medoff also found unionization may raise the wages of nonunionized work forces. In large nonunion organizations, for example, the presence of unions nearby may lead the employer to provide higher wages and benefits to maintain its nonunion status; such increases in wages and benefits may also occur in non-unionized work forces where unionization is threatened.[35]

2. Unions Reduce Employee Turnover

Compared to nonunion workers paid the same wages, the estimated reduction in turnover is estimated at between 31% and 65%. The reduction appears to be greatest among service workers (39%), among workers above 50 years of age (38%), and those with less than a high school education (39%).[36] The reduction is due primarily to the fact that unionized workers have a way of voicing their complaints through grievance arbitration, and that they have greater job stability through seniority rights established in union contracts.[37]

3. Unionized Workers Report Lower Job Satisfaction

This seems contradictory in that one would normally expect lower levels of job satisfaction to be associated with higher levels of turnover. Yet this is not the case for unionized workers. Unions provide employees with a safe channel through which to voice dissatisfaction; unions members are even encouraged to voice this dissatisfaction. This may, in itself, increase the employees' level of dissatisfaction. The particular source of unionized employees' dissatisfaction appears to be supervisors, followed by working conditions.[38]

4. Unions Have a Beneficial Effect on Productivity

This has been supported in studies of selected industries such as manufacturing and construction with productivity gains estimated at between 9% and 39%.[39] It should be noted, however, that the data are not consistent for all industries and there is no information concerning service-related sectors. In addition, while productivity gains are noted for blue-collar workers, unionization appears to have a modest negative effect on productivity for unionized white-collar workers.

Three factors may explain why unions have a generally positive effect on productivity. First, the fact that union members can voice their concerns appears to lower employee turnover, which in turn fosters greater job stability. Second, although unions can create conflict they also can create stable and positive labor relations. A positive labor climate is positively associated with productivity; conversely, poor labor relations, unionized or not, are usually associated with poor productivity. Third, the presence of a union may in fact *improve* managerial performance because it forces management to plan and develop rational management practices, helping the organization run more efficiently and effectively.[40]

5. Unions Significantly Increase Labor Costs

Employees enjoy better wages and benefits, but the net result is that unions have a negative effect on profitability. Estimates in business and industry suggest that profits may be affected by as much as 17% to 37%.[41]

Unions in the Public Sector

The data analyzed by Freeman and Medoff were from the 1970s. The 1980s have seen a retrenchment with private employers even forcing givebacks, or wage reductions, in some industries. This has not been as significant a factor in the public sector. In the private sector as many as 20% of the contracts involved wage concessions, while in the public sector only 4% contained such concessions.[42]

There is some reason to believe that public employees are, overall, doing better than employees in the private sector. For example, while pay increases in 1985 and 1986 averaged 2.6% and 2.1% respectively for the private sector, increases in the public sector were 5.7% and 5.2%.[43] In addition, there does appear to be a wage effect: unionized public employees reap greater wage rewards than nonunionized employees, but the size of the effect is less than in the private sector. The effect becomes more pronounced for benefits, with unionized public employees tending to have more benefits than nonunionized employees.[44] Evidence also suggests that unionization has boosted the average pay of government workers *beyond* that of what they would receive if they were in the private sector.[45]

The Effects of Unions in Libraries

There is little research on the effect of unions on library employers and employees. Rosenthal, in the most current review of the literature, breaks down what little research there is into five broad areas:[46]

* Factors that influence union formation
* The attitudes of librarian and library school students toward unionization
* Collective bargaining agreements themselves
* The impact of unions on productivity
* The impact of library unions on wages and salaries.

Her review suggests that unions are more appealing to younger librarians, that librarians are concerned with professional issues as well as wages and benefits, and that there is reason to believe that unionization does increase wages and benefits. Productivity appeared to be unrelated to the presence of a union.[47] Certainly, some librarians believe that unionization provides substantial benefits. Carmack and Olsgaard noted that unionized librarians believed that their unions had improved their situation in at least three areas: due process (the ability to appeal unfair treatment), salaries, and fringe benefits.[48] Again, it should be noted that the amount of research in these areas is slight and definitive conclusions are impossible at this time. Nonetheless, it is consistent with the sparse data for the public sector indicating little or no relationship between productivity and unionization.[49]

Salaries and Benefits
From the employees' perspective perhaps the single most important effect of library unions is in raising salaries and benefits. Guyton noted that dissatisfaction with wages and working conditions were powerful reasons for early unionization, and that the same issues are still important today.[50] Getz, in an analysis of 31 of the largest public libraries in the late 1970s found a significant difference in the salaries of unionized and nonunionized libraries, with the average salary being approximately 16% higher in the union settings. This differential was greatest for experienced librarians and for clerical workers. No differences were found for entry level librarians. In addition, a positive association

between unions and improved benefits was found.[51] Rosenthal, in a study of 114 public libraries with annual budgets of $100,000 or more, did find that unions made some differences. She found that the presence of a librarian's union explained 5% to 14% of the variation in wages for librarians. The presence of a professional librarian's union, however, had *no* impact on the salaries of either clerical workers or department heads in the same libraries. Conversely, when library unions representing nonlibrarian employees were analyzed, the union presence explained 11% to 17% of the variance in clerical salaries. The presence of such unions had *no* effect on the salaries of librarians or department heads.[52] Rosenthal, in a separate study of Minnesota public libraries, found similar results with unionized libraries having higher salaries and a larger number of paid sick days and holidays than nonunion libraries.[53]

The evidence suggests, then, that library unions do increase salaries and benefits. But the research is sparse and not without contrary findings. Guyton, in his analysis of six public libraries, found that there was no statistically significant difference in salaries in unionized libraries, nor were there any differences in fringe benefits.[54] Kusack, in a study of support staff in academic libraries, failed to find statistically significant differences in the wages or fringe benefits provided to unionized and nonunionized employees.[55] Ehrenberg et al. in a study of more than 270 municipal libraries found no association between higher wages and collective bargaining agreements.[56]

Library Unions, Job Satisfaction, and Worker Productivity
Guyton found that, consistent with the findings of Freeman and Medoff, the job satisfaction of librarians in unionized settings was lower, especially with wages and benefits, than those of nonunionized librarians. Guyton suggested that the greater dissatisfaction is caused by contact with union leaders, newsletters, and programs, which tend to emphasize the negative aspects of the employer.[57]

Only one study has been conducted on productivity. It involved 256 municipal libraries using basic output measures such as number of information requests, number of borrowers, number of interlibrary loans, total circulation, and book and periodical circulation.[58] With the exception of interlibrary loans, no relationship between productivity and collective bargaining was found.[59] This is consistent with Carmack and Olsgaard's finding that library unions tend to focus on personal rather than organizational goals. They found that academic librarians perceived that the quality of service had *worsened* after unionization.[60] The lack of relationship between unionization and productivity is further supported by Caynon. In his study of professional development activities of academic librarians, he analyzed the relationship of unionization to professional membership in associations, attendance at professional conferences, number of library journals and books read, attendance at workshops and seminars, and publications. Overall, he found no relationship between professional involvement and union membership.[61]

The lack of evidence that professional service or development improves with unionization may be a result of the traditional attention that unions pay to "bread and butter" issues. Ballard observes that the tendency of library unions to affiliate with national unions such as the AFL-CIO and the American Federation of State, County, and Municipal Employees (AFSCME) may increase this problem, because the history of such unions is to focus on salaries and benefits, not on professional issues.[62] But the blame for a lack of professional focus must be shared by the public employer. In many instances, it is a result of state law that expressly excludes or inhibits bargaining on some professional issues, especially those that might involve participatory decision making; such decision making may be perceived as violating the basic management rights and responsibilities of the public employer.

Despite these factors, some union contracts do attempt to deal with professional concerns. Five of the more common issues dealt with in contracts are professional leave, faculty status, evaluation and promotion, selection and censorship of the library collection, and selection of the director.[63] The effect of such provisions on professional performance is unknown.

THE LEGAL CONTEXT OF UNIONIZATION

Federal Guidelines

Library staff working for private employers are covered by the National Labor Relations Act (NLRA). Public employees, on the other hand, may be covered by state collective bargaining bills. Some states have no such legislation and public employees wishing to bargain must then rely on the courts.

The Great Depression was a formative period of labor-management relations. The labor unrest created by hard economic times prompted the Congress to pass the NLRA, sometimes referred to as the Wagner Act, in 1935. This act deals with employees in the private sector, focusing on the orderly creation of unions, and the regulation of conduct during collective bargaining. Its intent was to promote industrial peace by resolving disputes through a collective bargaining process in which the rights of the employer and employee were clearly defined. The act gave employees the right to form labor unions and to bargain collectively regarding the terms and conditions of employment. It also created the

National Labor Relations Board (NLRB) to decide issues of representation and conduct. In doing so, it significantly restricted management use of interference and coercion to prevent unionization. The results were dramatic. Union membership in the five-year period from 1933 to 1938 jumped from approximately 2 million to more than 7.5 million.[64]

At the time the NLRA was passed, no similar constraints were placed on the unionized employees. In the 1940s, it was feared that this power imbalance might lead to significant work stoppages that could detrimentally affect peacetime economic growth. Focus shifted from issues involving the organization of unions to issues involving conflict resolution. As a consequence, the NLRA was amended in 1947 by the Labor Management Relations Act (LMRA) also known as the Taft-Hartley Act. Its intent was to reduce union bargaining power and establish procedures for resolving conflicts through mediation and conciliation.[65] Unions as well as employers became accountable for unfair labor practices. These regulations did not, however, diminish union membership, which peaked in 1955 with 33% of the labor force.[66] Further regulation of union activities occurred in 1959 with the passage of the Labor Management Reporting and Disclosure Act, the Landrum-Griffin Act, which was designed to ensure that unions operated in a democratic fashion.

None of these laws affected government workers. Federal workers were not protected until 1962, when President Kennedy issued Executive Order 10988 which permitted government employees to bargain collectively. The order had significant impact on the unionization of public employees; union membership of public employees rose more than 100% from 1960 to 1968.[67] It also set the stage for state laws which reflected the new Federal attitude toward labor-management relations.

Aspects of State Collective Bargaining Laws

Because of the large number of librarians who are subject to state collective bargaining laws, the ensuing discussion of collective bargaining will be conducted primarily in the context of these laws. About three-fourths of the states have some type of collective bargaining legislation affecting at least some public employees.[68] More than 940,000 employees are covered in 470 bargaining units. Generally, the bargaining units split along occupational (e.g. teachers, nurses) rather than departmental lines.[69]

There are three basic foci of state collective bargaining laws:

- Provisions related to the creation and certification of employee organizations and their representatives
- Provisions related to the negotiation process, including unfair labor practices

- Provisions related to impasses in which disputes cannot be resolved.

As might be expected, there is great variety in collective bargaining legislation from state to state. Even within a state there may be several collective bargaining statutes e.g., one for teachers or faculty members, and one for other public employees. However, some important common features are shared (Appendix D). Among them are the following:

1. Identification of Who Is Eligible to Join the Union

State legislation usually identifies who is eligible to be represented by a union, and who is excluded. Generally speaking there are certain groups of individuals who are not eligible to be part of a public employee union. The groups most often excluded are confidential and managerial employees.[70] Both of these groups often participate in negotiating for the employer or have access to confidential communications regarding the negotiations. Other groups that are usually excluded are elected and appointed officials and their staffs, supervisory employees, members of the state militia, students, and seasonal, temporary, or casual employees.[71] Part-time employees may also be excluded. Some state legislation may also exclude certain types of workers whose activities are deemed vital to survival. These might include fire fighters, paramedics, and police officers. Sometimes, such individuals are included in the collective bargaining bill, but their rights are restricted, e.g., not permitted to strike.

Disputes over which individuals meet the various definitions of excluded employees and which do not are common. For example, disputes often arise as to which individuals are supervisors. Ohio law, for example, defines a supervisor as

> ...any individual who has authority, in the interest of the public employer, to hire, transfer, suspend, lay off, recall, promote, discharge, assign, reward, or discipline other public employees; to responsibly direct them; to adjust their grievances; or to effectively recommend such action, if the exercise of that authority is not of a merely routine or clerical nature but requires the use of independent judgment...[72]

Such a definition might be quite clear for the head of a large department, but what of the assistant to the head? What if supervision constitutes only a small percentage of an individual's duties? What if the individual's supervision involves only one person, or just a few students shelving books? What if supervision occurs during only part of a year? In Ohio, such supervisors may well be included in bargaining units.[73] In some states, supervisors are eligible to form an employee organization, but they must be separate from nonsupervisory employees; in other states, they can be together in the same unit.[74]

Similar problems can arise when trying to define a management level or confidential employee. Management level employees may be seen as individuals who formulate, direct, and implement policy on behalf of the employer, or who participate in collective bargaining on behalf of the employer. Confidential employees are individuals who work closely with public officers or administrators or who handle documents related to collective bargaining, e.g., secretary to the director. In either case, these are employees whose responsibilities do not fit neatly into the definitions.

2. Identification of the Bargaining Unit

State legislation also attempts to provide some guidance as to what constitutes a bargaining unit. This is an important aspect of the collective bargaining legislation because it defines who can be represented by the union. A bargaining unit is a specific group of employees who have a "community of interest," that is, they have similar wants and needs in terms of their jobs and can be reasonably represented as a group by a union. Although many public employees may be eligible to join an employee organization, not all may be eligible to be in the same bargaining unit. For example, legislation may prohibit professional and support staff from being in the same bargaining unit. This is a logical restriction because the wants and needs of professional librarians may be quite different from those of support staff. As noted above, supervisors and nonsupervisors may also be forced into different bargaining units.

Public librarians are found in one of three types of bargaining units: municipal employees, which is the broadest type of unit; public library employees, in which librarians and other library employees may be lumped together; and distinct units, in which professionals are separated from other classifications. Academic librarians also find themselves in three types of units: faculty, library employees, and librarians.[75]

Public employee bargaining units are represented by a variety of employee organizations. In 24 states with collective bargaining laws, affiliates of the American Federation of State, County, and Municipal Employees (AFSCME) are found. Similarly, state employee associations are recognized in 13 states. Other national unions with affiliates include the Communications Workers of America which represents the largest number of employees, the International Federation of Professional and Technical Engineers, and the Service Employees International Union. Professional unions such as the American Federation of Teachers, the National Education Association, the American Association of University Professors, and the American Nurses Association also have affiliates in libraries.[76]

3. Statement of Employee Rights

One of the primary purposes of collective bargaining legislation is to identify clearly the rights of public employees in regard to unionization. Such legislation gives public employees the right to form, join (or not to join), and participate in an employee organization. In addition, it gives them the right to bargain collectively for wages, hours, and other terms and conditions of employment, to be represented exclusively by one employee organization for a specified period, and to file grievances if violation of the contract is charged.

4. Methods of Securing Representation

Under state legislation various options may be available in order to obtain recognition of an employee union as an exclusive representative. Two common means are either through voluntary recognition by the employer, or by conducting an election. In the former case, a request for exclusive representation is made to the employer with evidence that a majority of employees in a given bargaining unit wish to be represented by a specific employee organization. If the employer agrees, then representation is secured. In the latter case, the legislation sets out the process by which employees may petition an employer for an election which is usually conducted under the watchful eye of the employee relations board established by law to oversee such elections.

5. Creation of an Employee Relations Board

In order to settle disputes between employer and employees, the state collective bargaining laws establish labor relations boards similar to the NLRB established for private employees under the Wagner Act. The duties of these boards include adjudicating disputes involving eligibility for representation, the formation of collective bargaining units, and charges of unfair labor practices. They are also responsible for overseeing union elections, certifying unions, and promulgating rules, regulations, and procedures for implementing the collective bargaining legislation.

6. Defining the Subjects of Bargaining

The legislation will likely contain a statement that the employer has a duty to bargain with the recognized union on certain subjects, sometimes called mandatory subjects. These subjects generally include wages and hours, as well as terms and conditions of employment. Certain subjects are often expressly excluded from negotiation such as the administration of the civil service system. The law may also establish certain subjects on which the employer may choose to bargain; these are referred to as permissive subjects (see "The Scope of Negotiations" on page 253).

7. Defining Unfair Labor Practices

Unfair labor practices are actions taken by the employer or employee in violation of federal or state employment relations acts.[77] Some areas identified in state legislation as unfair labor practices for *management* include:

- Attempts to interfere with, or coerce employees in exercising their collective bargaining rights
- Attempts to interfere with, or dominate, the formation or administration of an employee organization
- Discrimination in regard to hire or other terms or conditions of employment of individuals exercising their collective bargaining rights
- Discharging an employee for union activities
- Refusing to bargain with union representatives
- Refusing to deal with grievances in a timely fashion
- "Locking out" employees, that is, prohibiting employees from entering the place of work, in order to force capitulation to the terms of management
- Making threats or reprisals.

Unions are subject to similar unfair labor practice restrictions. They, too, cannot coerce employees or refuse to bargain in the exercise of their collective bargaining rights. Other unfair labor practices for unions include encouraging workers to strike or boycott an employer in violation of the provisions of the state law; causing an employer to discriminate in hiring or tenure; violating election rules; and picketing to compel an employer to recognize an employee organization.

8. Dispute Resolution and Strike Provisions

State collective bargaining laws play a particularly important role when an employer and the union are unable to come to agreement regarding the provisions of a contract. This is referred to as an impasse. When such an impasse is reached, a series of steps may be required under the law before a strike may be called. Among the possible alternatives are conciliation, mediation, and arbitration. Conciliation and mediation are sometimes used synonymously, other times they are distinguished. *Conciliation* involves the use of a neutral third party who, in an informal fashion, tries to encourage the parties to resolve their differences. Usually, the conciliator tries not to get into too much detail but attempts to cajole both sides to work together. *Mediation* involves a neutral third party who is more actively involved in the resolution of the dispute. The use of such individuals may be required by statute before further union action can be taken. The mediation process is more formal; the mediator meets with representatives of both groups together or individually. The mediator may make recommendations regarding a resolution, although the recommendations are not binding on the parties.[78] *Arbitration* involves a neutral third party who hears the arguments from both sides and makes decisions regarding the settlement of the dispute. During arbitration a formal fact-finding process occurs in which both sides present arguments and evidence supporting their positions.

Arbitration can take many forms. It may be compulsory, that is, required by law; or it may be voluntary, that is, the disputing parties mutually agree that they will abide by the arbitrator's decision. A common form of arbitration is called binding or interest arbitration. In this type of arbitration the disputing parties present their respective positions to the arbitrator who makes a decision regarding the disputed issues.

Depending on how arbitration is defined by the appropriate statutes, the arbitrator may be forced to choose either the union or management position, or the arbitrator may be able to forge a new resolution by combining aspects of both sides. The latter type of interest arbitration has been criticized because it can inspire exaggerated union claims in hopes that the arbitrator will "split the difference." It can also foster what is called a "narcotic effect" in which the parties develop a habit of arbitration, reducing the likelihood of serious collective bargaining.[79]

An alternative type of interest arbitration which reduces some of these problems is called "final offer arbitration" in which the arbitrator is forced to choose between the management and labor positions. In some states, the law may not permit interest arbitration in which the arbitrator can make any final determination because it is considered a usurpation of the powers of the duly elected or appointed authorities who govern the public organization. In this case, another type of arbitration, called advisory arbitration, can be used in which the arbitrator makes recommendations regarding the settlement of the dispute.[80]

In the public sector two types of interest arbitration usually occur. These are "item by item" in which the arbitrator rules on each disputed item in the contract, or "total package" arbitration in which the arbitrator chooses either the total union or total management contract proposal.[81] Evidence suggests that the use of interest arbitration reduces the number of strikes.[82] Holman, however, warns that binding arbitration is a very serious matter for public libraries. The arbitrator's decision may impose impossible economic burdens on the library, or may disrupt the policy and authority of boards who traditionally have broad statutory authority to make and implement policy.[83] Binding arbitration places a tremendous amount of power in the hands of a third party.

Nonetheless, dispute resolution procedures are a vital part of the collective bargaining process. Some state laws create procedures that are very complicated, time-consuming, cumbersome, and threatening to the fiscal well-being of the library. On the other hand, if the law permits, both sides can mutually agree to more efficient voluntary dispute resolution procedures. For libraries, these alternative procedures may include, but are not limited to:

* Appointing a federal mediator to assist in negotiations
* Using arbitration for all unsettled issues in which the arbitrator is not limited to the final offers of either side, but may forge his own resolution
* Using arbitration in which the arbitrator is limited to either the labor or management position.[84]

If no agreement is reached after dispute resolution procedures have been used, the collective bargaining law may permit public employees to go on strike. In such cases, the law regulates the procedures by which an employee organization notifies the employer of its intent to strike. Some classifications of public employees such as police or fire fighters may be prohibited from striking under any circumstances. These workers may be forced to go to binding arbitration to settle their disputes.

The right of public employees to strike has been a controversial issues for many years, and there is little doubt that the use of the strike as a weapon has changed the way many perceive public employees, for example, teachers. Holman summarized the basic arguments both for and against giving public employees the right to strike.[85]

In favor
* Public employees should have the same right to strike as those in private industry
* Collective bargaining is of little value unless the threat of a strike is available
* Strikes do not occur often enough to justify their restriction, and seldom really threaten public health and safety

Against
* Public employees provide essential services which should not be disrupted by a strike
* Public employees are not like private sector employees who are part of the free market system
* Strikes could seriously affect public health and safety

The issue seems to be resolving in favor of most public employees having the right to strike under state collective bargaining laws.

THE COLLECTIVE BARGAINING PROCESS

Although there is a general pattern to the collective bargaining process, no situation is the same as any other. The results of collective

bargaining emerge from a delicate interaction of a variety of factors.[86]
These include:

1. The Attitude and Personality of the Individuals

The individuals involved in collective bargaining bring to the bargaining
table their distinct personalities, attitudes, past history, values, interpersonal and group skills. How each individual reacts to conflict,
confrontation, flattery, even long hours of work, may have substantial
impact on the outcome of negotiations.

2. Situational Influences

Of considerable importance is the power relationship that exists
between the parties. The more equal the power, the more effective the
bargaining process.[87] The general attitudes of the union membership,
administration, and board provide a context for the bargaining process.
Strongly negative attitudes could impede effective negotiations; strongly positive ones could promote it.

There is a tendency for collective bargaining to be perceived as a
negative process. It is natural for employers to oppose unions. At the
very least, unions are a threat to management's ability to control the
workplace. When there is no union, the employer can act autonomously
so long as the actions are within legal bounds. In addition, the employer
may feel that the creation of a union will create divisions within the
organization that were not there before. Problems that could be resolved
informally, and in a friendly fashion are turned into formal grievances
which must be processed under strict rules and regulations. Managerial
discretion is reduced, and an adversarial relationship is created.
Employers, especially public ones, may also feel that the creation of a
union diverts management from its goals of service. Instead of time
spent on developing and maintaining public services, time and money
is spent on negotiating union contracts, and settling grievances and
charges of unfair labor practices.

The negative attitude toward the bargaining process persists on
both sides. Colosi and Berkeley characterize this as Theory U and
Theory M after Douglas McGregor's Theory X and Theory Y. Unions
operate under Theory U which includes the assumptions that:

- management tries to pay employees as little as possible for the maximum
  amount of work
- management will introduce any technological improvements that make
  employees work harder
- management inhibits the formation of unions through deceptive and coercive tactics

- management will punish union supporters whenever they can
- management's lack of flexibility is the cause of strikes.

Management, on the other hand, holds completely different assumptions (Theory M) including:

- employees continually ask for more money and less work
- unions block all forms of progressive technological changes
- unions engage in deceptive and coercive tactics
- strikes are caused by unreasonable demands on the part of unions.[88]

These underlying values may affect the negotiating process and attempts should be made to limit the potential negative impact of such beliefs.

3. Environmental Factors
These include the provisions of the relevant state collective bargaining laws; the financial condition of the institution, the goals and mission of the organization, the organizational climate, the local, state, and national economic environment; and the history of labor relations in the organization prior to unionization.

4. Negotiating Strategies and Skills
The techniques and approaches used in the collective bargaining process will determine the outcome. Negotiation strategies based on distrust and deceptive communication are likely to produce difficult bargaining. How each side presents its case, uses its power, and communicates, plays an important role.[89]

5. Bargaining Philosophy
How management bargains should depend in part on a broader management philosophy, and an understanding of the political and fiscal realities in which the library functions. Rather than taking a negative attitude based on unfriendly assumptions about unions, management should take a positive approach emphasizing the importance of high quality service and high standards of professional performance. It is important to remember that although management may reserve the right to make planning, policy, and personnel decisions, management is not prohibited from consulting employees on these matters, and developing strong communication links with staff so that the quality of decisions improves. A labor contract that preserves management rights but alienates staff serves little purpose if the result is poorer service and reduced productivity.

The Duty to Bargain in Good Faith

The heart of collective bargaining is the negotiation process. This process requires both sides to sit down at the bargaining table and sincerely attempt to resolve their differences in good faith. This is referred to as the *Duty to Bargain.*

Once a union has been certified, the employer is obligated to bargain with that union; the union is obligated to bargain as well. The employer may not bargain independently with the employees in the bargaining unit, but only with the union representatives. Bargaining in good faith means that the parties agree to meet at reasonable times and bargain concerning wages, hours, and the terms and conditions of employment, leading to a written contract. The employer is obligated to show genuine interest and to maintain an open mind.[90] It does not imply that either the employer or union agrees to make particular concessions, but an employer or union who refuses to bargain is subject to an unfair labor practice charge.

In order to demonstrate good faith, Clark suggests that management follow some basic guidelines including:[91]

- Appoint negotiators who have meaningful authority
- Provide relevant information in a timely manner as requested by the union
- Avoid taking unilateral actions
- "Take it or leave it" proposals should be avoided
- Do not attempt to circumvent the union representatives by going directly to the employees
- Do not make statements that suggest that management has no intention of signing a contract.

The Scope of Negotiations

As noted above, bargaining issues are defined by the respective state collective bargaining law. There are three types of issues: mandatory, prohibited, and permissive. The subjects on which the employer *must* bargain are referred to as the mandatory subjects and usually include wages, hours, and terms and conditions of employment. Prohibited subjects are those which would constitute violations of law, or which are prohibited by the collective bargaining law itself.

Permissive subjects are those subjects that can be raised by either management or labor but on which either side can refuse to bargain. It is on these subjects that management must be especially careful not to bargain away its authority. For example, management must not bargain away what is referred to as its "management prerogative" or "management rights." These are rights traditionally recognized as those that reside in management. In Ohio, for example, management is given the following rights:[92]

1) To determine matters of inherent managerial policy which include, but are not limited to areas of discretion of policy such as the functions and programs of the public employer, standards of services, its overall budget, utilization of technology, and organizational structure;

2) To direct, supervise, evaluate, or hire employees;

3) To maintain and improve the efficiency and effectiveness of governmental operations;

4) To determine the overall methods, process, means, or personnel by which governmental operations are to be conducted;

5) To suspend, discipline, demote, or discharge for just cause, or lay off, transfer, assign, schedule, promote, or retain employees;

6) To determine the adequacy of the work force;

7) To determine the overall mission of the employer as a unit of government;

8) To effectively manage the work force;

9) To take actions to carry out the mission of the public employer as a governmental unit.

Naturally, many of the rights given to management are ones of great interest to unions. How individuals are promoted, transferred, and disciplined is of legitimate concern to union members and the union will make concerted efforts to erode management's right to make these decisions.

STAGES OF COLLECTIVE BARGAINING

Collective bargaining goes through several stages before a final contract is signed.

Stage I: Prenegotiation

This stage involves preparing for negotiations with the union. Among the preparatory steps that should be taken are:

1. Establish a management bargaining team. Levy recommends that this team have a chief spokesperson, legal counsel, administrators (including the personnel officer), and an individual with financial acumen. Levy also notes that the director is in a stronger position when *not* part of the bargaining team and therefore removed from personal disputes.[93] Some smaller government agencies hire an industrial relations specialist who serves as the chief negotiator until the negotiation ends.[94]
2. Review the current contract with special attention to the grievances that have been filed. This will help identify future demands of the union. If the first contract is being negotiated, management should still try to identify areas of common complaint voiced by staff.

3. Review the contract for problem areas in the contract itself. Perhaps some sections were unclear, or resulted in great cost to the library. These areas should be identified as areas for potential change in the new contract.

4. Collect information on costs associated with the current contract. These include wage and benefits costs, as well as the cost of sick time, absenteeism, and accidents.

5. Collect demographic information on the current staff and the number of individuals in each job classification. This will be needed to project accurately the costs of additional benefits and wages proposed by the union.

6. Collect information on other collective bargaining agreements and trends. It is important to monitor developments in other libraries and to identify trends. This may help anticipate the demands of the union.

7. Anticipate and analyze those demands on which the union will push hardest. Determine the cost of each demand and its effect on administrative power and authority.

8. Project the budget and anticipated revenues to meet the costs of an anticipated contract and to maintain a competitive position in the labor market.

9. Establish a communication structure so that the administration, board and negotiating team are able to deal with issues quickly and effectively as they arise in negotiation. In some cases, the union attempts to circumvent the management bargaining team by going directly to Board members. Good communication minimizes the effect of such a strategy. It is also important that the management bargaining team have good communication with supervisors. Because supervisors often have direct and close links with employees, they can provide vital information regarding the attitudes of employees as negotiations proceed.[95]

10. Develop contingency plans in case a settlement is not reached and a strike results.[96, 97]

Stage II: Proposal Formulation and Bargaining

During this stage both union and management may offer their own proposals and counter-proposals. Traditionally, the union is the first to offer a proposal. Management may respond through counterproposals to the union, or it may submit an entirely new set of proposals based on management's view of the situation. In either case, by laying the proposals on the table, management and labor are able to identify what issues are important to both sides and the potential areas for quick agreement or protracted negotiation. A certain amount of posturing may occur at this point, both sides wishing to establish their respective positions.

The bargaining stage actually is composed of three segments. First is *distributive bargaining* which occurs early in the bargaining process and in which the parties attempt to test the limits of the other side's position by expressing their demands in uncompromising language and style. This may reveal itself in argumentative or confrontational tactics. The second stage is *integrative bargaining* in which the parties demonstrate greater flexibility and show a willingness to move from their established positions. Language and nonverbal skills play an increasingly important role at this stage. The tone of the negotiations may change, and a more cooperative or conciliatory atmosphere may develop. The third stage is *decision making and action*. At this stage the issues are clear and both sides have to make decisions regarding what is acceptable and what is not.[98]

Although this may have the appearance of "game playing," such posturing may be important. Clark observes that, historically, public administrators often made negotiating too easy for unions, putting too much on the table too early in the bargaining process.[99] That was not always desirable because unions needed to be perceived by their constituents as winning concessions from management, otherwise they were suspected of not getting enough. Union attorneys and negotiators, who often come from the private sector, expected difficult and protracted negotiations.

Generally less important topics should be negotiated first because it is likely to create an atmosphere of cooperation and compromise; money issues should be decided last.[100] Clark also advises that concessions in the final stages of negotiation should be made only if they are contingent on a final agreement, and to try to get the initiative by focusing on management proposals rather than the union's.[101]

Under good conditions, the result of the bargaining process is a written agreement. In the public sector, the parties who do the bargaining are usually not in and of themselves empowered to accept the contract. Rather, each side must have the contract ratified. The management team must have the contract ratified by the governing board or council; the union must have the pact ratified by its membership. There can be, of course, many reasons why the union membership might not ratify a contract. They may feel that it is inadequate, or there may be political infighting in which some union members wish to repudiate the current union leadership. If approval is forthcoming, then the bargaining process, for all practical purposes is completed. If the contract is not approved, then it is up to management to decide if it wishes to return to the bargaining table. Management must be particularly careful about this, because it might send a message that management is not firm in its final offers.[102]

An alternative to renegotiation is to implement unilaterally management's final offer. That is, the employer begins administering the new contract or specific provisions of the contract as though the union had accepted them. Because unilateral action may be seen as a violation of the duty to bargain in good faith, the employer should only implement a final offer after a real attempt has been made to bargain and a genuine impasse has been reached. In addition, unilaterial implementation may be restricted only to the subjects involved in the impasse. If bargaining is still occurring on some subject, unilateral action on those subjects is not permitted.[103] In any case, unilaterial acts should be reviewed by legal counsel before action is taken.

Stage III: Contract Administration

Once agreement has been reached, the contract must be administered. In this stage, the parties to the agreement enforce the provisions of the contract. It is a difficult and important part of the collective bargaining process because the actions taken during administration of the contract can preserve or threaten the rights secured by the management negotiators.

No contract is perfect; there are always ambiguities in language. Woodford notes that the contract takes on concrete significance through three activities: implementation, interpretation, and incorporation. *Implementation* involves the actual exercise of the provisions of the contract, e.g., increasing wages. Implementing some parts of the contract may be straightforward, while others will require interpretation. *Interpretation* is needed in situations for which there is no clear statement in the contract. Matters for interpretation arise when there are differences in how a particular provision of the contract is understood, hence the possibility of strong disagreement between union and management. Such differences could ultimately lead to the filing of a grievance, or unfair labor practice. *Incorporation* consists of the precedents and practices that are established during the implementation of the contract. How the contract is implemented and interpreted establishes these precedents and practices.[104]

Supervisors play a critical role at this stage because their actions or inactions establish a body of precedents that affect how the contract is understood. Management must make every effort to ensure that supervisors are well trained to interpret and implement the labor contract. This is the best way to ensure that management preserves the rights secured in the contract and can enforce the contract in a fair manner.

When disagreements arise concerning the implementation or interpretation of a contract, the contract provides for the filing of grievances either by management or labor, although it is usually used by labor. If the grievance cannot be resolved by the disputing parties based on the procedures for internal resolution, then the contract may provide for grievance arbitration. This process is similar to interest arbitration; a third party hears the dispute and makes decisions on the merits of the arguments presented.

PROVISIONS OF THE UNION CONTRACT

The content of union contracts will vary substantially depending on the local conditions as well as the size and type of library. There are, however, some common features which are likely to appear. The reader should keep in mind that the items below are not meant to constitute an exhaustive list of contract issues, but to serve as examples.

1. Statement of Purpose

Such a statement includes the names of the official parties to the contract. It may also include statements regarding the fundamental purpose of the agreement such as "to promote beneficial relationships between the employer and the union," or "to provide effective service without interruptions." Management should also include a statement in this section indicating that the agreement reached supercedes all previous agreements.

2. Statement of Recognition

In this section, the union is officially recognized as the bargaining agent for the employees. Of critical importance is the definition of who is included in the bargaining unit represented and who is excluded from this unit. Generally, the bargaining unit is defined by job classification or job title. This can be a problem, especially when job titles change or new jobs are created. Describing the *type* of work rather than just the job title is one recommendation for dealing with this problem.[105] Management also needs to make very clear who is *not* included in the bargaining unit.

3. Authority and Limitations of the Contract

Public employee contracts are made within a broader context of state and federal laws, as well as regulations which are part of the larger but local governmental unit such as city or county council. The contract usually contains an explicit statement that any specific provisions of the contract found in violation of such laws and regulations are invalid. A "savings clause" is also included which means that if a particular provision is declared unlawful, the remaining portion of the contract remains in force. Additional provisions include a "zipper clause," which prohibits attempts to reopen negotiations during the life of a contract, and a statement that subjects not covered by the contract are governed by existing personnel policies and practices.

4. Statement of Management Rights

The contract usually contains a statement of what rights management reserves to itself. As noted earlier, it is critical that management not yield its rights and responsibility to manage the library. It should explicitly identify its right to plan, direct, and control, the policies of the library and the conditions of employment. Because specific state laws may already identify and protect these rights, some contracts quote directly from these state provisions.

5. Statement of Nondiscrimination

The contract may include an explicit statement that under no circumstances will either the union or employer make employment decisions because of race, national origin, handicap, religion, sex, age, marital status, or status as a veteran. In addition there may be provisions indicating that the employer will not retaliate against individuals who wish to join or take part in union activities.

6. Negotiation Procedures

The contract may spell out exactly how negotiations are to proceed and how disputes may be settled. This section may spell out such issues as:

* who can initiate negotiations
* the dates when proposals must be submitted
* the time limits for response to proposals
* the date when actual negotiations must commence
* the form of the final agreement
* dispute resolution procedures if the parties do not agree.

7. Strike or "Lockout" Provisions

Depending on the provisions established in the section on negotiation procedures, this section discusses whether strikes are allowable, under what conditions, and the procedure for beginning a strike. If binding arbitration has been established in the contract, then it is likely that the contract will contain a prohibition against striking for the life of the contract. Similarly, management agrees not to lock out employees.

8. Statement of Union Rights

In this section, the rights of the union and its membership are secured. Among the subjects that might appear are:

* the use of bulletin boards, or internal mail system for communicating with employees
* the right of union members to attend board meetings
* agreements by the employer to subtract union dues by automatically deducting amounts from employees' paychecks
* identification of when and where the union may conduct its business on library premises

- the right of employees to inspect their personnel files, and to challenge or respond to derogatory material in them.

Two areas of note relate to the use of bulletin boards, and when and where union business can be conducted. From the management perspective, some contracts indicate that the use of designated bulletin boards should be only for the posting of notices regarding union meetings, elections, and appointments. Derogatory materials about management may be expressly prohibited. Similarly, the contract may limit the conduct of union business, including the receiving or making of telephone calls, to breaks, meal periods, or other nonwork time.

9. Individual Rights
The contract may contain provisions stating that individuals are free to join or *not* to join a union, and to participate or refuse to participate in union activities without threat or intimidation by either union or management.

10. Job Vacancies, Promotion, and Probationary Appointment
These provisions deal with how employees may apply for job vacancies (sometimes referred to as job bidding), how job decisions are reached, and the employment status of new employees. Generally, the process for how vacancies are posted and the time limits for application are specified. Of particular importance to management is making sure that proper criteria for selection are stated. In the interest of quality service, management should make every effort to assure that the knowledge, skill, ability, and motivation of the employee be considered over and above seniority, although seniority may be an important factor, all other things being equal.

Concerning new employees, usually there is a probationary period established in the contract, e.g. six months, along with statements limiting the rights of probationary employees. For example, the probationary employee may not have the right to file a grievance, to accrue vacation or sick time, or to accrue seniority. Provisions may also be made for establishing a probationary period for newly promoted employees.

11. Hours of Work
Contract provisions may also define the normal work week. For libraries, a full-time work week varies, usually between 35 and 40 hours. The contract should clearly define the work week indicating the number of hours a day required for full-time employment, and the number of days of work required for each week. It is probably best not to identify the specific days, e.g. Monday through Friday, because weekend work is often required. The employer should also make sure that there is

nothing in the contract that guarantees an employee that they will work a specific number of hours or days within a given week.

Additional provisions should indicate the length of lunches and breaks, and compensation for overtime. Because of wage and hour laws, usually overtime is compensated at time-and-a-half for each hour of overtime worked. Some states may allow the employee to elect to take compensation time, that is, get subsequent time off instead of monetary compensation. Such time is usually accrued at the time-and-a-half rate. Similarly, there may be provisions for how overtime is offered. Voluntary overtime, for example, may be offered on a rotating basis beginning with the most senior employee in the department. Involuntary overtime is generally offered on a rotating basis beginning with the least senior member. The issue of Sunday hours may require additional provisions, especially in regard to whether the assignment to work Sundays is voluntary, who gets first choice to work and the rate of pay.

12. Wages and Benefits

A central part of the union contract deals with wages. Usually, the specific job classifications are identified along with the minimum rates of pay. Provisions concerning subsequent raises including the percentage of the raise and when the raise is to go into effect may also be included. Other provisions may indicate differences in pay for employees who work split shifts, those on leave of absence, as well as how merit pay may be assigned.

The contract spells out the benefits available, the criteria for eligibility, and the amount that the library contributes in premiums for various kinds of benefit coverage.

13. Separation from Employment

The contract establishes the terms under which an employee leaves the organization. Provisions for resignation and retirement are common, including the amount of notice that must be given and whether the notice should be in writing. In addition, information regarding the payment of accumulated benefit time to the employee may be part of the contract. There may be a section on "abandonment," which clarifies that if an employee is absent for a given number of days without prior approval or giving notification of absence, this can be viewed as a voluntary resignation.

14. Layoffs

The contract will very likely contain provisions for the layoff of employees. Often seniority is considered the chief criteria within a given job classification. Employees with the longest tenure are the last to be laid off, while probationary and low tenure employees are the first. In addition, bumping rights may be established. Bumping is the process by which an employee with greater seniority in a higher job classification may displace a worker with less seniority in the next lowest job classification, rather than be laid off. Management must stipulate that bumping can occur only if the senior employee possesses the required knowledge, skill, and ability to perform the job.

15. Leaves of Absence

The contract may contain provisions regarding the procedures and conditions under which an employee may take a leave of absence. Generally, a leave is considered an approved absence for one day or more. Among the common types of leaves are maternity/paternity leave, sick and disability leave, educational leave, military leave, jury duty leave, emergency leave, personal leave, and funeral leave.

16. Vacation and Holiday Time

The contract should contain formulas for how vacation time is accrued. Because these formulas tend to get confusing, the contract should provide employees with examples. The contract usually identifies specifically which holidays are recognized, and which ones will be celebrated as floating holidays: one in which the employee comes to work on the holiday, but is given a day off either before or after.

17. Discipline

Some contracts may contain explicit provisions regarding the use of discipline. For example they may specify a system of progressive discipline (see chapter 4). In addition, there may be statements regarding the right of the employee to file a grievance on the basis of a disciplinary action, the right to union representation in a dispute over disciplinary actions, and whether disciplinary materials are placed in employees' personnel files.

18. Grievance Procedures

A fundamental part of the contract involves the handling of grievances. A critical part of this section involves the definition of a grievance. The union may attempt to negotiate a broad definition implying that any action of the employer deemed to be unfair or unjust is a subject for a grievance. Management should consider keeping the definition narrow, and specifically related to the contract. Grievances should be seen as complaints that specific provisions of the contract were violated or misinterpreted. In addition, specific exclusions may be advisable. For example, management should consider provisions that exclude performance evaluations from grievance procedures.

Generally, the grievance procedure identifies the series of specific steps which the grievant and employer must take in handling a complaint. It is best that time limits of relatively short duration be included so that grievances do not pile up. When the parties appear to be unable to resolve the grievance, the contract may include provisions for grievance arbitration. This process is similar to interest arbitration. Provisions are set out for the selection of the arbitrator, who serves as a neutral third party, e.g. a member of the American Arbitration Association. The arbitrator reviews the facts, conducts a hearing, and makes a decision that is binding on all concerned.

19. Professional Development and Training

Because librarianship requires continuous education and training, the contract may identify the conditions under which library employees may acquire additional knowledge and skill. This may involve payment by the employer of registration fees and expenses for conferences, seminars or workshops, or the payment of tuition for more extensive courses at a college, university, or vocational training program.

20. Labor-Management Committee

Establishing a regular conduit for official communications promotes a stable work environment. For this reason, a contract may contain provisions for a committee composed of labor and management who meet in an ongoing fashion to discuss issues of concern to both sides during the length of the contract.

21. Miscellaneous Issues

Video Display Terminals: The safety of VDTs has become an issue in recent years, most notably because of the low level radiation emitted by the screen, and the physical discomfort that arises after prolonged use. The effects of prolonged VDT use include eye strain, backache, carpal tunnel syndrome, and headaches. In some cases, VDTs have been cited as the cause of miscarriages. The contract may contain provisions for the use of terminals if the employee is pregnant, the number of continuous hours that an employee may work at a terminal, the length and frequency of breaks, and the conditions under which job reassignment may occur.

Intellectual Freedom: Some contracts may contain provisions that protect employees from retaliation if they write articles for publication. In return for noninterference by management, the contract may require that employees include a statement that they speak for themselves only and not for the library.

The items above are representative of some things contained within the union contract. Depending on the history and situation, the number and type of issues negotiated vary. In the final analysis, most of the issues found in a union contract are the same issues an employer must deal with without a union. The difference is that the union has a formal and important role to play in the shaping of the policies.

AVOIDING LIBRARY UNIONS

There is little doubt that most employers would prefer to avoid unions if they could. There are two basic approaches to avoiding union-ization successfully. The first is to make a determined effort to fight unions when they attempt to organize staff. Some research suggests that when management wages an intense antiunion campaign they are able to avoid unionization in 78% of the cases.[106] There is also evidence that in a closely contested election, the use of a professional consultant can change the results.[107] This approach, however, seems to miss the basic point of avoiding unions; that is the need to remedy problems in the organization that lead to unionization.

The second approach is to create conditions within the library that make unionization unnecessary. Bucalo has identified several factors that tend to stimulate the development of unions in the general labor force. They include:[108]

- A feeling that management does not treat the employees well and with respect
- Poor communication
- Failure to provide wages and benefits that are competitive, or that adequately reward years of service
- Unfair treatment or favoritism, especially in regard to discipline and promotion
- Lack of effective channels to voice grievances
- Dangerous or unhealthy working conditions, and
- Poor training.

The library work force, both past and present, is interested in many of the things that all employees want. It is clear then, what the library employer must do:

- Have wages and benefits that provide a decent living and are competitive with similar job classifications in the general labor market
- Maximize the opportunities for employees to participate formally and informally in making decisions that affect them
- Ensure that the system of rewards, evaluation, discipline, and promotion are fairly administered
- Provide a formal and informal means by which grievances can be handled efficiently and fairly

- Ensure that the workplace is clean and safe for library workers
- Ensure that workers receive the proper training both in their specific job, and in relation to the goals of the organization as a whole
- Ensure that employees receive timely and accurate communication on all subjects related to the library. These communications can be both written and oral. Also, make sure that the right person does the communicating. Employees should not be hearing information from colleagues that they should have heard first from their supervisor, or from the director.

One wonders whether there is any one organization that can satisfy all these criteria. But a library should strive to meet these goals if it hopes to prevent unionization, especially in communities where labor unions are already present and active.

Theoretically, there is one other union-avoidance technique which is really a union removal strategy. This is called *decertification*. Decertification is the legal means by which employees can terminate their relationship with the union that currently represents them. The process of decertification is similar to that of certifying a union and involves an election by the employees in the bargaining unit. The decertification process has become quite popular in the private sector. Decertification elections have increased from 453 in 1976 to 892 in 1982; in 75% of the elections, decertification resulted.[109] Currently this technique is not in general use in libraries, perhaps because library unionization is relatively new and there has been little time for disillusionment, or little need for it. In the future, however, it may become more common.

FACTORS RELATED TO UNIONIZATION

1. There is a general trend toward increasing unionization among public employees.

2. Collective bargaining takes place in a complex legal enironment. Obtaining competent legal counsel is essential.

3. Librarians join unions primarily because of needs for increased salaries and wages, dissatisfaction with library administrations, lack of job security, and the desire to increase involvement in decision making.

4. Research on unions in general suggests that they have the effect of increasing wages, benefits and productivity, reducing employee turnover, and decreasing levels of job satisfaction and profitability.

5. Limited research on library unions indicates that library unions increase wages and benefits, decrease job satisfaction, and are unrelated to productivity.

6. Library managers should attempt to preserve "management rights" when engaged in collective bargaining.

7. The collective bargaining process is dependent on a variety of factors including the attitudes and personalities of the partici- pants, relevant state and local laws, previous history of labor relations, and negotiating strategies.

8. Employers have a duty to bargain in good faith with the union.

9. Employers should be scrupulously aware of what constitutes unfair labor practices.

10. Employers should prepare for negotiations by establishing a management team, reviewing the current contract, anticipating union demands, projecting costs, and examining contracts from other libraries.

11. Employers should beware of provisions that give final decision making power to a third party arbitrator.

12. The employer should have a contingency plan if negotiations reach an impasse.

13. Implementation and interpretation of the contract while the contract is in force is an extention of the collective bargaining process. Supervisors must be well trained in how to implement the provisions of the contract so that important management rights are not lost.

14. The best way to prevent unionization is by creating a work environment that makes unionization unnecessary. Other methods include engaging in a strong anti-union compaign, and hiring a consultant.

Endnotes

1. There is still considerable argument in the labor literature concerning whether state collective bargaining laws *caused* the increase in collective bargaining activity, or whether they were primarily a *result* of increasing agitation by public employees to unionize. See for example, John F. Burton, Jr. and Terry Thomason's "The Extent of Collective Bargaining in the Public Sector," 17-27, in *Public Sector Bargaining*, edited by Benjamin Aaron, Joyce M. Najita and James L. Stern, Washington, D.C.: BNA, 1988.
2. Duane E. Leigh and Stephen M. Hills, "Public Sector-Private Sector Differences in Reasons Underlying Expressed Union Preferences," *Journal of Collective Negotiations* 16 (1987): 4.
3. Duane E. Leigh and Stephen M. Hills, "Male-Female Differences in the Potential for Union Growth Outside Traditionally Unionized Industries," *Journal of Labor Research* 8 (Spring 1987): 138-139.
4. Leigh and Hills: 5-9.
5. Burton and Thomason: 5.
6. John A. Fossum, "Labor Relations: Research and Practice in Transition," *Journal of Management* 13 (Summer 1987): 285.
7. Burton and Thomason: 5.
8. Daniel J.B. Mitchell, "Collective Bargaining and Compensation in the Public Sector": 124, in *Public Sector Bargaining*, edited by Benjamin Aaron, Joyce M. Najita, and James L. Stern, Washington, D.C.: BNA, 1988.
9. Burton and Thomason: 28.
10. Burton and Thomason: 5.
11. Edward C. Kokkelenberg and Donna R. Sockell, "Union Membership in the United States, 1973-1981," *Industrial and Labor Relations Review* 38 (July 1985): 504.
12. Burton and Thomason: 34.
13. Robert C. O'Reilly and Marjorie I. O'Reilly, *Librarians and Labor Relations: Employment Under Union Contracts*, Westport, Conn.: Greenwood, 1981: xiii.
14. *Unionization in ARL Libraries*, Spec Kit 118, Washington, D.C.: Association of Research Libraries, 1985: 5-6.
15. Bob Carmack and John N. Olsgaard, "Collective Bargaining Among Academic Librarians: A Survey of ACRL Members," *College and Research Libraries* 43 (March 1982): 141.
16. Joseph J. Mika, "Collective Bargaining: Still a Relevant Issue," *Catholic Library World* 57 (January-February 1986): 181.
17. Theodore Lewis Guyton, *Unionization: The Viewpoint of Librarians*, Chicago: American Library Association, 1975: 156.
18. James M. Kusack, *Unions for Academic Library Support Staff*, Westport, Conn.: Greenwood, 1986: 86.
19. Bernard Berelson, "Library Unionization", *Library Quarterly* 9 (October 1939): 492.
20. Berelson: 478.
21. Katherine Todd, "Collective Bargaining and Professional Associations in the Library Field," *Library Quarterly* 55 (July 1985): 288.

22. Guyton:11-12.
23. Berelson: 485.
24. Guyton: 19.
25. Kusack: 10.
26. Kusack: 11.
27. Kusack: 12-13.
28. Todd: 288.
29. O'Reilly and O'Reilly: 3-4.
30. American Library Association, "The American Library Association and Library Collective Bargaining," Position Paper adopted by the Library Administration Division, Board of Directors January 21, 1970.
31. Todd: 290.
32. "Collective Bargaining," A Statement of Policy, Adopted by ALA Council, January 21, 1980.
33. Richard B. Freeman and James L. Medoff, *What Do Unions Do?*, New York: Basic Books, 1984: 46-51.
34. Freeman and Medoff: 64-65.
35. Freeman and Medoff: 160-161.
36. Freeman and Medoff: 95-99.
37. Freeman and Medoff: 105-107.
38. Freeman and Medoff: 137-142.
39. Freeman and Medoff: 166.
40. Freeman and Medoff: 174-180.
41. Freeman and Medoff: 187.
42. Mitchell: 129, 134.
43. Mitchell: 125.
44. Mitchell: 144-147.
45. Mitchell: 138.
46. Mary Rosenthal, "The Impact of Unions on Salaries in Public Libraries," *Library Quarterly* 55 (January 1985):54-56.
47. Rosenthal: 54-58.
48. Carmack and Olsgaard: 141.
49. Mitchell: 158.
50. Guyton: 112-115.
51. Malcolm Getz, *Public Libraries: An Economic View*, Baltimore: John's Hopkins, 1980: 70-71.
52. Rosenthal: 61-66.
53. Rosenthal: 55.
54. Guyton: 117-119.
55. Kusack: 60-68.
56. Ronald G. Ehrenberg, Daniel R. Sherman, and Joshua L. Schwarz, "Unions and Productivity in the Public Sector: A Study of Municipal Libraries," *Industrial and Labor Relations Review* 36 (January 1983): 213.
57. Guyton: 116-120.
58. Ehrenberg, Sherman, and Schwarz: 203.
59. Ehrenberg, Sherman, and Schwarz: 213.
60. Carmack and Olsgaard: 141.

61. William Caynon, "Collective Bargaining and Professional Development of Academic Librarians," *College and Research Libraries* 43 (March 1982): 137-138.
62. Thomas H. Ballard, "Public Library Unions--The Fantasy and the Reality," *American Libraries* 13 (September 1982): 508.
63. Margaret Chaplan and Charles Maxey, "The Scope of Faculty Bargaining: Implications for Academic Librarians," *Library Quarterly* 46 (July 1976): 244-246.
64. *Collective Bargaining: Democracy on the Job*, American Federation of Labor, Congress of Industrial Organizations, n.d.: 13.
65. John A. Fossum, "Labor Relations: Research and Practice in Transition," *Journal of Management* 13 (Summer 1987): 281.
66. Fossum: 281.
67. Guyton: 141.
68. Steve Barr, "Risk Aversion and Negotiator Behavior in Public Sector Arbitration," *Journal of Collective Negotiations* 16 (1987): 99.
69. Helene S. Tanimoto and Gail F. Inaba, "State Employee Bargaining: Policy and Organization," *Monthly Labor Review* 108 (April 1985): 51-52.
70. Tanimoto and Inaba: 52.
71. Tanimoto and Inaba: 52.
72. Public Employees' Collective Bargaining, Ohio Revised Code, 4117.01, Section F.
73. Tanimoto and Inaba: 52.
74. Tanimoto and Inaba: 53-54.
75. John W. Weatherford, *Librarians' Agreements: Bargaining for a Heterogeneous Profession*, Metuchen, N.J.: Scarecrow, 1988: 9-10.
76. Tanimoto and Inaba: 54-55.
77. Labor Relations Training Center, Bureau of Training, U.S. Civil Service Commission, "Glossary of Collective Bargaining Terms," in *Collective Bargaining in Libraries*, edited by Frederick A. Schlipf, Urbana, Ill.: University of Illinois Graduate School of Library and Information Science, 1975: 175.
78. Thomas R. Colosi and Arthur Eliot Berkeley, *Collective Bargaining: How It Works and Why*, New York: American Arbitration Association, 1986: 121-122.
79. Barr: 100.
80. Barr: 100.
81. Colosi and Berkeley: 130.
82. Fossum: 290.
83. Norman Holman, "Collective Bargaining in Public Libraries: Preserving Management Prerogatives," in Critical Issues in Library Personnel Management, edited by Richard Rubin, Urbana, IL.: University of Illinois, 1989: 17.
84. Holman: 5-6.
85. Holman: 9-10.
86. J.Y. Cousins and M.B. McCall, "The Professional Approach to Collective Bargaining," *Management Decision* 24 (1986): 41-44.
87. Cousins and McCall: 41.
88. Colosi and Berkeley: 18-28.
89. Cousins and McCall: 42.

90. R. Theodore Clark, Jr., "The Duty to Bargain," in *Collective Bargaining in Libraries*, edited by Frederick A. Schlipf, University of Illinois, Urbana 1975: 58.
91. Clark: 59.
92. Ohio Revised Code, "Public Employees' Collective Bargaining," Section 4117.08, Subsection C.
93. Howard A. Levy, "Collective Bargaining by a Public Library," Presentation given to the Ohio Library Association, November 3, 1988, Columbus, Ohio.
94. Milton Derber, "Management Organization for Collective Bargaining in the Public Sector," in *Public Sector Bargaining*, edited by Benjamin Aaron, Joyce M. Najita, and James L. Stern, Washington, D.C.: BNA, 1988: 104.
95. Joseph J. Woodford, *Supervisor's Guide to Contract Administration and Grievance Handling*, Crestline, Calif.: Advisory Publishing, 1986: 9.
96. R. Theodore Clark, Jr., *Drafting the Public Sector Labor Agreement*, Chicago: Public Personnel Association, No. 13, 1969: 4-5.
97. Colosi and Berkeley: 90-91.
98. Cousins and McCall: 43-44.
99. Clark, *Drafting...*: 7.
100. Colosi and Berkeley: 140.
101. Clark, *Drafting...*: 7-8.
102. Colosi and Berkeley: 108.
103. Steven C. Kahn, Barbara A. Brown, and Brent E. Zepke, *Personnel Director's Legal Guide*, Boston: Warren, Gorham, and Lamont, 1984: 14-33---14.34.
104. Woodford: 14.
105. Clark, *Drafting...*: 8.
106. Fossum: 285.
107. John J. Lawler, "The Influence of Management Consultants on the Outcome of Union Certification Elections," *Industrial and Labor Relations Review* 38 (October 1984): 49.
108. John P. Bucalo, Jr., "Successful Employee Relations," *Personnel Administrator* 31 (April 1986): 63-64.
109. Francis T. Coleman, "Once a Union, Not Always a Union," *Personnel Journal* 63 (March 1985): 42.

7

Human Factors and Human Performance

There is no more complicated area of managing libraries than dealing with the human forces that affect job performance. Each person is different, and each job entails its own tasks and work environment. In addition, supervisors react uniquely to each employee. Library managers have discovered time and again that there is no simple formula that relieves them of trying to understand employees as people. This is good in one sense, because it forces the manager to treat employees as individuals, but it also makes it hard to create general policies and programs for all employees. It places special and difficult demands on the supervisor to be personally responsive to individual needs. Underlying all the concern for employees must be the fundamental goal of productivity; the manager must ask, "How do I structure the workplace to get the most out of my staff?"

The manager's task is daunting: he or she is expected to stimulate high productivity among the staff while simultaneously maintaining high job satisfaction and morale and keeping turnover, absenteeism, and conflict low. All of this requires an understanding of not one but three fundamental concepts: job satisfaction, human motivation, and job commitment. The job of the library manager would be easier if these concepts had a simple relationship in the workplace: that happy library workers were also productive and committed workers. But this is not the case. Consider for a moment four types of workers:

Type I: The Happy, Motivated, Committed, and
Productive Library Worker
This person is the manager's delight. The worker gets along well with others, loves work, puts in a full day's work (and more), and does all the work well.

Type II: The Happy, but Unmotivated and
Unproductive Library Worker
Some poor workers may be quite happy. For example, the tasks of the
job may be very easy, there may be little supervision, little is expected,
and there may be regular opportunity for the employees to avoid work
by talking to others or taking numerous breaks. In these circumstances,
the employee may be quite happy, but little work is getting done;
productivity and worker satisfaction are unrelated.

Type III: The Unhappy, Productive Library Worker
Sometimes workers do not like their work for a variety of reasons. Maybe
they dislike their supervisor or working conditions. But these workers
may be motivated to be productive for other reasons. They may have a
strong work ethic which motivates them to work even in the absence of
environmental blandishments. Some workers may take an "I'll show
you" attitude in which their anger toward the supervisor, colleagues,
organization, or others, motivates them to perform at high levels. In any
case, a worker can be unhappy, but still be quite productive. Interestingly, there is also some evidence that the unhappy worker may serve
an important role in the productive organization. Individuals with
negative attitudes may be more suitable for certain job situations
requiring critical faculties, while positive work attitudes such as enthusiasm and energy may be appropriate for other types of jobs.[1]

Type IV: The Uncommitted Productive Library Worker
Some workers may have no particular commitment to their job or the
workplace, but they have tremendous talent that allows them to complete tasks successfully with little effort. Such an individual's productivity may be quite high, but commitment is low. Similarly, commitment
can take on many forms. A librarian may be committed to the profession
but uncommitted to a particular organization. The result may be high
productivity to satisfy professional ideals, but a lack of commitment to
the particular library. There is a strong possibility that such an individual may have a good work record but will leave if an opportunity arises
in another library.

In each case, we see the complexity of dealing with people in the
workplace. What is it that the library manager wants—satisfied workers? Motivated workers? Committed workers? Of course, the answer is
all of these. But which is *most* important? If we must sacrifice one for
the other, which do we sacrifice? Sometimes it seems that supervisors
sacrifice productivity for satisfaction; they may allow employees extra
time off, or schedule them at their convenience instead of basing the
schedule on the needs of the library.

The goal of human resource management is fostering productivity, and this should form the underlying rationale for a library's personnel policies and procedures. This responsibility is both political and ethical. Certainly, a productive work force is likely to engender support on the part of the public and this, in turn, improves the chances for the library's prosperity. It is also a civic duty of the library to use its resources wisely; the purpose of public agencies is to serve the people in the most efficient and effective manner.

HUMAN FACTORS THAT INCREASE PRODUCTIVITY

Productivity appears to be mediated by a variety of situational and individual factors including level of intelligence and ability, possession of necessary information to perform the job, budget support, energy level, self-confidence, dependence on the work of others, preparation for the tasks, time available, tools and equipment, and other environmental conditions such as temperature and lighting.[2, 3, 4] Two basic approaches describe how best to increase human performance. One is the dispositionalist approach in which human performance is attributed to personality and genetic factors; the other is the behavioralist/environmentalist approach, in which human performance depends on factors present in the workplace.

The Dispositionalists

The dispositionalists argue that there are certain personality traits consistently associated with high levels of performance. Among them are intellectual ability (such as problem solving skills), socioeconomic status, and level of career aspirations (challenging or unchallenging career goals).[5] This disposition is formed by genetic factors such as intelligence or physical skill, and by personality characteristics that are formed early in life. Longitudinal research has revealed that such dispositions are stable over long periods of time. Indeed, the stability of worker attitudes was found not only over time in the same jobs but also when individuals changed jobs, and even when they changed occupations.[6]

From the dispositionalist's perspective, work redesign and organizational development may not in fact affect employees in the way the programs are intended. Such programs, designed with the purpose of substantially and consistently increasing worker productivity, may not be sufficiently tailored to the personalities of the individuals.[7] Rather, the dispositionalists argue that organizations should be devoting at least as much energy to ensuring the hiring of staff with the appropriate disposition to perform the needed work. This is not to say that motivational programs are useless, only that considerable energy and resources are needed if the powerful dispositional traits of the unproductive worker are to be overcome. Managers, the dispositionalists warn, should not have high expectations for such programs.

The Disposition of Librarians

If the dispositionalists are correct, then personality traits have a substantial effect on worker performance. What then is the disposition of the librarian? The stereotypes of television and literature have not painted an especially positive picture. Bean characterizes this image as "that little old lady with bun and pince-nez glasses who, with rubber stamp in hand, delivers a firm 'shhh' to any and all disturbances in the sanctity of the library."[8] In fact, there has been relatively little research over the years on the personality of librarians. The findings suggest that the overall personality of librarians is "normal," but that certain troubling features do emerge; features that tend to confirm rather than deny the stereotype.

As early as 1948, Bryan, in the *Public Library Inquiry,* attempted to assess the personality of public librarians using a personality inventory. Her conclusion was that both male and female librarians tended to be submissive and lack leadership abilities.[9] Later studies of public and academic librarians as well as library school students have tended to support this picture, describing librarians as lacking in aggressiveness and competitiveness, lacking the desire to lead, make decisions, be autonomous, or exercise initiative. Additional research has also described librarians as self-effacing or abasing, inclined toward nurturance, and resistant to change.[10] The faith one puts in such findings depends on the faith one puts in personality inventories. From the perspective of the human resources manager, one must ask if such individuals are best suited to librarianship. Can individuals who possess these traits be highly motivated and productive for the library? Certainly, there is something attractive about those who tend toward the docile, especially in bureaucracies where following the dictates of the hierarchy is desirable; but, doesn't the modern library need creative, energetic, and active individuals to meet the changing information environment? Doesn't library productivity depend on encouraging individuals with different traits to become part of the profession?

Why would librarianship attract the more submissive individual? To some extent, it must be remembered that career choices are often based on *perceptions* of the career, not necessarily actual experience. Perhaps the powerful stereotype of the librarian attracts submissive individuals. Whether such individuals are best for librarianship is a subject for debate. But it does raise important questions for the library manager. How does one find good people for tasks that require atypical characteristics? If the dispositionalists are at least partially right, then jobs requiring high levels of autonomy, initiative and leadership, such as upper-level management, may require searching from a larger, more varied, labor pool.

The library manager who accepts the dispositionalist position must decide what characteristics are desired for a particular position, and look for those traits in hiring or promoting workers to those positions. That the profession, as a whole, would benefit from having individuals who are dynamic, creative, and forceful cannot be doubted; at the very least, it would help dispel the stereotype that has likely helped to keep the status and pay of librarians low. But this also means that the *jobs* librarians do must in fact demand creative and dynamic people. If they do not, then there will be a mismatch between the disposition of the librarian and the job to be done, which will inevitably cause consternation and turnover. If different dispositions are desired, then recruitment practices must be re-examined. If a library wants energetic people, its recruiting must focus on individuals who demonstrate such characteristics. Given the stereotype of the profession, considerable resources may be needed to accomplish this task.

The Behavioralist/Environmentalists

The position of the behavioralist/environmentalists is that worker attitudes and performance can be affected by structuring the workplace appropriately. It relies primarily on the ability and willingness of the organization to alter the work situation, including the environment, job tasks, and reward systems so that productivity will increase. Despite the arguments of the dispositionalists, there is evidence that situational factors do play a substantial role in job performance.[11] Research on professionals, such as accountants, suggests that in some cases job conditions and competent management, not dispositional variables, have a stronger relationship to performance.

In order to structure the workplace to maximize the employees' productivity, it is vital that managers understand basic psychological and sociological needs of workers. Once the concepts of worker satisfaction, motivation, and commitment are understood, it is possible to identify and design those aspects of the workplace that will have positive effects on work performance.

JOB SATISFACTION

There is evidence, albeit anecdotal, that high worker satisfaction is associated with some of the more productive companies. A study of 100 fast-growing small and midsize companies noted that they were characterized by high levels of satisfaction and motivation among their workers.[12] Unfortunately, the evidence associating job satisfaction with productivity is unconvincing.[13] Does this mean that a discussion of job satisfaction is superfluous? On the contrary, it provides revealing and useful information to the library administrator. No theory concerning the development of productive workers is complete without discussing it.[14]

There are many reasons why the concept of job satisfaction should be considered by library managers. Among them:

- Job satisfaction is often a critical variable in the employee's decision to leave the organization. Job satisfaction is strongly correlated negatively with turnover decisions.[15] The greater the employee's satisfaction, the less the chance the employee will decide to leave. Because of the considerable cost of turnover to any organization, this factor alone would justify concern.

- Job satisfaction or dissatisfaction may reveal organizational deficiencies that can create further problems. For example, studying satisfaction can reveal problems with salary, supervisory or communication styles, or problems with the work environment. Each of these areas can produce corollary legal, health, public relations, and labor relations problems for the employer.

- Employee job satisfaction makes the tasks of the administrator and supervisor easier. If employees are satisfied, there are fewer grievances, or complaints, and less absenteeism. The workplace, which when unpleasant can become a source of stress to all, can also be a place of enjoyment.

- Concern with job satisfaction is ethically right. Even if one cannot establish a clear link between employee satisfaction and worker productivity, it is proper that human beings enjoy their lives. People should be important as people. Hopkins, in her work on job satisfaction in the public sector put it this way:

> Work occupies almost half of the waking hours of most Americans. The quality of life of most workers is dramatically influenced by the nature of that employment. The reactions of workers to their jobs alter their basic self-perceptions and self-esteem. To most individuals, work is one of the key elements of their lives.[16]

It is a troubling finding that the job satisfaction of workers has declined over the years. The most satisfied groups appear to be farmers, professional and technical workers, salespeople, managers and administrators. Some of the least satisfied workers include laborers, clerical, and service workers.[17] The fact that service workers appear to be dissatisfied is troubling because they comprise such a large percentage of the library work force.

The Concept of Job Satisfaction

What do we mean when we use the term *job satisfaction*? In its simplest sense, it is asking the question: "What makes employees happy?" It is important to remember that job satisfaction is an emotional state, rather than an intellectual condition. It is a *feeling* about one's work. There are three ways in which job satisfaction has been regarded in the past. First, satisfaction can be regarded as being part of the job itself. That is, a job is intrinsically satisfying. There is a sense in which we intuitively understand this notion. For example, it may be difficult to consider the tasks of a garbage collector or rest-room attendant as intrinsically satisfying. On the other hand, we may perceive the work of a pediatric surgeon as especially satisfying because of the precious lives that are saved. Second, job satisfaction can be regarded as residing solely within the individual. The tasks of the job are not relevant, only the subjective state of the individual is important. Job satisfaction is an attitude of mind and is not inherent in the specific tasks to be performed. A third view is called the *interactionist* perspective. In this view, job satisfaction arises from the interaction of the job environment with the subjective state of the worker.[18]

In some sense, the interactionist view is a restatement of the observation that people are different, and their reactions to work environments vary. There is little doubt that workers, in fact, place different values on various aspects of work.[19] Jobs that we, as managers, believe should produce satisfaction may not produce such satisfaction in each worker. For example, we may have a position that is challenging, requiring creative thinking, planning, and individual initiative, but the employee filling the position is dissatisfied. It is possible that the worker does not want a challenge or to think creatively; he or she may want unambiguous direction. Similarly, we may have a productive worker who is quite satisfied in one position, but finds that he or she is quite unhappy when changing positions. This may occur when a productive nonsupervisory worker is moved to a supervisory position. Many workers find that supervising people requires certain skills and responsibilities that they can perform only with great stress and personal conflict. The manager must realize that a satisfied worker may become dissatisfied when a change in job occurs. The interactionist view requires us to understand the entire context of the work environment, the person, the tasks, and the organizational environment in which the worker functions.

Defining What a Job Is

Our first notion of a job is often confined to the specific tasks that we perform—the duties described in our job description. But a job is much more complex, and concerns not only the tasks but the social and physical surroundings in which these tasks are performed. A job may be seen as a composite of:

- The tasks of the specific job
- Relations with coworkers
- Relations with subordinates
- Relations with supervisors
- Organizational factors such as pay, benefits, opportunity for promotion, opportunity for decision making
- Relationship with broader professional and social values.

The concept of a job in this more catholic perspective demands greater sensitivity of the manager. When employees indicate that they dislike their job they may be referring to specific job tasks or anxiety about working with a particular colleague, supervisor, or subordinate; or they may be expressing discontent with remuneration, lack of communication, or chance for promotion. Similarly, when they say they are satisfied with a job, they may be expressing a pleasure more with "doing library work" or "helping people," than with anything specifically related to the organization itself.

The challenge to the manager is to assess accurately the expectations, wants, needs, and values of particular employees, and to place them in positions in which they can satisfy those wants while, at the same time, accomplishing the tasks of the job. This challenge becomes even more complex, because the individual must not only have a job that meets his or her wants, needs, and expectations, but must also *perceive* that the job satisfies these requirements. For example, a librarian who wants and *has* good employee benefits may not *perceive* that they are good, and may thus be dissatisfied.

So far, the individual character of job satisfaction has been emphasized. This emphasis may overwhelm the human resource manager, who is seemingly condemned to the infinite diversity of employees. How could it be possible to satisfy all these individuals. Fortunately, it is also possible to identify certain factors that are commonly associated with the production of job satisfaction.

Variables of Job Satisfaction

Many researchers have attempted to identify and define the variables that affect the job satisfaction of workers. Their findings are revealing to the library manager. Dunnette, Campbell, and Hakel, in a study of job satisfaction among six occupational groups (not including librarians), identified a variety of factors that affect the satisfaction of workers:

- Achievement: completing a job successfully
- Recognition: to be singled out
- The work tasks themselves
- The level of responsibility for one's own work or the work of others
- Opportunities for advancement through promotion
- Salary increases
- Changes in the job that enrich personal or professional growth
- Working conditions
- The effect of the job on the employee's personal life
- Increases in status
- Job security
- Interpersonal relations with coworkers, subordinates, and superiors
- Skills of supervisors
- Company policy and administration.[20]

Among these characteristics, six were found to be most important: achievement, responsibility, the work itself, opportunity for advancement, relations with coworkers, and supervision.

Intrinsic and Extrinsic Rewards

The importance of many of these characteristics has been confirmed in numerous studies. One approach in understanding the variables has been to divide them into those that are *intrinsic* rewards, e.g. those that relate directly to the job itself, and those that are *extrinsic*, such as pay and benefits. Research suggests that workers place greatest importance on intrinsic rewards such as the interesting character of the job, challenge, the ability to take responsibility and direct one's own work, variety, creativity, ability to use one's talents, and opportunity for feedback. This suggests that the strongest influences on job satisfaction are meaningful, interesting, and challenging work. This is followed in importance by extrinsic social rewards such as the ability to develop good relationships with coworkers and supervisors and organizational rewards such as pay, promotion, fringe benefits, and job security.[21]

The fact that pay is not considered a primary reward illustrates the complex nature of job satisfaction. The evidence regarding pay and its relationship to job satisfaction is unclear. Perhaps most important is not the absolute value of the pay, but the *perceived* equity or inequity of the pay. Employees who think that their level of remuneration is unfair may become dissatisfied. Employers should therefore keep in mind that there is a distinction between "unfair" and "not enough." Few employees believe that they are being paid as much as they deserve; but this is different from employees who see that others who work less hard or who perform less well are receiving disproportionately higher salaries or merit increments. The level of dissatisfaction will generally be much more intense in the latter case than in the former. This underscores the need not only to have an effective wage and salary compensation system, but also an effective communications system so that employees understand that their pay is adequate and fair.

Despite the overall importance of intrinsic over extrinsic rewards, managers should note that the importance of rewards may vary depending on whether the individual is in a blue-collar or white-collar occupation.[22] In blue-collar occupations, extrinsic organizational rewards such as pay play a significantly greater role in predicting job satisfaction. As tenure in such positions increases, these rewards increase in importance.[23] For this reason, the library manager should consider that the sources of satisfaction for the professional librarian may vary substantially from those of the clerical worker or bookmobile driver.

Occupation may not be the only factor that affects satisfaction on the job. Another factor may involve the career or life cycle stage of the employee. For those in the early stages of careers, satisfaction is related to the need for freedom, participation, self-esteem, and variety; those in the middle stages of their career value professionalism, involvement in their work, collegiality, and high pay; those in the late stages value the ability to serve as mentors.[24] Library managers need to assess the career stages of their employees so that the work environment can be best adapted for increased satisfaction.

Managers should also note that the quality of immediate supervision appears to have substantial impact on job satisfaction. This is logical because workers often find themselves in proximity with the supervisor for a large portion of the workday. Although upper-level administrators may make final decisions regarding an employee's future, it is the immediate supervisor who sets the tone for the department, hires colleagues, and makes work assignments. If, as noted above, job tasks play an important role in job satisfaction, then the supervisor plays a potent role in increasing or decreasing levels of satisfaction. One extensive review of the job satisfaction literature identified immediate supervision as the *most* important single variable in job satisfaction.[25]

Workspace characteristics may also have a significant influence on job satisfaction. Such factors as lighting in the work area, the number of enclosures surrounding employee work areas, the proximity of seating in an office, and the number of employees occupying an office, appear to influence both job satisfaction and turnover.[26] One study suggested that noise and lighting appear to have substantial effects on job satisfaction, although no difference in actual performance could be detected.[27]

Gender and Satisfaction

A question of interest to library managers is the effect of gender on possible differences in job satisfaction. The relationship between gender and job satisfaction has had only limited study. Underlying this question is the suspicion that men and women may differ in their attitude and experience of the work environment. Differences in socialization, marital and family roles, career goals, evaluation of rewards, personal investment in their work, and need for fulfillment through the job may be gender related. Same or similar work circumstances may have different effects on men and women.[28]

Generally, overall levels of job satisfaction are similar for men and women, but some of the factors that are important in producing satisfaction differ. Men tend to place greater importance on external rewards including benefits, pay, job security, opportunity for promotion, and autonomy. Women place greater emphasis on good relations with colleagues, supervisors, and interesting work.[29] This is found to be especially true for workers in blue-collar occupations.[30] Men also place greater importance on their position in the organizational hierarchy than do women,[31] while females find time pressures affect their levels of satisfaction to a greater extent.[32]

The library manager should also be aware that professionally-educated women are especially sensitive to the job components that allow them to express their ability to use the talents they possess. Women who are better educated and work in urban environments are more dissatisfied with their work than their male counterparts. This may be due to the fact that women, like men, aspire to challenging jobs with complex tasks and responsibilities, but are less likely to receive them.[33] The fact that women may experience a substantial amount of underutilization highlights the need for library managers to exploit to the fullest the potential of their female employees. The connection between feeling that one's own abilities are not being used and job dissatisfaction is considerable for both men and women. One major study of job satisfaction among American workers revealed that 36% of the respondents felt that they were underutilized.[34]

Librarians and Job Satisfaction

It is fair for the library manager to ask if the information on job satisfaction in the general labor force can be applied to libraries. One might suspect, for example, that those entering public employment have different concerns or needs than those in the private sector. There is some support for this. For example, publicly employed executives place much greater emphasis on job security, stability, and benefits, as well as the usefulness of their work, than those in the private sector who value the pleasure of the work itself.[35] This suggests that the job values of public employees may be substantially different. Numerous studies of job satisfaction among librarians have been undertaken in the last 20 years. In general, the results from these studies confirm those of the management literature.

Of primary importance to job satisfaction in libraries are aspects of the work itself. D'Elia found that job satisfaction of new librarians is related to job characteristics and to supervisory climate. He noted in particular that satisfaction was related to such factors as ability to achieve, to be creative, to have responsibility, and to be recognized.[36] He surmises that as opportunity for individual initiative and professional judgment increase, satisfaction increases. D'Elia recommends a participatory management style that permits librarians to develop mastery of their own jobs.[37]

Plate and Stone suggest that the factors that create job satisfaction in libraries are different from those that create dissatisfaction. The factors that produced job satisfaction included the job tasks themselves, and the ability to achieve and to be recognized; the factors that were responsible for job dissatisfaction were institutional policies, supervision, and interpersonal relations.[38]

Some library studies have suggested that there may be differences in satisfaction between professional and nonprofessional staff. Lynch and Verdin in their study of academic librarians found that different aspects of the work environment affect professionals and nonprofessionals. For example, job satisfaction among professionals was significantly correlated with their supervisory level, and the strength of their commitment to continue working in the library. The higher the supervisory level and the stronger the commitment, the greater the satisfaction. Among nonprofessionals, job satisfaction was correlated with age and job tenure, the youngest being the least satisfied.[39] The fact that tenure and age are related to satisfaction suggests that younger workers, professional or nonprofessional, may not be getting the challenge needed to keep them happy. Scamell and Stead have observed that the relationship between age, tenure, and job satisfaction is complex. They found that older librarians experienced greater dissatisfaction with supervision, and younger librarians experienced greater dissatisfaction with pay.[40]

Limited attention has been focused on departmental differences in job satisfaction and the evidence for such differences is inconclusive. Lynch and Verdin found that those working in academic reference departments had higher levels of satisfaction than those working in most other departments, especially among nonprofessionals.[41] In a related study, D'Elia found that different types of librarians are affected by different factors. For example, school librarians appear to get greater satisfaction from the ability to be creative, technical services librarians place more importance on having autonomy in their jobs, and public service librarians on performing service.[42] Chwe, in a study of job satisfaction among reference librarians and catalogers, found no overall differences in job satisfaction, although like D'Elia, he found a higher need for creativity, social service, and variety among reference librarians.[43] Vaughn and Dunn found no differences in job satisfaction among academic library departments on five dimensions of supervision, pay, work, people, and promotion.[44]

Marchant, in a study of job satisfaction in academic libraries, found that administrators using a participatory management style tended to have staff with higher job satisfaction. Marchant asserted a relationship between satisfaction, participation, and productivity; that libraries in which employees were involved in management, had more satisfied employees, and actually provided better service.[45] He noted that the major factors that produced job satisfaction were the assigned duties of the job, supervisory relations, opportunities for salary increases, and relations with clients.[46] This link between satisfaction and participation is consistent with other research; however, the assertion that greater productivity resulted is problematic. Attempts, for example, to replicate the model of productivity and satisfaction used by Marchant, were unsuccessful in at least one follow-up study.[47]

Another area that has received limited attention has been the relationship of role ambiguity and role conflict to job satisfaction in libraries. Role ambiguity develops when employees are unclear as to their job responsibilities; role conflict develops when an individual's job involves incompatible tasks. Stead and Scamell found that both role ambiguity and role conflict are significantly related to overall levels of job satisfaction in libraries. They suggest that managers need to make departmental and organizational objectives more clear, and to be more precise about how librarians can fulfill these objectives.[48]

Gender and Job Satisfaction in Libraries

In general, the evidence in the library literature indicates that there is no difference in the levels of job satisfaction between men and women.[49-52] However, Wahba did find both lower levels of satisfaction among females, and differences in the factors that affect satisfaction. Among academic librarians, Wahba found that women had generally lower levels of satisfaction than men. Men and women attached equal significance to such factors as security, social relations, and need for self-esteem, but women had less need for autonomy and self-actualization.[53] Wabha attributes this to the prevailing social mores which emphasize male dominance. In another study, Rockman found that female faculty members and librarians experience less satisfaction than male librarians. Rockman also found that different factors may affect satisfaction among males and females; males place stronger emphasis on autonomy than females, while females place greater emphasis on decision-making opportunities.[54] Despite these findings, there is insufficient information to conclude that there are substantial gender differences in job satisfaction among librarians.

WORKER MOTIVATION

If a perusal of American popular magazines and newspapers is any measure, Americans are deeply concerned that our business and industrial sector is falling behind those of other countries; that the American worker is far less productive than in the past. Our workers, it is said, are more concerned with salaries and benefits, which increase labor costs, than they are with producing sufficient quantities of high-quality products. Certainly, workers have expressed declining satisfaction with their work in such areas as challenge, financial reward, and comfort.[55] But it is unclear whether the jobs themselves have changed for the worse, or whether American workers have come to expect more and more from their employers. Whatever the case, library managers must be concerned about hiring and retaining motivated workers. This is especially true because, as a group, service workers seem to have less job satisfaction than many other job categories.[56]

It is important to distinguish motivation from satisfaction. Satisfaction involves an emotional evaluation of the employee's job. Motivation tells us how *hard* the employee is willing to work. Measuring satisfaction tells us whether employees like or dislike their jobs. Motivation involves the employees' desire to do something. From the manager's perspective, that "something" is to perform the tasks of a job.

Characteristics of Motivation

Employers want motivated workers, but what does this mean? Maehr and Braskamp note that there are several characteristics that motivated workers demonstrate when they work.[57] These include:

1. Direction
Employees are motivated to do many things; motivation can, to some extent, be assessed by what choices employees make. If an employee chooses librarianship over teaching, then it is likely the individual has a stronger motivation to do library work. If an employee chooses to stand at the water cooler rather than work at the reference desk, then the lack of motivation for library work is similarly evident.

2. Persistence

A motivated worker will spend more time on a task than one with less motivation. In library work it is easy to find examples of the highly motivated, persistent librarian. One need only think of the reference librarian who, in response to a reference question, may spend hours seeking the answer.

3. Continuing Motivation

A motivated worker will return to a task even after interruptions. Children's librarians often demonstrate continuing motivation. These highly motivated professionals, even after a full day's work, spend their evenings making additional preparations. Such examples are also common among library managers and directors whose dedication often exceeds the normal bounds of the workday.

4. Intensity

Motivated workers are more likely to work intensely; their concentration will be focused, less subject to distraction, and their energies will be specifically directed to the job tasks. Such workers may appear constantly busy.

5. Performance

There are, of course, other reasons why an employee performs well even when motivation is not present. But good performance may also be an exhibition of high motivation. An employee who is directed toward work, persistent, intense, and willing to work during nonwork hours is more likely to be a good performer.

THEORIES OF MOTIVATION

Maslow's Hierarchy of Needs

Perhaps the best known and most often cited theory of motivation is based on the work of Abraham Maslow. Maslow argued that the basis of human motivation is the satisfaction of certain human needs and that these needs are arranged in a hierarchical order. The individual works to satisfy the most basic needs first, and once satisfied, would move to the next level of need. The hierarchy consisted of the following, from lowest to highest:

- Physiological needs: the need for food, clothing, shelter
- Safety needs: the need to be protected from bodily harm or threatening conditions
- Social needs: the need for love, affection, the need to belong

- Esteem needs: the need for self-esteem or self-respect; the need to have status and recognition from others
- Self-Actualization: the need for self-fulfillment, to be creative and at peace with oneself.[58]

The influence of Maslow's hierarchy is considerable both in the management and library literature. Unfortunately, evidence supporting the hierarchical relationship of needs has not been forthcoming. There is general support for the view that basic physiological and security needs must be satisfied in order for the individual to seek higher-order needs, but there is little evidence that a hierarchical relationship exists above basic security needs. Rather, it is postulated that higher-order needs occur simultaneously.[59] This is not to say that Maslow's hierarchy is not helpful in understanding human motivation. It is clear, for example, that library management must first provide a work situation that pays sufficiently to provide adequate food, clothing, and shelter, and to provide safe and secure working conditions. Attempts to stimulate motivation through other means without satisfying these basic conditions are bound to fail. But it is also clear that management cannot concentrate on only one need at any given time; the complex nature of human beings demands that many factors be considered simultaneously if the manager is to create the greatest amount of motivation.

Hertzberg's Hygiene-Motivator Theory

Frederick Hertzberg proposed that the factors that produce satisfaction and positive motivation to work are separate and distinct from those that cause dissatisfaction in the worker. This is called a dual-factor view. It implies that the opposite of job satisfaction is not job *dis*satisfaction, but no job satisfaction; the opposite of job dissatisfaction is not job satisfaction but no dissatisfaction.

Hertzberg's studies revealed that the motivator factors, those that created satisfaction and motivation, involved characteristics related to the work itself. These included the job tasks, opportunities for achievement, recognition, responsibility, and for growth and advancement. On the other hand, different factors, which he called hygiene factors, were found to be external to the job tasks, and were the causes of job *dis*satisfaction. These included company policies and administration, supervision, interpersonal relations, salary, status, security, and working conditions.[60] The implications for Hertzberg were that if an organization wanted to motivate its workers, it must focus on those factors that produce satisfaction (motivators), rather than emphasize aspects that produce dissatisfaction (hygiene factors). This would involve enriching the worker's job by increasing opportunities to work with few controls, to exercise greater responsibility and authority, to encourage the developing mastery over one's work, and to provide increasingly difficult and challenging tasks.[61] In this view, the use of traditional motivators such as increased wages would not produce motivation or satisfaction, although they might *reduce dissatisfaction*.[62]

Although Hertzberg's theory, like Maslow's, has provided tremendous stimulus for further research, convincing evidence to support it has not been forthcoming.[63] A particularly weak aspect of the theory is that it does not take into account how individual characteristics of the worker interact with the many variables affecting work attitude and performance. Some employees might be motivated by "hygiene" factors. Pay may motivate some individuals, while for others, recognition or increased responsibility might motivate. Nonetheless, Hertzberg's model again reminds us of the complexity of human motivation and the variety of factors that affect work attitudes.

McClelland's Achievement and Power Motivation

Another model of motivation was developed by McClelland beginning in the 1940s, and popularized in the 1960s. McClelland's particular interest in motivation was cross-cultural, anticipating today's preoccupation with the economic competition created by foreign countries. Among the questions he asked was why do certain countries have slower or faster economic growth than others; what accounts for entrepreneurial growth in one country but not another?[64] McClelland was interested in determining if there were common motivating factors for high performance among different cultures and among different individuals. His work revealed that individuals differed in the extent to which they valued three needs: the need to achieve, the need for power, and the need to affiliate. Achievement was defined as the attainment of moderately difficult goals; power as the ability to influence others or activities in the organization, and affiliation as the need to maintain friendships and be liked by others. McClelland found, for example, that successful entrepreneurial business managers exhibited higher levels of achievement motivation. Such individuals were motivated by the achievement of challenging goals.

Among the characteristics of individuals motivated by achievement were:

- They like to take personal responsibility for finding solutions to problems and they welcome challenging positions that test their skill and ability
- They like to set moderate goals and are willing to take risks
- They have a strong desire to know exactly how they are doing by clear feedback.[65]

For McClelland, the fact that achievement motivation was closely correlated to business success underlined the need to hire individuals with strong achievement motivation and to develop programs that might stimulate such motivations in others.

Although achievement motivation was found to be of considerable importance in a productive organization, McClelland also found that the need for power was a substantial motivator for critical individuals. In fact, McClelland discovered that the independent spirit that characterized the person motivated by achievement was not the best quality if the individual needed to supervise others or lead the organization. While achievement-motivated individuals tended to concentrate on themselves and their own needs, power motivated individuals wished to influence the behavior of others for the good of the organization. These individuals were found to be the most successful top level managers.[66] This is not surprising. Many hard working individuals who like challenging tasks (achievement-oriented) are not necessarily good managers. The good manager, according to McClelland, was an individual who gave subordinates their own feeling of responsibility and who organized and rewarded subordinates in such a way that they performed better.[67] These managers wanted the power to influence others; their effectiveness was based on building team spirit and commitment to organizational goals, not on a dictatorial approach or self-aggrandizement.

Interestingly, the individuals motivated by power were not necessarily interested in being liked by their staffs. McClelland found only a small percentage of the successful "power" individuals had a strong need for maintaining friendships.[68] In fact, managers who were motivated by the need to be liked (affiliation motivation) were found to have subordinates who took little responsibility and who took little pride in their work.[69] This does not mean that power motivated individuals can or should be *disliked* by their staffs to be effective; only that they do not exhibit a high need for friendships.

The implications of McClelland's work for library managers are significant. Different types of individuals are required for different positions. Individuals motivated by achievement may be best at jobs that require clear tasks and goals, where autonomy, recognition, and challenge can be provided. Evidence in the library literature is that librarians, as a group, value challenge, recognition, and autonomy, and there are many appropriate library positions for such individuals, professional and otherwise. However, for positions requiring strong leadership and supervisory skills, a different type of individual should be sought: one who is motivated by the need to influence people and events, rather than to accomplish tasks. The error of promoting an achievement motivated individual into supervisory or leadership roles occurs all too frequently in libraries, e.g. the expert reference librarian promoted to department head. McClelland's model helps explain why such individuals often have difficulty in their new positions.

Goal-Based Motivation

Goal-based motivation, whose chief proponent is Edwin Locke, contends that increases in motivation can be accomplished through goal-setting. It is a promising theory which appears to have considerable support in the research. Locke contends that motivation increases if specific, challenging, and difficult goals are established for workers. Over 100 experimental studies have been conducted to test this view.[70] As a result of these studies, Locke and Latham estimate that the average increase in performance attributed to goal-setting is 17%.[71]

Although most studies of goal-based motivation have been of workers who perform repetitive tasks, the results have been consistent. Workers who were assigned hard goals generally did better than those who were assigned moderate to easy goals. Similarly, workers who were given specific goals that challenged their ability, performed better than those who were given vague goals, such as "do your best."[72]

Interestingly, even some of the commonly accepted motivators were found to be mediated by goal setting. For example, pay was found to be a motivator only if the reward was associated with the attainment of specific goals.[73] A similar finding was made concerning participative goal setting. Participation was found to increase motivation only when the participation resulted in the setting of more difficult goals.[74] Locke has noted that it is not *how* a goal is set that is important, rather it is *that* a goal is set.[75] Setting the right goal is critical. The goal must be difficult, but it must also be perceived as attainable by the employee. Difficulty can be understood from several perspectives. A task can be difficult because it requires special skills, or because the time to accomplish it has been shortened. Similarly, the difficulty can be affected by increasing the amount of work to be accomplished. Not only must the goal be difficult, it must also be clear so the employee knows exactly what is expected. Goal clarity is not, in itself, enough to increase performance, but it is a necessary element. Having clear goals helps reduce the number of extraneous activities that employees might undertake because they did not understand what task was to be accomplished.[76] Finally, it is best that a goal is measurable so that its attainment can be easily ascertained by the employee. When the employee realizes that the goal has been met, it automatically provides needed feelings of accomplishment.[77]

If goal setting is to be successful, certain other factors must also exist in the workplace. Of special importance is the need for commitment to the goals on the part of the workers. If commitment is not present, the motivation to obtain difficult goals is seriously impaired.[78] Goal commitment can also be enhanced by increasing the degree of participation on the part of the employees in goal-setting. Participation in goal-setting appears to be most important for relatively unskilled and uneducated workers, more so than educated workers, because it gives them a degree of control over their work situation which they seldom experience otherwise.[79] These factors underscore the importance of the supervisor in the goal-setting process. Regardless of whether a goal is set jointly, or stipulated by the supervisor, the supervisor must be seen as trying to help the employee attain the goal rather than using it as a basis for judgment or criticism.

Worker Commitment

The need to build goal commitment highlights the more general issue of worker commitment to the organization as a whole. As an employer, it is certainly beneficial to have satisfied and motivated employees; but it is especially important that such employees be committed to your particular institution. Workers who do not develop a bond with the organization may end up going elsewhere to make their contribution. To the extent an employee loses commitment, the library may become the victim of unproductive behaviors known as withdrawal behaviors. These behaviors involve attempts by employees to avoid the workplace either physically or emotionally and include absenteeism, tardiness, laziness, sabotage, and employee turnover. Of course, the organization should not try to maintain commitment from all its workers. It may be desirable that some workers, especially those who are unproductive, experience little commitment. The organizational structure must be designed to strengthen the bonds with good workers, and weaken the bonds with poor ones.

As with the concepts of satisfaction and motivation, defining commitment is not easy. Mowday, Porter and Steers, in reviewing definitions of worker commitment, identified three chief characteristics. A worker is committed to the extent that he or she endorses and feels attached to the goals and values of the organization; desires to work hard for the organization; and feels a strong desire to remain with the organization.[80]

Greater employee commitment is required in certain types of organizations. These are organizations where:

- Quality of work is critical, especially service jobs
- There are positions that are not easily replaced
- There are positions that are not easily supervised
- There are positions where public contact is required
- There is an environment in which change and uncertainty are commonplace.[81]

It is obvious that almost all the members of a public library staff satisfy these criteria. All or most library staff are in service positions and are in contact with the public; many library positions have limited direct supervision; and many are exposed to major technological innovations on a regular basis. Commitment is, therefore, a vital aspect of the library workplace.

Characteristics that Build Commitment

A variety of characteristics have generally been associated with increasing or lessening job commitment. Organizations need to build commitment beginning with the first contacts with a prospective employee, and continuing over the employee's career. Employees tend to pass through various career stages if they remain with an organization and the factors that influence their desire to stay or leave change. Consider how commitment factors change over the following stages:

Pre-Entry Stage
This stage occurs before the employee actually enters the organization. At this point, the employee's level of commitment may be extremely high. He or she can be very excited about coming to work, has high expectations for success, and is probably unaware of the negative aspects of the workplace. The factors that affect early commitment may include treatment during the interviews, initial phone or written contacts, first contacts with staff members and the supervisor. If the employee is coming to work for an organization that performs a service valued by the employee (this is certainly true of many library workers), then commitment may also be based on the employee's perception of the worthiness of the job itself. Because early commitment is based on little actual knowledge of the realities of the particular workplace, the level of commitment is fragile and may be significantly and adversely affected by a small number of negative experiences.

Entry or Initiation Stage
Once the employee begins work, the factors that affect commitment are early contacts with fellow workers and supervisor, adequacy of training and orientation, and the tasks of the job itself. Employees expect and desire interesting, challenging work at this stage; they want a chance to participate, to be free from the tethers of bureaucracy, and to find a place in the organization.[82] The first year of service is a critical time in building commitment. Employees who experience dissatisfaction early in their employment have little to lose in changing jobs; they are yet to be tied down by friends and pensions. Some studies have found that

more than 40% of voluntary turnovers occur in the first year of service.[83] Rubin, in a study of employee turnover of full-time public librarians found that 25% of the turnovers occurred in the first three years of service.[84]

Career-Development Stage

Once employees have become oriented to the organization, they enter the career-development stage. In this stage there is high commitment to their profession and the development of their professional reputation. Such individuals are likely to work long hours, value their work groups, and desire high pay and autonomy.[85] Promotion and professional participation in national or state organizations are valued. Sustaining commitment may require the organization to offer opportunities for professional growth through attendance at conferences or training programs. It should reward high performance through merit pay, and should allow the individual professional autonomy unfettered by close supervision. Similarly, because this stage is vulnerable to burnout due to overwork, the organization should respond to evidence that the employee is under too much strain.

Entrenchment Stage

At this stage, the employee has been working for years. To some extent, although the employee may have a strong attachment to the library, it is not professional growth or aspiration that is the source of this commitment. Rather, such factors as the building of a social network of friends and colleagues may link them to the organization; retirement plans and a high salary may also make looking for other jobs undesirable. Generally, these factors may be such powerful incentives to stay, that the employer need do little to retain them. By the same token, such factors do not necessarily lead to greater productivity. The organization should always be looking for opportunities to use the talent and experience of such individuals. Consider, for example, using entrenched employees as mentors. This would provide useful knowledge to those in earlier career stages, and provide increased self-esteem and importance to entrenched workers who may feel that the knowledge which they have acquired over the years is a valuable untapped resource.[86]

DESIGNING A PRODUCTIVE WORK ENVIRONMENT

The three concepts of satisfaction, motivation, and job commitment play a vital role in the health of any organization. All three concepts must be dealt with simultaneously if high-quality productivity is to be accomplished.[87] In this light, how does the library manager design the workplace to maintain and increase productivity?

Job Redesign

Perhaps the most influential organizational approach is job redesign. Job redesign presupposes that the work must provide three basic needs to the worker, it must fulfill:

- the need to have meaningful work
- the need to feel responsible for the product of the work
- the need to get feedback concerning the results of their work.[88]

Meaningfulness is provided by assigning jobs that require a variety of skills and talents, that can be perceived by the employee as an identifiable unit, and that can be perceived by the employee as having a significant impact on the organization and on people. *Responsibility* is felt by the degree to which the employee is free to control the work. This includes control over scheduling, and the manner by which tasks are completed. *Feedback* is the amount of information the employee gets about the level of work performance from the job itself.[89] This is distinct from feedback from the supervisor and is derived from getting direct information from the individual served. In the case of a library, a reference librarian gets direct feedback when a patron tells the librarian that they are pleased with the information received.

There are two basic ways in which a job can be redesigned: *job enlargement* involves "horizontally" increasing the number and variety of tasks; *job enrichment* involves expanding the job "vertically" by increasing the employees' participation in management activities such as planning and controlling their own work.[90] Hertzberg emphasizes job enrichment rather than job enlargement to motivate workers through work redesign. This includes removing some managerial controls over the employee, thus increasing the employee's sense of responsibility and achievement; putting a person in charge of a complete unit of work which increases his or her sense of responsibility; granting the employee additional authority; allowing the worker to make reports to other workers thus increasing levels of recognition; and assigning increasingly difficult tasks that require specialization so that the employee becomes an expert.[91] This last suggestion is an especially notable one for libraries given their increasing reliance on automation, and the opportunity of both professional and support staff to develop special expertise in various technologies.

Of course, as with all motivational strategies, there is a complex interaction between worker and work environment. Although the basic principles of work redesign are useful, some employees may not respond as hoped. Some employees have a greater need for recognition, autonomy, responsibility, and feedback from the job than others. Individuals with a stronger need for growth are liable to respond more positively to work enrichment than those who feel little need to grow.[92]

Mentoring

Enriching employees' jobs may also occur by creating a supportive environment in which they can learn and grow professionally. Mentoring programs are designed particularly for new entrants, or those aspiring to administrative or directorial positions. Mentoring is a process in which experienced managers (mentors) give less experienced individuals (proteges) the benefit of their knowledge and influence in the organization. The mentor serves many roles including teacher, counselor, master, supporter, coach, boss, and sponsor.

From a sociological perspective, mentoring is very important because it provides employees with role models. Often, the mentor-protege relationship is an informal one; a manager and an employee develop a strong bond through common interests or values. Because few libraries have developed formal mentorship programs, almost all mentorship in the profession is done informally. In the private sector, however, there has been concerted effort to develop formal mentoring programs.

There are many advantages to mentoring. For the protege, it provides an opportunity to increase self-confidence, to learn how the organization functions, to make important contacts with other individuals of influence, and to increase opportunities for promotion. Research suggests that most successful male executives owe at least some of their success to a mentor who guided their career.[93] Similarly many top level women managers had at least one mentor in their careers who was vital to their success.[94, 95] Mentoring also has its advantage to the mentor. It satisfies and confirms that the mentor's knowledge and experience is valuable, and it provides new opportunities for challenge as the mentor takes on a new role.[96] In addition, the organization benefits because of the increased skills the protege receives, and the more efficient use of talent among older workers.

Historically, mentoring has been problematical for women for at least two reasons: first, there are fewer women managers who can serve as role models for other women; second, men who have the potential to serve as mentors may be reluctant to sponsor female proteges because the relationship might seem to be more than just professional. Fortunately, although men still occupy a disproportionate number of managerial positions, there are now substantial numbers of female library managers capable of serving as mentors.

If a library decides to develop a mentoring program several factors should be kept in mind regarding both the mentor and the protege:

- *Age*: Generally, the mentor should be older and possess considerable experience. However, the age gap should not be too great, perhaps 8 to 15 years.[97]
- *Success*: The mentor should be successful in his or her field. There is little reason to assign proteges to individuals who are not competent role models. The protege should be an individual who has demonstrated or who has the capacity to demonstrate high performance.
- *Gender*: Mentor and protege should be of the same sex if possible. This decreases the possibility of sexual relationships developing and diminishes the chance that stereotypes will be imposed in the relationship.
- *Power*: The mentor should be highly placed in the organization and proteges should be secure enough not to be threatened by the success of the mentor.[98]
- *Performance*: The protege should be an employee who has demonstrated high performance or the capacity for such performance. Noe suggests that the best proteges are those who believe that their success will depend on their own performance.[99]

Employers who decide to implement a mentoring program must realize that the mentoring process is a dynamic one. As the protege matures, the relationship passes through several stages. Kram has identified four stages:[100]

- *Initiation stage*: The initiation stage usually involves the first 6 to 12 months. This period is characterized by the protege's admiration and respect for the mentor. The relationship is characterized by support.
- *Cultivation stage*: This stage occurs for approximately 2 to 5 years. The mentor provides the greatest benefit during this period as he or she helps develop the protege's career, sponsoring the employee for promotions, providing challenges on the job, and protecting the employee from those who might try to damage the protege's career.
- *Separation stage*: This is a stage in which a new equilibrium is established. The protege begins to develop both a psychological, professional and, in some cases, geographical independence. This can cause strains on the mentor as the dependency of the protege is significantly diminished. The mentor may even feel threatened by the increasing success of the protege. In rare cases, the mentor may begin to block promotional opportunities of the protege.
- *Redefinition stage*: If the mentoring has been successful, this stage leads the mentor and protege to see each other as equals. It may take some time before both are comfortable in the peer relationship that develops. Often this leads to a strong friendship. In some cases, the redefined relationship is not positive. The protege may feel estranged from the mentor and anger and hostility may result.

Although mentoring can be an extremely beneficial process, it is clear from the above discussion that there are several potential pitfalls as well. Among the areas the employer must monitor are the following:

1. Ensure that eligibility for mentoring programs is based on objective criteria. Because a disproportionate number of administrative and managerial positions are held by males, employers should be scrupulous about avoiding an "old boys network" when offering opportunities for mentorships. In addition, opportunities for mentoring should not be based on pre-established friendships or family relationships.
2. Attempt to assign mentors to individuals with complementary personalities. Mentoring requires the development of close bonds and loyalties; individuals who are not compatible are likely to develop destructive relationships.
3. The responsibilities of the protege should be substantial. Mentors should not be permitted to use employees as errand runners, to fill in for vacant positions, or to perform busy-work. The purpose of mentoring is to develop and train the employee.
4. Mentors should be selected for their knowledge, managerial, and interpersonal skills. Individuals who are inclined to punish, to be possessive, or to be dictatorial should be avoided.
5. Cross-gender mentorships, usually male mentors and female proteges, should be avoided if possible. As noted above, successful mentor relationships involve the development of emotional as well as professional bonds. The possibility that such relationships could lead to romantic entanglements, or the perception of such entanglements, could create serious problems. This is not to say that cross-gender mentorships should be prohibited; they may be necessary in many libraries. Nonetheless, employers should be aware of the special problems. If a male-female mentorship is involved, several steps can be taken to diminish potential problems. First, the mentor should provide opportunities for other managers to observe the performance of the protege, and to work with her. If the mentor subsequently recommends promotion for the protege, others will have observed the quality of the protege's performance themselves. This lessens the possibility that the mentor's recommendation will be perceived as based on sexual, rather than professional reasons. Second, discourage after-hours, or extended, or unscheduled private meetings that provide fodder for inappropriate speculation by others. Third, avoid pet expressions, names, or inside jokes signifying a more-than-professional relationship. Fourth, avoid touching, hugging, or other forms of intimacy with the protege. Although these actions may be perfectly innocent, it jeopardizes the perceived objectivity of the mentor and the abilities of the protege.[101]

Despite the pitfalls of mentoring, there is little doubt that it offers one of the best opportunities for employees to develop the necessary contacts and skills for career development. As such, library managers should seriously consider developing such programs, and encouraging informal mentoring in their absence.

Job Sharing

Although traditional approaches to job enrichment imply an expansion of job responsibilities, another recent trend has been to staff a full-time position with two employees who share the responsibilities of the job. This is referred to as job sharing. Job sharing is actually not a new idea. It was popularized in the 1930s during the Great Depression when reducing the work week was proposed as a less draconian alternative to eliminating workers.[102] Today, different factors have precipitated interest in job sharing. These factors often revolve around female employees who are the most frequent participants in job sharing. Among the factors involved are:

- The increasing numbers of women in the workplace.
- The need for women to balance family responsibilities with work requiring more flexible, part-time employment.
- The need for female professionals who temporarily leave the work force, often for family reasons, to reenter the work force. This reentry is stimulated by a desire to maintain professional contact, and a feeling of accomplishment. Often this reentry is gradual and requires part-time employment for extended periods.
- The need to overcome the social stigma of staying at home, which many professional women experience.[103]

Other factors are also at work stimulating interest in job sharing. The post-World War II baby boom produced a large number of workers who must be absorbed by a relatively sluggish economy. Under these circumstances, job sharing provides one, albeit small, means of alleviating the problem of unemployment by increasing the size of an organization's work force. In addition, with federal legislation protecting older workers from forced retirement, there is an increasing trend for older workers to remain in the workplace. Job sharing can provide a transition for the older employee who has worked full-time for many years, to make the transition out of the work force, while simultaneously serving as a trainer or mentor to the individual sharing the job.[104]

There are advantages to work sharing for both employee and employer. For employees, especially women, the flexibility of part-time employment enhances their ability to harmonize the responsibilities of family and professional life. The benefits for the employer can also be considerable. They include lower employee turnover, better employee morale, improved ability to provide a substitute when one employee is absent, higher productivity, reductions in stress, and a larger pool of employees from which to draw for promotions.[105, 106]

There are potential disadvantages to job sharing as well. These include increased administrative and training costs, and increased costs for benefits such as Social Security and worker compensation.[107] The employees involved in job sharing may also experience negative effects. Employees who share a job often find that they have difficulty maintaining adequate organizational communication. In addition they may experience jealousy from other colleagues, or perceive that they are not being treated as equals.[108] Finally, if the partners are mismatched, the resulting personality and work conflicts can produce serious problems.

Developing a Job Sharing Policy

Job sharing policies should be carefully written to ensure that participants understand their obligations. A policy should at least include:

- A statement defining job sharing, which might also include the philosophy of the organization toward job sharing.
- Identification of who is eligible to apply for job sharing, and what types of positions can be shared. For example, supervisory positions should not, in general, be considered for job sharing. In addition, information on how pairs are assigned should be provided. For example, are pair assignments based on the preferences of the employee or the employer. Because of the critical need for teamwork, employee preferences should generally be respected.
- Procedures for applying for job sharing. This may involve determining whether two individuals must apply together as a team.
- Information on scheduling. This should include an estimate of the total number of hours to be worked by each participant, whether overlap is required so that communication can occur between the job sharers. In addition, the policy might include information on how the various responsibilities of the job are divided.
- Statement on wages benefits. The policy should indicate how the wage and fringe benefits are determined. Generally, fringe benefits should be prorated including sick and vacation time. Job sharers should, when feasible, also be entitled to enroll in the health and life insurance programs.
- Statement on employee evaluations. The policy should indicate how performance evaluations should be conducted; whether the employees are evaluated as a team or as individuals. In general, performance should be evaluated individually, but with special attention on the ability of the team members to effectively coordinate their activities.
- Statement on resignation and termination. The policy should indicate how one person resigns from a job sharing position, and what happens if one member of the team resigns. When a resignation occurs, there are two options, either allow the remaining employee to fill the position in a full-time capacity, or fill the open position with another employee.

Of course, the greatest difficulty arises, if the remaining employee does not wish a full-time position and the part-time vacancy has no qualified applicants. The employer's policy should state clearly that the library has the right to terminate the job sharing arrangement with proper notice. In order to assure clarity on these important matters, some organizations obtain a signed agreement with the job sharing team, indicating the terms and conditions of the job sharing program.

Despite the potential pitfalls of job sharing, it could have substantial advantages for libraries. This is especially true because of the largely female work force whose talents are best harnessed when the workplace can adapt to the conflicting demands of family and profession. The flexible scheduling provided in job sharing would seem to be a logical alternative.

Quality of Work-Life

Another application of job enrichment principles is through attention to a worker's quality of work life (QWL). Martell has developed this concept for libraries. Citing the work of Levine, Taylor and Davis, Martell identifies the factors that define an employee's QWL. These include:

* The manner in which employees are treated by supervisors
* The degree to which job variety, challenge, and self-esteem are present
* The extent to which the present job provides future opportunities
* The relationship of outside life to current work
* The degree to which the work contributes to society.[109]

Martell argues that there is a direct relationship between the quality of work life in a library and the employees' performance, and he expresses concern that the quality of work life in libraries does not promote peak performance.[110] Martell notes that present day libraries are structured to centralize managerial authority and decision making and cannot respond quickly and effectively to user needs. Librarians must have an organizational structure that places more responsibility and decision-making power on the librarians in contact with the patron.[111] This in effect, decreases centralized administrative control and increases participatory decision making. In terms of job tasks, the results would be consistent with job enrichment strategies that increase responsibility, autonomy, and meaningfulness of the work for librarians. Martell refers to the transformed library organizational structure as the "Client-Centered" organization. Such an organization, when properly run, places greater emphasis on teamwork, productivity, autonomy, results, hard work, competition, and productivity.[112]

The emphasis that Martell places on organizational restructuring is only one of several approaches that could enrich and therefore motivate workers, but it is one of the few systematic analyses of the library workplace and worker productivity. The message is clear that the overall climate in which library employees work is important. Whether restructuring the organization would actually increase library productivity is an unanswered question; there is no substantive research in libraries on this issue.

Stress

The subject of stress in the library workplace is another major environmental issue for librarians. If the number of articles is any measure of the significance of a problem, stress is a serious problem in librarianship. Stress and its most negative effect, burnout, have been the subject of considerable discussion in the library literature. Particular attention has been focused on library workers who deal with the public, especially reference librarians. Of course, stress itself is not necessarily bad. In its simplest sense, stress is simply any demand on the person; any time an individual needs to adapt to an environmental circumstance, stress is created. Anything in the environment that creates stress is called a stressor. The effect of stressors can be quite constructive, for example, when an individual is challenged and excited by a new job assignment, then the stress that is created is positive. Indeed, the relationship of productivity and stress is shaped like an inverted "U"; that is, too little stress leads to a lackadaisical attitude; too much stress leads to anxiety or depression. Moderate levels tend to stimulate peak performances.[113]

There may also be gender-related issues in regard to stress. For example, the clash of family and work roles may produce stress. The female who feels that she must succeed both at work and at home may place herself at considerable risk of burnout.[114] Other gender-related sources of stress may arise from segregating females into certain jobs, job discrimination, and hormonal imbalances which produce mood changes.[115]

When environmental demands create negative effects on the individual, then the individual experiences *dis*tress. The symptoms of distress are many and varied. They include:

- Feelings of helplessness
- Short-temper and irritation with simple problems
- Anxiety
- Increased physical complaints
- Lack of energy
- Inability to concentrate
- Resistance to change.

These symptoms often have negative outcomes including job dissatisfaction, increased absenteeism and turnover, lowered productivity, susceptibility to error and accidents, lowered morale, and increased levels of conflict among employees.

When the symptoms and effects of stress become severe then the individual is said to be suffering from burnout. The symptoms of burnout are simply extensions of the general symptoms of stress. They include mental and physical exhaustion, physical or emotional withdrawal from work, serious depression, apathy, boredom, rigidity, and inflexibility.[116] Generally, distress passes through several stages before actual burnout develops.

Sources of Stress in Libraries

The sources of stress in the library work environment are many and varied. Bunge, in a study of librarians and support staff identified numerous areas of concern. Overall, the greatest source of stress was patrons. This was followed by excessive workloads, inadequate supervisors or managers, unpredictable and unrealistic work schedules, lack of positive feedback from supervisors, the public, or the organization, and incompetent or difficult coworkers. Interestingly, Bunge noted that the sources of stress were similar to the factors identified by librarians as the sources of satisfaction as well (e.g. patrons!).[117] This is not surprising. Public librarians place great importance on public service, therefore, positive responses from the public should be quite edifying; conversely if public contacts are negative, then significant dissatisfaction is likely to result.

Although many sources of stress are the same for all library staff, Bunge's analysis also revealed differences in stressors by type of department, and level of position (i.e. professional or support staff). For example, a significant stressor for reference librarians was "feelings of inadequacy" because of inability to provide high quality reference service. On the other hand, technical service librarians did not identify patrons as a source of stress, but placed work load as the primary stressor, and considered fragmentation of work as significant. Support staff, in addition to work load, identified lack of positive feedback, coworkers, supervisors, and managers as additional stressors.[118] These findings suggest that attempts to intervene to control stress in the library workplace may, like other psychosocial issues, require different programs for workers in different departments and on different levels. For example, reference librarians may need to focus on coping strategies with difficult patrons, while technical service librarians may need to focus on time management and realistic goal setting. Stress programs for support staff may need to focus on supervisory training and departmental communications.

The physical environment as well as work expectations and job tasks themselves can be a source of psychological stress in the library workplace. Among the stressors for staff are a constant demand for accuracy; the performance of repetitious, routine, and monotonous tasks; overcrowded work areas; and the introduction of new technologies.

In addition, Gann suggests that library managers should be especially sensitive to sources of stress for new employees. Stress may result from disappointed expectations, especially if their high ideals of public service clash with work realities.[119] It is important however to note that much of the library literature on stress does not measure the actual stress felt by librarians. Although many stressors exist, is there actual evidence that they have an especially negative impact on librarians, or that librarians are suffering burnout?

Some research suggested that the issue of burnout may be exaggerated. Smith and Nelson, in a study of burnout among academic reference librarians found that they were not experiencing burnout. They suggested that librarianship is not a particularly stressful occupation when compared with others and that librarians tend to be well satisfied with their work.[120]

Subsequent research, however, has suggested that burnout may be more prevalent, especially in public librarianship. Birch, Marchant and Smith conducted a study of public reference librarians and found that almost 35% of the respondents were experiencing high levels of burnout. The authors suggested that part of the reason for burnout may be perceived role conflicts and role ambiguity in the workplace.[121] In addition, younger workers tended to experience burnout because of lack of personal accomplishment, while older workers experienced burnout because of feelings of depersonalization. This suggests that stressors differ for younger and older workers; younger workers may need freedom and opportunity to achieve; older librarians need a greater feeling of belonging, of self-esteem. Interestingly, burnout appeared to decline overall with the age of the librarian, and when the librarian was married.[122] In another study of reference librarians, Haack, Jones and Roos measured the stress levels of 92 public reference librarians and found that 14% were experiencing severe burnout and an additional 28% were suffering from above average stress levels.[123] Haack et al. concluded that librarians undergo burnout at approximately the same rate as those in occupations such as health professionals and retail clerks.[124] It is important to note, however, that the research by Haack was a pilot study using a small sample, so the results must be treated with caution.

Numerous suggestions have been offered to adapt the library work environment so that stress is alleviated. Among the suggestions are:

- Making jobs more interesting by varying the tasks, allowing greater flexibility in hours, permitting more group activities, or tasks that foster creativity and autonomy
- Alternating intense work with less demanding work
- Reducing the total amount of work that is especially stressful and assigning only a reasonable work load
- Designing the workplace to be more comfortable and attractive; avoiding crowded, dark, noisy work environments, or work areas that are too hot or cold
- Encouraging workers to take their vacations
- Training workers on how to cope with stress
- Providing formal counseling services when needed.[125, 126]

Special attention should be focused on new employees whose early expectations are bound to be quite high and who may experience frustration because of routine tasks, less than polite patrons, and bureaucracies that are not immediately responsive to new ideas. Special attention should also be given to high-level performers who are the most frequent victims of burnout. It must be cautioned that there is no actual research evidence in librarianship that these techniques work to reduce stress and burnout. Nonetheless, they represent logical recommendations based on experiences in other occupations.

Of course, sources of stress do not lie wholly in the workplace. Employees may be experiencing stress from outside sources such as family and friends. Although these factors cannot be ignored, the control that the organization exercises over them is relatively limited. Attempts to assist employees to gain greater control of these outside forces have led some organizations to initiate Employee Assistance Programs which provide low cost or free counseling.

There is certainly sufficient evidence of stress among library workers to cause concern. Employers must be concerned for their staffs *and* for the fiscal viability of their institution. There are increasing numbers of legal claims on employers for stress related problems. These cases often make a causal connection between stress on the job and subsequent injury or illness. State workers' compensation laws are increasingly accepting stress claims for compensation.[127] Library supervisors and managers play a key role in the management of stress. It is they who often control the assignment, type, and scheduling of job tasks, as well as the level of work expectation. For this reason, library managers must be trained to recognize, inhibit, and deal with worker stress and burnout. Employees experiencing distress and burnout are going to be less productive.

Resistance to Technological Change

In the library literature, the analysis of employee attitudes toward technological change is an area closely related to stress. The library environment has experienced a major influx of new technologies in the last decade. The introduction of automated cataloging, circulation, acquisitions, information retrieval systems, and microcomputers has redefined not only the tasks of the staff, but also the organizational structure and the physical workplace. The adaptations which employees must undergo in order to accommodate such developments are considerable and, as noted above, the demand to adapt is inherently stressful. Whether or not the stress will be positive or negative depends at least in part on how the organization deals with the effects of change on the library staff. There is little doubt that recognizing and addressing this stress is crucial.

The subject of technological change has been widely discussed in the general management literature, but there is a dearth of research that deals specifically with psychosocial aspects of technological change in the library environment. If some of the personality studies of librarians are correct, then one could predict significant resistance to such changes. Conroy has, in fact, predicted substantial turnover as traditional librarians find the new technological environment undesirable.[128]

Controlling resistance to change requires an understanding of the individual's perception of change, and of the fears that may underlie it. Fine, in a major study of resistance to change among librarians, points out that resistance is not in and of itself a problem; it can serve a positive as well as negative function.[129] The goal for the manager is not to eliminate fear but to harness it in a constructive fashion; fear in itself may lead to growth on the part of the employee and the organization.

Often, for example, resistance to technological change manifests itself in criticism. The organization should be structured so that this criticism is channeled beneficially. For example, criticism may expose problems that might otherwise have gone unrecognized and therefore it improves the end product. Similarly criticism may be based on misunderstandings or misconceptions, which when voiced, can be clarified. Criticism is also a form of participation; if the critics can be brought into the deliberative process, their involvement can serve as a form of personal growth and development. In essence, critics help slow the process down so that greater deliberation from a variety of viewpoints can be obtained.

Fearing technological change is not, in itself, irrational. There are real reasons for apprehension. It is clear, for example, that such changes can radically alter the workplace. It is also true that many managers are not equipped to meet the needs of the staff when such changes occur.

In these circumstances, why shouldn't an employee have trepidations about the future? Schraml, in a review of the psychosocial literature on resistance to technology, has identified several fears that may promote resistance to change in the library setting.[130] These include:

1. Fear of Changes in the Job
The technological innovation may lead to changes in the nature of the individual's job. Changing job duties may lead to changes in physical location, in supervisors, and in coworkers. Related to a change in jobs is the fear that retraining will be necessary, and employees may feel that they are not capable of learning the new knowledge.

2. Fear of Job Loss
The fear that automation will replace workers has been around for a long time. As a general rule, few employees have actually lost their jobs due to technological innovation.[131] Nonetheless, without a guarantee from management, employees are bound to feel uneasy about their positions.

3. Fear that the Technology Will Alter the Organizational Structure
The introduction of computers often leads to the creation of new positions that may substantially change the lines of authority and responsibility. The new positions may be filled by individuals who are paid considerably more than the typical librarian and have direct lines of communication to the highest organizational positions. Similarly, the physical, as well as the organizational structure of the library may be affected. New rooms may be created, space may be lost, crowding may occur. Resistance may build as the employees perceive that the computer is getting favored treatment. When computers get air conditioned and nicely carpeted rooms, while staff members work in hot, crowded quarters, there is bound to be a feeling of resentment.

In addition to these factors, Fine notes that the introduction of new technologies can threaten feelings of professional competence and worth.[132] The employee may question whether the goals of the library have changed. Certainly, when employees perceive that the organization is devoting large amounts of money and time to computers, money which they believe could be spent on library materials and salaries, it is logical for them to wonder whether basic assumptions about library service are being changed. Because there is a close relationship between organizational values and job commitment, failure to reaffirm the traditional library values while introducing innovations could precipitate the turnover of valued employees.

There are several steps the organization can take to limit resistance to change among staff. Among these are:

1. Involve All Staff in Major Technological Changes

Involvement of staff supports a fundamental psychological need for control; the broader the participation the better. When employees feel that they have lost control they are much more likely to perceive the change as threatening.[133] Participation increases the opportunity for worker recognition and commitment. Further, it improves the quality of problem solving because diverse and numerous points of view are gathered before decisions are made.[134] Managers should involve staff at the beginning of any major technological innovation and continue their involvement throughout. If staff members are not brought in at the beginning, they may feel that the important decisions have already been made, and that soliciting their opinion at a later date is meant more to salve egos than to hear their viewpoint. Such a situation could become quite destructive in the library setting. If employees feel that they are politically subordinated and alienated from the organization, sabotage could result.[135]

2. Begin Communicating Early and Often

A fundamental cause for resistance to change is that the announced innovation comes as a surprise to the employees. A natural reaction is to become defensive and negative. When employees are uncertain about what is happening, they are going to resist until they know the full implications of the change.[136]

3. Create A Positive and Constructive Management Attitude

It is too easy for managers themselves to become cynical about a technological change, or to become cynical about the potential of their staff to make the necessary adaptations. In both cases, the staff members are bound to increase their resistance. The library manager must exhibit enthusiasm for the change and confidence in the staff, consistently reaffirming that the purpose and values of the library have not changed.

4. Devote Sufficient Human and Fiscal Resources to Training

The importance of training cannot be overestimated. One study of 300 automation projects revealed that 50% of the costs were for training.[137] One-time demonstrations are seldom adequate, and there must be an established routine for training new employees as they enter the organization. In addition, employees must feel free to seek additional assistance as the need arises. Management must also be responsive to suggestions from staff regarding modifications of training techniques and content. It is crucial that managers understand that although the content of training is important, there is the deeper aspect of self-esteem at stake. If the employer cares enough to devote money and time to staff members, they are more likely to respond with good will and effort. Failure to recognize this psychological dimension will diminish the enthusiasm and motivation of library workers.

5. Protect the Health and Well-being of Staff

The introduction of VDTs has caused considerable concern among workers, especially in regard to prolonged exposure to low-level radiation. The automated work station has also produced ergonomic concerns regarding the proper height of work surfaces, proper seating, and appropriate lighting. Employers must demonstrate that they care about employees' health. It should be remembered that health and safety needs must be satisfied before workers will be motivated by higher-order needs. If employees feel that their health is being threatened, they are not likely to be motivated to work hard to meet broader organizational goals.

Staff Development

Increased productivity may also be accomplished through staff development. Staff development is similar to training and many of the characteristics that make training successful are the same for successful staff development (See chapter 2). Staff development differs from training in that it does not have to deal directly with the specific tasks of the job. Rather, it may involve developing the employees' understanding of the organization or of themselves so that they are better employees regardless of their specific position. This distinction, however, is artificial. Many aspects of training, such as employee orientation, are often considered to be part of staff development.

Staff development should not be seen as isolated from other organizational processes and purposes, rather it should be perceived as a tool for motivation. From this perspective, staff development must be perceived by both the employee and employer as a meaningful and useful process. There is little point to an employer offering programs that develop staff members unless those programs contribute to the accomplishment of organizational goals. By the same token, staff members must perceive that the education provided meets their own professional goals.

Staff development may be especially important in organizations where there is a need to cultivate employees for future management and supervisory positions. Similarly, it can be quite helpful in libraries where the work environment is changing—e.g., the introduction of technological innovations. The library must determine what organizational needs can be met by staff development programs. This requires regular *needs assessments*. Needs assessments may include surveys of staff members or the creation of a staff development committee comprised of staff members who generate, as well as solicit, ideas from colleagues. Obtaining ideas from staff can help promote the effectiveness of staff development programs in that the participation in selecting program topics increases the sense of ownership in the development process. Ideas for staff development may also come from sources other than committees and surveys, for example, from administrators, supervisors and middle managers, individual staff members, outside consultants and trainers, or from performance appraisals.

Employees in different job classifications may require or want different types of programs. Library managers or prospective managers may desire programs quite different from support staff. Sample topics that could be considered for staff development include the following:

Management and Administration
- Fundraising
- Marketing library services
- Leadership
- Planning
- Organizational communications
- Proposal and grant writing
- Personnel issues

Staff
- Health programs including stress management, weight reduction, and smoking cessation
- Time management
- Dealing with problem patrons
- Library policies and procedures
- Record keeping and maintenance
- Library services and departments
- Dealing with automation and change

Although there are numerous ways to provide staff development, managers should be aware it can sometimes be accomplished informally. For example, employees can, from time to time, be assigned especially challenging tasks which may require and help develop important skills such as planning, co-ordination with other departments, or supervision. By assigning job responsibilities that enhance the employee's potential, the organization is creating a pool of qualified candidates when important vacancies arise.

Some staff development opportunities should be open to all interested employees; however, other types of staff development could be used as rewards to increase and sustain motivation, especially when only one or two individuals are able to participate. Opportunities to attend workshops or conferences might be directly connected to demonstrations of excellent performance. The use of staff development as a form of recognition can be seen in this sense as a merit component of the total compensation package. This is consistent with the notion that when employees perceive a direct connection between performance and rewards, their productivity improves.

Among the formal types of staff development are the following:

Organizational Development through Committee Work: The library may attempt to develop employees by creating a variety of internal committees on which staff members serve. The committees often broaden an employee's perspective of the organization and develop important skills such as interpersonal communication, report writing, data collection, program planning, and political acumen.

Internal Programs or Workshops: Staff development may take the form of library programs or workshops which are given by employees of the library or by outside trainers. The focus of such programs determines the audience. It is conceivable, for example, that a staff development program could be designed for the entire staff—a program on library security is one example. Other programs might be targeted to narrower interests. For example, a program on patron relations might be held for public service employees only.

The use of internal programs or workshops as staff development has several advantages. There is greater control over the content of the material which can be adapted to particular organizational needs; there is greater knowledge of the skills of the trainer; and the cost per employee is lower. Among the disadvantages are: there is usually a narrower perspective provided since outside experiences are not included; the skills of the trainers may be limited; and, there are more opportunities for interruptions and distractions which may detract from the effectiveness of the program.

Continuing Education: Continuing education can take many forms including formal classes at colleges or universities, or attendance at outside workshops or institutes which may last from a few hours to several days. Continuing education differs from most internal staff development programming in that it usually involves only a few employees. This is sometimes due to the cost of such programs or the fact that there is often considerable disruption in scheduling when employees decide to take a class that may continue for months.

In some cases, continuing education may extend well beyond a single course. This is especially true for employees who wish to obtain their masters of library science. In these circumstances, the library should consider the writing of specific leave policies or the development of special programs that encourage workers to obtain their degrees. For example, a staff development policy might provide financial support for an employee working on a master's degree. Such a policy could be used as a recruiting tool for increasing the number of minorities in professional positions.

Attendance or Participation at Conferences: Usually this form of development is aimed at librarians and generally involves attendance at conferences given by ALA, the Association of Research Libraries (ARL), or the American Society of Information Scientists (ASIS). The type of staff development that occurs in these settings varies from attendance or participation in programs to meeting and talking with other professionals and developing a network which can serve as a professional resource in the future.

As with training, the effectiveness of staff development programs should be evaluated. Unfortunately, evaluation of staff development is more difficult than evaluation of training. Evaluating training that is directed to a particular task is relatively easy; one can observe the performance of the employee. The aim of staff development is not as easily measured and verified because the goal of staff development is more diffuse and long-term and may not become obvious for months or years. The usual means to measure the success of such programs, the use of a questionnaire which the participant completes at the end of the program, provides little real information. Such forms measure attitudes, not actual use of the information. This is not to say that the feelings of employees are unimportant. On the contrary, employees who are unhappy about a program are not likely to use the information provided in it, but the fact that the program was received positively is no guarantee than the information will be used. Consequently, those responsible for staff development should make an effort to identify measurable organizational outcomes. If, for example, the desired outcome of a staff development professional education program is more minority professionals, then a yearly analysis of the library's labor force would be a satisfactory measure. If the purpose of a staff development program is to develop and promote the writing of grant applications, then a yearly count of proposals written and monies received would be a satisfactory measure. Not all programs are as easily evaluated, in part because the organizational goal may itself be more difficult to measure. Lipow suggests, for example, that a valid staff development goal might be that patrons are satisfied with library service whether or not the desired information is provided. She notes that this might be measured by decreases in the number of patron complaints or increases in support from donors. The need for objective measures highlights the necessity of identifying clear organizational goals before undertaking these programs. Vague goals are likely to lead to an inability to determine whether staff development programs are effective.

The Productive Work Force: A Summary

Dealing with the human factors that affect the workplace requires special sensitivity on the part of the library manager. Among the actions the library employer should take to provide for a productive work force are the following:

1. Realistic Job Previews for Incoming Employees

Employees who are misinformed during the hiring or promotion stage regarding their job tasks, potential for advancement, working conditions, and pay, will rapidly experience reductions in their levels of satisfaction, commitment, and motivation. Scrupulous attention to information provided in the interview, by the supervisor, and others will help reduce the possibility of unrealistic expectations.

2. Clarify Organizational Goals and Values

Employees need to know that they are engaged in *meaningful* and important work; that they are accomplishing organizational goals that are valued by all. Clearly stated goals and organizational values do influence organizational performance.[138]

3. Make Job Tasks Interesting

Individuals have personal preferences regarding the specific work they would like to do, but generally speaking, jobs should be challenging, enriching, and provide variety. Librarians place considerable importance on the tasks of the job itself. The focus should be on responding to the employees' need for achievement, responsibility, recognition, and professional growth. Such jobs are bound to increase satisfaction, motivation, and productivity in many workers.

4. Expose the New Employee to Work that Develops Commitment

Give the employee interesting work from the very beginning. A common error is to assign employees to the most routine tasks first, with the rationale that they must learn the job "from the ground up." This often results in tedious and repetitive work that lowers employees' job satisfaction, disappoints their expectations, and decreases their commitment at the point where the need for commitment is greatest. Library employees' early experience should involve the most interesting aspects of the job rather than the least interesting.

5. Set Challenging Goals

There is a temptation, especially in a bureaucracy, to set similar goals for similar jobs. Although this may appear to be a good idea, goals must be tailored to individual abilities. Goals must be sufficiently difficult and challenging so that workers have a sense of achievement when the tasks are completed. Managers must challenge their employees and set objectives that are not easily obtained. Of course, the setting of challenging goals is made more difficult in libraries because service goals are often hard to quantify. This should not prevent managers from seeking definable tasks for each employee that are both difficult and challenging.

6. Provide Opportunities for Employees to Demonstrate Commitment

Employees should be given a chance to demonstrate their commitment voluntarily and publicly. That is, there should be times when they are able to voluntarily make sacrifices, e.g. come in on a day off to help out; work an extra evening. Such sacrifices, when they are voluntary, and are known by others, including the supervisor, can provide a powerful statement that they are committed to their work. Of course, such opportunities should not be used merely as a subterfuge to get more work out of employees; they are meant to provide a statement by the employee of the value of the work being done and of the institution.

7. Provide Responsible Jobs

Workers need to feel that they are responsible for accomplishing broader organizational goals. This is sometimes referred to as felt responsibility. Because of specialization of job tasks and departmentalization, employees often feel that they are not connected to the organization as a whole. These feelings alienate them from organizational goals, and obscure their role in accomplishing those goals. Supervisors must pay special attention to ensuring that employees understand how important their work is to the greater organization. This begins at the point of hire. Workers who feel the interconnectedness of their job and their dependence on others are bound to feel a greater sense of commitment to the organization.

8. Create Opportunities for Building Social Bonds

Employees need to develop links with others in the organization. As those links increase in number and deepen in intensity, it becomes more difficult for the employee to leave. This is especially true for talented and productive workers; if they perceive themselves as loners, if they think that their success does not depend on the work of others, then they are more likely to leave. For this reason, the organization should provide opportunities for group contact. This might involve library committee activities, departmental or institutional programs, or social occasions that increase chances for interaction. Group cohesiveness can also be increased by permitting participatory decision making on the departmental level, and for the setting of group (departmental) performance goals as well as individual goals.

9. Create Fair Evaluation and Compensation Systems

Compensation systems must be perceived as fair and connected to high levels of performance. Performance evaluation systems must provide for accurate and regular feedback. Feedback has been found to be especially important to people who want to achieve.[139] Use the performance review system as an opportunity to set challenging goals. Similarly, the reward and promotion system should be based on the productivity of the worker. Workers should perceive that those who work hard reap the greatest benefits, and those who perform poorly are not rewarded for their substandard effort.

10. Good Orientation, Training, and Staff Development

Workers want and deserve to know how to perform their jobs, and to feel that the development of their career and abilities is important to the organization. Workers who experience early criticism of their work, especially when they perceive the cause of their problem as centered in the organization and not themselves, are not likely to respond positively to the organization, especially in their first year of service when they have little to lose by leaving.

11. Design Motivational Programs for Different Career Stages

Pay close attention to orientation and interesting job tasks for entrants; to professional development, participation, and autonomy in the career development stage; and to benefit programs and recognizing and using the collective wisdom of senior employees.

FACTORS RELATED TO JOB SATISFACTION, COMMITMENT AND MOTIVATION

1. The quality of supervision is a critical aspect of job satisfaction.

2. Worker satisfaction, commitment, and motivation are not identical. Each concept must be understood.

3. The purpose of stimulating job satisfaction, commitment and motivation is to increase library productivity.

4. Job satisfaction among librarians is linked to the tasks of the job itself as well as the opportunity to achieve and be recognized.

5. There is no clear relationship between gender and job satisfaction in librarianship.

6. The setting of difficult and challeging goals for employees is directly related to increasing employee productivity.

7. Developing worker commitment is especially important in service occupations such as librarianship.

8. The reasons for job commitment vary depending on career stage. Younger workers seek challenges, middle-career workers seek professional development, older workers seek the security of friends and benefits, and want to be appreciated for their years of experience.

9. A worker's general disposition to work remains relatively stable over time. It is important that employers hire individuals whose dispositions fit the needs of the job.

10. Environmental factors that may help stimulate productivity include job enrichment, attention to quality of worklife, and stress management.

11. Employers should make a special effort to study worker turnover including the calculation of annual turnover rates, and analysis of reasons why employees stay with or leave the library.

12. Not all turnovers are bad. It is important to focus on the turnover of employees who were productive workers to determine if anything could have been done to prevent such turnover.

13. Turnover rates of librarians are low compared to other occupations. This highlights the need for library employers to hire the right person for any given job.

14. The decision to quit is often a result of a series of intermediate decisions which can occur over an extended period of time. The final reason for quitting may not be the same as the reason that started the employee thinking about quitting.

15. Exit interviews should be conducted with as many employees as is practical.

Endnotes

1. Barry M. Staw and Jerry Ross, "Stability in the Midst of Change: A Dispositional Approach to Job Attitudes," *Journal of Applied Psychology* 70 (1985): 479.
2. Barry M. Staw, "The Pursuit of the Happy/Productive Worker," *California Management Review* 28 (Summer 1986): 46.
3. Lawrence H. Peters and Edward J. O'Connor, "Situational Constraints and Work Outcomes: The Influences of a Frequently Overlooked Construct," *Academy of Management Review* 5 (1980): 396.
4. Edward J. O'Connor, Lawrence H. Peters, Abdullah Pooyan, Jeff Weekley, Frank Blake, and Bruce Erenkrantz, "Situational Constraint Effects on Performance, Affective Reactions, and Turnover: A Field Replication and Extension," *Journal of Applied Psychology* 69 (1984): 669-670.
5. Stephen M. Colarelli, Roger A. Dean, and Constantine Konstans, "Comparative Effects of Personal and Situational Influences on Job Outcomes of New Professionals," *Journal of Applied Psychology* 72 (November 1987): 558.
6. Staw: 44.
7. Staw and Ross: 478.
8. Estelle S. Bean, "Polish-up Your Image," *Catholic Library World* 58 (March/April 1987): 232.
9. *The Public Library Inquiry*, p. 48 as cited in John Agada, "Studies of the Personality of Librarians," *Drexel Library Quarterly* 20 (1984): 31.
10. John Agada, "Studies of the Personality of Librarians," *Drexel Library Quarterly* 20 (Spring 1984): 24-45.
11. Colarelli, Dean, and Konstans: 563.
12. Curtis Hartman and Steven Pearlstein, "The Joy of Working," *INC.* 9 (November 1987): 61.
13. Anne Hopkins, *Work and Job Satisfaction in the Public Sector*, Totowa, N.J.: Rowman and Allanheld, 1983: 19.
14. Jon L. Pierce, "Job Design In Perspective," *Personnel Administrator* 25 (December 1980): 68.
15. James L. Price, *The Study of Turnover,* Iowa State University, Ames, Iowa: 1977: 79.
16. Hopkins: 1.
17. Graham L. Staines and Robert P. Quinn, "American Workers Evaluate the Quality of Their Jobs," *Monthly Labor Review* 102 (January 1979): 5.
18. Edwin Locke, "What is Job Satisfaction," *Organizational Behavior and Human Performance* 4 (1969): 309.
19. Clifford J. Mottaz, "The Relative Importance of Intrinsic and Extrinsic Rewards as Determinant of Work Satisfaction," *The Sociological Quarterly* 26 (Fall 1985): 367.
20. Marvin D. Dunnette, John P. Campbell, and Milton D. Hakel, "Factors Contributing to Job Satisfaction and Job Dissatisfaction in Six Occupational Groups," *Organizational Behavior and Human Performance* 2 (May 1967): 143, 146-147.
21. Mottaz: 373-375.

22. Mottaz: 373.
23. Mottaz: 378-379.
24. Joseph A. Raelin, "Work Patterns in the Professional Life- Cycle," *Journal of Occupational Psychology* 58 (September 1985): 185-186.
25. W.W. Ronan, "Individual and Situation Variables Relating to Job Satisfaction," *Journal of Applied Psychology Monograph* 54 (February 1970): 28.
26. Greg R. Oldham and Yitzhak Fried, "Employee Reactions to Workspace Characteristics," *Journal of Applied Psychology* 72 (February 1987): 78.
27. Jeanne M. Isacco, "Work Spaces, Satisfaction and Productivity in Libraries," *Library Journal* 110 (May 1, 1985): 27-30.
28. Joanne Miller, "Individual and Occupational Determinants of Job Satisfaction," *Sociology of Work and Occupations* 7 (August 1980): 338.
29. Clifford J. Mottaz, "Gender Differences in Work Satisfaction, Work-Related Rewards and Values, and the Determinants of Work Satisfaction," *Human Relations* 39 (April 1986): 360.
30. Mottaz, "Gender Differences...": 366.
31. Miller: 350.
32. Miller: 359.
33. Miller: 347.
34. Graham L. Staines and Robert P. Quinn, "American Workers Evaluate the Quality of Their Jobs, *Monthly Labor Review* 102 (January 1979): 9.
35. Fred W. Grupp, Jr. and Allan R. Richards, "Job Satisfaction Among State Executives in the U.S.," *Public Personnel Management* (March-April 1975): 106.
36. George P. D'Elia, "The Determinants of Job Satisfaction Among Beginning Librarians," *Library Quarterly* 49 (July 1979): 297.
37. D'Elia: 300-301.
38. Kenneth H. Plate and Elizabeth W. Stone, "Factors Affecting Librarians' Job Satisfaction: A Report of Two Studies," *Library Quarterly* 44 (April 1974): 103.
39. Beverly P. Lynch and Jo Ann Verdin, "Job Satisfaction in Libraries: Relationships of the Work Itself, Age, Sex, Occupational Group, Tenure, Supervisory Level, Career Commitment and Library Department," *Library Quarterly* 53 (October 1983): 442-443.
40. Richard W. Scamell and Bette Ann Stead, "A Study of Age and Tenure as It pertains to Job Satisfaction," *Journal of Library Administration* 1 (Spring 1980): 14.
41. Lynch and Verdin: 442.
42. D'Elia: 292-293.
43. Steven Seokho Chwe, "A Comparative Study of Job Satisfaction: Catalogers and Reference Librarians in University Libraries," *Journal of Academic Librarianship* 4 (July 1978): 141.
44. William J. Vaughn and J.D. Dunn, "A Study of Job Satisfaction In Six University Libraries," *College and Research Libraries* 35 (May 1974): 177.
45. Maurice Marchant, "Participative Management, Job Satisfaction, and Service," *Library Journal* 107 (April 15, 1982): 783-784.
46. Maurice P. Marchant, "Managing Motivation and Job Satisfaction," in *Strategies for Library Administration: Concepts and Approaches*, edited

by Charles R. McClure and Alan Samuels, Littleton, Colo.: Libraries Unlimited, 1982: 262-263.

47. D. S. Bengston and D.M. Shields, "A Test of Marchant's Predictive Formulas Involving Job Satisfaction," *Journal of Academic Librarianship* 11 (May 1985): 88-92.

48. Bette Ann Stead and Richard W. Scamell, "A Study of the Relationship of Role Conflict, The Need for Role Clarity, and Job Satisfaction for Professional Librarians, *Library Quarterly* 50 (July 1980): 319.

49. Lynch and Verdin: 442-443.

50. Chwe: 141.

51. D'Elia: 300-301.

52. Beverly P. Lynch and Jo Ann Verdin, "Job Satisfaction in Libraries: A Replication," *Library Quarterly* 57 (1987):190-202.

53. Susanne Patterson Wahba, "Job Satisfaction of Librarians: A Comparison between Men and Women," *College and Research Libraries* 36 (January 1975): 50.

54. Ilene F. Rockman, "Job Satisfaction Among Faculty and Librarians, *Journal of Library Administration* 5 (Fall 1984): 55.

55. Graham L. Staines and Robert P. Quinn, "American Workers Evaluate the Quality of Their Jobs," *Monthly Labor Review* 102 (January 1979): 4.

56. Staines and Quinn: 5.

57. Martin L. Maehr and Larry A. Braskamp, *The Motivation Factor: A Theory of Personal Investment*, Lexington, Mass.: D.C. Heath, 1986: 2-6.

58. Abraham H. Maslow, *Motivation and Personality*, New York: Harper, 1954: 80-92.

59. Lyman W. Porter, Edward E. Lawler III, and J. Richard Hackman, *Behavior in Organizations*, New York: McGraw-Hill, 1975: 43-44.

60. Frederick Hertzberg,"One More Time: How Do You Motivate Employees?" in *Harvard Business Review* 65 (September-October 1987): 113.

61. Hertzberg, "One More Time...": 114.

62. Hertzberg, "One More Time...": 111.

63. See for example, Donald P. Schwab, H. William DeVitt, and Larry L. Cummings, "A Test of the Adequacy of the Two Factor Theory as a Predictor of Self-Report Performance Effects," *Personnel Psychology* 24 (Summer 1971): 302.

64. David C. McClelland, "Business Drive and National Achievement," *Harvard Business Review* 40 (July-August 1962): 99.

65. McClelland: 103-105.

66. David C. McClelland and David H. Burnham, "Power is the Great Motivator," *Harvard Business Review* 54 (March-April 1976): 101.

67. McClelland, "Power...": 102.

68. McClelland, "Power...": 102.

69. McClelland, "Power...": 104.

70. Edwin A. Locke and Richard L. Somers, "The Effects of Goal Emphasis on Performance on a Complex Task," *Journal of Management Studies* 24 (July 1987): 405.

71. Gary P. Latham and Edwin A. Locke, "Goal Setting—A Motivational Technique That Works," in *Contemporary Problems in Personnel*, 3rd

ed., edited by Kenneth Pearlman, Frank L. Schmidt, and W. Clay Hamner, New York: John Wiley, 1983: 319.

72. Latham and Locke: 314.
73. Latham and Locke: 313.
74. Latham and Locke: 318.
75. Latham and Locke: 318.
76. Edwin A. Locke, Dong-OK Chah, Scott Harrison, and Nancy Lustgarten, "Separating the Effects of Goal Specificity from Goal Level," *Organizational Behavior and Human Decision Processes* 43 (April 1989): 282-283.
77. Latham and Locke: 316.
78. Miriam Erez and Isaac Zidon, "Effect of Goal Acceptance on the Relationship of Goal Difficulty to Performance," *Journal of Applied Psychology* 69 (February 1984): 76.
79. Latham and Locke: 322.
80. Richard T. Mowday, Lyman W. Porter, and Richard M. Steers, *Employee-Organization Linkages: The Psychology of Commitment, Absenteeism, and Turnover*, New York: Academic Press, 1982.
81. Mowday, Porter, and Steers: 206-210.
82. For a fuller discussion of life-cycle patterns see Joseph Raelin, "Work Patterns in the Professional Life-Cycle," *Journal of Occupational Psychology* 58 (September 1985): 177-187.
83. John P. Wanous, Stephen A. Stumpf, and Hrach Bedrosian, "Job Survival of New Employees," *Personnel Psychology* 32 (Autumn 1979): 657.
84. Richard E. Rubin, "Employee Turnover of Librarians," *Library Quarterly* 59 (January 1989): 34.
85. Raelin: 186.
86. Raelin: 187.
87. Jon L. Pierce, "Job Design in Perspective," *Personnel Administrator* 25 (December 1980): 68.
88. Richard J. Hackman, *Work Redesign*, New York: Addison-Wesley, 1979: 73.
89. Hackman: 77-80.
90. Pierce: 68.
91. Hertzberg: 114.
92. Hackman: 85.
93. David Marshall Hunt and Carol Michael, "Mentoring: A Career Training and Development Tool," *Academy of Management Review* 8 (1983): 475.
94. Hunt and Michael: 476.
95. Raymond A. Noe, "Women and Mentoring: A Review and Research Agenda," *Academy of Management Review* 13 (1988): 66.
96. Hunt and Michael: 478.
97. Hunt and Michael: 479.
98. Hunt and Michael: 480-482.
99. Raymond A. Noe, "An Investigation of the Determinants of Successful Assigned Mentoring Relationships," *Personnel Psychology* 41 (Autumn 1988):461.
100. Kathy E. Kram, "Phases of the Mentor Relationship," *Academy of Management Journal* 26 (1983): 608-625.

101. James G. Clawson and Kathy E. Kram, "Managing Cross- Gender Mentoring," *Business Horizons* 27 (May/June 1984): 29.
102. Fred Best, *Work Sharing: Issues, Policy Options and Prospects*, Kalamazoo, Mich.: W.E. Upjohn Institute, 1981: 3.
103. *Job Sharing: An Alternative to Traditional Employment Patterns*, Arlington, Va.: Educational Research Service: 4.
104. Gretl S. Meier, *Job Sharing: A New Pattern for Quality of Work and Life*, Kalamazoo, Mich.: W.E. Upjohn Institute: 9-10.
105. Educational Research Service: 6-7.
106. Meier: 83.
107. Educational Research Service: 8.
108. Meier: 81-82.
109. Charles Martell, "Automation, Quality of Work Life, and Middle Managers," *Library Administration and Management* 1 (September 1987): 135.
110. Charles Martell, "Achieving High Performance in Library Work," in *Critical Issues in Library Personnel Management*, edited by Richard Rubin, Urbana, Ill.: University of Illinois, 1989: 83.
111. Martell: 21-22.
112. Martell: 21-22.
113. Vandra L. Huber, "Managing Stress for Increased Productivity," *Supervisory Management* 26 (December 1981): 3-4.
114. Judy Lynn Bube, "Stress in the Library Environment," *Technicalities* 5 (July 1985): 8.
115. Leonard H. Chusmir and Douglas E. Durand, "Stress and the Working Woman," *Personnel* 64 (May 1987): 39.
116. Nathan M. Smith and Veneese C. Nelson, "Burnout: A Survey of Academic Reference Librarians," *College and Research Libraries* 44 (May 1983): 245.
117. Charles A. Bunge, "Stress in the Library," *Library Journal* 112 (September 15, 1987): 47-48.
118. Bunge: 49-51.
119. Maxine Laure Gann, "The Role of Personality Factors and Job Characteristics in Burnout: A Study of Social Service Workers," Ph.D. dissertation, University of California at Berkeley, 1979, cited in "Burnout: A Survey of Academic Reference Librarians," Nathan M. Smith and Veneese C. Nelson, *College and Research Libraries* 44 (May 1983): 245.
120. Smith and Nelson: 249.
121. Nancy Birch, Maurice P. Marchant, and Nathan M. Smith, "Perceived Role Conflict, Role Ambiguity, and Reference Librarian Burnout in Public Libraries," *Library and Information Science Research* 8 (January-March 1986): 53.
122. Birch, Marchant, and Smith: 62.
123. Mary Haack, John W. Jones, and Tina Roos, "Occupational Burnout Among Librarians," *Drexel Library Quarterly* 20 (Spring 1984): 51.
124. Haack et al.: 68.
125. Charles A. Bunge, "Stress in the Library Workplace," in *Critical Issues in Library Personnel Management*, edited by Richard Rubin, Urbana, Ill.: University of Illinois, 1989: 97-101.
126. Bube: 9-10.

127. John M. Ivancevich, Michael T. Matteson, and Edward P. Richards III, "Who's Liable for Stress on the Job," *Harvard Business Review* 63 (March/April 1985): 60.

128. Barbara Conroy, "The Human Element in the Electronic Library," *Drexel Library Quarterly* 17 (Fall 1981): 94.

129. Sara Fine, "Terminal Paralysis, or Showdown at the Interface," in *Human Aspects of Library Automation: Helping Staff and Patrons Cope* (Papers presented at the 22nd Annual Clinic on Library Applications of Data Processing, 14-16 April 1985), edited by Debora Shaw. Urbana-Champaign: University of Illinois, Graduate School of Library and Information Science, 1985: 3-15

130. Mary L. Schraml, "The Psychological Impact of Automation on Library and Office Workers," *Special Libraries* 72 (April 1981): 149-150.

131. Jerome A. Mark, "Technological Change and Employment: Some Results from BLS Research," *Monthly Labor Review* 110 (April 1987): 27.

132. Sara F. Fine, "Technological Innovation, Diffusion and Resistance: An Historical Perspective," *Journal of Library Administration* 7 (Spring 1986): 98.

133. Rosabeth Moss Kanter, "Managing the Human Side of Change," *Management Review* 74 (April 1985): 52.

134. Fine: 97.

135. Carolyn M. Gray, "Technology and the Academic Library Staff or the Resurgence of the Luddites," in *Professional Competencies: Technology and the Librarian* (Papers presented at the 20th Annual Clinic on Library Applications of Data Processing, 24-26 April 1983), edited by Linda C. Smith, Urbana-Champaign: University of Illinois, Graduate School of Library and Information Science, 1983: 69-76.

136. Kanter: 53-54.

137. Margaret Myers, "Personnel Consideration in Library Automation," in *Human Aspects of Library Automation: Helping Staff and Patrons Cope* (Papers presented at the 22nd Annual Clinic on Library Applications of Data Processing, 14-16 April 1985), edited by Debora Shaw. Urbana-Champaign: University of Illinois, Graduate School of Library and Information Science, 1985: 30-45.

138. Barry Z. Posner, James M. Kouzes, and Warren H. Schmidt, "Shared Values Make a Difference: An Empirical Test of Corporate Culture," Human Resources Management 24 (Fall 1985): 303.

139. David C. McClelland, "Business Drive and National Achievement," *Harvard Business Review* 40 (July/August 1962): 105.

8

Employee Retention and Turnover

When workers are dissatisfied, unmotivated, uncommitted, or unproductive, a common result is employee turnover. This process can prove both expensive and damaging to library service. For this reason, the subjects of worker retention and turnover are important. Unfortunately, retention and turnover are seldom studied in a systematic or objective fashion; in librarianship they are seldom studied at all. There are several reasons why turnover analysis has been difficult and unproductive, among them:

1. Folklore

Turnover analysis is often based on folklore and observations by vested interests, rather than objective information. Folklore develops in many ways. Sometimes it is revealed in oft repeated statements such as "Turnover has been high here for years," or "This library can't keep good people." Such observations are often incorrect, but they lead to a conclusion that there is a turnover problem.

2. Vested Interest

Vested interest often plays a role because analysis of retention is often based on the observations of those who have a strong interest in painting the best picture of themselves. Easy explanations that are not self-critical are usually desired, not only by the supervisor but by administrators as well because they are less threatening.

3. Negative Focus

Turnover analysis often focuses on resignations and the leavers' stated reasons for leaving, rather than on stayers and their reasons for staying. Resignation is the end of the employment process. Although it is important and useful to analyze why people resigned, it is equally, perhaps even more important, to analyze why people *stay*. Those who have resigned may have many reasons for not giving an honest answer as to why they are leaving. The stated reasons for leaving seldom reflect totally or accurately why the person has decided to go. Focusing on those who stay has many benefits not the least of which is that they can be part of an ongoing analysis of retention.

4. Not People-Centered

Turnover analysis often focuses on turnover rates rather than on the type of individuals leaving. The temptation to look at simple quantitative turnover measures to determine retention performance is misleading. The analysis in retention should focus on two questions: Are you losing your good workers? and: Are you retaining your poor workers? The size of the turnover rate is less important than *who* is turning over.

5. Failure to Individualize

Turnover solutions often treat all workers in the same way. There is a tendency to introduce programs that encourage *all* workers to stay, rather than only those who *should* stay. For example, a program that recognizes years of service may help retain employees, but if the program recognizes all staff regardless of their level of performance, then it is not functioning to retain only the good workers.

DEFINING TURNOVER

There are many types of turnover. This can best be understood by examining definitions that reveal this variety. In general, turnover is the departure of an employee from the organization. When an employee resigns or is terminated, it is a turnover. But there are more subtle ways to define turnover that help us understand whether we are building commitment among the right type of workers. Among the definitions that are useful for the manager are the following:

Voluntary Turnover

A voluntary turnover occurs when employees leave by their own decision. This concept is not always as precise as it may seem. For example, when an employer and employee agree that the employee should leave by mutual agreement, is it a voluntary turnover? To some extent, it may depend on whether the employee would have been terminated if he or she had refused to resign.

Involuntary Turnover

An involuntary turnover occurs when employees leave by a decision other than their own, usually through termination by the employer. But other possibilities do arise, such as an individual who is sentenced to jail.

Controllable Turnover

A controllable turnover is one that can be affected by the employer. This is an especially useful definition for the employer who may be seeking ways to retain employees. It asks the question: Could I have done otherwise and kept this employee?

Uncontrollable Turnover

An uncontrollable turnover is one that could not be affected by the employer. Obviously, there are certain circumstances which make employer intervention useless. When an employee must resign to take care of an ill parent or when a spouse relocates for a better position; these circumstances often make employer actions useless.

Functional Turnover

Functional turnover occurs when the employee's departure benefits the organization: such as when a poor performer or disruptive employee leaves. This concept is quite useful to the library manager because it suggests that not all turnovers are cause for concern. Sometimes they are evidence that the organization is working quite well.

Dysfunctional Turnover

Dysfunctional turnover arises when the employee's departure is not in the best interest of the organization. These turnovers should be of special concern to the library manager, especially if the turnover is both dysfunctional and controllable. Retention programs should be focused on minimizing such turnovers.

THE ADVANTAGES OF TURNOVER

The variety of definitions suggests that turnover can be viewed from many perspectives; turnovers can be beneficial as well as damaging. Among the advantages are:

Introduction of New Ideas

Employee turnover gives the library a chance to bring in new employees who may contribute important new ideas. Oftentimes this fresh perspective is appreciated by both management and coworkers.

Increased Productivity

Although new workers often need some time before they can be productive, their level of energy and enthusiasm is often quite high. The productivity of others may increase when the new employee has the effect of motivating coworkers. In addition, new workers may quickly bolster productivity especially if they are replacing individuals who worked many years and who were experiencing burnout. Indeed, the belief that performance increases with years of experience has been questioned. In occupations involving public service, performance has been described as an inverted U, with productivity rising in early years, reaching a plateau and then declining.[1]

Reduced Conflict

The departing employee may have been an individual who caused personal and professional disruptions in the workplace. The loss of such a person may result in happier supervisors and coworkers, and reductions in the numbers of complaints and grievances.

Improved Morale

Sometimes new employees possess characteristics that improve the overall esprit de corps of the department. This is especially true if, by contrast, the previous employee was a poor performer and difficult to deal with.

Reduced Labor Costs

Bringing in a new employee may result in savings if the former employee had many years of service. Savings in salary alone often results as well as increasing cost-effectiveness due to the higher motivation of the new employee.

Opportunity To Promote Good Workers

Except for increasing the number of positions, employee turnover is one of the few ways to move good performers into new positions. In this sense, turnover is an opportunity to provide recognition and reward.

THE DISADVANTAGES OF TURNOVER

Turnover also has some substantial negative effects on organizations including:

Cost

Although turnover costs in libraries have not been calculated for many library settings, one study conducted by Roos and Shelton estimated the cost of hiring one academic librarian to be between $13,000 and $15,000.[2] Of course, the hiring process is not the only source of costs when turnovers occur. Other sources include:

- The costs of employee separation including the costs of exit interview, of processing the necessary papers, of providing job counseling, of continuing benefits, of separation pay or pay for unused benefit time.
- The costs of replacing the employee including advertising, recruiting, reviewing applications, interviewing, and selecting the new employee.
- The costs of training the new employee including providing orientation to the organization and the department, training to perform the particular job, the costs of literature about the organization, and the need for increased supervision and evaluation time for the new employee.
- The costs in loss of productivity including the productivity lost in the early period of the new employee, and loss of productivity in the departing worker in the period just before his or her departure.

Lower Morale

Some turnovers may decrease rather than increase morale. Such decreases occur if the employee who left was valued by the staff. Under such circumstances, the remaining employees may feel that the library can not retain good workers, or does not respect good work. Such attitudes may result in additional turnovers. There is evidence, for example, that turnovers do not occur independently, but rather occur in clusters that often follow the pattern of social networks or work groups.[3]

Poor Public Relations

If the number of turnovers becomes too high, or well-known individuals leave the library, then the public may become concerned about the ability of the library to retain good workers. Given most library's reliance on public funding, such a reputation could be seriously damaging.

Disruptions in Library Activities and Services

The loss of a good worker, especially one who has acquired high levels of special skills, can damage library service and programs. These disruptions can involve not only quality of service, but also work schedules and job duties which in turn could affect the job satisfaction of those who remain.

Disruptions to the Social Network

Organizations are not simply composed of separate individuals, they are also composed of social groups who work with each other as colleagues and friends. Different employees fulfill different social roles: some might serve as mentors or counselors, others as listeners or sources of amusement. When valued employees leave, their place in that social structure also becomes vacant and the employees must readjust their social network in response. Sometimes, this may not be easy and equilibrium may be difficult to reestablish. Under such circumstances, employees may lose their feeling of interconnectedness which in turn could result in job dissatisfaction and turnover.

Whether a turnover is functional or dysfunctional depends to a great extent on weighing the advantages and disadvantages experienced for a given turnover. No one can predict exactly what will happen when an individual leaves, but the library manager must make an attempt to characterize the effects that turnovers have on the organization. This will help them determine whether the organization's health is being adversely affected or improved by the type and number of turnovers occurring.

MEASURING TURNOVER

One type of turnover analysis is to determine a turnover rate. Such measures provide some information on how many turnovers are occurring within a specified period of time, e.g. one year. Different types of rates reveal different information about the organization. Among the different rates are the following:

Crude Turnover Rate

$$\frac{\text{The number of employees who leave in a given period}}{\text{The average number of employees in the same period}}$$

The crude turnover rate is the percentage of the work force that left the organization in a given period. A common procedure is to calculate the turnover rate on an annual basis using the Crude Annual Turnover Rate. It must be kept in mind that such a rate does not indicate whether different *positions* turned over, or whether the same positions turned over many times. Crude turnover measures can be calculated not only for the institution as a whole, but for various job classifications (e.g. professional, clerk-typist). It can also be used to determine if men and women leave the library at similar or different rates.

Cohort Wastage Rate

The number of employees who leave during a given period

The number of employees hired at the beginning of the period

This ratio measures the attrition within a given group (cohort). For example, a manager could determine what percentage of the individuals who were hired in 1985 (the 1985 cohort) have already left the organization. This is useful in determining the rate at which new entrants subsequently leave.

Mean Tenure of Leavers

The total number of years worked by those who left

The total number of leavers

This measure provides information on how long employees stay with the organization before they leave. Low mean tenures would suggest that new entrants are not being sufficiently exposed to factors that increase commitment.

Mean Tenure of Stayers

The total number of years worked by current staff

The total number of staff

This ratio is a complement to the mean tenure of leavers and measures the average length of service of the individuals who remain with the organization. If, for example, the mean tenure of stayers was high and the mean tenure of leavers very low, it might suggest that the organization protects the status quo, and discourages new workers.

Gender and Turnover Rates

In a profession that is numerically dominated by women, the question is bound to arise: "Do women have higher turnover rates than men?" There is certainly a tenacious conviction in the general labor force that women demonstrate weaker job commitments because of their child-bearing or family responsibilities.[4] Such beliefs have the potential of reducing opportunities for promotion and hire among women.

Research on the general labor market in the 1970s revealed that turnover rates of women were generally higher than those of men. In addition, women had a greater tendency to leave the work force when quitting than their male counterparts.[5] Although subsequent research verified higher turnover rates among women, further analysis revealed that the reason for the higher turnover rates had nothing to do with gender. Rather, it was related to the number of years of service and lower salaries which females receive. When these factors were taken into account, female rates were *lower* than male rates.[6, 7] There is no evidence that women are less committed workers than men.

THE DECISION TO LEAVE

Using quantitative measures of turnover represents only a small portion of turnover analysis. The qualitative process which an employee undergoes before making the final decision to leave is significant. The final decision to quit is often a result of a lengthy deliberative process on the part of the employee; sometimes it can be a matter of years before the final decision to quit is made. There are several stages that the employee passes through before such decisions are reached; these stages are called intermediate linkages.

The process involves several distinct steps, which in effect, require independent decisions which could be separated by lengthy periods of time. The following steps in the turnover process are adaptations from a turnover decision model proposed by Mobley.[8]

Step 1: Experiencing Dissatisfaction on the Job which Leads the Employee to Think of Quitting
This may be the result of a particular event (e.g. being disciplined, or not receiving a raise), or it may be based on an accumulation of events such as negative stress resulting from public service work.

Step 2: Making a Judgment that One Should Search for a New Job
Although one may be dissatisfied, it is another matter to decide that it is worthwhile looking for other employment. Inertial factors such as the time required to conduct such a search must be overcome before the decision to search would be made.

Step 3: Actually Searching for Job Prospects
At this stage, the employee has decided that it is worth the time to search. The search itself may be affected by the job market and opportunities for employment. Job searching may stop not only because the current job may in fact be better than what is available, but also because there is no appropriate alternative employment.

Step 4: Evaluating the Advantages and Disadvantages of the Job Prospects

As the employee becomes more serious about the search, a process of analyzing the strengths and weaknesses of prospective employment occurs. Looking for jobs is distinct from seriously beginning to ask the question: What will this new job do for me?

Step 5: Comparing the Job Prospects to the Current Job

If employees determine that acceptable alternative employment is available, then they will also reevaluate the current job as well, determining what is lost if alternative employment is accepted.

Step 6: Intending to Quit

If the analysis of current and alternative jobs results in a positive evaluation in favor of the alternative, then the employee develops an intention to quit. This intention could be made public or be kept secret.

Step 7: Actual Quitting

The employee turns in a resignation and leaves the organization.

The employer can intervene at any point in this process to identify and modify the organizational sources of dissatisfaction on the part of the employee. It also highlights the fact that the *final* reasons for quitting may be unrelated to the reasons that initiated the turnover decision process. For example, the fact that an employee at the time of resignation says he or she is leaving for a position with higher pay, does not mean that pay was the original motivation to seek alternative employment. This is why focusing only on the stated reasons for resignation is an incomplete way of understanding the causes of turnover.

TURNOVER IN LIBRARIES

Very little is actually known about turnover in libraries. Most of what is known deals with turnover rates. Neal, in a study of 68 ARL libraries, noted that less than 50% of these libraries even calculated crude turnover rates.[9] In the same study, Neal calculated the turnover rate of *support* staff in these libraries and reported a rate of 20.1%.[10] In another study, Neal collected data from 98 ARL libraries and 1,658 librarians. An annual turnover rate of 7.4% was found.[11] No analysis by gender was attempted. Similar results have been found for public libraries, although research is similarly sparse. Rubin conducted a study of 31 public libraries of varying sizes in the U.S. His findings indicate the average turnover of public librarians to be 7.1%. When male

and female turnover rates were analyzed in the same study, no significant differences were found (males: 7.6%; females 7.4%).[12]

Turnover rates of librarians appear to be very low when compared
to other occupations. Compare the 7% turnover rate of librarians to the
industrial divisions in Table 8-1. Such a comparison suggests high levels
of job stability in the library profession. There are many possible reasons
for this including lack of perceived opportunities for movement, the
presence of family responsibilities, and the need for additional income
to support a family. Nonetheless, if one presumes that job satisfaction
and job turnover are closely related, the low turnover rate of librarians
suggests that they are happier in their jobs than many other workers.

TABLE 8-1. Annual Crude Separation Rates for Five Types of Organizations*[13]

Industrial Division	Median Rate
Manufacturing	54
Mining	38
Communication	22
Service	21
Government	23

*Annual turnovers per 100 employees

The low turnover rate also underscores the need to make sound
hiring decisions. Because there are few opportunities to replace librarians, each hire becomes critical. Library employees are likely to stay
with the organization for many years.

Reasons Why Librarians Leave

There is little research on why librarians or support staff decide to
leave their jobs. Rubin, in his analysis of full-time public librarians
found that both men and women most often leave either to retire or take
other library positions.[14] This pattern is probably repeated in academic
libraries although there is no hard information to support this.

Interestingly, the general labor force pattern of females more often
leaving for family related reasons than their male counterparts is also
supported by library research. Support for the propensity of women to
identify family and personal reasons has been found in several sources.
Heim and Estabrook in a study of ALA members, Braunagel's study of
academic librarians, and Dickson's study of reentering librarians all
confirm this characteristic of female library turnover.[15, 16, 17] Rubin
found that among public librarians, females were more likely to leave

the work force than their male counterparts, usually for family reasons.[18] However, *no* differences in the overall turnover rates of males and females were found. The library manager must therefore not assume that women have less commitment to their jobs, rather, leaving for family reasons substitutes for other reasons. It also must be remembered that the number of men leaving for family reasons may be underreported because men may find it less acceptable to admit to leaving for this reason.

Among academic librarians there is support for the view that the employees who stay or leave differ as to the importance of specific workplace factors. Allison and Sartori, in a study of librarians leaving the University of Nebraska-Lincoln library from 1974 to 1984, noted for example that leavers placed greater importance on such factors as the need for intellectual stimulation from colleagues, while stayers placed greater emphasis on the adequacy of support staff, family considerations, the competence of colleagues, and the relationship with immediate supervisors. Both stayers and leavers found the stimulation of the work or lack thereof, relationships with coworkers, opportunity to make decisions, career goals, and future salary prospects important factors in their decisions to stay or leave.[19]

Among support staff, only one study has been conducted regarding reasons for leaving. Neal queried academic library administrators as to why they felt support staff left. The major reasons cited were:

- To follow a graduating spouse
- To return to school
- Dissatisfaction with salary
- Relocation
- No opportunities for advancement.[20]

Unfortunately, none of these studies explore in sufficient detail or depth the factors that begin and sustain the desire to look for alternative employment or leave the library work force. It is clear that much more research is necessary to reach intelligent decisions about why library employees leave their jobs. Overall, however, one can say that librarians, both male and female, place considerable importance on their work and careers. More often than not, they leave to take other library positions. Although women are much more likely than men to leave their jobs to meet family obligations, their job commitment appears to be the same as men.

THE EXIT INTERVIEW

One means by which an employer can gather information from those who are about to leave is to conduct exit interviews with departing employees. There is little information on the extent to which libraries conduct exit interviews. Neal reports that of 150 North American University libraries, 50% conduct them regularly, 36% sometimes, and 14% never. Of those that conducted interviews, in 60% of the instances, personnel officers or their designated representatives carried out the interviews, the balance were conducted by administrators or immediate supervisors.[21]

There are some good reasons for conducting an exit interview. The exit interview:

1. Allows Employees to Speak Their Minds
The exit interview gives employees one last opportunity to talk about their opinions of their jobs and the library. Sometimes this provides a safety valve for the employees' dissatisfaction; sometimes it simply provides employees with a chance to say things that are important to them.

2. Provides an Opportunity to Get Information on the Strengths and Weaknesses of the Organization
The interview may provide constructive information about problems in the organization such as defective policies and practices, poor supervision and training, or problems with coworkers. It can also provide information on what the organization is doing right.

3. Provides Termination Information to the Employee
The interview can provide information concerning continued benefits, the payment of unused vacation or sick leave, the opportunity for career or retirement counseling, and eligibility for rehire.

4. Serves a Public Relations Function
As the employee becomes another taxpayer, it is good to create a positive impression. If possible, the genuine interest expressed during an exit interview provides a constructive and positive atmosphere for the departing employee. To some extent, such an interview gives the employee a sense of closure.

5. Provides Information for Subsequent Legal Actions
From time-to-time an employee may file a suit against the employer. Obtaining stated reasons for leaving and discussing problems that have

arisen in the workplace provide a record as to what was reported to the employer.

An exit interview should be a *voluntary* discussion between the employee and the employer. It is critical that employees perceive the interview in a constructive way; that they are performing a service by talking with the employer, and that the information they provide is valuable and will be used judiciously. Emphasis in the interview should be on the perceptions of the employee toward the organization and the job. *It should not be:*

- A mandatory meeting in which employees are forced to provide information before they are allowed to get their paychecks
- A performance appraisal in which employees' work is evaluated for the last time
- An interrogation in which employees are cross-examined concerning their activities or the activities of others
- An informal discussion in which a great deal of social chat occurs but little information is gained concerning the organization.

Who Conducts the Exit Interview?

Many different individuals may conduct the exit interview including the immediate supervisor, the payroll officer, personnel staff, regional or departmental managers, directors, and outside consultants. The most important consideration is to create the best situation to gather the most information. For this reason, it is generally a poor idea for the immediate supervisor to conduct such an interview. The potential for defensive reactions, and misinterpretation or reinterpretation of the information is too great. Obviously, if the reason for departure is poor supervision or poor relations with the supervisor, the departing employee is not likely to provide such information directly to the supervisor, and the supervisor is not likely to be objective when recording the information.

Generally, the individual conducting the interview should be as removed from the immediate work environment as possible. In larger organizations, this should be someone from the personnel staff. Such individuals are more likely to have developed questioning skills that elicit the maximum amount of job-related information, especially if they have the opportunity to conduct several exit interviews each year. Generally, only one or two individuals should conduct all interviews. In this way, the interviewer can get a larger picture of what's happening, as well as developing questioning skills.

Who Should Be Interviewed?

It is desirable to interview all individuals before they leave, even those who are being terminated, or who are part-time. Unfortunately, this is not possible in many libraries because of lack of time and personnel. For this reason, priorities should be established. A top priority should be administrators and professional librarians, as well as individuals serving in other critical capacities such as computer programmers. This should be followed by support staff including clerical, custodial, and maintenance, and pages. If it is pertinent, even departing volunteers can provide useful information, especially if the library has a large volunteer work force.

When Should the Interviews Be Conducted?

The literature is not in agreement as to when exit interviews should be conducted. Some contend it should be done on the last day; others believe it should be done in the last week or so. To some extent, this depends on the perception of the function of such an interview. If the interview is perceived primarily as a time for employees to talk about their work, then performing the interview sometime in the last week is advisable. The last day of work is then reserved for more clerical functions such as giving information about benefits, collecting keys, library cards, ID badges, and processing any needed paperwork. Such an approach tends to clarify the purpose of the exit interview and, perhaps, increases the perceived importance of employees' opinions of the workplace. Under no circumstances should the interview be conducted as a last-minute procedure which gives the employee the impression that it is a perfunctory rather than an important part of the termination process. Woods and MacCauley, following a survey of 27 organizations in the private sector concluded that the best time is sometime in the last week, but not on the last day.[22]

How Should Interviews Be Conducted?

The context in which the exit interview is placed is as important as the interview itself.

1. Scheduling
The interview should be scheduled in advance so that employees have an opportunity to think about their attitudes toward the workplace. If the interviewer is working from a written checklist or set of questions, it may be advisable to give these questions to the employee in advance to help focus the interview. Of course, there is always the danger that

by knowing the questions, employees may be less spontaneous and perhaps less honest about their responses. This is offset by the possibility that employees will give more thoughtful and informative answers.

2. Type of Interview

The interview should be conducted face-to-face, rather than by telephone. The face-to-face interview is more personal and allows the interviewer to interpret body language as well as words. The interview should be conducted in a nonthreatening manner and should focus on getting at the *real* reasons for leaving not just the superficial ones. The interview must try to get at what prompted the individual to think about quitting in the first place as well as the final reasons for leaving.

3. Preparation

The interviewer should be well prepared before going into the interview. A review of employees' records should be made, and a written interview list of questions should be prepared so that all the pertinent information can be obtained. Generally, similar interview questions should be used for all employees so that an opportunity for comparison is possible.

4. Confidentiality

An especially sensitive area for exit interviewing is what to do with the information. It is obviously wrong to take a specific piece of criticism and immediately confront another employee with it. This would severely diminish the chance that exiting employees would be forthright in the interview. But if the employer fails to use the information obtained in the interview, then there would be no point to such an interview. The employee must be assured that the information provided will be treated as confidential, and that it will be used in a general way, perhaps to alter policies and procedures, and that whatever changes occur will not be associated with the employee.

5. Format

The exit interview should proceed in a well-organized fashion, and should be designed to elicit the maximum amount of information with maximum comfort to all concerned. Embrey, Mondy, and Noe have proposed a logical format designed to accomplish this objective. They suggest seven stages

- Establishing rapport
- Discussion of purpose of the interview
- Discussion of attitudes regarding the old job
- Examining the reasons for leaving
- Comparing the old job with the new one
- Soliciting recommended changes
- Concluding the interview.[23]

FIGURE 8-1.   Major Areas To Be Covered in an Exit Interview

GENERAL
What did you enjoy most about working in the library?
What did you like least about working in the library?
Were your expectations for working here realized?

ASPECTS OF THE NEW JOB
Does the new position offer:
* more money,
* more responsibility,
* more interesting work,
* different type of work,
* new location?

OPPORTUNITIES FOR PROMOTION
Were opportunities provided for promotion?
Was the employee treated fairly in regard to consideration for promotion?
Were more opportunities needed?

POLICIES AND PROCEDURES
Were the organizational and departmental policies perceived as reasonable and fair?

PROPOSED CHANGES
What needs to be changed to improve the organization?
* More salary and benefits,
* More opportunity for promotion,
* Better supervision,
* More challenging and meaningful work,
* More responsibility,
* Better work environment?

SALARIES AND BENEFITS
Was the employee satisfied with the salary?
Was the compensation system (e.g. merit) perceived as fair?
Was the employee satisfied with benefits such as:
* health plan
* life insurance
* vacation pay
* sick pay?

FIGURE 8-1. Major Areas To Be Covered in an Exit Interview

SPECIFIC REASONS FOR LEAVING
Money and benefits?
Continue education?
Relocation with spouse?
Health reasons?
Family circumstances?
Poor working conditions?
Did not like the tasks of the job?
Difficulty with coworkers?
Difficulty with supervisor?
Unhappiness with policies and procedures?

SUPERVISION
Was supervisor fair and supportive?
Were performance expectations clear and reasonable?
Were performance evaluations conducted fairly and professionally?
Were communication channels open?
Were instructions clear?
Was feedback given for work performance?
Were complaints resolved quickly and effectively?
Were suggestions welcomed?
Were policies applied evenhandedly and consistently?

WORK ENVIRONMENT
Was morale good?
Was there a cooperative atmosphere in the department?
Were you trained and oriented to your job and to the organization as a
   whole?
Was too much or too little expected?
Was the work environment safe and clean?

WORK LOAD AND RESPONSIBILITIES
Were duties fairly distributed?
Was scheduling fair and reasonable?
Was work interesting?
• Meaningful?
• Challenging?
• Varied?
Were responsibilities clearly stated?

The Content of Exit Interviews

What areas should be addressed in the exit interview? The central aspect of any exit interview is an assessment of employees' perceptions of the library and an exploration of the reasons why employees decided to leave. The outline in Figure 8-1 provides a list of some of the areas that could be covered. At the end of the interview, some record should be made concerning the mood of the employee and any notable observations that require a response on the part of others, for example, a supervisor, in the library.

Are Exit Interviews Effective?

Assessing the effectiveness of exit interviews depends on the primary goal of the interviewing process. It is likely that much valuable information regarding the strengths and weaknesses of the library can be obtained in a well-conducted interview. Employers should pay closest attention to criticisms and try to avoid defensiveness. On the other side, it must be realized that only one point-of-view is being heard. The employer should not move too quickly on critical information without confirmation from other sources.

If the exit interview is being used primarily to determine actual reasons for leaving, then the employer must be especially cautious. The information obtained in such interviews is not necessarily reliable. One study which examined the stated reasons for leaving of employees at the time of departure, and their stated reasons 18 months later, revealed substantial differences. For example, at the time of departure, 4% blamed inadequate supervision as the reason for leaving, 18 months later, 24% blamed supervision. Interestingly, the same group identified inadequate salary and benefits as the reason for leaving at the time of their departure, but this dropped to only 12%, eighteen months later![24]

There are many reasons why employees might hesitate to give honest answers in the exit interview. Among them are:

- Fear of retaliation: employees may feel that they would not get good recommendations from an employer whom they criticized
- Fear of retaliation on others: employees may feel that valued coworkers might be punished for their remarks
- Reluctance to criticize: some employees simply feel uncomfortable saying negative things about other people
- Desire to be rehired: employees may feel that opportunities for rehire would be damaged because of their criticisms
- Need for self-esteem: employees may be unwilling to admit that their own inabilities led to failure in the position.

In order to help validate the information provided in the exit interview, it may be advisable to talk with immediate supervisors regarding their perceptions as to why employees left. In some cases, such discussion might also involve coworkers.[25] In no case, however, should information given in the exit interview be shared with these employees, unless the departing employee specifically requested or consented in its dissemination.

The Post-Exit Interview

Because the reasons for leaving may be distorted at the time of departure, some organizations conduct post-exit interviews. Generally, outside consultants are recommended for such processes.[26] These consultants may contact the former employee by telephone or in writing. Such processes are expensive, but given the generally low turnover rates of librarians, the expense may not be too great, and the information obtained could be quite valuable.

FACTORS AFFECTING TURNOVER

1. Employers should make a special effort to study worker turnover including the calculation of annual turnover rates, and analysis of reasons why employees stay with or leave the library.

2. Not all turnovers are bad. It is important to focus on the turnover of employees who were productive workers to determine if anything could have been done.

3. Turnover rates of librarians are low compared to other occupations. This highlights the need for library employers to hire the right person for any given job.

4. The decision to quit is often a result of a series of intermediate decisions which can occur over an extended period of time. The final reason for quitting may not be the same as the reason that started the employee thinking about quitting.

5. Exit interviews should be conducted with as many employees as is practical.

Endnotes

1. Barry M. Staw, "The Consequence of Turnover," *Journal of Occupational Behavior* 1 (1980): 259-260.
2. Tedine J. Roos and Diana W. Shelton, "The Cost of Hiring an Academic Librarian," *Journal of Library Administration* 8 (Summer 1987): 89.
3. David Krackhardt and Lyman Porter, "The Snowball Effect: Turnover Embedded in Communication Networks," *Journal of Applied Psychology* 71 (February 1986): 54-55.
4. W. Kip Viscusi, "Sex Differences in Worker Quitting," *Review of Economics and Statistics* 62 (August 1980):388-398.
5. William F. Barnes and Ethel B. Jones, "Differences in Male and Female Quitting," *Journal of Human Resources* 9 (Fall 1974): 449-451.
6. Viscusi: 388-395.
7. Sheldon Haber, Enrique J. Lamas, and Gordon Green, "A New Method for Estimating Job Separations by Sex and Race," *Monthly Labor Review* 106 (June 1983): 23.
8. William H. Mobley, *Employee Turnover: Causes, Consequences, and Control*, Reading, Mass.: Addison-Wesley, 1982: 123.
9. James G. Neal, "Staff Turnover and the Academic Library," in *Options for the 80s: Proceedings of the Second National Conference of the Association of College and Research Libraries*, edited by Michael D. Kathman and Virgil F. Massman, Greenwich Conn.: JAI, 1982: 101.
10. Neal: 102.
11. James Neal, "Employee Turnover and the Exit Interview," Presentation given at the Allerton Institute, November 7, 1987, University of Illinois at Urbana-Champaign.
12. Richard Rubin, "Employee Turnover Among Full-Time Public Librarians," *Library Quarterly* 59 (January 1989): 37-38.
13. James L. Price, *The Study of Turnover*, Ames, Iowa: Iowa State University, 1977.
14. Rubin: 39.
15. Kathleen Heim and Leigh Estabrook, *Career Profiles and Sex Discrimination in the Library Profession*, Chicago: ALA, 1983.
16. Judith Braunagel, "Job Mobility as Related to Career Progression of Female Academic Librarians in the South," Ph.D. dissertation, Florida State University, 1975.
17. Katherine Murphy Dickson, *Librarians Re-Entering the Work Force*, Chicago: ALA, 1985.
18. Rubin: 36.
19. Dee Ann Allison and Eva Sartori, "Professional Staff Turnover in Academic Libraries: A Case Study," *College and Research Libraries* 49 (March 1988): 144.
20. Neal, "Staff Turnover... ": 104.
21. Neal, "Employee Turnover... ": 3.
22. Robert H. Woods and James F. MacCauley, "Exit Interviews: How to Turn a File Filler into a Management Tool," *Cornell Hotel and Restaurant Administration Quarterly* 28 (November 1987): 46.

23. Wanda R. Embrey, R. Wayne Mondy, and Robert M. Noe, "Exit Interview: A Tool for Personnel Development," *The Personnel Administrator* 24 (May 1979): 46.
24. Joseph Zarandona and Michael Camuso, "A Study of Exit Interviews: Does the Last Word Count?" *Personnel* 62 (March 1985): 47-48.
25. Zarandona and Camuso: 48.
26. Woods and MacCauley: 46.

Appendixes

APPENDIX A-1

Equal Pay Act
Title 29, Section 206(d)

No employer having employees subject to any provisions of this section
shall discriminate, within any establishment in which such employees
are employed, between employees on the basis of sex by paying wages
to employees in such establishment at a rate less than the rate at
which he pays wages to employees of the opposite sex in such establishment for equal work on jobs the performance of which requires equal
skill, effort, and responsibility, and which are performed under similar
working conditions, except where such payment is made pursant to (i)
a seniority system; (ii) a merit system; (iii) a system which measures
earnings by quantity or quality of production; or (iv) a differential
based on any other factor other than sex: Provided, that an employer
who is paying a wage rate differential in violation of this subsection
shall not, in order to comply with the provisions of this subsection,
reduce the wage rate of any employee.

APPENDIX A-2

Civil Rights Act
Title 42, Section 2000e-3(a)

It shall be an unlawful employment practice for an employer:
(1) to fail or refuse to hire or to discharge any individual, or otherwise
to discriminate against any individual with respect to his compensation, terms, conditions, or privileges of employment, because of such
individual's race, color, religion, sex, or national origin; or

(2) to limit, segregate, or classify his employees or applicants for
employment in any way which would deprive or tend to deprive any
individual of employment opportunities or otherwise adversely affect
his status as an employee, because of such individual's race, color, religion, sex, or national origin.

APPENDIX A-3

Age Discrimination In Employment Act
Title 29, Section 623(a)

It shall be unlawful for an employer:
(1) to fail or refuse to hire or to discharge any individual or otherwise discriminate against any individual with respect to his compensation, terms, conditions, or privileges of employment, because of such individual's age;
(2) to limit, segregate, or classify his employees in any way which would deprive or tend to deprive any individual of employment opportunities or otherwise adversely affect his status as an employee, because of such individual's age; or
(3) to reduce the wage rate of any employee in order to comply with this chapter.

APPENDIX A-4

Rehabilitation Act
Title 29, Section 794

No otherwise qualified handicapped individual in the United States, as defined in section 706(8) of this title, shall, solely by reason of his handicap, be excluded from the participation in, be denied the benefits of, or be subjected to discrimination under any program or activity conducted by any Executive agency or by the United States Postal Service. The head of each such agency shall promulgate such regulations as may be necessary to carry out the amendments to this section made by the Rehabilitation, Comprehensive Services, and Developmental Disabilities Act of 1978. Copies of any proposed regulation shall be submitted to appropriate authorizing committees of the Congress, and such regulation may take effect no earlier than the thirtieth day after the date on which such regulation is so submitted to such committees.

APPENDIX B-1.   EEOC Guidelines on Sex Discrimination 29 CFR 1604.

§ 1604.2

PART 1604—GUIDELINES ON DISCRIMINATION BECAUSE OF SEX

Sec.
1604.1 General principles.
1604.2 Sex as a bona fide occupational qualification.
1604.3 Separate lines of progression and seniority systems.
1604.4 Discrimination against married women.
1604.5 Job opportunities advertising.
1604.6 Employment agencies.
1604.7 Pre-employment inquiries as to sex.
1604.8 Relationship of Title VII to the Equal Pay Act.
1604.9 Fringe benefits.
1604.10 Employment policies relating to pregnancy and childbirth.
1604.11 Sexual harassment.

APPENDIX—QUESTIONS AND ANSWERS ON THE PREGNANCY DISCRIMINATION ACT, PUB. L. 95-555, 92 STAT. 2076 (1978)

AUTHORITY: Sec. 713(b), 78 Stat. 265, 42 U.S.C. 2000e-12.

SOURCE: 37 FR 6836, April 5, 1972, unless otherwise noted.

§ 1604.1 General principles.

(a) References to "employer" or "employers" in this Part 1604 state principles that are applicable not only to employers but also to labor organizations and to employment agencies insofar as their action or inaction may adversely affect employment opportunities.

(b) To the extent that the views expressed in prior Commission pronouncements are inconsistent with the views expressed herein, such prior views are hereby overruled.

(c) The Commission will continue to consider particular problems relating to sex discrimination on a case-by-case basis.

§ 1604.2 Sex as a bona fide occupational qualification.

(a) The commission believes that the bona fide occupational qualification exception as to sex should be interpreted narrowly. Label—"Men's jobs" and "Women's jobs"—tend to deny employment opportunities unnecessarily to one sex or the other.

(1) The Commission will find that the following situations do not warrant the application of the bona fide occupational qualification exception:

(i) The refusal to hire a woman because of her sex based on assumptions of the comparative employment characteristics of women in general. For example, the assumption that the turnover rate among women is higher than among men.

(ii) The refusal to hire an individual based on stereotyped characterizations of the sexes. Such stereotypes include, for example, that men are less capable of assembling intricate equipment; that women are less capable of aggressive salesmanship. The principle of nondiscrimination requires that individuals be considered on the basis of individual capacities and not on the basis of any characteristics generally attributed to the group.

(iii) The refusal to hire an individual because of the preferences of coworkers, the employer, clients or customers except as covered specifically in paragraph (a)(2) of this section.

(2) Where it is necessary for the purpose of authenticity or genuineness, the Commission will consider sex to be a bona fide occupational qualification, e.g., an actor or actress.

(b) Effect of sex-oriented State employment legislation.

APPENDIX B-1. EEOC Guidelines on Sex Discrimination 29 CFR 1604.

§ 1604.3

(1) Many States have enacted laws or promulgated administrative regulations with respect to the employment of females. Among these laws are those which prohibit or limit the employment of females, e.g., the employment of females in certain occupations, in jobs requiring the lifting or carrying of weights exceeding certain prescribed limits, during certain hours of the night, for more than a specified number of hours per day or per week, and for certain periods of time before and after childbirth. The Commission has found that such laws and regulations do not take into account the capacities, preferences, and abilities of individual females and, therefore, discriminate on the basis of sex. The Commission has concluded that such laws and regulations conflict with and are superseded by title VII of the Civil Rights Act of 1964. Accordingly, such laws will not be considered a defense to an otherwise established unlawful employment practice or as a basis for the application of the bona fide occupational qualification exception.

(2) The Commission has concluded that State laws and regulations which discriminate on the basis of sex with regard to the employment of minors are in conflict with and are superseded by title VII to the extent that such laws are more restrictive for one sex. Accordingly, restrictions on the employment of minors of one sex over and above those imposed on minors of the other sex will not be considered a defense to an otherwise established unlawful employment practice or as a basis for the application of the bona fide occupational qualification exception.

(3) A number of States require that minimum wage and premium pay for overtime be provided for female employees. An employer will be deemed to have engaged in an unlawful employment practice if:

(i) It refuses to hire or otherwise adversely affects the employment opportunities of female applicants or employees in order to avoid the payment of minimum wages or overtime pay required by State law; or

(ii) It does not provide the same benefits for male employees.

29 CFR Ch. XIV (7-1-89 Edition)

(4) As to other kinds of sex-oriented State employment laws, such as those requiring special rest and meal periods or physical facilities for women, provision of these benefits to one sex only will be a violation of title VII. An employer will be deemed to have engaged in an unlawful employment practice if:

(i) It refuses to hire or otherwise adversely affects the employment opportunities of female applicants or employees in order to avoid the provision of such benefits; or

(ii) It does not provide the same benefits for male employees. If the employer can prove that business necessity precludes providing these benefits to both men and women, then the State law is in conflict with and superseded by title VII as to this employer. In this situation, the employer shall not provide such benefits to members of either sex.

(5) Some States require that separate restrooms be provided for employees of each sex. An employer will be deemed to have engaged in an unlawful employment practice if it refuses to hire or otherwise adversely affects the employment opportunities of applicants or employees in order to avoid the provision of such restrooms for persons of that sex.

§ 1604.3 Separate lines of progression and seniority systems.

(a) It is an unlawful employment practice to classify a job as "male" or "female" or to maintain separate lines of progression or separate seniority lists based on sex where this would adversely affect any employee unless sex is a bona fide occupational qualification for that job. Accordingly, employment practices are unlawful which arbitrarily classify jobs so that:

(1) A female is prohibited from applying for a job labeled "male," or for a job in a "male" line of progression; and vice versa.

(2) A male scheduled for layoff is prohibited from displacing a less senior female on a "female" seniority list; and vice versa.

(b) A Seniority system or line of progression which distinguishes between "light" and "heavy" jobs constitutes an unlawful employment practice if it

APPENDIX B-1.   EEOC Guidelines on Sex Discrimination 29 CFR 1604.

Equal Employment Opportunity Comm.

operates as a disguised form of classification by sex, or creates unreasonable obstacles to the advancement by members of either sex into jobs which members of that sex would reasonably be expected to perform.

§ 1604.4 Discrimination against married women.

(a) The Commission has determined that an employer's rule which forbids or restricts the employment of married women and which is not applicable to married men is a discrimination based on sex prohibited by title VII of the Civil Rights Act. It does not seem to us relevant that the rule is not directed against all females, but only against married females, for so long as sex is a factor in the application of the rule, such application involves a discrimination based on sex.

(b) It may be that under certain circumstances, such a rule could be justified within the meaning of section 703(e)(1) of title VII. We express no opinion on this question at this time except to point out that sex as a bona fide occupational qualification must be justified in terms of the peculiar requirements of the particular job and not on the basis of a general principle such as the desirability of spreading work.

§ 1604.5 Job opportunities advertising.

It is a violation of title VII for a help-wanted advertisement to indicate a preference, limitation, specification, or discrimination based on sex unless sex is a bona fide occupational qualification for the particular job involved. The placement of an advertisement in columns classified by publishers on the basis of sex, such as columns headed "Male" or "Female," will be considered an expression of a preference, limitation, specification, or discrimination based on sex.

§ 1604.6 Employment agencies.

(a) Section 703(b) of the Civil Rights Act specifically states that it shall be unlawful for an employment agency to discriminate against any individual because of sex. The Commission has determined that private employment agencies which deal exclusively with one sex are engaged in an unlawful

§ 1604.8

employment practice, except to the extent that such agencies limit their services to furnishing employees for particular jobs for which sex is a bona fide occupational qualification.

(b) An employment agency that receives a job order containing an unlawful sex specification will share responsibility with the employer placing the job order if the agency fills the order knowing that the sex specification is not based upon a bona fide occupational qualification. However, an employment agency will not be deemed to be in violation of the law, regardless of the determination as to the employer, if the agency does not have reason to believe that the employer's claim of bona fide occupations qualification is without substance and the agency makes and maintains a written record available to the Commission of each such job order. Such record shall include the name of the employer, the description of the job and the basis for the employer's claim of bona fide occupational qualification.

(c) It is the responsibility of employment agencies to keep informed of opinions and decisions of the Commission on sex discrimination.

§ 1604.7 Pre-employment inquiries as to sex.

A pre-employment inquiry may ask "Male........, Female........"; or "Mr. Mrs. Miss," provided that the inquiry is made in good faith for a nondiscriminatory purpose. Any pre-employment inquiry in connection with prospective employment which expresses directly or indirectly any limitation, specification, or discrimination as to sex shall be unlawful unless based upon a bona fide occupational qualification.

§ 1604.8 Relationship of title VII to the Equal Pay Act.

(a) The employee coverage of the prohibitions against discrimination based on sex contained in title VII is coextensive with that of the other prohibitions contained in title VII and is not limited by section 703(h) to those employees covered by the Fair Labor Standards Act.

(b) By virtue of section 703(h), a defense based on the Equal Pay Act may

APPENDIX B-1.   EEOC Guidelines on Sex Discrimination 29 CFR 1604.

§ 1604.9

be raised in a proceeding under title VII.

(c) Where such a defense is raised the Commission will give appropriate consideration to the interpretations of the Administrator, Wage and Hour Division, Department of Labor, but will not be bound thereby.

§ 1604.9 Fringe benefits.

(a) "Fringe benefits," as used herein, includes medical, hospital, accident, life insurance and retirement benefits; profit-sharing and bonus plans; leave; and other terms, conditions, and privileges of employment.

(b) It shall be an unlawful employment practice for an employer to discriminate between men and women with regard to fringe benefits.

(c) Where an employer conditions benefits available to employees and their spouses and families on whether the employee is the "head of the household" or "principal wage earner" in the family unit, the benefits tend to be available only to male employees and their families. Due to the fact that such conditioning discriminatorily affects the rights of women employees, and that "head of household" or "principal wage earner" status bears no relationship to job performance, benefits which are so conditioned will be found a prima facie violation of the prohibitions against sex discrimination contained in the act.

(d) It shall be an unlawful employment practice for an employer to make available benefits for the wives and families of male employees where the same benefits are not made available for the husbands and families of female employees; or to make available benefits for the wives of male employees which are not made available for female employees; or to make available benefits to the husbands of female employees which are not made available for male employees. An example of such an unlawful employment practice is a situation in which wives of male employees receive maternity benefits while female employees receive no such benefits.

(e) It shall not be a defense under title VII to a charge of sex discrimination in benefits that the cost of such benefits is greater with respect to one sex than the other.

(f) It shall be an unlawful employment practice for an employer to have a pension or retirement plan which establishes different optional or compulsory retirement ages based on sex, or which differentiates in benefits on the basis of sex. A statement of the General Counsel of September 13, 1968, providing for a phasing out of differentials with regard to optional retirement age for certain incumbent employees is hereby withdrawn.

§ 1604.10 Employment policies relating to pregnancy and childbirth.

(a) A written or unwritten employment policy or practice which excludes from employment applicants or employees because of pregnancy, childbirth or related medical conditions is in prima facie violation of Title VII.

(b) Disabilities caused or contributed to by pregnancy, childbirth, or related medical conditions, for all job-related purposes, shall be treated the same as disabilities caused or contributed to by other medical conditions, under any health or disability insurance or sick leave plan available in connection with employment. Written or unwritten employment policies and practices involving matters such as the commencement and duration of leave, the availability of extensions, the accrual of seniority and other benefits and privileges, reinstatement, and payment under any health or disability insurance or sick leave plan, formal or informal, shall be applied to disability due to pregnancy, childbirth or related medical conditions on the same terms and conditions as they are applied to other disabilities. Health insurance benefits for abortion, except where the life of the mother would be endangered if the fetus were carried to term or where medical complications have arisen from an abortion, are not required to be paid by an employer; nothing herein, however, precludes an employer from providing abortion benefits or otherwise affects bargaining agreements in regard to abortion.

(c) Where the termination of an employee who is temporarily disabled is caused by an employment policy under

APPENDIX B-1.   EEOC Guidelines on Sex Discrimination 29 CFR 1604.

Equal Employment Opportunity Comm.

which insufficient or no leave is available, such a termination violates the Act if it has a disparate impact on employees of one sex and is not justified by business necessity.

(d)(1) Any fringe benefit program, or fund, or insurance program which is in effect on October 31, 1978, which does not treat women affected by pregnancy, childbirth, or related medical conditions the same as other persons not so affected but similar in their ability or inability to work, must be in compliance with the provisions of § 1604.10(b) by April 29, 1979. In order to come into compliance with the provisions of 1604.10(b), there can be no reduction of benefits or compensation which were in effect on October 31, 1978, before October 31, 1979 or the expiration of a collective bargaining agreement in effect on October 31, 1978, whichever is later.

(2) Any fringe benefit program implemented after October 31, 1978, must comply with the provisions of § 1604.10(b) upon implementation.

[44 FR 23805, Apr. 20, 1979]

§ 1604.11   Sexual harassment.

(a) Harassment on the basis of sex is a violation of Sec. 703 of Title VII.[1] Unwelcome sexual advances, requests for sexual favors, and other verbal or physical conduct of a sexual nature constitute sexual harassment when (1) submission to such conduct is made either explicitly or implicitly a term or condition of an individual's employment, (2) submission to or rejection of such conduct by an individual is used as the basis for employment decisions affecting such individual, or (3) such conduct has the purpose or effect of unreasonably interfering with an individual's work performance or creating an intimidating, hostile, or offensive working environment.

(b) In determining whether alleged conduct constitutes sexual harassment, the Commission will look at the record as a whole and at the totality of the circumstances, such as the nature of the sexual advances and the

---

[1]The principles involved here continue to apply to race, color, religion or national origin.

§ 1604.11

context in which the alleged incidents occurred. The determination of the legality of a particular action will be made from the facts, on a case by case basis.

(c) Applying general Title VII principles, an employer, employment agency, joint apprenticeship committee or labor organization (hereinafter collectively referred to as "employer") is responsible for its acts and those of its agents and supervisory employees with respect to sexual harassment regardless of whether the specific acts complained of were authorized or even forbidden by the employer and regardless of whether the employer knew or should have known of their occurrence. The Commission will examine the circumstances of the particular employment relationship and the job junctions performed by the individual in determining whether an individual acts in either a supervisory or agency capacity.

(d) With respect to conduct between fellow employees, an employer is responsible for acts of sexual harassment in the workplace where the employer (or its agents or supervisory employees) knows or should have known of the conduct, unless it can show that it took immediate and appropriate corrective action.

(e) An employer may also be responsible for the acts of non-employees, with respect to sexual harassment of employees in the workplace, where the employer (or its agents or supervisory employees) knows or should have known of the conduct and fails to take immediate and appropriate corrective action. In reviewing these cases the Commission will consider the extent of the employer's control and any other legal responsibility which the employer may have with respect to the conduct of such non-employees.

(f) Prevention is the best tool for the elimination of sexual harassment. An employer should take all steps necessary to prevent sexual harassment from occurring, such as affirmatively raising the subject, expressing strong disapproval, developing appropriate sanctions, informing employees of their right to raise and how to raise the issue of harassment under Title

APPENDIX B-1.   EEOC Guidelines on Sex Discrimination 29 CFR 1604.

Pt. 1604, App.

VII, and developing methods to sensitize all concerned.

(g) Other related practices: Where employment opportunities or benefits are granted because of an individual's submission to the employer's sexual advances or requests for sexual favors, the employer may be held liable for unlawful sex discrimination against other persons who were qualified for but denied that employment opportunity or benefit.

(Title VII, Pub. L. 88–352, 78 Stat. 253 (42 U.S.C. 2000e et seq.))

[45 FR 74677, Nov. 10, 1980]

APPENDIX—QUESTIONS AND ANSWERS ON THE PREGNANCY DISCRIMINATION ACT, PUB. L. 95–555, 92 STAT. 2076 (1978)

INTRODUCTION

On October 31, 1978, President Carter signed into law the *Pregnancy Discrimination Act* (Pub. L. 95–955). The Act is an amendment to Title VII of the Civil Rights Act of 1964 which prohibits, among other things, discrimination in employment on the basis of sex. The *Pregnancy Discrimination Act* makes it clear that "because of sex" or "on the basis of sex", as used in Title VII, includes "because of or on the basis of pregnancy, childbirth or related medical conditions." Therefore, Title VII prohibits discrimination in employment against women affected by pregnancy or related conditions.

The basic principle of the Act is that women affected by pregnancy and related conditions must be treated the same as other applicants and employees on the basis of their ability or inability to work. A woman is therefore protected against such practices as being fired, or refused a job or promotion, merely because she is pregnant or has had an abortion. She usually cannot be forced to go on leave as long as she can still work. If other employees who take disability leave are entitled to get their jobs back when they are able to work again, so are women who have been unable to work because of pregnancy.

In the area of fringe benefits, such as disability benefits, sick leave and health insurance, the same principle applies. A woman unable to work for pregnancy-related reasons is entitled to disability benefits or sick leave on the same basis as employees unable to work for other medical reasons. Also, any health insurance provided must cover expenses for pregnancy-related conditions on the same basis as expenses for other medical conditions. However, health insurance for expenses arising from abortion is not re-

29 CFR Ch. XIV (7-1-89 Edition)

quired except where the life of the mother would be endangered if the fetus were carried to term, or where medical complications have arisen from an abortion.

Some questions and answers about the *Pregnancy Discrimination Act* follow. Although the questions and answers often use only the term "employer," the Act—and these questions and answers—apply also to unions and other entities covered by Title VII.

1. Q. What is the effective date of the Pregnancy Discrimination Act?

A. The Act became effective on October 31, 1978, except that with respect to fringe benefit programs in effect on that date, the Act will take effect 180 days thereafter, that is, April 29, 1979.

To the extent that Title VII already required employers to treat persons affected by pregnancy-related conditions the same as persons affected by other medical conditions, the Act does not change employee rights arising prior to October 31, 1978, or April 29, 1979. Most employment practices relating to pregnancy, childbirth and related conditions—whether concerning fringe benefits or other practices—were already controlled by Title VII prior to this Act. For example, Title VII has always prohibited an employer from firing, or refusing to hire or promote, a woman because of pregnancy or related conditions, and from failing to accord a woman on pregnancy-related leave the same seniority retention and accrual accorded those on other disability leaves.

2. Q. If an employer had a sick leave policy in effect on October 31, 1978, by what date must the employer bring its policy into compliance with the Act?

A. With respect to payment of benefits, an employer has until April 29, 1979, to bring into compliance any fringe benefit or insurance program, including a sick leave policy, which was in effect on October 31, 1978. However, any such policy or program created after October 31, 1978, must be in compliance when created.

With respect to all aspects of sick leave policy other than payment of benefits, such as the terms governing retention and accrual of seniority, credit for vacation, and resumption of former job on return from sick leave, equality of treatment was required by Title VII without the Amendment.

3. Q. Must an employer provide benefits for pregnancy-related conditions to an employee whose pregnancy begins prior to April 29, 1979, and continues beyond that date?

A. As of April 29, 1979, the effective date of the Act's requirements, an employer must provide the same benefits for pregnancy-related conditions as it provides for other conditions, regardless of when the pregnancy began. Thus, disability benefits must be

APPENDIX B-1.   EEOC Guidelines on Sex Discrimination 29 CFR 1604.

---

paid for all absences on or after April 29, 1979, resulting from pregnancy-related temporary disabilities to the same extent as they are paid for absences resulting from other temporary disabilities. For example, if an employee gives birth before April 29, 1979, but is still unable to work on or after that date, she is entitled to the same disability benefits available to other employees. Similarly, medical insurance benefits must be paid for pregnancy-related expenses incurred on or after April 29, 1979.

If an employer requires an employee to be employed for a predetermined period prior to being eligible for insurance coverage, the period prior to April 29, 1979, during which a pregnant employee has been employed must be credited toward the eligibility waiting period on the same basis as for any other employee.

As to any programs instituted for the first time after October 31, 1978, coverage for pregnancy-related conditions must be provided in the same manner as for other medical conditions.

4. Q. Would the answer to the preceding question be the same if the employee became pregnant prior to October 31, 1978?

A. Yes.

5. Q. If, for pregnancy-related reasons, an employee is unable to perform the functions of her job, does the employer have to provide her an alternative job?

A. An employer is required to treat an employee temporarily unable to perform the functions of her job because of her pregnancy-related condition in the same manner as it treats other temporarily disabled employees, whether by providing modified tasks, alternative assignments, disability leaves, leaves without pay, etc. For example, a woman's primary job function may be the operation of a machine, and, incidental to that function, she may carry materials to and from the machine. If other employees temporarily unable to lift are relieved of these functions, pregnant employees also unable to lift must be temporarily relieved of the function.

6. Q. What procedures may an employer use to determine whether to place on leave as unable to work a pregnant employee who claims she is able to work or deny leave to a pregnant employee who claims that she is disabled from work?

A. An employer may not single out pregnancy-related conditions for special procedures for determining an employee's ability to work. However, an employer may use any procedure used to determine the ability of all employees to work. For example, if an employer requires its employees to submit a doctor's statement concerning their inability to work before granting leave or paying sick benefits, the employer may require employees affected by pregnancy-related conditions to submit such statement. Similarly,

if an employer allows its employees to obtain doctor's statements from their personal physicians for absences due to other disabilities or return dates from other disabilities, it must accept doctor's statements from personal physicians for absences and return dates connected with pregnancy-related disabilities.

7. Q. Can an employer have a rule which prohibits an employee from returning to work for a predetermined length of time after childbirth?

A. No.

8. Q. If an employee has been absent from work as a result of a pregnancy-related condition and recovers, may her employer require her to remain on leave until after her baby is born?

A. No. An employee must be permitted to work at all times during pregnancy when she is able to perform her job.

9. Q. Must an employer hold open the job of an employee who is absent on leave because she is temporarily disabled by pregnancy-related conditions?

A. Unless the employee on leave has informed the employer that she does not intend to return to work, her job must be held open for her return on the same basis as jobs are held open for employees on sick or disability leave for other reasons.

10. Q. May an employer's policy concerning the accrual and crediting of seniority during absences for medical conditions be different for employees affected by pregnancy-related conditions than for other employees?

A. No. An employer's seniority policy must be the same for employees absent for pregnancy-related reasons as for those absent for other medical reasons.

11. Q. For purposes of calculating such matters as vacations and pay increases, may an employer credit time spent on leave for pregnancy-related reasons differently than time spent on leave for other reasons?

A. No. An employer's policy with respect to crediting time for the purpose of calculating such matters as vacations and pay increases cannot treat employees on leave for pregnancy-related reasons less favorably than employees on leave for other reasons. For example, if employees on leave for medical reasons are credited with the time spent on leave when computing entitlement to vacation or pay raises, an employee on leave for pregnancy-related disability is entitled to the same kind of time credit.

12. Q. Must an employer hire a woman who is medically unable, because of a pregnancy-related condition, to perform a necessary function of a job?

A. An employer cannot refuse to hire a women because of her pregnancy-related condition so long as she is able to perform the major functions necessary to the job.

APPENDIX B-1. EEOC Guidelines on Sex Discrimination 29 CFR 1604.

Pt. 1604, App.

Nor can an employer refuse to hire her because of its preferences against pregnant workers or the preferences of co-workers, clients, or customers.

13. Q. May an employer limit disability benefits for pregnancy-related conditions to married employees?

A. No.

14. Q. If an employer has an all female workforce or job classification, must benefits be provided for pregnancy-related conditions?

A. Yes. If benefits are provided for other conditions, they must also be provided for pregnancy-related conditions.

15. Q. For what length of time must an employer who provides income maintenance benefits for temporary disabilities provide such benefits for pregnancy-related disabilities?

A. Benefits should be provided for as long as the employee is unable to work for medical reasons unless some other limitation is set for all other temporary disabilities, in which case pregnancy-related disabilities should be treated the same as other temporary disabilities.

16. Q. Must an employer who provides benefits for long-term or permanent disabilities provide such benefits for pregnancy-related conditions?

A. Yes. Benefits for long-term or permanent disabilities resulting from pregnancy-related conditions must be provided to the same extent that such benefits are provided for other conditions which result in long-term or permanent disability.

17. Q. If an employer provides benefits to employees on leave, such as installment purchase disability insurance, payment of premiums for health, life or other insurance, continued payments into pension, saving or profit sharing plans, must the same benefits be provided for those on leave for pregnancy-related conditions?

A. Yes, the employer must provide the same benefits for those on leave for pregnancy-related conditions as for those on leave for other reasons.

18. Q. Can an employee who is absent due to a pregnancy-related disability be required to exhaust vacation benefits before receiving sick leave pay or disability benefits?

A. No. If employees who are absent because of other disabling causes receive sick leave pay or disability benefits without any requirement that they first exhaust vacation benefits, the employer cannot impose this requirement on an employee absent for a pregnancy-related cause.

18(A). Q. Must an employer grant leave to a female employee for childcare purposes after she is medically able to return to work following leave necessitated by pregnancy, childbirth or related medical conditions?

A. While leave for childcare purposes is not covered by the Pregnancy Discrimina-

29 CFR Ch. XIV (7-1-89 Edition)

tion Act, ordinary Title VII principles would require that leave for childcare purposes be granted on the same basis as leave which is granted to employees for other non-medical reasons. For example, if an employer allows its employees to take leave without pay or accrued annual leave for travel or education which is not job related, the same type of leave must be granted to those who wish to remain on leave for infant care, even though they are medically able to return to work.

19. Q. If state law requires an employer to provide disability insurance for a specified period before and after childbirth, does compliance with the state law fulfill the employer's obligation under the Pregnancy Discrimination Act?

A. Not necessarily. It is an employer's obligation to treat employees temporarily disabled by pregnancy in the same manner as employees affected by other temporary disabilities. Therefore, any restrictions imposed by state law on benefits for pregnancy-related disabilities, but not for other disabilities, do not excuse the employer from treating the individuals in both groups of employees the same. If, for example, a state law requires an employer to pay a maximum of 26 weeks benefits for disabilities other than pregnancy-related ones but only six weeks for pregnancy-related disabilities, the employer must provide benefits for the additional weeks to an employee disabled by pregnancy-related conditions, up to the maximum provided other disabled employees.

20. Q. If a State or local government provides its own employees income maintenance benefits for disabilities, may it provide different benefits for disabilities arising from pregnancy-related conditions than for disabilities arising from other conditions?

A. No. State and local governments, as employers, are subject to the Pregnancy Discrimination Act in the same way as private employers and must bring their employment practices and programs into compliance with the Act, including disability and health insurance programs.

21. Q. Must an employer provide health insurance coverage for the medical expenses of pregnancy-related conditions of the spouses of male employees? Of the dependents of all employees?

A. Where an employer provides no coverage for dependents, the employer is not required to institute such coverage. However, if an employer's insurance program covers the medical expenses of spouses of female employees, then it must equally cover the medical expenses of spouses of male employees, including those arising from pregnancy-related conditions.

But the insurance does not have to cover the pregnancy-related conditions of other

APPENDIX B-1.   EEOC Guidelines on Sex Discrimination 29 CFR 1604.

Equal Employment Opportunity Comm.

dependents as long as it excludes the pregnancy-related conditions of the dependents of male and female employees equally.

22. Q. Must an employer provide the same level of health insurance coverage for the pregnancy-related medical conditions of the spouses of male employees as it provides for its female employees?

A. No. It is not necessary to provide the same level of coverage for the pregnancy-related medical conditions of spouses of male employees as for female employees. However, where the employer provides coverage for the medical conditions of the spouses of its employees, then the level of coverage for pregnancy-related medical conditions of the spouses of male employees must be the same as the level of coverage for all other medical conditions of the spouses of female employees. For example, if the employer covers employees for 100 percent of reasonable and customary expenses sustained for a medical condition, but only covers dependent spouses for 50 percent of reasonable and customary expenses for their medical conditions, the pregnancy-related expenses of the male employee's spouse must be covered at the 50 percent level.

23. Q. May an employer offer optional dependent coverage which excludes pregnancy-related medical conditions or offers less coverage for pregnancy-related medical conditions where the total premium for the optional coverage is paid by the employee?

A. No. Pregnancy-related medical conditions must be treated the same as other medical conditions under any health or disability insuran⊂⸗ or sick leave plan *available in connection with employment*, regardless of who pays the premiums.

24. Q. Where an employer provides its employees a choice among several health insurance plans, must coverage for pregnancy-related conditions be offered in all of the plans?

A. Yes. Each of the plans must cover pregnancy-related conditions. For example, an employee with a single coverage policy cannot be forced to purchase a more expensive family coverage policy in order to receive coverage for her own pregnancy-related condition.

25. Q. On what basis should an employee be reimbursed for medical expenses arising from pregnancy, childbirth or related conditions?

A. Pregnancy-related expenses should be reimbursed in the same manner as are expenses incurred for other medical conditions. Therefore, whether a plan reimburses the employees on a fixed basis, or a percentage of reasonable and customary charge basis, the same basis should be used for reimbursement of expenses incurred for pregnancy-related conditions. Furthermore, if medical costs for pregnancy-related conditions increase, reevaluation of the reim-

bursement level should be conducted in the same manner as are cost reevaluations of increases for other medical conditions.

Coverage provided by a health insurance program for other conditions must be provided for pregnancy-related conditions. For example, if a plan provides major medical coverage, pregnancy-related conditions must be so covered. Similarly, if a plan covers the cost of a private room for other conditions, the plan must cover the cost of a private room for pregnancy-related conditions. Finally, where a health insurance plan covers office visits to physicians, pre-natal and post-natal visits must be included in such coverage.

26. Q. May an employer limit payment of costs for pregnancy-related medical conditions to a specified dollar amount set forth in an insurance policy, collective bargaining agreement or other statement of benefits to which an employee is entitled?

A. The amounts payable for the costs incurred for pregnancy-related conditions can be limited only to the same extent as are costs for other conditions. Maximum recoverable dollar amounts may be specified for pregnancy-related conditions if such amounts are similarly specified for other conditions, and so long as the specified amounts in all instances cover the same proportion of actual costs. If, in addition to the scheduled amount for other procedures, additional costs are paid for, either directly or indirectly, by the employer, such additional payments must also be paid for pregnancy-related procedures.

27. Q. May an employer impose a different deductible for payment of costs for pregnancy-related medical conditions than for costs of other medical conditions?

A. No. Neither an additional deductible, an increase in the usual deductible, nor a larger deductible can be imposed for coverage for pregnancy-related medical costs, whether as a condition for inclusion of pregnancy-related costs in the policy or for payment of the costs when incurred. Thus, if pregnancy-related costs are the first incurred under the policy, the employee is required to pay only the same deductible as would otherwise be required had other medical costs been the first incurred. Once this deductible has been paid, no additional deductible can be required for other medical procedures. If the usual deductible has already been paid for other medical procedures, no additional deductible can be required when pregnancy-related costs are later incurred.

28. Q. If a health insurance plan excludes the payment of benefits for any conditions existing at the time the insured's coverage becomes effective (pre-existing condition clause), can benefits be denied for medical

APPENDIX B-1.   EEOC Guidelines on Sex Discrimination 29 CFR 1604.

Pt. 1604, App.

costs arising from a pregnancy existing at the time the coverage became effective?

A. Yes. However, such benefits cannot be denied unless the pre-existing condition clause also excludes benefits for other pre-existing conditions in the same way.

29. Q. If an employer's insurance plan provides benefits after the insured's employment has ended (i.e. extended benefits) for costs connected with pregnancy and delivery where conception occurred while the insured was working for the employer, but not for the costs of any other medical condition which began prior to termination of employment, may an employer (a) continue to pay these extended benefits for pregnancy-related medical conditions but not for other medical conditions, or (b) terminate these benefits for pregnancy-related conditions?

A. Where a health insurance plan currently provides extended benefits for other medical conditions on a less favorable basis than for pregnancy-related medical conditions, extended benefits must be provided for other medical conditions on the same basis as for pregnancy-related medical conditions. Therefore, an employer can neither continue to provide less benefits for other medical conditions nor reduce benefits currently paid for pregnancy-related medical conditions.

30. Q. Where an employer's health insurance plan currently requires total disability as a prerequisite for payment of extended benefits for other medical conditions but not for pregnancy-related costs, may the employer now require total disability for payment of benefits for pregnancy-related medical conditions as well?

A. Since extended benefits cannot be reduced in order to come into compliance with the Act, a more stringent prerequisite for payment of extended benefits for pregnancy-related medical conditions, such as a requirement for total disability, cannot be imposed. Thus, in this instance, in order to comply with the Act, the employer must treat other medical conditions as pregnancy-related conditions are treated.

31. Q. Can the added cost of bringing benefit plans into compliance with the Act be apportioned between the employer and employee?

A. The added cost, if any, can be apportioned between the employer and employee in the same proportion that the cost of the fringe benefit plan was apportioned on October 31, 1978, if that apportionment was nondiscriminatory. If the costs were not apportioned on October 31, 1978, they may not be apportioned in order to come into compliance with the Act. However, in no circumstance may male or female employees be required to pay unequal apportionments on the basis of sex or pregnancy.

29 CFR Ch. XIV (7-1-89 Edition)

32. Q. In order to come into compliance with the Act, may an employer reduce benefits or compensation?

A. In order to come into compliance with the Act, benefits or compensation which an employer was paying on October 31, 1978 cannot be reduced before October 31, 1979 or before the expiration of a collective bargaining agreement in effect on October 31, 1978, whichever is later.

Where an employer has not been in compliance with the Act by the times specified in the Act, and attempts to reduce benefits, or compensation, the employer may be required to remedy its practices in accord with ordinary Title VII remedial principles.

33. Q. Can an employer self-insure benefits for pregnancy-related conditions if it does not self-insure benefits for other medical conditions?

A. Yes, so long as the benefits are the same. In measuring whether benefits are the same, factors other than the dollar coverage paid should be considered. Such factors include the range of choice of physicians and hospitals, and the processing and promptness of payment of claims.

34. Q. Can an employer discharge, refuse to hire or otherwise discriminate against a woman because she has had an abortion?

A. No. An employer cannot discriminate in its employment practices against a woman who has had an abortion.

35. Q. Is an employer required to provide fringe benefits for abortions if fringe benefits are provided for other medical conditions?

A. All fringe benefits other than health insurance, such as sick leave, which are provided for other medical conditions, must be provided for abortions. Health insurance, however, need be provided for abortions only where the life of the woman would be endangered if the fetus were carried to term or where medical complications arise from an abortion.

36. Q. If complications arise during the course of an abortion, as for instance excessive hemorrhaging, must an employer's health insurance plan cover the additional cost due to the complications of the abortion?

A. Yes. The plan is required to pay those additional costs attributable to the complications of the abortion. However, the employer is not required to pay for the abortion itself, except where the life of the mother would be endangered if the fetus were carried to term.

37. Q. May an employer elect to provide insurance coverage for abortions?

A. Yes. The Act specifically provides that an employer is not precluded from providing benefits for abortions whether directly or through a collective bargaining agreement, but if an employer decides to cover the costs of abortion, the employer must do so in the same manner and to the same degree as it covers other medical conditions.

[44 FR 23805, Apr. 20, 1979]

APPENDIX B-2. EEOC Guidelines for Age Discrimination 29 CFR 1625.

PART 1625—AGE DISCRIMINATION IN EMPLOYMENT ACT

Subpart A—Interpretations

Sec.
1625.1 Definitions.
1625.2 Discrimination between individuals protected by the Act.
1625.3 Employment agency.
1625.4 Help wanted notices or advertisements.
1625.5 Employment applications.
1625.6 Bona fide occupational qualifications.
1625.7 Differentiations based on reasonable factors other than age.
1625.8 Bona fide seniority systems.
1625.9 Prohibition of involuntary retirement.
1625.10 Costs and benefits under employee benefit plans.
1625.11 Exemption for employees serving under a contract of unlimited tenure.
1625.12 Exemption for bona fide executive or high policymaking employees.
1625.13 Apprenticeship programs.

Subpart B—Substantive Regulations [Reserved]

AUTHORITY: 81 Stat. 602; 29 U.S.C. 621, 5 U.S.C. 301, Secretary's Order No. 10–68; Secretary's Order No. 11–68; Sec. 12, 29 U.S.C. 631, Pub. L. No. 99–592, 100 Stat. 3342; Sec. 2, Reorg. Plan No. 1 of 1978, 43 FR 19807.

SOURCE: 46 FR 47726, Sept. 29, 1981, unless otherwise noted.

Subpart A—Interpretations

§ 1625.1 Definitions.

The Equal Employment Opportunity Commission is hereinafter referred to as the "Commission". The terms "person", "employer", "employment agency", "labor organization", and "employee" shall have the meanings set forth in Section 11 of the Age Discrimination in Employment Act of 1967, as amended, 29 U.S.C. 621 et seq., hereinafter referred to as the "Act". References to "employers" in this part state principles that are applicable not only to employers but also to labor organizations and to employment agencies.

§ 1625.2 Discrimination between individuals protected by the Act.

(a) It is unlawful in situations where this Act applies, for an employer to discriminate in hiring or in any other way by giving preference because of age between individuals 40 and over. Thus, if two people apply for the same position, and one is 42 and the other 52, the employer may not lawfully turn down either one on the basis of age, but must make such decision on the basis of some other factor.

(b) The extension of additional benefits, such as increased severance pay, to older employees within the protected group may be lawful if an employer has a reasonable basis to conclude that those benefits will counteract problems related to age discrimination. The extension of those additional benefits may not be used as a means to accomplish practices otherwise prohibited by the Act.

[46 FR 47726, Sept. 29, 1981, as amended at 53 FR 5972, Feb. 29, 1988]

§ 1625.3 Employment agency.

(a) As long as an employment agency regularly procures employees for at least one covered employer, it qualifies under section 11(c) of the Act as an employment agency with respect to all of its activities whether or not such activities are for employers covered by the act.

(b) The prohibitions of section 4(b) of the Act apply not only to the referral activities of a covered employment agency but also to the agency's own employment practices, regardless of the number of employees the agency may have.

§ 1625.4 Help wanted notices or advertisements.

(a) When help wanted notices or advertisements contain terms and phrases such as "age 25 to 35," "young," "college student," "recent college graduate," "boy," "girl," or others of a similar nature, such a term or phrase deters the employment of older persons and is a violation of the Act, unless one of the exceptions applies. Such phrases as "age 40 to 50," "age over 65," "retired person," or "supplement your pension" discriminate against others within the protected group and, therefore, are prohibited unless one of the exceptions applies.

APPENDIX B-2.   EEOC Guidelines for Age Discrimination 29 CFR 1625.

Equal Employment Opportunity Comm.   **§ 1625.7**

(b) The use of the phrase "state age" in help wanted notices or advertisements is not, in itself, a violation of the Act. But because the request that an applicant state his age may tend to deter older applicants or otherwise indicate discrimination based on age, employment notices or advertisements which include the phrase "state age," or any similar term, will be closely scrutinized to assure that the request is for a lawful purpose.

§ 1625.5   Employment applications.

A request on the part of an employer for information such as "Date of Birth" or "State Age" on an employment application form is not, in itself, a violation of the Act. But because the request that an applicant state his age may tend to deter older applicants or otherwise indicate discrimination based on age, employment application forms which request such information will be closely scrutinized to assure that the request is for a permissible purpose and not for purposes proscribed by the Act. That the purpose is not one proscribed by the statute should be made known to the applicant, either by a reference on the application form to the statutory prohibition in language to the following effect:

The Age Discrimination in Employment Act of 1967 prohibits discrimination on the basis of age with respect to individuals who are at least 40 years of age," or by other means. The term "employment applications," refers to all written inquiries about employment or applications for employment or promotion including, but not limited to, résumés or other summaries of the applicant's background. It relates not only to written preemployment inquiries, but to inquiries by employees concerning terms, conditions, or privileges of employment as specified in section 4 of the Act.

[46 FR 47726, Sept. 29, 1981, as amended at 53 FR 5972, Feb. 29, 1988]

§ 1625.6   Bona fide occupational qualifications.

(a) Whether occupational qualifications will be deemed to be "bona fide" to a specific job and "reasonably necessary to the normal operation of the particular business, " will be determined on the basis of all the pertinent facts surrounding each particular situation. It is anticipated that this concept of a bona fide occupational qualification will have limited scope and application. Further, as this is an exception to the Act it must be narrowly construed.

(b) An employer asserting a BFOQ defense has the burden of proving that (1) the age limit is reasonably necessary to the essence of the business, and either (2) that all or substantially all individuals excluded from the job involved are in fact disqualified, or (3) that some of the individuals so excluded possess a disqualifying trait that cannot be ascertained except by reference to age. If the employer's objective in asserting a BFOQ is the goal of public safety, the employer must prove that the challenged practice does indeed effectuate that goal and that there is no acceptable alternative which would better advance it or equally advance it with less discriminatory impact.

(c) Many State and local governments have enacted laws or administrative regulations which limit employment opportunities based on age. Unless these laws meet the standards for the establishment of a valid bona fide occupational qualification under section 4(f)(1) of the Act, they will be considered in conflict with and effectively superseded by the ADEA.

§ 1625.7   Differentiations based on reasonable factors other than age.

(a) Section 4(f)(1) of the Act provides that

* * * it shall not be unlawful for an employer, employment agency, or labor organization * * * to take any action otherwise prohibited under paragraphs (a), (b), (c), or (e) of this section * * * where the differentiation is based on reasonable factors other than age * * *.

(b) No precise and unequivocal determination can be made as to the scope of the phrase "differentiation based on reasonable factors other than age." Whether such differentiations exist must be decided on the basis of all the particular facts and circumstances surrounding each individual situation.

(c) When an employment practice uses age as a limiting criterion, the de-

APPENDIX B-2.   EEOC Guidelines for Age Discrimination 29 CFR 1625.

---

§ 1625.8

fense that the practice is justified by a reasonable factor other than age is unavailable.

(d) When an employment practice, including a test, is claimed as a basis for different treatment of employees or applicants for employment on the grounds that it is a "factor other than" age, and such a practice has an adverse impact on individuals within the protected age group, it can only be justified as a business necessity. Tests which are asserted as "reasonable factors other than age" will be scrutinized in accordance with the standards set forth at Part 1607 of this title.

(e) When the exception of "a reasonable factor other than age" is raised against an individual claim of discriminatory treatment, the employer bears the burden of showing that the "reasonable factor other than age" exists factually.

(f) A differentiation based on the average cost of employing older employees as a group is unlawful except with respect to employee benefit plans which qualify for the section 4(f)(2) exception to the Act.

§ 1625.8 Bona fide seniority systems.

Section 4(f)(2) of the Act provides that

* * * It shall not be unlawful for an employer, employment agency, or labor organization * * * to observe the terms of a bona fide seniority system * * * which is not a subterfuge to evade the purposes of this Act except that no such seniority system * * * shall require or permit the involuntary retirement of any individual specified by section 12(a) of this Act because of the age of such individual. * * *

(a) Though a seniority system may be qualified by such factors as merit, capacity, or ability, any bona fide seniority system must be based on length of service as the primary criterion for the equitable allocation of available employment opportunities and prerogatives among younger and older workers.

(b) Adoption of a purported seniority system which gives those with longer service lesser rights, and results in discharge or less favored treatment to those within the protection of the

Act, may, depending upon the circumstances, be a "subterfuge to evade the purposes" of the Act.

(c) Unless the essential terms and conditions of an alleged seniority system have been communicated to the affected employees and can be shown to be applied uniformly to all of those affected, regardless of age, it will not be considered a bona fide seniority system within the meaning of the Act.

(d) It should be noted that seniority systems which segregate, classify, or otherwise discriminate against individuals on the basis of race, color, religion, sex, or national origin, are prohibited under Title VII of the Civil Rights Act of 1964, where that Act otherwise applies. The "bona fides" of such a system will be closely scrutinized to ensure that such a system is, in fact, bona fide under the ADEA.

[53 FR 15673, May 3, 1988]

§ 1625.9 Prohibition of involuntary retirement.

(a)(1) As originally enacted in 1967, section 4(f)(2) of the Act provided: "It shall not be unlawful * * * to observe the terms of a bona fide seniority system or any bona fide employee benefit plan such as a retirement, pension, or insurance plan, which is not a subterfuge to evade the purposes of this Act, except that no such employee benefit plan shall excuse the failure to hire any individual * * *." The Department of Labor interpreted the provision as "Authoriz[ing] involuntary retirement irrespective of age: *Provided*, That such retirement is pursuant to the terms of a retirement or pension plan meeting the requirements of section 4(f)(2)." *See* 34 FR 9709 (June 21, 1969). The Department took the position that in order to meet the requirements of section 4(f)(2), the involuntary retirement provision had to be (i) contained in a bona fide pension or retirement plan, (ii) required by the terms of the plan and not optional, and (iii) essential to the plan's economic survival or to some other legitimate business purpose—i.e., the provision was not in the plan as the result of arbitrary discrimination on the basis of age.

APPENDIX B-2.   EEOC Guidelines for Age Discrimination 29 CFR 1625.

Equal Employment Opportunity Comm.

(2) As revised by the 1978 amendments, section 4(f)(2) was amended by adding the following clause at the end: "and no such seniority system or employee benefit plan shall require or permit the involuntary retirement of any individual specified by section 12(a) of this Act because of the age of such individual * * *." The Conference Committee Report expressly states that this amendment is intended "to make absolutely clear one of the original purposes of this provision, namely, that the exception does not authorize an employer to require or permit involuntary retirement of an employee within the protected age group on account of age" (H.R. Rept. No. 95-950, p. 8).

(b)(1) The amendment applies to all new and existing seniority systems and employee benefit plans. Accordingly, any system or plan provision requiring or permitting involuntary retirement is unlawful, regardless of whether the provision antedates the 1967 Act or the 1978 amendments.

(2) Where lawsuits pending on the date of enactment (April 6, 1978) or filed thereafter challenge involuntary retirements which occurred either before or after that date, the amendment applies.

(c)(1) The amendment protects all individuals covered by section 12(a) of the Act. Section 12(a) was amended in October of 1986 by the Age Discrimination in Employment Amendments of 1986, Pub. L. 99-592, 100 Stat. 3342 (1986), which removed the age 70 limit. Section 12(a) provides that the Act's prohibitions shall be limited to individuals who are at least forty years of age. Accordingly, unless a specific exemption applies, an employer can no longer force retirement or otherwise discriminate on the basis of age against an individual because (s)he is 70 or older.

(2) The amendment to section 12(a) of the Act became effective on January 1, 1987, except with respect to any employee subject to a collective bargaining agreement containing a provision that would be superseded by such amendment that was in effect on June 30, 1986, and which terminates after January 1, 1987. In that case, the amendment is effective on the termi-

§ 1625.10

nation of the agreement or January 1, 1990, whichever comes first.

(d) Neither section 4(f)(2) nor any other provision of the Act makes it unlawful for a plan to permit individuals to elect early retirement at a specified age at their own option. Nor is it unlawful for a plan to require early retirement for reasons other than age.

[46 FR 47726, Sept. 29, 1981, as amended at 52 FR 23811, June 25, 1987; 53 FR 5973, Feb. 29, 1988]

§ 1625.10   Costs and benefits under employee benefit plans.

(a)(1) *General.* Section 4(f)(2) of the Act provides that it is not unlawful for an employer, employment agency, or labor organization "to observe the terms of * * * any bona fide employee benefit plan such as a retirement, pension, or insurance plan, which is not a subterfuge to evade the purposes of this Act, except that no such employee benefit plan shall excuse the failure to hire any individual, and no such * * * employee benefit plan shall require or permit the involuntary retirement of any individual specified by section 12(a) of this Act because of the age of such individuals." The legislative history of this provision indicates that its purpose is to permit age-based reductions in employee benefit plans where such reductions are justified by significant cost considerations. Accordingly, section 4(f)(2) does not apply, for example, to paid vacations and uninsured paid sick leave, since reductions in these benefits would not be justified by significant cost considerations. Where employee benefit plans do meet the criteria in section 4(f)(2), benefit levels for older workers may be reduced to the extent necessary to achieve approximate equivalency in cost for older and younger workers. A benefit plan will be considered in compliance with the statute where the actual amount of payment made, or cost incurred, in behalf of an older worker is equal to that made or incurred in behalf of a younger worker, even though the older worker may thereby receive a lesser amount of benefits or insurance coverage. Since section 4(f)(2) is an exception from the general non-discrimination provi-

APPENDIX B-2. EEOC Guidelines for Age Discrimination 29 CFR 1625.

§ 1625.10

sions of the Act, the burden is on the one seeking to invoke the exception to show that every element has been clearly and unmistakably met. The exception must be narrowly construed. The following sections explain three key elements of the exception: (i) What a "bona fide employee benefit plan" is; (ii) what it means to "observe the terms" of such a plan; and (iii) what kind of plan, or plan provision, would be considered "a subterfuge to evade the purposes of [the] Act." There is also a discussion of the application of the general rules governing all plans with respect to specific kinds of employee benefit plans.

(2) *Relation of section 4(f)(2) to sections 4(a), 4(b) and 4(c).* Sections 4(a), 4(b) and 4(c) prohibit specified acts of discrimination on the basis of age. Section 4(a) in particular makes it unlawful for an employer to "discriminate against any individual with respect to his compensation, terms, conditions, or privileges of employment, because of such individual's age * * *." Section 4(f)(2) is an exception to this general prohibition. Where an employer under an employee benefit plan provides the same level of benefits to older workers as to younger workers, there is no violation of section 4(a), and accordingly the practice does not have to be justified under section 4(f)(2).

(b) *"Bona fide employee benefit plan."* Section 4(f)(2) applies only to bona fide employee benefit plans. A plan is considered "bona fide" if its terms (including cessation of contributions or accruals in the case of retirement income plans) have been accurately described in writing to all employees and if it actually provides the benefits in accordance with the terms of the plan. Notifying employees promptly of the provisions and changes in an employee benefit plan is essential if they are to know how the plan affects them. For these purposes, it would be sufficient under the ADEA for employers to follow the disclosure requirements of ERISA and the regulations thereunder. The plan must actually provide the benefits its provisions describe, since otherwise the notification of the provisions to employees is misleading and inaccurate. An "employee benefit plan" is a plan,

such as a retirement, pension, or insurance plan, which provides employees with what are frequently referred to as "fringe benefits." The term does not refer to wages or salary in cash; neither section 4(f)(2) nor any other section of the Act excuses the payment of lower wages or salary to older employees on account of age. Whether or not any particular employee benefit plan may lawfully provide lower benefits to older employees on account of age depends on whether all of the elements of the exception have been met. An "employee-pay-all" employee benefit plan is one of the "terms, conditions, or privileges of employment" with respect to which discrimination on the basis of age is forbidden under section 4(a)(1). In such a plan, benefits for older workers may be reduced only to the extent and according to the same principles as apply to other plans under section 4(f)(2).

(c) *"To observe the terms" of a plan.* In order for a bona fide employee benefit plan which provides lower benefits to older employees on account of age to be within the section 4(f)(2) exception, the lower benefits must be provided in "observ[ance of] the terms of" the plan. As this statutory text makes clear, the section 4(f)(2) exception is limited to otherwise discriminatory actions which are actually prescribed by the terms of a bona fide employee benefit plan. Where the employer, employment agency, or labor organization is not required by the express provisions of the plan to provide lesser benefits to older workers, section 4(f)(2) does not apply. Important purposes are served by this requirement. Where a discriminatory policy is an express term of a benefit plan, employees presumably have some opportunity to know of the policy and to plan (or protest) accordingly. Moreover, the requirement that the discrimination actually be prescribed by a plan assures that the particular plan provision will be equally applied to all employees of the same age. Where a discriminatory provision is an optional term of the plan, it permits individual, discretionary acts of discrimination, which do not fall within the section 4(f)(2) exception.

APPENDIX B-2.   EEOC Guidelines for Age Discrimination 29 CFR 1625.

Equal Employment Opportunity Comm.

(d) *"Subterfuge."* In order for a bona fide employee benefit plan which prescribes lower benefits for older employees on account of age to be within the section 4(f)(2) exception, it must not be "a subterfuge to evade the purposes of [the] Act." In general, a plan or plan provision which prescribes lower benefits for older employees on account of age is not a "subterfuge" within the meaning of section 4(f)(2), provided that the lower level of benefits is justified by age-related cost considerations. (The only exception to this general rule is with respect to certain retirement plans. See paragraph (f)(4) of this section.) There are certain other requirements that must be met in order for a plan not to be a subterfuge. These requirements are set forth below.

(1) *Cost data—general.* Cost data used in justification of a benefit plan which provides lower benefits to older employees on account of age must be valid and reasonable. This standard is met where an employer has cost data which show the actual cost to it of providing the particular benefit (or benefits) in question over a representative period of years. An employer may rely on cost data for its own employees over such a period, or on cost data for a larger group of similarly situated employees. Sometimes, as a result of experience rating or other causes, an employer incurs costs that differ significantly from costs for a group of similarly situated employees. Such an employer may not rely on cost data for the similarly situated employees where such reliance would result in significantly lower benefits for its own older employees. Where reliable cost information is not available, reasonable projections made from existing cost data meeting the standards set forth above will be considered acceptable.

(2) *Cost data—Individual benefit basis and "benefit package" basis.* Cost comparisons and adjustments under section 4(f)(2) must be made on a benefit-by-benefit basis or on a "benefit package" basis, as described below.

(i) *Benefit-by-benefit basis.* Adjustments made on a benefit-by-benefit basis must be made in the amount or level of a specific form of benefit for a

§ 1625.

specific event or contingency. For example, higher group term life insurance costs for older workers would justify a corresponding reduction in the amount of group term life insurance coverage for older workers, on the basis of age. However, a benefit-by-benefit approach would not justify the substitution of one form of benefit for another, even though both forms of benefit are designed for the same contingency, such as death. See paragraph (f)(1) of this section.

(ii) *"Benefit package" basis.* As an alternative to the benefit-by-benefit basis, cost comparisons and adjustments under section 4(f)(2) may be made on a limited "benefit package" basis. Under this approach, subject to the limitations described below, cost comparisons and adjustments can be made with respect to section 4(f)(2) plans in the aggregate. This alternative basis provides greater flexibility than a benefit-by-benefit basis in order to carry out the declared statutory purpose "to help employers and workers find ways of meeting problems arising from the impact of age on employment." A "benefit package" approach is an alternative approach consistent with this purpose and with the general purpose of section 4(f)(2) only if it is not used to reduce the cost to the employer or the favorability to the employees of overall employee benefits for older employees. A "benefit package" approach used for either of these purposes would be a subterfuge to evade the purposes of the Act. In order to assure that such a "benefit package" approach is not abused and is consistent with the legislative intent, it is subject to the limitations described in paragraph (f), which also includes a general example.

(3) *Cost data—five year maximum basis.* Cost comparisons and adjustments under section 4(f)(2) may be made on the basis of age brackets of up to 5 years. Thus a particular benefit may be reduced for employees of any age within the protected age group by an amount no greater than that which could be justified by the additional cost to provide them with the same level of the benefit as younger employees within a specified five-year age group immediately preceding

APPENDIX B-2. EEOC Guidelines for Age Discrimination 29 CFR 1625.

---

§ 1625.10

theirs. For example, where an employer chooses to provide unreduced group term life insurance benefits until age 60, benefits for employees who are between 60 and 65 years of age may be reduced only to the extent necessary to achieve approximate equivalency in costs with employees who are 55 to 60 years old. Similarly, any reductions in benefit levels for 65 to 70 year old employees cannot exceed an amount which is proportional to the additional costs for their coverage over 60 to 65 year old employees.

(4) *Employee contributions in support of employee benefit plans*—(i) *As a condition of employment.* An older employee within the protected age group may not be required as a condition of employment to make greater contributions than a younger employee in support of an employee benefit plan. Such a requirement would be in effect a mandatory reduction in take-home pay, which is never authorized by section 4(f)(2), and would impose an impediment to employment in violation of the specific restrictions in section 4(f)(2).

(ii) *As a condition of participation in a voluntary employee benefit plan.* An older employee within the protected age group may be required as a condition of participation in a voluntary employee benefit plan to make a greater contribution than a younger employee only if the older employee is not thereby required to bear a greater proportion of the total premium cost (employer-paid and employee-paid) than the younger employee. Otherwise the requirement would discriminate against the older employee by making compensation in the form of an employer contribution available on less favorable terms than for the younger employee and denying that compensation altogether to an older employee unwilling or unable to meet the less favorable terms. Such discrimination is not authorized by section 4(f)(2). This principle applies to three different contribution arrangements as follows:

(A) *Employee-pay-all plans.* Older employees, like younger employees, may be required to contribute as a condition of participation up to the full premium cost for their age.

(B) *Non-contributory* ("employer-pay-all") *plans.* Where younger employees are not required to contribute any portion of the total premium cost, older employees may not be required to contribute any portion.

(C) *Contributory plans.* In these plans employers and participating employees share the premium cost. The required contributions of participants may increase with age so long as the *proportion* of the total premium required to be paid by the participants does not increase with age.

(iii) *As an option in order to receive an unreduced benefit.* An older employee may be given the option, as an individual, to make the additional contribution necessary to receive the same level of benefits as a younger employee (provided that the contemplated reduction in benefits is otherwise justified by section 4(f)(2)).

(5) *Forfeiture clauses.* Clauses in employee benefit plans which state that litigation or participation in any manner in a formal proceeding by an employee will result in the forfeiture of his rights are unlawful insofar as they may be applied to those who seek redress under the Act. This is by reason of section 4(d) which provides that it is unlawful for an employer, employment agency, or labor organization to discriminate against any individual because such individual "has made a charge, testified, assisted, or participated in any manner in an investigation, proceeding, or litigation under this Act."

(6) *Refusal to hire clauses.* Any provision of an employee benefit plan which requires or permits the refusal to hire an individual specified in section 12(a) of the Act on the basis of age is a subterfuge to evade the purposes of the Act and cannot be excused under section 4(f)(2).

(7) *Involuntary retirement clauses.* Any provision of an employee benefit plan which requires or permits the involuntary retirement of any individual specified in section 12(a) of the Act on the basis of age is a subterfuge to evade the purpose of the Act and cannot be excused under section 4(f)(2).

(e) *Benefits provided by the Government.* An employer does not violate

APPENDIX B-2. EEOC Guidelines for Age Discrimination 29 CFR 1625.

Equal Employment Opportunity Comm.　　　　　　**§ 1625.10**

the Act by permitting certain benefits to be provided by the Government, even though the availability of such benefits may be based on age. For example, it is not necessary for an employer to provide health benefits which are otherwise provided to certain employees by Medicare. However, the availability of benefits from the Government will not justify a reduction in employer-provided benefits if the result is that, taking the employer-provided and Government-provided benefits together, an older employee is entitled to a lesser benefit of any type (including coverage for family and/or dependents) than a similarly situated younger employee. For example, the availability of certain benefits to an older employee under Medicare will not justify denying an older employee a benefit which is provided to younger employees and is not provided to the older employee by Medicare.

(f) *Application of section 4(f)(2) to various employee benefit plans*—(1) *Benefit-by-benefit approach.* This portion of the interpretation discusses how a benefit-by-benefit approach would apply to four of the most common types of employee benefit plans.

(i) *Life insurance.* It is not uncommon for life insurance coverage to remain constant until a specified age, frequently 65, and then be reduced. This practice will not violate the Act (even if reductions start before age 65), provided that the reduction for an employee of a particular age is no greater than is justified by the increased cost of coverage for that employee's specific age bracket encompassing no more than five years. It should be noted that a total denial of life insurance, on the basis of age, would not be justified under a benefit-by-benefit analysis. However, it is not unlawful for life insurance coverage to cease upon separation from service.

(ii) *Long-term disability.* Under a benefit-by-benefit approach, where employees who are disabled at younger ages are entitled to long-term disability benefits, there is no cost—based justification for denying such benefits altogether, on the basis of age, to employees who are disabled at older ages. It is not unlawful to cut off long-term

disability benefits and coverage on the basis of some non-age factor, such as recovery from disability. Reductions on the basis of age in the level or duration of benefits available for disability are justifiable only on the basis of age-related cost considerations as set forth elsewhere in this section. An employer which provides long-term disability coverage to all employees may avoid any increases in the cost to it that such coverage for older employees would entail by reducing the level of benefits available to older employees. An employer may also avoid such cost increases by reducing the duration of benefits available to employees who become disabled at older ages, without reducing the level of benefits. In this connection, the Department would not assert a violation where the level of benefits is not reduced and the duration of benefits is reduced in the following manner:

(A) With respect to disabilities which occur at age 60 or less, benefits cease at age 65.

(B) With respect to disabilities which occur after age 60, benefits cease 5 years after disablement. Cost data may be produced to support other patterns of reduction as well.

(iii) *Retirement plans*—(A) *Participation.* No employee hired prior to normal retirement age may be excluded from a defined contribution plan. With respect to defined benefit plans not subject to the Employee Retirement Income Security Act (ERISA), Pub. L. 93-406, 29 U.S.C. 1001, 1003 (a) and (b), an employee hired at an age more than 5 years prior to normal retirement age may not be excluded from such a plan unless the exclusion is justifiable on the basis of cost considerations as set forth elsewhere in this section. With respect to defined benefit plans subject to ERISA, such an exclusion would be unlawful in any case. An employee hired less than 5 years prior to normal retirement age may be excluded from a defined benefit plan, regardless of whether or not the plan is covered by ERISA. Similarly, any employee hired after normal retirement age may be excluded from a defined benefit plan.

APPENDIX B-2.   EEOC Guidelines for Age Discrimination 29 CFR 1625.

§ 1625.10

(2) *"Benefit package" approach.* A "benefit package" approach to compliance under section 4(f)(2) offers greater flexibility than a benefit-by-benefit approach by permitting deviations from a benefit-by-benefit approach so long as the overall result is no lesser cost to the employer *and* no less favorable benefits for employees. As previously noted, in order to assure that such an approach is used for the benefit of older workers and not to their detriment, and is otherwise consistent with the legislative intent, it is subject to limitations as set forth below:

(i) *A benefit package approach shall apply only to employee benefit plans which fall within section 4(f)(2).*

(ii) *A benefit package approach shall not apply to a retirement or pension plan.* The 1978 legislative history sets forth specific and comprehensive rules governing such plans, which have been adopted above. These rules are not tied to actuarially significant cost considerations but are intended to deal with the special funding arrangements of retirement or pension plans. Variations from these special rules are therefore not justified by variations from the cost-based benefit-by-benefit approach in other benefit plans, nor may variations from the special rules governing pension and retirement plans justify variations from the benefit-by-benefit approach in other benefit plans.

(iii) *A benefit package approach shall not be used to justify reductions in health benefits greater than would be justified under a benefit-by-benefit approach.* Such benefits appear to be of particular importance to older workers in meeting "problems arising from the impact of age" and were of particular concern to Congress. Therefore, the "benefit package" approach may not be used to reduce health insurance benefits by more than is warranted by the increase in the cost to the employer of those benefits alone. Any greater reduction would be a subterfuge to evade the purpose of the Act.

(iv) *A benefit reduction greater than would be justified under a benefit-by-benefit approach must be offset by another benefit available to the same employees.* No employees may be deprived because of age of one benefit

29 CFR Ch. XIV (7-1-89 Edition)

without an offsetting benefit being made available to them.

(v) *Employers who wish to justify benefit reductions under a benefit package approach must be prepared to produce data to show that those reductions are fully justified.* Thus employers must be able to show that deviations from a benefit-by-benefit approach do not result in lesser cost to them or less favorable benefits to their employees. A general example consistent with these limitations may be given. Assume two employee benefit plans, providing Benefit "A" and Benefit "B." Both plans fall within section 4(f)(2), and neither is a retirement or pension plan subject to special rules. Both benefits are available to all employees. Age-based cost increases would justify a 10% decrease in both benefits on a benefit-by-benefit basis. The affected employees would, however, find it more favorable—that is, more consistent with meeting their needs—for no reduction to be made in Benefit "A" and a greater reduction to be made in Benefit "B." This "trade-off" would not result in a reduction in health benefits. The "trade-off" may therefore be made. The details of the "trade-off" depend on data on the relative cost to the employer of the two benefits. If the data show that Benefit "A" and Benefit "B" cost the same, Benefit "B" may be reduced up to 20% if Benefit "A" is unreduced. If the data show that Benefit "A" costs only half as much as Benefit "B", however, Benefit "B" may be reduced up to only 15% if Benefit "A" is unreduced, since a greater reduction in Benefit "B" would result in an impermissible reduction in total benefit costs.

(g) *Relation of ADEA to State laws.* The ADEA does not preempt State age discrimination in employment laws. However, the failure of the ADEA to preempt such laws does not affect the issue of whether section 514 of the Employee Retirement Income Security Act (ERISA) preempts State laws which related to employee benefit plans.

[44 FR 30658, May 25, 1979, as amended at 52 FR 8448, Mar. 18, 1987. Redesignated and

APPENDIX B-2. EEOC Guidelines for Age Discrimination 29 CFR 1625.

Equal Employment Opportunity Comm.　　　　§ 1625.11

amended at 52 FR 23812, June 25, 1987; 53 FR 5973, Feb. 29, 1988]

§ 1625.11 Exemption for employees serving under a contract of unlimited tenure.

(a)(1) Section 12(d) of the Act, added by the 1986 amendments, provides:

Nothing in this Act shall be construed to prohibit compulsory retirement of any employee who has attained 70 years of age, and who is serving under a contract of unlimited tenure (or similar arrangement providing for unlimited tenure) at an institution of higher education (as defined by section 1201(a) of the Higher Education Act of 1965).

(2) This exemption from the Act's protection of covered individuals took effect on January 1, 1987, and is repealed on December 31, 1993 (see section 6 of the Age Discrimination in Employment Act Amendments of 1986, Pub. L. No. 99-592, 100 Stat. 3342). The Equal Employment Opportunity Commission is required to enter into an agreement with the National Academy of Sciences, for the conduct of a study to analyze the potential consequences of the elimination of mandatory retirement on institutions of higher education.

(b) Since section 12(d) is an exemption from the nondiscrimination requirements of the Act, the burden is on the one seeking to invoke the exemption to show that every element has been clearly and unmistakably met. Moreover, as with other exemptions from the ADEA, this exemption must be narrowly construed.

(c) Section 1201(a) of the Higher Education Act of 1965, as amended, and set forth in 20 U.S.C. 1141(a), provides in pertinent part:

The term "institution of higher education" means an educational institution in any State which (1) admits as regular students only persons having a certificate of graduation from a school providing secondary education, or the recognized equivalent of such a certificate, (2) is legally authorized within such State to provide a program of education beyond secondary education, (3) provides an educational program for which it awards a bachelor's degree or provides not less than a two-year program which is acceptable for full credit toward such a degree, (4) is a public or other nonprofit institution, and (5) is accredited by a nationally recognized accrediting agency or associa-

tion or, if not so accredited, (A) is an institution with respect to which the Commissioner has determined that there is satisfactory assurance, considering the resources available to the institution, the period of time, if any, during which it has operated, the effort it is making to meet the accreditation standards, and the purpose for which this determination is being made, that the institution will meet the accreditation standards of such an agency or association within a reasonable time, or (B) is an institution whose credits are accepted, on transfer, by not less than three institutions which are so accredited, for credit on the same basis as if transferred from an institution so accredited.

The definition encompasses almost all public and private universities and two and four year colleges. The omitted portion of the text of section 1201(a) refers largely on one-year technical schools which generally do not grant tenure to employees but which, if they do, are also eligible to claim the exemption.

(d)(1) Use of the term "any employee" indicates that application of the exemption is not limited to teachers, who are traditional recipients of tenure. The exemption may also be available with respect to other groups, such as academic deans, scientific researchers, professional librarians and counseling staff, who frequently have tenured status.

(2) The Conference Committee Report on the 1978 amendments expressly states that the exemption does not apply to Federal employees covered by section 15 of the Act (H.R. Rept. No. 95-950, p. 10).

(e)(1) The phrase "unlimited tenure" is not defined in the Act. However, the almost universally accepted definition of academic "tenure" is an arrangement under which certain appointments in an institution of higher education are continued until retirement for age of physical disability, subject to dismissal for adequate cause or under extraordinary circumstances on account of financial exigency or change of institutional program. Adopting that definition, it is evident that the word "unlimited" refers to the duration of tenure. Therefore, a contract (or other similar arrangement) which is limited to a specific term (for example, one year or 10

APPENDIX B-2.   EEOC Guidelines for Age Discrimination 29 CFR 1625.

---

§ 1625.11

years) will not meet the requirements of the exemption.

(2) The legislative history shows that Congress intented the exemption to apply only where the minimum rights and privileges traditionally associated with tenure are guaranteed to an employee by contract or similar arrangement. While tenure policies and practices vary greatly from one institution to another, the minimum standards set forth in the 1940 Statement of Principles on Academic Freedom and Tenure, jointly developed by the Association of American Colleges and the American Association of University Professors, have enjoyed widespread adoption or endorsement. The 1940 Statement of Principles on academic tenure provides as follows:

(a) After the expiration of a probationary period, teachers or investigators should have permanent or continuous tenure, and their service should be terminated only for adequate cause, except in the case of retirement for age, or under extraordinary circumstances because of financial exigencies. In the interpretation of this principle it is understood that the following represents acceptable academic practice:

(1) The precise terms and conditions of every appointment should be stated in writing and be in the possession of both institution and teacher before the appointment is consummated.

(2) Beginning with appointment to the rank of full-time instructor or a higher rank, the probationary period should not exceed seven years, including within this period full-time service in all institutions of higher education; but subject to the proviso that when, after a term of probationary service of more than three years in one or more institutions, a teacher is called to another institution it may be agreed in writing that his new appointment is for a probationary period of not more than four years, even though thereby the person's total probationary period in the academic profession is extended beyond the normal maximum of seven years. Notice should be given at least one year prior to the expiration of the probationary period if the teacher is not to be continued in service after the expiration of that period.

(3) During the probationary period a teacher should have the academic freedom that all other members of the faculty have.

(4) Termination for cause of a continuous appointment, or the dismissal for cause of a teacher previous to the expiration of a term appointment, should, if possible, be considered by both a faculty committee and the governing board of the institution. In all cases where the facts are in dispute, the accused teacher should be informed before the hearing in writing of the charges against him and should have the opportunity to be heard in his own defense by all bodies that pass judgment upon his case. He should be permitted to have with him an advisor of his own choosing who may act as counsel.There should be a full stenographic record of the hearing available to the parties concerned. In the hearing of charges of incompetence the testimony should include that of teachers and other scholars, either from his own or from other institutions. Teachers on continuous appointment who are dismissed for reasons not involving moral turpitude should receive their salaries for at least a year from the date of notification of dismissal whether or not they are continued in their duties at the institution.

(5) Termination of a continuous appointment because of financial exigency should be demonstrably bona fide.

(3) A contract or similar arrangement which meets the standards in the 1940 Statement of Principles will satisfy the tenure requirements of the exemption. However, a tenure arrangement will not be deemed inadequate solely because it fails to meet these standards in every respect. For example, a tenure plan will not be deemed inadequate solely because it includes a probationary period somewhat longer than seven years. Of course, the greater the deviation from the standards in the 1940 Statement of Principles, the less likely it is that the employee in question will be deemed subject to "unlimited tenure" within the meaning of the exemption. Whether or not a tenure arrangement is adequate to satisfy the requirements of the exemption must be determined on the basis of the facts of each case.

(f) Employees who are not assured of a continuing appointment either by contract of unlimited tenure or other similar arrangement (such as a state statute) would not, of course, be exempted from the prohibitions against compulsory retirement, even if they perform functions identical to those performed by employees with appropriate tenure.

(g) An employee within the exemption can lawfully be forced to retire on account of age at age 70 (see (a)(1) above). In addition, the employer is free to retain such employees, either in the same position or status or in a

APPENDIX B-2. EEOC Guidelines for Age Discrimination 29 CFR 1625.

Equal Employment Opportunity Comm.

§ 1625.12

different position or status: *Provided,* That the employee voluntarily accepts this new position or status. For example, an employee who falls within the exemption may be offered a nontenured position or part-time employment. An employee who accepts a nontenured position or part-time employment, however, may not be treated any less favorably, on account of age, than any similarly situated younger employee (unless such less favorable treatment is excused by an exception to the Act).

[44 FR 66799, Nov. 21, 1979; 45 FR 43704, June 30, 1980; 45 FR 51547, Aug. 4, 1980, as amended at 53 FR 5973, Feb. 29, 1988]

§ 1625.12 Exemption for bona fide executive or high policymaking employees.

(a) Section 12(c)(1) of the Act, added by the 1978 amendments and as amended in 1984 and 1986, provides: "Nothing in this Act shall be construed to prohibit compulsory retirement of any employee who has attained 65 years of age, and who, for the 2-year period immediately before retirement, is employed in a bona fide executive or higher policymaking position, if such employee is entitled to an immediate nonforfeitable annual retirement benefit from a pension, profit-sharing, savings, or deferred compensation plan, or any combination of such plans, of the employer of such employee which equals, in the aggregate, at least $44,000."

(b) Since this provision is an exemption from the non-discrimination requirements of the Act, the burden is on the one seeking to invoke the exemption to show that every element has been clearly and unmistakably met. Moreover, as with other exemptions from the Act, this exemption must be narrowly construed.

(c) An employee within the exemption can lawfully be forced to retire on account of age at age 65 or above. In addition, the employer is free to retain such employees, either in the same position or status or in a different position or status. For example, an employee who falls within the exemption may be offered a position of lesser status or a part-time position. An employee who accepts such a new status or position, however, may not be treat-

ed any less favorably, on account of age, than any similarly situated younger employee.

(d)(1) In order for an employee to qualify as a "bona fide executive," the employer must initially show that the employee satisfies the definition of a bona fide executive set forth in § 541.1 of this chapter. Each of the requirements in paragraphs (a) through (e) of § 541.1 must be satisfied, regardless of the level of the employee's salary or compensation.

(2) Even if an employee qualifies as an executive under the definition in § 541.1 of this chapter, the exemption from the ADEA may not be claimed unless the employee also meets the further criteria specified in the Conference Committee Report in the form of examples (see H.R. Rept. No. 95-950, p. 9). The examples are intended to make clear that the exemption does not apply to middle-management employees, no matter how great their retirement income, but only to a very few top level employees who exercise substantial executive authority over a significant number of employees and a large volume of business. As stated in the Conference Report (H.R. Rept. No. 95-950, p. 9):

Typically the head of a significant and substantial local or regional operation of a corporation [or other business organization], such as a major production facility or retail establishment, but not the head of a minor branch, warehouse or retail store, would be covered by the term "bona fide executive." Individuals at higher levels in the corporate organizational structure who possess comparable or greater levels of responsibility and authority as measured by established and recognized criteria would also be covered.

The heads of major departments or divisions of corporations [or other business organizations] are usually located at corporate or regional headquarters. With respect to employees whose duties are associated with corporate headquarters operations, such as finance, marketing, legal, production and manufacturing (or in a corporation organized on a product line basis, the management of product lines), the definition would cover employees who head those divisions.

In a large organization the immediate subordinates of the heads of these divisions sometimes also exercise executive authority, within the meaning of this exemption. The conferees intend the definition to cover

APPENDIX B-2.   EEOC Guidelines for Age Discrimination 29 CFR 1625.

---

§ 1625.12

such employees if they possess responsibility which is comparable to or greater than that possessed by the head of a significant and substantial local operation who meets the definition.

(e) The phrase "high policymaking position," according to the Conference Report (H.R. Rept. No. 95-950, p. 10), is limited to "* * * certain top level employees who are not 'bona fide executives' * * *." Specifically, these are:

* * * individuals who have little or no line authority but whose position and responsibility are such that they play a significant role in the development of corporate policy and effectively recommend the implementation thereof.

For example, the chief economist or the chief research scientist of a corporation typically has little line authority. His duties would be primarily intellectual as opposed to executive or managerial. His responsibility would be to evaluate significant economic or scientific trends and issues, to develop and recommend policy direction to the top executive officers of the corporation, and he would have a significant impact on the ultimate decision on such policies by virtue of his expertise and direct access to the decisionmakers. Such an employee would meet the definition of a "high policymaking" employee.

On the other hand, as this description makes clear, the support personnel of a "high policymaking" employee would not be subject to the exemption even if they supervise the development, and draft the recommendation, of various policies submitted by their supervisors.

(f) In order for the exemption to apply to a particular employee, the employee must have been in a "bona fide executive or high policymaking position," as those terms are defined in this section, for the two-year period immediately before retirement. Thus, an employee who holds two or more different positions during the two-year period is subject to the exemption only if each such job is an executive or high policymaking position.

(g) The Conference Committee Report expressly states that the exemption is not applicable to Federal employees covered by section 15 of the Act (H.R. Rept. No. 95-950, p. 10).

(h) The "annual retirement benefit," to which covered employees must be entitled, is the sum of amounts payable during each one-year period from

29 CFR Ch. XIV (7-1-89 Edition)

the date on which such benefits first become receivable by the retiree. Once established, the annual period upon which calculations are based may not be changed from year to year.

(i) The annual retirement benefit must be immediately available to the employee to be retired pursuant to the exemption. For purposes of determining compliance, "immediate" means that the payment of plan benefits (in a lump sum or the first of a series of periodic payments) must occur not later than 60 days after the effective date of the retirement in question. The fact that an employee will receive benefits only after expiration of the 60-day period will not preclude his retirement pursuant to the exemption, if the employee could have elected to receive benefits within that period.

(j)(1) The annual retirement benefit must equal, in the aggregate, at least $44,000. The manner of determining whether this requirement has been satisfied is set forth in §1627.17(c).

(2) In determining whether the aggregate annual retirement benefit equals at least $44,000, the only benefits which may be counted are those authorized by and provided under the terms of a pension, profit-sharing, savings, or deferred compensation plan. (Regulations issued pursuant to section 12(c)(2) of the Act, regarding the manner of calculating the amount of qualified retirement benefits for purposes of the exemption, are set forth in § 1627.17 of this chapter.)

(k)(1) The annual retirement benefit must be "nonforfeitable." Accordingly, the exemption may not be applied to any employee subject to plan provisions which could cause the cessation of payments to a retiree or result in the reduction of benefits to less than $44,000 in any one year. For example, where a plan contains a provision under which benefits would be suspended if a retiree engages in litigation against the former employer, or obtains employment with a competitor of the former employer, the retirement benefit will be deemed to be forfeitable. However, retirement benefits will not be deemed forfeitable solely because the benefits are discontinued or suspended for reasons permitted

APPENDIX B-2.   EEOC Guidelines for Age Discrimination 29 CFR 1625.

Equal Employment Opportunity Comm.

under section 411(a)(3) of the Internal Revenue Code.

(2) An annual retirement benefit will not be deemed forfeitable merely because the minimum statutory benefit level is not guaranteed against the possibility of plan bankruptcy or is subject to benefit restrictions in the event of early termination of the plan in accordance with Treasury Regulation 1.401–4(c). However, as of the effective date of the retirement in question, there must be at least a reasonable expectation that the plan will meet its obligations.

(Sec. 12(c)(1) of the Age Discrimination In Employment Act of 1967, as amended by Sec. 802(c)(1) of the Older Americans Act Amendments of 1984, Pub. L. 98–459, 98 Stat. 1792))

[44 FR 66800, Nov. 21, 1979; 45 FR 43704, June 30, 1980, as amended at 50 FR 2544, Jan. 17, 1985; 53 FR 5973, Feb. 29, 1988]

§ 1625.13. Apprenticeship programs.

Age limitations for entry into bona fide apprenticeship programs were not intended to be affected by the Act. Entry into most apprenticeship programs has traditionally been limited to youths under specified ages. This is in recognition of the fact that apprenticeship is an extension of the educational process to prepare young men and women for skilled employment. Accordingly, the prohibitions contained in the Act will not be applied to bona fide apprenticeship programs which meet the standards specified in §§ 521.2 and 521.3 of this chapter.

[46 FR 47726, Sept. 29, 1981; 52 FR 33809, Sept. 8, 1987]

APPENDIX B-3.   EEOC Guidelines for Religious Discrimination 29 CFR 1605.

PART 1605—GUIDELINES ON DISCRIMINATION BECAUSE OF RELIGION

Sec.

1605.1 "Religious" nature of a practice or belief.

1605.2 Reasonable accommodation without undue hardship as required by Section 701(j) of Title VII of the Civil Rights Act of 1964.

1605.3 Selection practices.

APPENDIX A TO §§ 1605.2 AND 1605.3—BACKGROUND INFORMATION

AUTHORITY: Title VII of the Civil Rights Act of 1964, as amended, 42 U.S.C. 2000e et seq.

SOURCE: 45 FR 72612, Oct. 31, 1980, unless otherwise noted.

§ 1605.1 "Religious" nature of a practice or belief.

In most cases whether or not a practice or belief is religious is not at issue. However, in those cases in which the issue does exist, the Commission will define religious practices to include moral or ethical beliefs as to what is right and wrong which are sincerely held with the strength of traditional religious views. This standard was developed in *United States* v. *Seeger*, 380 U.S. 163 (1965) and *Welsh* v. *United States*, 398 U.S. 333 (1970). The Commission has consistently applied this standard in its decisions.[1] The fact that no religious group espouses such beliefs or the fact that the religious group to which the individual professes to belong may not accept such belief will not determine whether the belief is a religious belief of the employee or prospective employee. The phrase "religious practice" as used in these Guidelines includes both religious observances and practices, as stated in Section 701(j), 42 U.S.C. 2000e(j).

---

[1]See CD 76-104 (1976), CCH ¶6500; CD 71-2620 (1971), CCH ¶6283; CD 71-779 (1970), CCH ¶6180.

§ 1605.2   Reasonable accommodation without undue hardship as required by Section 701(j) of Title VII of the Civil Rights Act of 1964.

(a) *Purpose of this section.* This section clarifies the obligation imposed by Title VII of the Civil Rights Act of 1964, as amended, (sections 701(j), 703 and 717) to accommodate the religious practices of employees and prospective employees. This section does not address other obligations under Title VII not to discriminate on grounds of religion, nor other provisions of Title VII. This section is not intended to limit any additional obligations to accommodate religious practices which may exist pursuant to constitutional, or other statutory provisions; neither is it intended to provide guidance for statutes which require accommodation on bases other than religion such as section 503 of the Rehabilitation Act of 1973. The legal principles which have been developed with respect to discrimination prohibited by Title VII on the bases of race, color, sex, and national origin also apply to religious discrimination in all circumstances other than where an accommodation is required.

(b) *Duty to accommodate.* (1) Section 701(j) makes it an unlawful employment practice under section 703(a)(1) for an employer to fail to reasonably accommodate the religious practices of an employee or prospective employee, unless the employer demonstrates that accommodation would result in undue hardship on the conduct of its business.[2]

(2) Section 701(j) in conjunction with section 703(c), imposes an obligation on a labor organization to reasonably accommodate the religious practices of an employee or prospective employee, unless the labor organization demonstrates that accommodation would result in undue hardship.

(3) Section 1605.2 is primarily directed to obligations of employers or labor organizations, which are the entities covered by Title VII that will most often be required to make an accommodation. However, the principles of

---

[2]See *Trans World Airlines, Inc.* v. *Hardison*, 432 U.S. 63, 74 (1977).

APPENDIX B-3.   EEOC Guidelines for Religious Discrimination 29 CFR 1605.

§ 1605.2 also apply when an accommodation can be required of other entities covered by Title VII, such as employment agencies (Section 703(b)) or joint labor-management committees controlling apprecticeship or other training or retraining (Section 703(d)). (See, for example, § 1605.3(a) "Scheduling of Tests or Other Selection Procedures.")

(c) *Reasonable accommodation.* (1) After an employee or prospective employee notifies the employer or labor organization of his or her need for a religious accommodation, the employer or labor organization has an obligation to reasonably accommodate the individual's religious practices. A refusal to accommodate is justified only when an employer or labor organization can demonstrate that an undue hardship would in fact result from each available alternative method of accommodation. A mere assumption that many more people, with the same religious practices as the person being accommodated, may also need accommodation is not evidence of undue hardship.

(2) When there is more than one method of accommodation available which would not cause undue hardship, the Commission will determine whether the accommodation offered is reasonable by examining:

(i) The alternatives for accommodation considered by the employer or labor organization; and

(ii) The alternatives for accommodation, if any, actually offered to the individual requiring accommodation. Some alternatives for accommodating religious practices might disadvantage the individual with respect to his or her employment opportunites, such as compensation, terms, conditions, or privileges of employment. Therefore, when there is more than one means of accommodation which would not cause undue hardship, the employer or labor organization must offer the alternative which least disadvantages the individual with respect to his or her employment opportunities.

(d) *Alternatives for accommodating religious practices.* (1) Employees and prospective employees most frequently request an accommodation because their religious practices conflict with

their work schedules. The following subsections are some means of accommodating the conflict between work schedules and religious practices which the Commission believes that employers and labor organizations should consider as part of the obligation to accommodate and which the Commission will consider in investigating a charge. These are not intended to be all-inclusive. There are often other alternatives which would reasonably accommodate an individual's religious practices when they conflict with a work schedule. There are also employment practices besides work scheduling which may conflict with religious practices and cause an individual to request an accommodation. See, for example, the Commission's finding number (3) from its Hearings on Religious Discrimination, in Appendix A to §§ 1605.2 and 1605.3. The principles expressed in these Guidelines apply as well to such requests for accommodation.

(i)   Voluntary   Substitutes   and "Swaps".

Reasonable accommodation without undue hardship is generally possible where a voluntary substitute with substantially similar qualifications is available. One means of substitution is the voluntary swap. In a number of cases, the securing of a substitute has been left entirely up to the individual seeking the accommodation. The Commission believes that the obligation to accommodate requires that employers and labor organizations facilitate the securing of a voluntary substitute with substantially similar qualifications. Some means of doing this which employers and labor organizations should consider are: to publicize policies regarding accommodation and voluntary substitution; to promote an atmosphere in which such substitutions are favorably regarded; to provide a central file, bulletin board or other means for matching voluntary substitutes with positions for which substitutes are needed.

(ii) Flexible Scheduling.

One means of providing reasonable accommodation for the religious practices of employees or prospective employees which employers and labor organizations should consider is the cre-

APPENDIX B-3.   EEOC Guidelines for Religious Discrimination 29 CFR 1605.

Equal Employment Opportunity Comm.

§ 1605.3

ation of a flexible work schedule for individuals requesting accommodation.

The following list is an example of areas in which flexibility might be introduced: flexible arrival and departure times; floating or optional holidays; flexible work breaks; use of lunch time in exchange for early departure; staggered work hours; and permitting an employee to make up time lost due to the observance of religious practices. [3]

(iii) Lateral Transfer and Change of Job Assignments.

When an employee cannot be accommodated either as to his or her entire job or an assignment within the job, employers and labor organizations should consider whether or not it is possible to change the job assignment or give the employee a lateral transfer.

(2) Payment of Dues to a Labor Organization.

Some collective bargaining agreements include a provision that each employee must join the labor organization or pay the labor organization a sum equivalent to dues. When an employee's religious practices do not permit compliance with such a provision, the labor organization should accommodate the employee by not requiring the employee to join the organization and by permitting him or her to donate a sum equivalent to dues to a charitable organization.

(e) *Undue hardship.* (1) Cost. An employer may assert undue hardship to justify a refusal to accommodate an employee's need to be absent from his or her scheduled duty hours if the employer can demonstrate that the accommodation would require "more than a *de minimis* cost". [4] The Commission will determine what constitutes "more than a *de minimis* cost" with due regard given to the identifiable cost in relation to the size and operating cost of the employer, and the number of individuals who will in fact need a particular accommodation. In general, the Commission interprets

this phrase as it was used in the *Hardison* decision to mean that costs similar to the regular payment of premium wages of substitutes, which was at issue in *Hardison,* would constitute undue hardship. However, the Commission will presume that the infrequent payment of premium wages for a substitute or the payment of premium wages while a more permanent accommodation is being sought are costs which an employer can be required to bear as a means of providing a reasonable accommodation. Further, the Commission will presume that generally, the payment of administrative costs necessary for providing the accommodation will not constitute more than a *de minimis* cost. Administrative costs, for example, include those costs involved in rearranging schedules and recording substitutions for payroll purposes.

(2) Seniority Rights. Undue hardship would also be shown where a variance from a bona fide seniority system is necessary in order to accommodate an employee's religious practices when doing so would deny another employee his or her job or shift preference guaranteed by that system. *Hardison, supra,* 432 U.S. at 80. Arrangements for voluntary substitutes and swaps (see paragraph (d)(1)(i) of this section) do not constitute an undue hardship to the extent the arrangements do not violate a bona fide seniority system. Nothing in the Statute or these Guidelines precludes an employer and a union from including arrangements for voluntary substitutes and swaps as part of a collective bargaining agreement.

§ 1605.3 Selection practices.

(a) Scheduling of Tests or Other Selection Procedures. When a test or other selection procedure is scheduled at a time when an employee or prospective employee cannot attend because of his or her religious practices, the user of the test should be aware that the principles enunciated in these guidelines apply and that it has an obligation to accommodate such employee or prospective employee unless undue hardship would result.

---

[3] On September 29, 1978, Congress enacted such a provision for the accommodation of Federal employees' religious practices. See Pub. L 95-390, 5 U.S.C. 5550a "Compensatory Time Off for Religious Observances."

[4] *Hardison, supra,* 432 U.S. at 84.

APPENDIX B-3. EEOC Guidelines for Religious Discrimination 29 CFR 1605.

§ 1605.3

(b) Inquiries Which Determine An Applicant's Availability to Work During An Employer's Scheduled Working Hours.

(1) The duty to accommodate pertains to prospective employees as well as current employees. Consequently, an employer may not permit an applicant's need for a religious accommodation to affect in any way its decision whether to hire the applicant unless it can demonstrate that it cannot reasonably accommodate the applicant's religious practices without undue hardship.

(2) As a result of the oral and written testimony submitted at the Commission's Hearings on Religious Discrimination, discussions with representatives of organizations interested in the issue of religious discrimination, and the comments received from the public on these Guidelines as proposed, the Commission has concluded that the use of pre-selection inquiries which determine an applicant's availability has an exclusionary effect on the employment opportunities of persons with certain religious practices. The use of such inquiries will, therefore, be considered to violate Title VII unless the employer can show that it:

(i) Did not have an exclusionary effect on its employees or prospective employees needing an accommodation for the same religious practices; or

(ii) Was otherwise-justified by business necessity.

Employers who believe they have a legitimate interest in knowing the availability of their applicants prior to selection must consider procedures which would serve this interest and which would have a lesser exclusionary effect on persons whose religious practices need accommodation. An example of such a procedure is for the employer to state the normal work hours for the job and, after making it clear to the applicant that he or she is not required to indicate the need for any absences for religious practices during the scheduled work hours, ask the applicant whether he or she is otherwise available to work those hours. Then, after a position is offered, but before the applicant is hired, the employer can inquire into the need for a religious accommoda-

29 CFR Ch. XIV (7-1-89 Edition)

tion and determine, according to the principles of these Guidelines, whether an accommodation is possible. This type of inquiry would provide an employer with information concerning the availability of most of its applicants, while deferring until after a position is offered the identification of the usually small number of applicants who require an accommodation.

(3) The Commission will infer that the need for an accommodation discriminatorily influenced a decision to reject an applicant when: (i) prior to an offer of employment the employer makes an i uiry into an applicant's availability without having a business necessity justification; and (ii) after the employer has determined the applicant's need for an accommodation, the employer rejects a qualified applicant. The burden is then on the employer to demonstrate that factors other than the need for an accommodation were the reason for rejecting the qualified applicant, or that a reasonable accommodation without undue hardship was not possible.

APPENDIX A TO §§ 1605.2 AND 1605.3—
BACKGROUND INFORMATION

In 1966, the Commission adopted guidelines on religious discrimination which stated that an employer had an obligation to accommodate the religious practices of its employees or prospective employees unless to do so would create a "serious inconvenience to the conduct of the business". 29 CFR 1605.1(a)(2), 31 FR 3870 (1966).

In 1967, the Commission revised these guidelines to state that an employer had an obligation to reasonably accommodate the religious practices of its employees or prospective employees, unless the employer could prove that to do so would create an "undue hardship". 29 CFR 1605.1(b)(c), 32 FR 10298.

In 1972, Congress amended Title VII to incorporate the obligation to accommodate expressed in the Commission's 1967 Guidelines by adding section 701(j).

In 1977, the United States Supreme Court issued its decision in the case of *Trans World Airlines, Inc.* v. *Hardison*, 432 U.S. 63 (1977). *Hardison* was brought under section 703(a)(1) because it involved facts occurring before the enactment of Section 701(j). The Court applied the Commission's 1967 Guidelines, but indicated that the result would be the same under Section 701(j). It stated that Trans World Airlines had made reasonable efforts to accommodate the religious needs

APPENDIX B-3.   EEOC Guidelines for Religious Discrimination 29 CFR 1605.

of its employee, Hardison. The Court held that to require Trans World Airlines to make further attempts at accommodations—by unilaterally violating a seniority provision of the collective bargaining agreement, paying premium wages on a regular basis to another employee to replace Hardison, or creating a serious shortage of necessary employees in another department in order to replace Hardison—would create an undue hardship on the conduct of Trans World Airlines' business, and would therefore, exceed the duty to accommodate Hardison.

In 1978, the Commission conducted public hearings on religious discrimination in New York City, Milwaukee, and Los Angeles in order to respond to the concerns raised by *Hardison.* Approximately 150 witnesses testified or submitted written statements.[1] The witnesses included employers, employees, representatives of religious and labor organizations and representatives of Federal, State and local governments.

The Commission found from the hearings that:

(1) There is widespread confusion concerning the extent of accommodation under the *Hardison* decision.

(2) The religious practices of some individuals and some groups of individuals are not being accommodated.

(3) Some of those practices which are not being accommodated are:

—Observance of a Sabbath or religious holidays;

—Need for prayer break during working hours;

—Practice of following certain dietary requirements;

—Practice of not working during a mourning period for a deceased relative;

—Prohibition against medical examinations;

—Prohibition against membership in labor and other organizations; and

—Practices concerning dress and other personal grooming habits.

(4) Many of the employers who testified had developed alternative employment practices which accommodate the religious practices of employees and prospective employees and which meet the employer's business needs.

(5) Little evidence was submitted by employers which showed actual attempts to accommodate religious practices with resultant unfavorable consequences to the employer's business. Employers appeared to have substantial anticipatory concerns but no, or very little, actual experience with the problems they theorized would emerge by providing reasonable accommodation for religious practices.

Based on these findings, the Commission is revising its Guidelines to clarify the obligation imposed by Section 701(j) to accommodate the religious practices of employees and prospective employees.

----

[1] The transcript of the Commission's Hearings on Religious Discrimination can be examined by the public at: The Equal Employment Opportunity Commission, 2401 E Street NW., Washington, D.C. 20506.

APPENDIX B-4.   EEOC Guidelines for Discrimination Because of
National Origin 29 CFR 1606.

**PART 1606—GUIDELINES ON DIS-
CRIMINATION BECAUSE OF NA-
TIONAL ORIGIN**

Sec.
1606.1 Definition of national origin discrimination.
1606.2 Scope of Title VII protection.
1606.3 The national security exception.
1606.4 The bona fide occupational qualification exception.
1606.5 Citizenship requirements.
1606.6 Selection procedures.
1606.7 Speak-English-only rules.
1606.8 Harassment.

AUTHORITY: Title VII of the Civil Rights
Act of 1964, as amended, 42 U.S.C. 2000e et
seq.

SOURCE: 45 FR 85635, Dec. 29, 1980, unless
otherwise noted.

§ 1606.1 Definition of national origin discrimination.

The Commission defines national
origin discrimination broadly as including, but not limited to, the denial
of equal employment opportunity because of an individual's, or his or her
ancestor's, place of origin; or because
an individual has the physical, cultural or linguistic characteristics of a national origin group. The Commission
will examine with particular concern
charges alleging that individuals
within the jurisdiction of the Commission have been denied equal employment opportunity for reasons which
are grounded in national origin considerations, such as (a) marriage to or association with persons of a national
origin group; (b) membership in, or association with an organization identified with or seeking to promote the interests of national origin groups; (c)
attendance or participation in schools,
churches, temples or mosques, generally used by persons of a national
origin group; and (d) because an individual's name or spouse's name is associated with a national origin group. In

207

APPENDIX B-4.   EEOC Guidelines for Discrimination Because of
National Origin 29 CFR 1606.

§ 1606.2

examining these charges for unlawful national origin discrimination, the Commission will apply general Title VII principles, such as disparate treatment and adverse impact.

§ 1606.2   Scope of Title VII protection.

Title VII of the Civil Rights Act of 1964, as amended, protects individuals against employment discrimination on the basis of race, color, religion, sex or national origin. The Title VII principles of disparate treatment and adverse impact apply equally to national origin discrimination. These Guidelines apply to all entities covered by Title VII (collectively referred to as "employer").

§ 1606.3   The national security exception.

It is not an unlawful employment practice to deny employment opportunities to any individual who does not fulfill the national security requirements stated in Section 703(g) of Title VII.[1]

§ 1606.4   The bona fide occupational qualification exception.

The exception stated in Section 703(e) of Title VII, that national origin may be a bona fide occupational qualification, shall be strictly construed.

§ 1606.5   Citizenship requirements.

(a) In those circumstances, where citizenship requirements have the purpose or effect of discriminating against an individual on the basis of national origin, they are prohibited by Title VII.[2]

(b) Some State laws prohibit the employment of non-citizens. Where these laws are in conflict with Title VII, they are superseded under Section 708 of the Title.

29 CFR Ch. XIV (7-1-89 Edition)

§ 1606.6   Selection procedures.

(a)(1) In investigating an employer's selection procedures (including those identified below) for adverse impact on the basis of national origin, the Commission will apply the *Uniform Guidelines on Employee Selection Procedures* (UGESP), 29 CFR part 1607. Employers and other users of selection procedures should refer to the UGESP for guidance on matters, such as adverse impact, validation and recordkeeping requirements for national origin groups.

(2) Because height or weight requirements tend to exclude individuals on the basis of national origin,[3] the user is expected to evaluate these selection procedures for adverse impact, regardless of whether the total selection process has an adverse impact based on national origin. Therefore, height or weight requirements are identified here, as they are in UGESP,[4] as exceptions to the "bottom line" concept.

(b) The Commission has found that the use of the following selection procedures may be discriminatory on the basis of national origin. Therefore, it will carefully investigate charges involving these selection procedures for both disparate treatment and adverse impact on the basis of national origin. However, the Commission does not consider these to be exceptions to the "bottom line" concept:

(1) Fluency-in-English requirements, such as denying employment opportunities because of an individual's foreign accent,[5] or inability to communicate well in English.[6]

[3] See CD 71-1529 (1971), CCH EEOC Decisions ¶6231, 3 FEP Cases 952; CD 71-1418 (1971), CCH EEOC Decisions ¶6223, 3 FEP Cases 580; CD 74-25 (1973), CCH EEOC Decisions ¶6400, 10 FEP Cases 260. *Davis* v. *County of Los Angeles,* 566 F. 2d 1334, 1341-42 (9th Cir., 1977) vacated and remanded as moot on other grounds, 440 U.S. 625 (1979). See also, *Dothard* v. *Rawlinson,* 433 U.S. 321 (1977).
[4] See Section 4C(2) of the *Uniform Guidelines on Employee Selection Procedures,* 29 CFR 1607.4C(2).
[5] See CD AL68-1-155E (1969), CCH EEOC Decisions ¶6008, 1 FEP Cases 921.
[6] See CD YAU9-048 (1969), CCH EEOC Decisions ¶6054, 2 FEP Cases 78.

[1] See also, 5 U.S.C. 7532, for the authority of the head of a federal agency or department to suspend or remove an employee on grounds of national security.
[2] See *Espinoza* v. *Farah Mfg. Co., Inc.,* 414 U.S. 86, 92 (1973). See also, E.O. 11935, 5 CFR Part 7.4; and 31 U.S.C. 699(b), for citizenship requirements in certain Federal employment.

APPENDIX B-4. EEOC Guidelines for Discrimination Because of National Origin 29 CFR 1606.

Equal Employment Opportunity Comm.

(2) Training or education requirements which deny employment opportunities to an individual because of his or her foreign training or education, or which require an individual to be foreign trained or educated.

§ 1606.7 Speak-English-only rules.

(a) *When applied at all times.* A rule requiring employees to speak only English at all times in the workplace is a burdensome term and condition of employment. The primary language of an individual is often an essential national origin characteristic. Prohibiting employees at all times, in the workplace, from speaking their primary language or the language they speak most comfortably, disadvantages an individual's employment opportunities on the basis of national origin. It may also create an atmosphere of inferiority, isolation and intimidation based on national origin which could result in a discriminatory working environment.[7] Therefore, the Commission will presume that such a rule violates Title VII and will closely scrutinize it.

(b) *When applied only at certain times.* An employer may have a rule requiring that employees speak only in English at certain times where the employer can show that the rule is justified by business necessity.

(c) *Notice of the rule.* It is common for individuals whose primary language is not English to inadvertently change from speaking English to speaking their primary language. Therefore, if an employer believes it has a business necessity for a speak-English-only rule at certain times, the employer should inform its employees of the general circumstances when speaking only in English is required and of the consequences of violating the rule. If an employer fails to effectively notify its employees of the rule and makes an adverse employment decision against an individual based on a violation of the rule, the Commission will consider the employer's application of the rule as evidence of discrimination on the basis of national origin.

§ 1606.8 Harassment.

(a) The Commission has consistently held that harassment on the basis of national origin is a violation of Title VII. An employer has an affirmative duty to maintain a working environment free of harassment on the basis

of national origin.[*]

§ 1606.8

(b) Ethnic slurs and other verbal or physical conduct relating to an individual's national origin constitute harassment when this conduct: (1) Has the purpose or effect of creating an intimidating, hostile or offensive working environment; (2) has the purpose or effect of unreasonably interfering with an individual's work performance; or (3) otherwise adversely affects an individual's employment opportunities.

(c) An employer is responsible for its acts and those of its agents and supervisory employees with respect to harassment on the basis of national origin regardless of whether the specific acts complained of were authorized or even forbidden by the employer and regardless of whether the employer knew or should have known of their occurrence. The Commission will examine the circumstances of the particular employment relationship and the job functions performed by the individual in determining whether an individual acts in either a supervisory or agency capacity.

(d) With respect to conduct between fellow employees, an employer is responsible for acts of harassment in the workplace on the basis of national origin, where the employer, its agents or supervisory employees, knows or should have known of the conduct, unless the employer can show that it took immediate and appropriate corrective action.

Part 1607

(e) An employer may also be responsible for the acts of non-employees with respect to harassment of employees in the workplace on the basis of national origin, where the employer, its agents or supervisory employees, knows or should have known of the conduct and fails to take immediate and appropriate corrective action. In reviewing these cases, the Commission will consider the extent of the employer's control and any other legal responsibility which the employer may have with respect to the conduct of such non-employees.

[*]See CD CL68-12-431 EU (1969), CCH EEOC Decisions ¶6085, 2 FEP Cases 295; CD 72-0621 (1971), CCH EEOC Decisions ¶6311, 4 FEP Cases 312; CD 72-1561 (1972), CCH EEOC Decisions ¶6354, 4 FEP Cases 852; CD 74-05 (1973), CCH EEOC Decisions ¶6387, 6 FEP Cases 834; CD 76-41 (1975), CCH EEOC Decisions ¶6632. See also, Amendment to *Guidelines on Discrimination Because of Sex,* § 1604.11(a) n. 1, 45 FR 7476 sy 74677 (November 10, 1980).

[7]See CD 71-446 (1970), CCH EEOC Decisions ¶6173, 2 FEP Cases, 1127; CD 72-0281 (1971), CCH EEOC Decisions ¶6293.

APPENDIX B-5. EEOC Guidelines for Handicapped Discrimination 29 CFR 1613, Subpart G.

Subpart G—Prohibition Against Discrimination Because of a Physical or Mental Handicap

AUTHORITY: 5 U.S.C. 7153; § 5.1 of the Civil Service Rules; 29 U.S.C. 791.

SOURCE: 43 FR 12295, Mar. 24, 1978. Redesignated at 43 FR 60901, Dec. 29, 1978, unless otherwise noted.

GENERAL PROVISIONS

§ 1613.701 Purpose and applicability.

(a) *Purpose.* This subpart sets forth the policy under which an agency shall establish a continuing program to assure nondiscrimination on account of physical or mental handicap and the regulations under which an agency will process complaints of discrimination based on a physical or mental handicap.

(b) *Applicability.* (1) This subpart applies to executive agencies as defined in section 105 of Title 5 of the United States Code and to those positions in the legislative and judicial branches of the Federal Government and the government of the District of Columbia which are in the competitive service. (2) This subpart applies to the U.S. Postal Service and Postal Rate Commission. (3) This subpart applies only to applicants and employees who have a handicap as defined in § 1613.702(a).

§ 1613.702 Definitions.

(a) "Handicapped person" is defined for this subpart as one who: (1) Has a physical or mental impairment which substantially limits one or more of such person's major life activities, (2) has a record of such an impairment, or (3) is regarded as having such an impairment.

(b) "Physical or mental impairment" means (1) any physiological disorder or condition, cosmetic disfigurement, or anatomical loss affecting one or more of the following body systems: Neurological; musculoskeletal; special sense organs; cardiovascular; reproductive; digestive; genito-urinary; hemic and lymphatic; skin; and endocrine; or (2) any mental or psychological disorder, such as mental retardation, organic brain syndrome, emotional or mental illness, and specific learning disabilities.

(c) "Major life activities" means functions, such as caring for one's self, performing manual tasks, walking, seeing, hearing, speaking, breathing, learning, and working.

(d) "Has a record of such an impairment" means has a history of, or has been classified (or misclassified) as having a mental or physical impairment that substantially limits one or more major life activities.

(e) "Is regarded as having such an impairment" means (1) has a physical or mental impairment that does not substantially limit major life activities but is treated by an employer as constituting such a limitation; (2) has a physical or mental impairment that substantially limits major life activities only as a result of the attitude of an employer toward such impairment; (3) or has none of the impairments defined in (b) of this section but is treated by an employer as having such an impairment.

(f) "Qualified handicapped person" means with respect to employment, a handicapped person who, with or without reasonable accommodation, can perform the essential functions of the position in question without endangering the health and safety of the individual or others and who, depending upon the type of appointing authority being used: (1) Meets the experience and/or education requirements (which may include passing a written test) of the position in question, or (2) meets the criteria for appointment under one of the special appointing authorities for handicapped persons.

§ 1613.703 General policy.

Agencies shall give full consideration to the hiring, placement, and advancement of qualified mentally and physically handicapped persons. The Federal Government shall become a model employer of handicapped individuals. An agency shall not discriminate against a qualified physically or mentally handicapped person.

§ 1613.704 Reasonable accommodation.

(a) An agency shall make reasonable accommodation to the known physical or mental limitations of a qualified handicapped applicant or employee unless the agency can demonstrate that the accommodation would impose an undue hardship on the operation of its program.

(b) Reasonable accommodation may include, but shall not be limited to: (1) Making facilities readily accessible to and usable by handicapped persons, and (2) job restructuring, part-time or modified work schedules, acquisition or modification of equipment or devices, appropriate adjustment or modification of examinations, the provision of readers and interpreters, and other similar actions.

(c) In determining pursuant to paragraph (a) of this section whether an accommodation would impose an undue hardship on the operation of the agency in question, factors to be considered include: (1) The overall size of the agency's program with respect to the number of employees, number

APPENDIX B-5. EEOC Guidelines for Handicapped Discrimination 29 CFR 1613, Subpart G.

---

§ 1613.705

and type of facilities and size of budget; (2) the type of agency operation, including the composition and structure of the agency's work force; and (3) the nature and the cost of the accommodation.

§ 1613.705 Employment criteria.

(a) An agency may not make use of any employment test or other selection criterion that screens out or tends to screen out qualified handicapped persons or any class of handicapped persons unless: (1) The test score or other selection criterion, as used by the agency, is shown to be job-related for the position in question, and (2) alternative job-related tests or criteria that do not screen out or tend to screen out as many handicapped persons are not shown by the Civil Service Commission's Director of Personnel Research and Development Center to be available.

(b) An agency shall select and administer tests concerning employment so as to insure that, when administered to an applicant or employee who has a handicap that impairs sensory, manual, or speaking skills, the test results accurately reflect the applicant's or employee's ability to perform the position or type of positions in question rather than reflecting the applicant's or employee's impaired sensory, manual, or speaking skills (except where those skills are the factors that the test purports to measure).

§ 1613.706 Preemployment inquiries.

(a) Except as provided in paragraphs (b) and (c) of this section, an agency may not conduct a preemployment medical examination and may not make preemployment inquiry of an applicant as to whether the applicant is a handicapped person or as to the nature or severity of a handicap. An agency may, however, make preemployment inquiry into an applicant's ability to meet the medical qualification requirements, with or without reasonable accommodation, of the position in question, i.e., the minimum abilities necessary for safe and efficient performance of the duties of the position in question. The Civil Service Commission may also make an inquiry

as to the nature and extent of a handicap for the purpose of special testing.

(b) Nothing in this section shall prohibit an agency from conditioning an offer of employment on the results of a medical examination conducted prior to the employee's entrance on duty, *Provided,* That: (1) All entering employees are subjected to such an examination regardless of handicap or when the preemployment medical questionnaire used for positions which do not routinely require medical examination indicates a condition for which further examination is required because of the job-related nature of the condition, and (2) the results of such an examination are used only in accordance with the requirements of this part. Nothing in this section shall be construed to prohibit the gathering of preemployment medical information for the purposes of special appointing authorities for handicapped persons.

(c) To enable and evaluate affirmative action to hire, place, or advance handicapped individuals, the agency may invite applicants for employment to indicate whether and to what extent they are handicapped, if: (1) The agency states clearly on any written questionnaire used for this purpose or makes clear orally, if no written questionnaire is used, that the information requested is intended for use solely in conjunction with affirmative action and (2) the agency states clearly that the information is being requested on a voluntary basis, that refusal to provide it will not subject the applicant or employee to any adverse treatment, and that it will be used only in accordance with this part.

(d) Information obtained in accordance with this section as to the medical condition or history of the applicant shall be kept confidential except that: (1) Managers, selecting officials, and others involved in the selection process or responsible for affirmative action may be informed that the applicant is a handicapped individual eligible for affirmative action; (2) supervisors and managers may be informed regarding necessary accommodations; (3) first aid and safety personnel may be informed, where appropriate, if the condition might require emergency

APPENDIX B-5.   EEOC Guidelines for Handicapped Discrimination 29 CFR 1613, Subpart G.

Equal Employment Opportunity Comm.   **§ 1613.801**

treatment; (4) government officials investigating compliance with laws, regulations, and instructions relevant to equal employment opportunity and affirmative action for handicapped individuals shall be provided information upon request; and (5) statistics generated from information obtained may be used to manage, evaluate, and report on equal employment opportunity and affirmative action programs.

[43 FR 12295, Mar. 24, 1978. Redesignated at 43 FR 60901, Dec. 29, 1978, and amended at 46 FR 11285, Feb. 6, 1981]

§ 1613.707 Physical access to buildings.

(a) An agency shall not discriminate against qualified handicapped applicants or employees due to the inaccessibility of its facility.

(b) For the purpose of this subpart, a facility shall be deemed accessible if it is in compliance with the Architectural Barriers Act of 1968.

AGENCY REGULATIONS FOR PROCESSING COMPLAINTS OF DISCRIMINATION

§ 1613.708 General.

An agency shall provide regulations governing the acceptance and processing of complaints of discrimination based on a physical or mental handicap which comply with the principles and requirements in §§ 1613.213 through 1613.283 and §§ 1613.601 through 1613.643. Nothing in the foregoing shall be construed to postpone the effective date of this rule.

[46 FR 51384, Oct. 20, 1981]

§ 1613.709 Coverage.

(a) An agency shall provide in its regulations for the acceptance of a complaint from any aggrieved employee or applicant for employment who believes that he or she has been discriminated against because of a handicap as defined in § 1613.702.

(b) An agency must process complaints of discrimination based on acts or actions that occurred 1 year prior to the effective date of these regulations Provided: (1) The complaint of discrimination was brought to the attention of the agency within 30 calendar days of the alleged discriminatory act, or, if a personnel action, within 30 calendar days of its effective date, (2) the complaint of discrimination was not adjudicated under some other grievance or appeals procedure, and (3) the complaint of discrimination is filed within 180 calendar days of the effective date of these regulations. Complaints of discrimination based on alleged discriminatory acts or personnel actions that occurred on or after the effective date of these regulations are subject to the time restraints set forth in § 1613.214(a).

(c) Notwithstanding the provision of subsection (b), a complainant may request an agency to process allegations of handicap discrimination which had been filed as a discrimination complaint or as a grievance, and were pending with the agency, the Civil Service Commission or in a Federal Court on April 10, 1978. Such requests for processing of allegations of handicap discrimination must be brought to the attention of the agency EEO counselor not later than 180 days from the publication of this subsection in final form in the FEDERAL REGISTER.

[43 FR 12295, Mar. 24, 1978. Redesignated at 43 FR 60901, Dec. 29, 1978, and amended at 45 FR 41634, June 20, 1980]

APPENDIX C. Part 1607, Uniform Guidelines on Employee Selection Procedures (1978).

Part 1607

29 CFR Ch. XIV (7-1-89 Edition)

PART 1607—UNIFORM GUIDELINES ON EMPLOYEE SELECTION PROCEDURES (1978)

COMPREHENSIVE TABLE OF CONTENTS

GENERAL PRINCIPLES

APPENDIX C.   Part 1607, Uniform Guidelines on Employee Selection Procedures (1978).

Equal Employment Opportunity Comm.   Part 1607

AUTHORITY: Secs. 709 and 713, Civil Rights Act of 1964 (78 Stat. 265) as amended by the Equal Employment Opportunity Act of 1972 (Pub. L. 92-261); 42 U.S.C. 2000e-8, 2000e-12.

APPENDIX C. Part 1607, Uniform Guidelines on Employee Selection Procedures (1978).

---

§ 1607.1

SOURCE: 43 FR 38295 and 43 FR 38312, Aug. 25, 1978, unless otherwise noted.

GENERAL PRINCIPLES

§ 1607.1 Statement of purpose.

A. *Need for uniformity—Issuing agencies.* The Federal government's need for a uniform set of principles on the question of the use of tests and other selection procedures has long been recognized. The Equal Employment Opportunity Commission, the Civil Service Commission, the Department of Labor, and the Department of Justice jointly have adopted these uniform guidelines to meet that need, and to apply the same principles to the Federal Government as are applied to other employers.

B. *Purpose of guidelines.* These guidelines incorporate a single set of principles which are designed to assist employers, labor organizations, employment agencies, and licensing and certification boards to comply with requirements of Federal law prohibiting employment practices which discriminate on grounds of race, color, religion, sex, and national origin. They are designed to provide a framework for determining the proper use of tests and other selection procedures. These guidelines do not require a user to conduct validity studies of selection procedures where no adverse impact results. However, all users are encouraged to use selection procedures which are valid, especially users operating under merit principles.

C. *Relation to prior guidelines.* These guidelines are based upon and supersede previously issued guidelines on employee selection procedures. These guidelines have been built upon court decisions, the previously issued guidelines of the agencies, and the practical experience of the agencies, as well as the standards of the psychological profession. These guidelines are intended to be consistent with existing law.

§ 1607.2 Scope.

A. *Application of guidelines.* These guidelines will be applied by the Equal Employment Opportunity Commission in the enforcement of title VII of the Civil Rights Act of 1964, as amended

29 CFR Ch. XIV (7-1-89 Edition)

by the Equal Employment Opportunity Act of 1972 (hereinafter "Title VII"); by the Department of Labor, and the contract compliance agencies until the transfer of authority contemplated by the President's Reorganization Plan No. 1 of 1978, in the administration and enforcement of Executive Order 11246, as amended by Executive Order 11375 (hereinafter "Executive Order 11246"); by the Civil Service Commission and other Federal agencies subject to section 717 of Title VII; by the Civil Service Commission in exercising its responsibilities toward State and local governments under section 208(b)(1) of the Intergovernmental-Personnel Act; by the Department of Justice in exercising its responsibilities under Federal law; by the Office of Revenue Sharing of the Department of the Treasury under the State and Local Fiscal Assistance Act of 1972, as amended; and by any other Federal agency which adopts them.

B. *Employment decisions.* These guidelines apply to tests and other selection procedures which are used as a basis for any employment decision. Employment decisions include but are not limited to hiring, promotion, demotion, membership (for example, in a labor organization), referral, retention, and licensing and certification, to the extent that licensing and certification may be covered by Federal equal employment opportunity law. Other selection decisions, such as selection for training or transfer, may also be considered employment decisions if they lead to any of the decisions listed above.

C. *Selection procedures.* These guidelines apply only to selection procedures which are used as a basis for making employment decisions. For example, the use of recruiting procedures designed to attract members of a particular race, sex, or ethnic group, which were previously denied employment opportunities or which are currently underutilized, may be necessary to bring an employer into compliance with Federal law, and is frequently an essential element of any effective affirmative action program; but recruitment practices are not considered by these guidelines to be selection proce-

APPENDIX C. Part 1607, Uniform Guidelines on Employee Selection Procedures (1978).

---

dures. Similarly, these guidelines do not pertain to the question of the lawfulness of a seniority system within the meaning of section 703(h), Executive Order 11246 or other provisions of Federal law or regulation, except to the extent that such systems utilize selection procedures to determine qualifications or abilities to perform the job. Nothing in these guidelines is intended or should be interpreted as discouraging the use of a selection procedure for the purpose of determining qualifications or for the purpose of selection on the basis of relative qualifications, if the selection procedure had been validated in accord with these guidelines for each such purpose for which it is to be used.

D. *Limitations.* These guidelines apply only to persons subject to Title VII, Executive Order 11246, or other equal employment opportunity requirements of Federal law. These guidelines do not apply to responsibilities under the Age Discrimination in Employment Act of 1967, as amended, not to discriminate on the basis of age, or under sections 501, 503, and 504 of the Rehabilitation Act of 1973, not to discriminate on the basis of handicap.

E. *Indian preference not affected.* These guidelines do not restrict any obligation imposed or right granted by Federal law to users to extend a preference in employment to Indians living on or near an Indian reservation in connection with employment opportunities on or near an Indian reservation.

§ 1607.3 Discrimination defined: Relationship between use of selection procedures and discrimination.

A. *Procedure having adverse impact constitutes discrimination unless justified.* The use of any selection procedure which has an adverse impact on the hiring, promotion, or other employment or membership opportunities of members of any race, sex, or ethnic group will be considered to be discriminatory and inconsistent with these guidelines, unless the procedure has been validated in accordance with these guidelines, or the provisions of section 6 below are satisfied.

B. *Consideration of suitable alternative selection procedures.* Where two or more selection procedures are available which serve the user's legitimate interest in efficient and trustworthy workmanship, and which are substantially equally valid for a given purpose, the user should use the procedure which has been demonstrated to have the lesser adverse impact. Accordingly, whenever a validity study is called for by these guidelines, the user should include, as a part of the validity study, an investigation of suitable alternative selection procedures and suitable alternative methods of using the selection procedure which have as little adverse impact as possible, to determine the appropriateness of using or validating them in accord with these guidelines. If a user has made a reasonable effort to become aware of such alternative procedures and validity has been demonstrated in accord with these guidelines, the use of the test or other selection procedure may continue until such time as it should reasonably be reviewed for currency. Whenever the user is shown an alternative selection procedure with evidence of less adverse impact and substantial evidence of validity for the same job in similar circumstances, the user should investigate it to determine the appropriateness of using or validating it in accord with these guidelines. This subsection is not intended to preclude the combination of procedures into a significantly more valid procedure, if the use of such a combination has been shown to be in compliance with the guidelines.

§ 1607.4 Information on impact.

A. *Records concerning impact.* Each user should maintain and have available for inspection records or other information which will disclose the impact which its tests and other selection procedures have upon employment opportunities of persons by identifiable race, sex, or ethnic group as set forth in subparagraph B below in order to determine compliance with these guidelines. Where there are large numbers of applicants and procedures are administered frequently, such information may be retained on a sample basis, provided that the sample

APPENDIX C. Part 1607, Uniform Guidelines on Employee Selection Procedures (1978).

---

§ 1607.4

is appropriate in terms of the applicant population and adequate in size.

B. *Applicable race, sex, and ethnic groups for recordkeeping.* The records called for by this section are to be maintained by sex, and the following races and ethnic groups: Blacks (Negroes), American Indians (including Alaskan Natives), Asians (including Pacific Islanders), Hispanic (including persons of Mexican, Puerto Rican, Cuban, Central or South American, or other Spanish origin or culture regardless of race), whites (Caucasians) other than Hispanic, and totals. The race, sex, and ethnic classifications called for by this section are consistent with the Equal Employment Opportunity Standard Form 100, Employer Information Report EEO-1 series of reports. The user should adopt safeguards to insure that the records required by this paragraph are used for appropriate purposes such as determining adverse impact, or (where required) for developing and monitoring affirmative action programs, and that such records are not used improperly. See sections 4E and 17(4), below.

C. *Evaluation of selection rates. The "bottom line."* If the information called for by sections 4A and B above shows that the total selection process for a job has an adverse impact, the individual components of the selection process should be evaluated for adverse impact. If this information shows that the total selection process does not have an adverse impact, the Federal enforcement agencies, in the exercise of their administrative and prosecutorial discretion, in usual circumstances, will not expect a user to evaluate the individual components for adverse impact, or to validate such individual components, and will not take enforcement action based upon adverse impact of any component of that process, including the separate parts of a multipart selection procedure or any separate procedure that is used as an alternative method of selection. However, in the following circumstances the Federal enforcement agencies will expect a user to evaluate the individual components for adverse impact and may, where appropriate, take enforcement action with respect to the individual components: (1)

---

29 CFR Ch. XIV (7-1-89 Edition)

Where the selection procedure is a significant factor in the continuation of patterns of assignments of incumbent employees caused by prior discriminatory employment practices, (2) where the weight of court decisions or administrative interpretations hold that a specific procedure (such as height or weight requirements or no-arrest records) is not job related in the same or similar circumstances. In unusual circumstances, other than those listed in (1) and (2) above, the Federal enforcement agencies may request a user to evaluate the individual components for adverse impact and may, where appropriate, take enforcement action with respect to the individual component.

D. *Adverse impact and the "four-fifths rule."* A selection rate for any race, sex, or ethnic group which is less than four-fifths (⅘) (or eighty percent) of the rate for the group with the highest rate will generally be regarded by the Federal enforcement agencies as evidence of adverse impact, while a greater than four-fifths rate will generally not be regarded by Federal enforcement agencies as evidence of adverse impact. Smaller differences in selection rate may nevertheless constitute adverse impact, where they are significant in both statistical and practical terms or where a user's actions have discouraged applicants disproportionately on grounds of race, sex, or ethnic group. Greater differences in selection rate may not constitute adverse impact where the differences are based on small numbers and are not statistically significant, or where special recruiting or other programs cause the pool of minority or female candidates to be atypical of the normal pool of applicants from that group. Where the user's evidence concerning the impact of a selection procedure indicates adverse impact but is based upon numbers which are too small to be reliable, evidence concerning the impact of the procedure over a longer period of time and/or evidence concerning the impact which the selection procedure had when used in the same manner in similar circumstances elsewhere may be considered in determining adverse impact. Where the user has not maintained data on adverse

214

APPENDIX C. Part 1607, Uniform Guidelines on Employee Selection Procedures (1978).

impact as required by the documentation section of applicable guidelines, the Federal enforcement agencies may draw an inference of adverse impact of the selection process from the failure of the user to maintain such data, if the user has an underutilization of a group in the job category, as compared to the group's representation in the relevant labor market or, in the case of jobs filled from within, the applicable work force.

E. *Consideration of user's equal employment opportunity posture.* In carrying out their obligations, the Federal enforcement agencies will consider the general posture of the user with respect to equal employment opportunity for the job or group of jobs in question. Where a user has adopted an affirmative action program, the Federal enforcement agencies will consider the provisions of that program, including the goals and timetables which the user has adopted and the progress which the user has made in carrying out that program and in meeting the goals and timetables. While such affirmative action programs may in design and execution be race, color, sex, or ethnic conscious, selection procedures under such programs should be based upon the ability or relative ability to do the work.

(Approved by the Office of Management and Budget under control number 3046-0017)

(Pub. L. No. 96–511, 94 Stat. 2812 (44 U.S.C. 3501 et seq.))

[43 FR 38295, 38312, Aug. 25, 1978, as amended at 46 FR 63268, Dec. 31, 1981]

§ 1607.5 General standards for validity studies.

A. *Acceptable types of validity studies.* For the purposes of satisfying these guidelines, users may rely upon criterion-related validity studies, content validity studies or construct validity studies, in accordance with the standards set forth in the technical standards of these guidelines, section 14 below. New strategies for showing the validity of selection procedures will be evaluated as they become accepted by the psychological profession.

B. *Criterion-related, content, and construct validity.* Evidence of the va-

lidity of a test or other selection procedure by a criterion-related validity study should consist of empirical data demonstrating that the selection procedure is predictive of or significantly correlated with important elements of job performance. See section 14B below. Evidence of the validity of a test or other selection procedure by a content validity study should consist of data showing that the content of the selection procedure is representative of important aspects of performance on the job for which the candidates are to be evaluated. See 14C below. Evidence of the validity of a test or other selection procedure through a construct validity study should consist of data showing that the procedure measures the degree to which candidates have identifiable characteristics which have been determined to be important in successful performance in the job for which the candidates are to be evaluated. See section 14D below.

C. *Guidelines are consistent with professional standards.* The provisions of these guidelines relating to validation of selection procedures are intended to be consistent with generally accepted professional standards for evaluating standardized tests and other selection procedures, such as those described in the Standards for Educational and Psychological Tests prepared by a joint committee of the American Psychological Association, the American Educational Research Association, and the National Council on Measurement in Education (American Psychological Association, Washington, D.C., 1974) (hereinafter "A.P.A. Standards") and standard textbooks and journals in the field of personnel selection.

D. *Need for documentation of validity.* For any selection procedure which is part of a selection process which has an adverse impact and which selection procedure has an adverse impact, each user should maintain and have available such documentation as is described in section 15 below.

E. *Accuracy and standardization.* Validity studies should be carried out under conditions which assure insofar as possible the adequacy and accuracy of the research and the report. Selec-

APPENDIX C. Part 1607, Uniform Guidelines on Employee Selection Procedures (1978).

---

tion procedures should be administered and scored under standardized conditions.

F. *Caution against selection on basis of knowledges, skills, or ability learned in brief orientation period.* In general, users should avoid making employment decisions on the basis of measures of knowledges, skills, or abilities which are normally learned in a brief orientation period, and which have an adverse impact.

G. *Method of use of selection procedures.* The evidence of both the validity and utility of a selection procedure should support the method the user chooses for operational use of the procedure, if that method of use has a greater adverse impact than another method of use. Evidence which may be sufficient to support the use of a selection procedure on a pass/fail (screening) basis may be insufficient to support the use of the same procedure on a ranking basis under these guidelines. Thus, if a user decides to use a selection procedure on a ranking basis, and that method of use has a greater adverse impact than use on an appropriate pass/fail basis (see section 5H below), the user should have sufficient evidence of validity and utility to support the use on a ranking basis. See sections 3B, 14B (5) and (6), and 14C (8) and (9).

H. *Cutoff scores.* Where cutoff scores are used, they should normally be set so as to be reasonable and consistent with normal expectations of acceptable proficiency within the work force. Where applicants are ranked on the basis of properly validated selection procedures and those applicants scoring below a higher cutoff score than appropriate in light of such expectations have little or no chance of being selected for employment, the higher cutoff score may be appropriate, but the degree of adverse impact should be considered.

I. *Use of selection procedures for higher level jobs.* If job progression structures are so established that employees will probably, within a reasonable period of time and in a majority of cases, progress to a higher level, it may be considered that the applicants are being evaluated for a job or jobs at the higher level. However, where job

progression is not so nearly automatic, or the time span is such that higher level jobs or employees' potential may be expected to change in significant ways, it should be considered that applicants are being evaluated for a job at or near the entry level. A "reasonable period of time" will vary for different jobs and employment situations but will seldom be more than 5 years. Use of selection procedures to evaluate applicants for a higher level job would not be appropriate:

(1) If the majority of those remaining employed do not progress to the higher level job;

(2) If there is a reason to doubt that the higher level job will continue to require essentially similar skills during the progression period; or

(3) If the selection procedures measure knowledges, skills, or abilities required for advancement which would be expected to develop principally from the training or experience on the job.

J. *Interim use of selection procedures.* Users may continue the use of a selection procedure which is not at the moment fully supported by the required evidence of validity, provided: (1) The user has available substantial evidence of validity, and (2) the user has in progress, when technically feasible, a study which is designed to produce the additional evidence required by these guidelines within a reasonable time. If such a study is not technically feasible, see section 6B. If the study does not demonstrate validity, this provision of these guidelines for interim use shall not constitute a defense in any action, nor shall it relieve the user of any obligations arising under Federal law.

K. *Review of validity studies for currency.* Whenever validity has been shown in accord with these guidelines for the use of a particular selection procedure for a job or group of jobs, additional studies need not be performed until such time as the validity study is subject to review as provided in section 3B above. There are no absolutes in the area of determining the currency of a validity study. All circumstances concerning the study, including the validation strategy used, and changes in the relevant labor

APPENDIX C.   Part 1607, Uniform Guidelines on Employee Selection Procedures (1978).

Equal Employment Opportunity Comm.   **§ 1607.7**

market and the job should be considered in the determination of when a validity study is outdated.

§ 1607.6   Use of selection procedures which have not been validated.

A. *Use of alternate selection procedures to eliminate adverse impact.* A user may choose to utilize alternative selection procedures in order to eliminate adverse impact or as part of an affirmative action program. See section 13 below. Such alternative procedures should eliminate the adverse impact in the total selection process, should be lawful and should be as job related as possible.

B. *Where validity studies cannot or need not be performed.* There are circumstances in which a user cannot or need not utilize the validation techniques contemplated by these guidelines. In such circumstances, the user should utilize selection procedures which are as job related as possible and which will minimize or eliminate adverse impact, as set forth below.

(1) *Where informal or unscored procedures are used.* When an informal or unscored selection procedure which has an adverse impact is utilized, the user should eliminate the adverse impact, or modify the procedure to one which is a formal, scored or quantified measure or combination of measures and then validate the procedure in accord with these guidelines, or otherwise justify continued use of the procedure in accord with Federal law.

(2) *Where formal and scored procedures are used.* When a formal and scored selection procedure is used which has an adverse impact, the validation techniques contemplated by these guidelines usually should be followed if technically feasible. Where the user cannot or need not follow the validation techniques anticipated by these guidelines, the user should either modify the procedure to eliminate adverse impact or otherwise justify continued use of the procedure in accord with Federal law.

§ 1607.7   Use of other validity studies.

A. *Validity studies not conducted by the user.* Users may, under certain circumstances, support the use of selection procedures by validity studies conducted by other users or conducted by test publishers or distributors and described in test manuals. While publishers of selection procedures have a professional obligation to provide evidence of validity which meets generally accepted professional standards (see section 5C above), users are cautioned that they are responsible for compliance with these guidelines. Accordingly, users seeking to obtain selection procedures from publishers and distributors should be careful to determine that, in the event the user becomes subject to the validity requirements of these guidelines, the necessary information to support validity has been determined and will be made available to the user.

B. *Use of criterion-related validity evidence from other sources.* Criterion-related validity studies conducted by one test user, or described in test manuals and the professional literature, will be considered acceptable for use by another user when the following requirements are met:

(1) *Validity evidence.* Evidence from the available studies meeting the standards of section 14B below clearly demonstrates that the selection procedure is valid;

(2) *Job similarity.* The incumbents in the user's job and the incumbents in the job or group of jobs on which the validity study was conducted perform substantially the same major work behaviors, as shown by appropriate job analyses both on the job or group of jobs on which the validity study was performed and on the job for which the selection procedure is to be used; and

(3) *Fairness evidence.* The studies include a study of test fairness for each race, sex, and ethnic group which constitutes a significant factor in the borrowing user's relevant labor market for the job or jobs in question. If the studies under consideration satisfy (1) and (2) above but do not contain an investigation of test fairness, and it is not technically feasible for the borrowing user to conduct an internal study of test fairness, the borrowing user may utilize the study until studies conducted elsewhere meeting the requirements of these guidelines show

217

APPENDIX C. Part 1607, Uniform Guidelines on Employee Selection Procedures (1978).

test unfairness, or until such time as it becomes technically feasible to conduct an internal study of test fairness and the results of that study can be acted upon. Users obtaining selection procedures from publishers should consider, as one factor in the decision to purchase a particular selection procedure, the availability of evidence concerning test fairness.

C. *Validity evidence from multiunit study.* if validity evidence from a study covering more than one unit within an organization statisfies the requirements of section 14B below, evidence of validity specific to each unit will not be required unless there are variables which are likely to affect validity significantly.

D. *Other significant variables.* If there are variables in the other studies which are likely to affect validity significantly, the user may not rely upon such studies, but will be expected either to conduct an internal validity study or to comply with section 6 above.

§ 1607.8 Cooperative studies.

A. *Encouragement of cooperative studies.* The agencies issuing these guidelines encourage employers, labor organizations, and employment agencies to cooperate in research, development, search for lawful alternatives, and validity studies in order to achieve procedures which are consistent with these guidelines.

B. *Standards for use of cooperative studies.* If validity evidence from a cooperative study satisfies the requirements of section 14 below, evidence of validity specific to each user will not be required unless there are variables in the user's situation which are likely to affect validity significantly.

§ 1607.9 No assumption of validity.

A. *Unacceptable substitutes for evidence of validity.* Under no circumstances will the general reputation of a test or other selection procedures, its author or its publisher, or casual reports of it's validity be accepted in lieu of evidence of validity. Specifically ruled out are: assumptions of validity based on a procedure's name or descriptive labels; all forms of promotional literature; data bearing on the

frequency of a procedure's usage; testimonial statements and credentials of sellers, users, or consultants; and other nonempirical or anecdotal accounts of selection practices or selection outcomes.

B. *Encouragement of professional supervision.* Professional supervision of selection activities is encouraged but is not a substitute for documented evidence of validity. The enforcement agencies will take into account the fact that a thorough job analysis was conducted and that careful development and use of a selection procedure in accordance with professional standards enhance the probability that the selection procedure is valid for the job.

§ 1607.10 Employment agencies and employment services.

A. *Where selection procedures are devised by agency.* An employment agency, including private employment agencies and State employment agencies, which agrees to a request by an employer or labor organization to device and utilize a selection procedure should follow the standards in these guidelines for determining adverse impact. If adverse impact exists the agency should comply with these guidelines. An employment agency is not relieved of its obligation herein because the user did not request such validation or has requested the use of some lesser standard of validation than is provided in these guidelines. The use of an employment agency does not relieve an employer or labor organization or other user of its responsibilities under Federal law to provide equal employment opportunity or its obligations as a user under these guidelines.

B. *Where selection procedures are devised elsewhere.* Where an employment agency or service is requested to administer a selection procedure which has been devised elsewhere and to make referrals pursuant to the results, the employment agency or service should maintain and have available evidence of the impact of the selection and referral procedures which it administers. If adverse impact results the agency or service should comply with these guidelines. If the agency or

APPENDIX C.   Part 1607, Uniform Guidelines on Employee Selection Procedures (1978).

---

service seeks to comply with these guidelines by reliance upon validity studies or other data in the possession of the employer, it should obtain and have available such information.

§ 1607.11   Disparate treatment.

The principles of disparate or unequal treatment must be distinguished from the concepts of validation. A selection procedure—even though validated against job performance in accordance with these guidelines—cannot be imposed upon members of a race, sex, or ethnic group where other employees, applicants, or members have not been subjected to that standard. Disparate treatment occurs where members of a race, sex, or ethnic group have been denied the same employment, promotion, membership, or other employment opportunities as have been available to other employees or applicants. Those employees or applicants who have been denied equal treatment, because of prior discriminatory practices or policies, must at least be afforded the same opportunities as had existed for other employees or applicants during the period of discrimination. Thus, the persons who were in the class of persons discriminated against during the period the user followed the discriminatory practices should be allowed the opportunity to qualify under less stringent selection procedures previously followed, unless the user demonstrates that the increased standards are required by business necessity. This section does not prohibit a user who has not previously followed merit standards from adopting merit standards which are in compliance with these guidelines; nor does it preclude a user who has previously used invalid or unvalidated selection procedures from developing and using procedures which are in accord with these guidelines.

§ 1607.12   Retesting of applicants.

Users should provide a reasonable opportunity for retesting and reconsideration. Where examinations are administered periodically with public notice, such reasonable opportunity exists, unless persons who have previously been tested are precluded from retesting. The user may however take

reasonable steps to preserve the security of its procedures.

§ 1607.13   Affirmative action.

A. *Affirmative action obligations.* The use of selection procedures which have been validated pursuant to these guidelines does not relieve users of any obligations they may have to undertake affirmative action to assure equal employment opportunity. Nothing in these guidelines is intended to preclude the use of lawful selection procedures which assist in remedying the effects of prior discriminatory practices, or the achievement of affirmative action objectives.

B. *Encouragement of voluntary affirmative action programs.* These guidelines are also intended to encourage the adoption and implementation of voluntary affirmative action programs by users who have no obligation under Federal law to adopt them; but are not intended to impose any new obligations in that regard. The agencies issuing and endorsing these guidelines endorse for all private employers and reaffirm for all governmental employers the Equal Employment Opportunity Coordinating Council's "Policy Statement on Affirmative Action Programs for State and Local Government Agencies" (41 FR 38814, September 13, 1976). That policy statement is attached hereto as appendix, section 17.

TECHNICAL STANDARDS

§ 1607.14   Technical standards for validity studies.

The following minimum standards, as applicable, should be met in conducting a validity study. Nothing in these guidelines is intended to preclude the development and use of other professionally acceptable techniques with respect to validation of selection procedures. Where it is not technically feasible for a user to conduct a validity study, the user has the obligation otherwise to comply with these guidelines. See sections 6 and 7 above.

A. *Validity studies should be based on review of information about the job.* Any validity study should be based upon a review of information

APPENDIX C. Part 1607, Uniform Guidelines on Employee Selection Procedures (1978).

---

about the job for which the selection procedure is to be used. The review should include a job analysis except as provided in section 14B(3) below with respect to criterion-related validity. Any method of job analysis may be used if it provides the information required for the specific validation strategy used.

B. *Technical standards for criterion-related validity studies.* (1) *Technical feasibility.* Users choosing to validate a selection procedure by a criterion-related validity strategy should determine whether it is technically feasible (as defined in section 16) to conduct such a study in the particular employment context. The determination of the number of persons necessary to permit the conduct of a meaningful criterion-related study should be made by the user on the basis of all relevant information concerning the selection procedure, the potential sample and the employment situation. Where appropriate, jobs with substantially the same major work behaviors may be grouped together for validity studies, in order to obtain an adequate sample. These guidelines do not require a user to hire or promote persons for the purpose of making it possible to conduct a criterion-related study.

(2) *Analysis of the job.* There should be a review of job information to determine measures of work behavior(s) or performance that are relevant to the job or group of jobs in question. These measures or criteria are relevant to the extent that they represent critical or important job duties, work behaviors or work outcomes as developed from the review of job information. The possibility of bias should be considered both in selection of the criterion measures and their application. In view of the possibility of bias in subjective evaluations, supervisory rating techniques and instructions to raters should be carefully developed. All criterion measures and the methods for gathering data need to be examined for freedom from factors which would unfairly alter scores of members of any group. The relevance of criteria and their freedom from bias are of particular concern when there are significant differences in measures

of job performance for different groups.

· (3) *Criterion measures.* Proper safeguards should be taken to insure that scores on selection procedures do not enter into any judgments of employee adequacy that are to be used as criterion measures. Whatever criteria are used should represent important or critical work behavior(s) or work outcomes. Certain criteria may be used without a full job analysis if the user can show the importance of the criteria to the particular employment context. These criteria include but are not limited to production rate, error rate, tardiness, absenteeism, and length of service. A standardized rating of overall work performance may be used where a study of the job shows that it is an appropriate criterion. Where performance in training is used as a criterion, success in training should be properly measured and the relevance of the training should be shown either through a comparison of the content of the training program with the critical or important work behavior(s) of the job(s), or through a demonstration of the relationship between measures of performance in training and measures of job performance. Measures of relative success in training include but are not limited to instructor evaluations, performance samples, or tests. Criterion measures consisting of paper and pencil tests will be closely reviewed for job relevance.

(4) *Representativeness of the sample.* Whether the study is predictive or concurrent, the sample subjects should insofar as feasible be representative of the candidates normally available in the relevant labor market for the job or group of jobs in question, and should insofar as feasible include the races, sexes, and ethnic groups normally available in the relevant job market. In determining the representativeness of the sample in a concurrent validity study, the user should take into account the extent to which the specific knowledges or skills which are the primary focus of the test are those which employees learn on the job.

Where samples are combined or compared, attention should be given to see that such samples are compara-

APPENDIX C. Part 1607, Uniform Guidelines on Employee Selection Procedures (1978).

---

ble in terms of the actual job they perform, the length of time on the job where time on the job is likely to affect performance, and other relevant factors likely to affect validity differences; or that these factors are included in the design of the study and their effects identified.

(5) *Statistical relationships.* The degree of relationship between selection procedure scores and criterion measures should be examined and computed, using professionally acceptable statistical procedures. Generally, a selection procedure is considered related to the criterion, for the purposes of these guidelines, when the relationship between performance on the procedure and performance on the criterion measure is statistically significant at the 0.05 level of significance, which means that it is sufficiently high as to have a probability of no more than one (1) in twenty (20) to have occurred by chance. Absence of a statistically significant relationship between a selection procedure and job performance should not necessarily discourage other investigations of the validity of that selection procedure.

(6) *Operational use of selection procedures.* Users should evaluate each selection procedure to assure that it is appropriate for operational use, including establishment of cutoff scores or rank ordering. Generally, if other factors reman the same, the greater the magnitude of .the relationship (e.g., correlation coefficient) between performance on a selection procedure and one or more criteria of performance on the job, and the greater the importance and number of aspects of job performance covered by the criteria, the more likely it is that the procedure will be appropriate for use. Reliance upon a selection procedure which is significantly related to a criterion measure, but which is based upon a study involving a large number of subjects and has a low correlation coefficient will be subject to close review if it has a large adverse impact. Sole reliance upon a single selection instrument which is related to only one of many job duties or aspects of job performance will also be subject to close review. The appropriateness of a selection procedure is best evaluated in each particular situation and there are no minimum correlation coefficients' applicable to all employment situations. In determining whether a selection procedure is appropriate for operational use the following considerations should also be taken into account: The degree of adverse impact of the procedure, the availability of other selection procedures of greater or substantially equal validity.

(7) *Overstatement of validity findings.* Users should avoid reliance upon techniques which tend to overestimate validity findings as a result of capitalization on chance unless an appropriate safeguard is taken. Reliance upon a few selection procedures or criteria of successful job performance when many selection procedures or criteria of performance have been studied, or the use of optimal statistical weights for selection procedures computed in one sample, are techniques which tend to inflate validity estimates as a result of chance. Use of a large sample is one safeguard: cross-validation is another.

(8) *Fairness.* This section generally calls for studies of unfairness where technically feasible. The concept of fairness or unfairness of selection procedures is a developing concept. In addition, fairness studies generally require substantial numbers of employees in the job or group of jobs being studied. For these reasons, the Federal enforcement agencies recognize that the obligation to conduct studies of fairness imposed by the guidelines generally will be upon users or groups of users with a large number of persons in a a job class, or test developers; and that small users utilizing their own selection procedures will generally not be obligated to conduct such studies because it will be technically infeasible for them to do so.

(a) *Unfairness defined.* When members of one race, sex, or ethnic group characteristically obtain lower scores on a selection procedure than members of another group, and the differences in scores are not reflected in differences in a measure of job performance, use of the selection procedure may unfairly deny opportunities to members of the group that obtains the lower scores.

APPENDIX C. Part 1607, Uniform Guidelines on Employee Selection Procedures (1978).

---

§ 1607.14

(b) *Investigation of fairness.* Where a selection procedure results in an adverse impact on a race, sex, or ethnic group identified in accordance with the classifications set forth in section 4 above and that group is a significant factor in the relevant labor market, the user generally should investigate the possible existence of unfairness for that group if it is technically feasible to do so. The greater the severity of the adverse impact on a group, the greater the need to investigate the possible existence of unfairness. Where the weight of evidence from other studies shows that the selection procedure predicts fairly for the group in question and for the same or similar jobs, such evidence may be relied on in connection with the selection procedure at issue.

(c) *General considerations in fairness investigations.* Users conducting a study of fairness should review the A.P.A. Standards regarding investigation of possible bias in testing. An investigation of fairness of a selection procedure depends on both evidence of validity and the manner in which the selection procedure is to be used in a particular employment context. Fairness of a selection procedure cannot necessarily be specified in advance without investigating these factors. Investigation of fairness of a selection procedure in samples where the range of scores on selection procedures or criterion measures is severely restricted for any subgroup sample (as compared to other subgroup samples) may produce misleading evidence of unfairness. That factor should accordingly be taken into account in conducting such studies and before reliance is placed on the results.

(d) *When unfairness is shown.* If unfairness is demonstrated through a showing that members of a particular group perform better or poorer on the job than their scores on the selection procedure would indicate through comparison with how members of other groups perform, the user may either revise or replace the selection instrument in accordance with these guidelines, or may continue to use the selection instrument operationally with appropriate revisions in its use to assure compatibility between the prob-

ability of successful job performance and the probability of being selected.

(e) *Technical feasibility of fairness studies.* In addition to the general conditions needed for technical feasibility for the conduct of a criterion-related study (see section 16, below) an investigation of fairness requires the following:

(i) An adequate sample of persons in each group available for the study to achieve findings of statistical significance. Guidelines do not require a user to hire or promote persons on the basis of group classifications for the purpose of making it possible to conduct a study of fairness; but the user has the obligation otherwise to comply with these guidelines.

(ii) The samples for each group should be comparable in terms of the actual job they perform, length of time on the job where time on the job is likely to affect performance, and other relevant factors likely to affect validity differences; or such factors should be included in the design of the study and their effects identified.

(f) *Continued use of selection procedures when fairness studies not feasible.* If a study of fairness should otherwise be performed, but is not technically feasible, a selection procedure may be used which has otherwise met the validity standards of these guidelines, unless the technical infeasibility resulted from discriminatory employment practices which are demonstrated by facts other than past failure to conform with requirements for validation of selection procedures. However, when it becomes technically feasible for the user to perform a study of fairness and such a study is otherwise called for, the user should conduct the study of fairness.

C. *Technical standards for content validity studies—(1) Appropriateness of content validity studies.* Users choosing to validate a selection procedure by a content validity strategy should determine whether it is appropriate to conduct such a study in the particular employment context. A selection procedure can be supported by a content validity strategy to the extent that it is a representative sample of the content of the job. Selection procedures which purport to

APPENDIX C. Part 1607, Uniform Guidelines on Employee Selection Procedures (1978).

ever it is feasible, appropriate statistical estimates should be made of the reliability of the selection procedure.

(6) *Prior training or experience.* A requirement for or evaluation of specific prior training or experience based on content validity, including a specification of level or amount of training or experience, should be justified on the basis of the relationship between the content of the training or experience and the content of the job for which the training or experience is to be required or evaluated. The critical consideration is the resemblance between the specific behaviors, products, knowledges, skills, or abilities in the experience or training and the specific behaviors, products, knowledges, skills, or abilities required on the job, whether or not there is close resemblance between the experience or training as a whole and the job as a whole.

(7) *Content validity of training success.* Where a measure of success in a training program is used as a selection procedure and the content of a training program is justified on the basis of content validity, the use should be justified on the relationship between the content of the training program and the content of the job.

(8) *Operational use.* A selection procedure which is supported on the basis of content validity may be used for a job if it represents a critical work behavior (i.e., a behavior which is necessary for performance of the job) or work behaviors which constitute most of the important parts of the job.

(9) *Ranking based on content validity studies.* If a user can show, by a job analysis or otherwise, that a higher score on a content valid selection procedure is likely to result in better job performance, the results may be used to rank persons who score above minimum levels. Where a selection procedure supported solely or primarily by content validity is used to rank job candidates, the selection procedure should measure those aspects of performance which differentiate among levels of job performance.

D. *Technical standards for construct validity studies—* (1) *Appropriateness of construct validity studies.* Construct validity is a more complex strategy than either criterion-related or

content validity. Construct validation is a relatively new and developing procedure in the employment field, and there is at present a lack of substantial literature extending the concept to employment practices. The user should be aware that the effort to obtain sufficient empirical support for construct validity is both an extensive and arduous effort involving a series of research studies, which include criterion related validity studies and which may include content validity studies. Users choosing to justify use of a selection procedure by this strategy should therefore take particular care to assure that the validity study meets the standards set forth below.

(2) *Job analysis for construct validity studies.* There should be a job analysis. This job analysis should show the work behavior(s) required for successful performance of the job, or the groups of jobs being studied, the critical or important work behavior(s) in the job or group of jobs being studied, and an identification of the construct(s) believed to underlie successful performance of these critical or important work behaviors in the job or jobs in question. Each construct should be named and defined, so as to distinguish it from other constructs. If a group of jobs is being studied the jobs should have in common one or more critical or important work behaviors at a comparable level of complexity.

(3) *Relationship to the job.* A selection procedure should then be identified or developed which measures the construct identified in accord with subparagraph (2) above. The user should show by empirical evidence that the selection procedure is validly related to the construct and that the construct is validly related to the performance of critical or important work behavior(s). The relationship between the construct as measured by the selection procedure and the related work behavior(s) should be supported by empirical evidence from one or more criterion-related studies involving the job or jobs in question which satisfy the provisions of section 14B above.

(4) *Use of construct validity study without new criterion-related evidence—(a) Standards for use.* Until

APPENDIX C.   Part 1607, Uniform Guidelines on Employee Selection Procedures (1978).

Equal Employment Opportunity Comm.   **§ 1607.14**

measure knowledges, skills, or abilities may in certain circumstances be justified by content validity, although they may not be representative samples, if the knowledge, skill, or ability measured by the selection procedure can be operationally defined as provided in section 14C(4) below, and if that knowledge, skill, or ability is a necessary prerequisite to successful job performance.

A selection procedure based upon inferences about mental processes cannot be supported solely or primarily on the basis of content validity. Thus, a content strategy is not appropriate for demonstrating the validity of selection procedures which purport to measure traits or constructs, such as intelligence, aptitude, personality, commonsense, judgment, leadership, and spatial ability. Content validity is also not an appropriate strategy when the selection procedure involves knowledges, skills, or abilities which an employee will be expected to learn on the job.

(2) *Job analysis for content validity.* There should be a job analysis which includes an analysis of the important work behavior(s) required for successful performance and their relative importance and, if the behavior results in work product(s), an analysis of the work product(s). Any job analysis should focus on the work behavior(s) and the tasks associated with them. If work behavior(s) are not observable, the job analysis should identify and analyze those aspects of the behavior(s) that can be observed and the observed work products. The work behavior(s) selected for measurement should be critical work behavior(s) and/or important work behavior(s) constituting most of the job.

(3) *Development of selection procedures.* A selection procedure designed to measure the work behavior may be developed specifically from the job and job analysis in question, or may have been previously developed by the user, or by other users or by a test publisher.

(4) *Standards for demonstrating content validity.* To demonstrate the content validity of a selection procedure, a user should show that the behavior(s) demonstrated in the selec-

tion procedure are a representative sample of the behavior(s) of the job in question or that the selection procedure provides a representative sample of the work product of the job. In the case of a selection procedure measuring a knowledge, skill, or ability, the knowledge, skill, or ability being measured should be operationally defined. In the case of a selection procedure measuring a knowledge, the knowledge being measured should be operationally defined as that body of learned information which is used in and is a necessary prerequisite for observable aspects of work behavior of the job. In the case of skills or abilities, the skill or ability being measured should be operationally defined in terms of observable aspects of work behavior of the job. For any selection procedure measuring a knowledge, skill, or ability the user should show that (a) the selection procedure measures and is a representative sample of that knowledge, skill, or ability; and (b) that knowledge, skill, or ability is used in and is a necessary prerequisite to performance of critical or important work behavior(s). In addition, to be content valid, a selection procedure measuring a skill or ability should either closely approximate an observable work behavior, or its product should closely approximate an observable work product. If a test purports to sample a work behavior or to provide a sample of a work product, the manner and setting of the selection procedure and its level and complexity should closely approximate the work situation. The closer the content and the context of the selection procedure are to work samples or work behaviors, the stronger is the basis for showing content validity. As the content of the selection procedure less resembles a work behavior, or the setting and manner of the administration of the selection procedure less resemble the work situation, or the result less resembles a work product, the less likely the selection procedure is to be content valid, and the greater the need for other evidence of validity.

(5) *Reliability.* The reliability of selection procedures justified on the basis of content validity should be a matter of concern to the user. When-

APPENDIX C. Part 1607, Uniform Guidelines on Employee Selection Procedures (1978).

Equal Employment Opportunity Comm.   **§ 1607.15**

such time as professional literature provides more guidance on the use of construct validity in employment situations, the Federal agencies will accept a claim of construct validity without a criterion-related study which satisfies section 14B above only when the selection procedure has been used elsewhere in a situation in which a criterion-related study has been conducted and the use of a criterion-related validity study in this context meets the standards for transportability of criterion-related validity studies as set forth above in section 7. However, if a study pertains to a number of jobs having common critical or important work behaviors at a comparable level of complexity, and the evidence satisfies subparagraphs 14B (2) and (3) above for those jobs with criterion-related validity evidence for those jobs, the selection procedure may be used for all the jobs to which the study pertains. If construct validity is to be generalized to other jobs. or groups of jobs not in the group studied, the Federal enforcement agencies will expect at a minimum additional empirical research evidence meeting the standards of subparagraphs section 14B (2) and (3) above for the additional jobs or ·groups of jobs.

(b) *Determination of common work behaviors.* In determining whether two or more jobs have one or more work behavior(s) in common, the user should compare the observed work behavior(s) in each of the jobs and should compare the observed work product(s) in each of the jobs. If neither the observed work behavior(s) in each of the jobs nor the observed work product(s) in each of the jobs are the same, the Federal enforcement agencies will presume that the work behavior(s) in each job are different. If the work behaviors are not observable, then evidence of similarity of work products and any other relevant research evidence will be considered in determining whether the work behavior(s) in the two jobs are the same.

DOCUMENTATION OF IMPACT AND
VALIDITY EVIDENCE

§ 1607.15 Documentation of impact and validity evidence.

A. *Required information.* Users of selection procedures other than those users complying with section 15A(1) below should maintain and have available for each job information on adverse impact of the selection process for that job and, where it is determined a selection process has an adverse impact, evidence of validity as set forth below.

(1) *Simplified recordkeeping for users with less than 100 employees.* In order to minimize recordkeeping burdens on employers who employ one hundred (100) or fewer employees, and other users not required to file EEO-1, et seq., reports, such users may satisfy the requirements of this section 15 if they maintain and have available records showing, for each year:

(a) The number of persons hired, promoted, and terminated for each job, by sex, and where appropriate by race and national origin;

(b) The number of applicants for hire and promotion by sex and where appropriate by race and national origin; and

(c) The selection procedures utilized (either standardized or not standardized).

These records should be maintained for each race or national origin group (see section 4 above) constituting more than two percent (2%) of the labor force in the relevant labor area. However, it is not necessary to maintain records by race and/or national origin (see § 4 above) if one race or national origin group in the relevant labor area constitutes more than ninety-eight percent (98%) of the labor force in the area. If the user has reason to believe that a selection procedure has an adverse impact, the user should maintain any available evidence of validity for that procedure (see sections 7A and 8).

(2) *Information on impact*—(a) *Collection of information on impact.* Users of selection procedures other than those complying with section 15A(1) above should maintain and have available for each job records or

225

APPENDIX C. Part 1607, Uniform Guidelines on Employee Selection Procedures (1978).

---

§ 1607.15

other information showing whether the total selection process for that job has an adverse impact on any of the groups for which records are called for by sections 4B above. Adverse impact determinations should be made at least annually for each such group which constitutes at least 2 percent of the labor force in the relevant labor area or 2 percent of the applicable workforce. Where a total selection process for a job has an adverse impact, the user should maintain and have available records or other information showing which components have an adverse impact. Where the total selection process for a job does not have an adverse impact, information need not be maintained for individual components except in circumstances set forth in subsection 15A(2)(b) below. If the determination of adverse impact is made using a procedure other than the "four-fifths rule," as defined in the first sentence of section 4D above, a justification, consistent with section 4D above, for the procedure used to determine adverse impact should be available.

(b) *When adverse impact has been eliminated in the total selection process.* Whenever the total selection process for a particular job has had an adverse impact, as defined in section 4 above, in any year, but no longer has an adverse impact, the user should maintain and have available the information on individual components of the selection process required in the preceding paragraph for the period in which there was adverse impact. In addition, the user should continue to collect such information for at least two (2) years after the adverse impact has been eliminated.

(c) *When data insufficient to determine impact.* Where there has been an insufficient number of selections to determine whether there is an adverse impact of the total selection process for a particular job, the user should continue to collect, maintain and have available the information on individual components of the selection process required in section 15(A)(2)(a) above until the information is sufficient to determine that the overall selection process does not have an adverse impact as defined in section 4

above, or until the job has changed substantially.

(3) *Documentation of validity evidence.—*(a) *Types of evidence.* Where a total selection process has an adverse impact (see section 4 above) the user should maintain and have available for each component of that process which has an adverse impact, one or more of the following types of documentation evidence:

(i) Documentation evidence showing criterion-related validity of the selection procedure (see section 15B, below).

(ii) Documentation evidence showing content validity of the selection procedure (see section 15C, below).

(iii) Documentation evidence showing construct validity of the selection procedure (see section 15D, below).

(iv) Documentation evidence from other studies showing validity of the selection procedure in the user's facility (see section 15E, below).

(v) Documentation evidence showing why a validity study cannot or need not be performed and why continued use of the procedure is consistent with Federal law.

(b) *Form of report.* This evidence should be compiled in a reasonably complete and organized manner to permit direct evaluation of the validity of the selection procedure. Previously written employer or consultant reports of validity, or reports describing validity studies completed before the issuance of these guidelines are acceptable if they are complete in regard to the documentation requirements contained in this section, or if they satisfied requirements of guidelines which were in effect when the validity study was completed. If they are not complete, the required additional documentation should be appended. If necessary information is not available the report of the validity study may still be used as documentation, but its adequacy will be evaluated in terms of compliance with the requirements of these guidelines.

(c) *Completeness.* In the event that evidence of validity is reviewed by an enforcement agency, the validation reports completed after the effective date of these guidelines are expected to contain the information set forth

APPENDIX C. Part 1607, Uniform Guidelines on Employee Selection Procedures (1978).

---

below. Evidence denoted by use of the word "(Essential)" is considered critical. If information denoted essential is not included, the report will be considered incomplete unless the user affirmatively demonstrates either its unavailability due to circumstances beyond the user's control or special circumstances of the user's study which make the information irrelevant. Evidence not so denoted is desirable but its absence will not be a basis for considering a report incomplete. The user should maintain and have available the information called for under the heading "Source Data" in sections 15B(11) and 15D(11). While it is a necessary part of the study, it need not be submitted with the report. All statistical results should be organized and presented in tabular or graphic form to the extent feasible.

B. *Criterion-related validity studies.* Reports of criterion-related validity for a selection procedure should include the following information:

(1) *User(s), location(s), and date(s) of study.* Dates and location(s) of the job analysis or review of job information, the date(s) and location(s) of the administration of the selection procedures and collection of criterion data, and the time between collection of data on selection procedures and criterion measures should be provided (Essential). If the study was conducted at several locations, the address of each location, including city and State, should be shown.

(2) *Problem and setting.* An explicit definition of the purpose(s) of the study and the circumstances in which the study was conducted should be provided. A description of existing selection procedures and cutoff scores, if any, should be provided.

(3) *Job anlysis or review of job information.* A description of the procedure used to analyze the job or group of jobs, or to review the job information should be provided (Essential). Where a review of job information results in criteria which may be used without a full job analysis (see section 14B(3)), the basis for the selection of these criteria should be reported (Essential). Where a job analysis is required a complete description of the work behavior(s) or work outcome(s),

and measures of their criticality or importance should be provided (Essential). The report should describe the basis on which the behavior(s) or outcome(s) were determined to be critical or important, such as the proportion of time spent on the respective behaviors, their level of difficulty, their frequency of performance, the consequences of error, or other appropriate factors (Essential). Where two or more jobs are grouped for a validity study, the information called for in this subsection should be provided for each of the jobs, and the justification for the grouping (see section 14B(1)) should be provided (Essential).

(4) *Job titles and codes.* It is desirable to provide the user's job title(s) for the job(s) in question and the corresponding job title(s) and code(s) from U.S. Employment Service's Dictionary of Occupational Titles.

(5) *Criterion measures.* The bases for the selection of the criterion measures should be provided, together with references to the evidence considered in making the selection of criterion measures (essential). A full description of all criteria on which data were collected and means by which they were observed, recorded, evaluated, and quantified, should be provided (essential). If rating techniques are used as criterion measures, the appraisal form(s) and instructions to the rater(s) should be included as part of the validation evidence, or should be explicitly described and available (essential). All steps taken to insure that criterion measures are free from factors which would unfairly alter the scores of members of any group should be described (essential).

(6) *Sample description.* A description of how the research sample was identified and selected should be included (essential). The race, sex, and ethnic composition of the sample, including those groups set forth in section 4A above, should be described (essential). This description should include the size of each subgroup (essential). A description of how the research sample compares with the relevant labor market or work force, the method by which the relevant labor market or work force was defined, and a discussion of the likely effects on validity of

APPENDIX C. Part 1607, Uniform Guidelines on Employee Selection Procedures (1978).

---

differences between the sample and the relevant labor market or work force, are also desirable. Descriptions of educational levels, length of service, and age are also desirable.

(7) *Description of selection procedures.* Any measure, combination of measures, or procedure studied should be completely and explicitly described or attached (essential). If commercially available selection procedures are studied, they should be described by title, form, and publisher (essential). Reports of reliability estimates and how they were established are desirable.

(8) *Techniques and results.* Methods used in analyzing data should be described (essential). Measures of central tendency (e.g., means) and measures of dispersion (e.g., standard deviations and ranges) for all selection procedures and all criteria should be reported for each race, sex, and ethnic group which constitutes a significant factor in the relevant labor market (essential). The magnitude and direction of all relationships between selection procedures and criterion measures investigated should be reported for each relevant race, sex, and ethnic group and for the total group (essential). Where groups are too small to obtain reliable evidence of the magnitude of the relationship, need not be reported separately. Statements regarding the statistical significance of results should be made (essential). Any statistical adjustments, such as for less then perfect reliability or for restriction of score range in the selection procedure or criterion should be described and explained; and uncorrected correlation coefficients should also be shown (essential). Where the statistical technique categorizes continuous data, such as biserial correlation and the phi coefficient, the categories and the bases on which they were determined should be described and explained (essential). Studies of test fairness should be included where called for by the requirements of section 14B(8) (essential). These studies should include the rationale by which a selection procedure was determined to be fair to the group(s) in question. Where test fairness or unfairness has been demonstrated on the basis of other studies, a

bibliography of the relevant studies should be included (essential). If the bibliography includes unpublished studies, copies of these studies, or adequate abstracts or summaries, should be attached (essential). Where revisions have been made in a selection procedure to assure compatability between successful job performance and the probability of being selected, the studies underlying such revisions should be included (essential). All statistical results should be organized and presented by relevant race, sex, and ethnic group (essential).

(9) *Alternative procedures investigated.* The selection procedures investigated and available evidence of their impact should be identified (essential). The scope, method, and findings of the investigation, and the conclusions reached in light of the findings, should be fully described (essential).

(10) *Uses and applications.* The methods considered for use of the selection procedure (e.g., as a screening device with a cutoff score, for grouping or ranking, or combined with other procedures in a battery) and available evidence of their impact should be described (essential). This description should include the rationale for choosing the method for operational use, and the evidence of the validity and utility of the procedure as it is to be used (essential). The purpose for which the procedure is to be used (e.g., hiring, transfer, promotion) should be described (essential). If weights are assigned to different parts of the selection procedure, these weights and the validity of the weighted composite should be reported (essential). If the selection procedure is used with a cutoff score, the user should describe the way in which normal expectations of proficiency within the work force were determined and the way in which the cutoff score was determined (essential).

(11) *Source data.* Each user should maintain records showing all pertinent information about individual sample members and raters where they are used, in studies involving the validation of selection procedures. These records should be made available upon request of a compliance agency. In the case of individual sample members

APPENDIX C.   Part 1607, Uniform Guidelines on Employee Selection Procedures (1978).

---

these data should include scores on the selection procedure(s), scores on criterion measures, age, sex, race, or ethnic group status, and experience on the specific job on which the validation study was conducted, and may also include such things as education, training, and prior job experience, but should not include names and social security numbers. Records should be maintained which show the ratings given to each sample member by each rater.

(12) *Contact person.* The name, mailing address, and telephone number of the person who may be contacted for further information about the validity study should be provided (essential).

(13) *Accuracy and completeness.* The report should describe the steps taken to assure the accuracy and completeness of the collection, analysis, and report of data and results.

C. *Content validity studies.* Reports of content validity for a selection procedure should include the following information:

(1) *User(s), location(s) and date(s) of study.* Dates and location(s) of the job analysis should be shown (essential).

(2) *Problem and setting.* An explicit definition of the purpose(s) of the study and the circumstances in which the study was conducted should be provided. A description of existing selection procedures and cutoff scores, if any, should be provided.

(3) *Job analysis—Content of the job.* A description of the method used to analyze the job should be provided (essential). The work behavior(s), the associated tasks, and, if the behavior results in a work product, the work products should be completely described (essential). Measures of criticality and/or importance of the work behavior(s) and the method of determining these measures should be provided (essential). Where the job analysis also identified the knowledges, skills, and abilities used in work behavior(s), an operational definition for each knowledge in terms of a body of learned information and for each skill and ability in terms of observable behaviors and outcomes, and the relationship between each knowledge, skill, or ability and each work behavior, as well as the method used to de-

termine this relationship, should be provided (essential). The work situation should be described, including the setting in which work behavior(s) are performed, and where appropriate, the manner in which knowledges, skills, or abilities are used, and the complexity and difficulty of the knowledge, skill, or ability as used in the work behavior(s).

(4) *Selection procedure and its content.* Selection procedures, including those constructed by or for the user, specific training requirements, composites of selection procedures, and any other procedure supported by content validity, should be completely and explicitly described or attached (essential). If commercially available selection procedures are used, they should be described by title, form, and publisher (essential). The behaviors measured or sampled by the selection procedure should be explicitly described (essential). Where the selection procedure purports to measure a knowledge, skill, or ability, evidence that the selection procedure measures and is a representative sample of the knowledge, skill, or ability should be provided (essential).

(5) *Relationship between the selection procedure and the job.* The evidence demonstrating that the selection procedure is a representative work sample, a representative sample of the work behavior(s), or a representative sample of a knowledge, skill, or ability as used as a part of a work behavior and necessary for that behavior should be provided (essential). The user should identify the work behavior(s) which each item or part of the selection procedure is intended to sample or measure (essential). Where the selection procedure purports to sample a work behavior or to provide a sample of a work product, a comparison should be provided of the manner, setting, and the level of complexity of the selection procedure with those of the work situation (essential). If any steps were taken to reduce adverse impact on a race, sex, or ethnic group in the content of the procedure or in its administration, these steps should be described. Establishment of time limits, if any, and how these limits are related to the speed with which duties

APPENDIX C. Part 1607, Uniform Guidelines on Employee Selection Procedures (1978).

---

§ 1607.15

must be performed on the job, should be explained. Measures of central tend- ency (e.g., means) and measures of dispersion (e.g., standard deviations) and estimates of realibility should be reported for all selection procedures if available. Such reports should be made for relevant race, sex, and ethnic subgroups, at least on a statistically reliable sample basis.

(6) *Alternative procedures investigated.* The alternative selection procedures investigated and available evidence of their impact should be identified (essential). The scope, method, and findings of the investigation, and the conclusions reached in light of the findings, should be fully described (essential).

(7) *Uses and applications.* The methods considered for use of the selection procedure (e.g., as a screening device with a cutoff score, for grouping or ranking, or combined with other procedures in a battery) and available evidence of their impact should be described (essential). This description should include the rationale for choosing the method for operational use, and the evidence of the validity and utility of the procedure as it is to be used (essential). The purpose for which the procedure is to be used (e.g., hiring, transfer, promotion) should be described (essential). If the selection procedure is used with a cutoff score, the user should describe the way in which normal expectations of proficiency within the work force were determined and the way in which the cutoff score was determined (essential). In addition, if the selection procedure is to be used for ranking, the user should specify the evidence showing that a higher score on the selection procedure is likely to result in better job performance.

(8) *Contact person.* The name, mailing address, and telephone number of the person who may be contacted for further information about the validity study should be provided (essential).

(9) *Accuracy and completeness.* The report should describe the steps taken to assure the accuracy and completeness of the collection, analysis, and report of data and results.

D. *Construct validity studies.* Reports of construct validity for a selec-

29 CFR Ch. XIV (7-1-89 Edition)

tion procedure should include the following information:

(1) *User(s), location(s), and date(s) of study.* Date(s) and location(s) of the job analysis and the gathering of other evidence called for by these guidelines should be provided (essential).

(2) *Problem and setting.* An explicit definition of the purpose(s) of the study and the circumstances in which the study was conducted should be provided. A description of existing selection procedures and cutoff scores, if any, should be provided.

(3) *Construct definition.* A clear definition of the construct(s) which are believed to underlie successful performance of the critical or important work behavior(s) should be provided (essential). This definition should include the levels of construct performance relevant to the job(s) for which the selection procedure is to be used (essential). There should be a summary of the position of the construct in the psychological literature, or in the absence of such a position, a description of the way in which the definition and measurement of the construct was developed and the psychological theory underlying it (essential). Any quantitative data which identify or define the job constructs, such as factor analyses, should be provided (essential).

(4) *Job analysis.* A description of the method used to analyze the job should be provided (essential). A complete description of the work behavior(s) and, to the extent appropriate, work outcomes and measures of their criticality and/or importance should be provided (essential). The report should also describe the basis on which the behavior(s) or outcomes were determined to be important, such as their level of difficulty, their frequency of performance, the consequences of error or other appropriate factors (essential). Where jobs are grouped or compared for the purposes of generalizing validity evidence, the work behavior(s) and work product(s) for each of the jobs should be described, and conclusions concerning the similarity of the jobs in terms of observable work behaviors or work products should be made (essential).

APPENDIX C.   Part 1607, Uniform Guidelines on Employee Selection Procedures (1978).

Equal Employment Opportunity Comm.

§ 1607.15

(5) *Job titles and codes.* It is desirable to provide the selection procedure user's job title(s) for the job(s) in question and the corresponding job title(s) and code(s) from the United States Employment Service's dictionary of occupational titles.

(6) *Selection procedure.* The selection procedure used as a measure of the construct should be completely and explicitly described or attached (essential). If commercially available selection procedures are used, they should be identified by title, form and publisher (essential). The research evidence of the relationship between the selection procedure and the construct, such as factor structure, should be included (essential). Measures of central tendency, variability and reliability of the selection procedure should be provided (essential). Whenever feasible, these measures should be completely provided separately for each relevant race, sex and ethnic group.

(7) *Relationship to job performance.* The criterion-related study(ies) and other empirical evidence of the relationship between the construct measured by the selection procedure and the related work behavior(s) for the job or jobs in question should be provided (essential). Documentation of the criterion-related study(ies) should satisfy the provisions of section 15B above or section 15E(1) below, except for studies conducted prior to the effective date of these guidelines (essential). Where a study pertains to a group of jobs, and, on the basis of the study, validity is asserted for a job in the group, the observed work behaviors and the observed work products for each of the jobs should be described (essential). Any other evidence used in determining whether the work behavior(s) in each of the jobs is the same should be fully described (essential).

(8) *Alternative procedures investigated.* The alternative selection procedures investigated and available evidence of their impact should be identified (essential). The scope, method, and findings of the investigation, and the conclusions reached in light of the findings should be fully described (essential).

(9) *Uses and applications.* The methods considered for use of the selection procedure (e.g., as a screening device with a cutoff score, for grouping or ranking, or combined with other procedures in a battery) and available evidence of their impact should be described (essential). This description should include the rationale for choosing the method for operational use, and the evidence of the validity and utility of the procedure as it is to be used (essential). The purpose for which the procedure is to be used (e.g., hiring, transfer, promotion) should be described (essential). If weights are assigned to different parts of the selection procedure, these weights and the validity of the weighted composite should be reported (essential). If the selection procedure is used with a cutoff score, the user should describe the way in which normal expectations of proficiency within the work force were determined and the way in which the cutoff score was determined (essential).

(10) *Accuracy and completeness.* The report should describe the steps taken to assure the accuracy and completeness of the collection, analysis, and report of data and results.

(11) *Source data.* Each user should maintain records showing all pertinent information relating to its study of construct validity.

(12) *Contact person.* The name, mailing address, and telephone number of the individual who may be contacted for further information about the validity study should be provided (essential).

E. *Evidence of validity from other studies.* When validity of a selection procedure is supported by studies not done by the user, the evidence from the original study or studies should be compiled in a manner similar to that required in the appropriate section of this section 15 above. In addition, the following evidence should be supplied:

(1) *Evidence from criterion-related validity studies.*—a. *Job information.* A description of the important job behavior(s) of the user's job and the basis on which the behaviors were determined to be important should be provided (essential). A full description of the basis for determining that these

APPENDIX C. Part 1607, Uniform Guidelines on Employee Selection Procedures (1978).

---

§ 1607.16

important work behaviors are the same as those of the job in the original study (or studies) should be provided (essential).

b. *Relevance of criteria.* A full description of the basis on which the criteria used in the original studies are determined to be relevant for the user should be provided (essential).

c. *Other variables.* The similarity of important applicant pool or sample characteristics reported in the original studies to those of the user should be described (essential). A description of the comparison between the race, sex and ethnic composition of the user's relevant labor market and the sample in the original validity studies should be provided (essential).

d. *Use of the selection procedure.* A full description should be provided showing that the use to be made of the selection procedure is consistent with the findings of the original validity studies (essential).

e. *Bibliography.* A bibliography of reports of validity of the selection procedure for the job or jobs in question should be provided (essential). Where any of the studies included an investigation of test fairness, the results of this investigation should be provided (essential). Copies of reports published in journals that are not commonly available should be described in detail or attached (essential). Where a user is relying upon unpublished studies, a reasonable effort should be made to obtain these studies. If these unpublished studies are the sole source of validity evidence they should be described in detail or attached (essential). If these studies are not available, the name and address of the source, an adequate abstract or summary of the validity study and data, and a contact person in the source organization should be provided (essential).

(2) *Evidence from content validity studies.* See section 14C(3) and section 15C above.

(3) *Evidence from construct validity studies.* See sections 14D(2) and 15D above.

F. *Evidence of validity from cooperative studies.* Where a selection procedure has been validated through a cooperative study, evidence that the study satisfies the requirements of sec-

tions 7, 8 and 15E should be provided (essential).

G. *Selection for higher level job.* If a selection procedure is used to evaluate candidates for jobs at a higher level than those for which they will initially be employed, the validity evidence should satisfy the documentation provisions of this section 15 for the higher level job or jobs, and in addition, the user should provide: (1) a description of the job progression structure, formal or informal; (2) the data showing how many employees progress to the higher level job and the length of time needed to make this progression; and (3) an identification of any anticipated changes in the higher level job. In addition, if the test measures a knowledge, skill or ability, the user should provide evidence that the knowledge, skill or ability is required for the higher level job and the basis for the conclusion that the knowledge, skill or ability is not expected to develop from the training or experience on the job.

H. *Interim use of selection procedures.* If a selection procedure is being used on an interim basis because the procedure is not fully supported by the required evidence of validity, the user should maintain and have available (1) substantial evidence of validity for the procedure, and (2) a report showing the date on which the study to gather the additional evidence commenced, the estimated completion date of the study, and a description of the data to be collected (essential).

(Approved by the Office of Management and Budget under control number 3046-0017)

(Pub. L. No. 96-511, 94 Stat. 2812 (44 U.S.C. 3501 et seq.))

[43 FR 38295, 38312, Aug. 25, 1978, as amended at 46 FR 63268, Dec. 31, 1981]

DEFINITIONS

§ 1607.16 Definitions.

The following definitions shall apply throughout these guidelines:

A. *Ability.* A present competence to perform an observable behavior or a behavior which results in an observable product.

APPENDIX C.   Part 1607, Uniform Guidelines on Employee Selection Procedures (1978).

Equal Employment Opportunity Comm.   **§ 1607.16**

B. *Adverse impact.* A substantially different rate of selection in hiring, promotion, or other employment decision which works to the disadvantage of members of a race, sex, or ethnic group. See section 4 of these guidelines.

C. *Compliance with these guidelines.* Use of a selection procedure is in compliance with these guidelines if such use has been validated in accord with these guidelines (as defined below), or if such use does not result in adverse impact on any race, sex, or ethnic group (see section 4, above), or, in unusual circumstances, if use of the procedure is otherwise justified in accord with Federal law. See section 6B, above.

D. *Content validity.* Demonstrated by data showing that the content of a selection procedure is representative of important aspects of performance on the job. See section 5B and section 14C.

E. *Construct validity.* Demonstrated by data showing that the selection procedure measures the degree to which candidates have identifiable characteristics which have been determined to be important for successful job performance. See section 5B and section 14D.

F. *Criterion-related validity.* Demonstrated by empirical data showing that the selection procedure is predictive of or significantly correlated with important elements of work behavior. See sections 5B and 14B.

G. *Employer.* Any employer subject to the provisions of the Civil Rights Act of 1964, as amended, including State or local governments and any Federal agency subject to the provisions of section 717 of the Civil Rights Act of 1964, as amended, and any Federal contractor or subcontractor or federally assisted construction contractor or subcontractor covered by Executive Order 11246, as amended.

H. *Employment agency.* Any employment agency subject to the provisions of the Civil Rights Act of 1964, as amended.

I. *Enforcement action.* For the purposes of section 4 a proceeding by a Federal enforcement agency such as a lawsuit or an administrative proceeding leading to debarment from or withholding, suspension, or termination of Federal Government contracts or the suspension or withholding of Federal Government funds; but not a finding of reasonable cause or a conciliation process or the issuance of right to sue letters under title VII or under Executive Order 11246 where such finding, conciliation, or issuance of notice of right to sue is based upon an individual complaint.

J. *Enforcement agency.* Any agency of the executive branch of the Federal Government which adopts these guidelines for purposes of the enforcement of the equal employment opportunity laws or which has responsibility for securing compliance with them.

K. *Job analysis.* A detailed statement of work behaviors and other information relevant to the job.

L. *Job description.* A general statement of job duties and responsibilities.

M. *Knowledge.* A body of information applied directly to the performance of a function.

N. *Labor organization.* Any labor organization subject to the provisions of the Civil Rights Act of 1964, as amended, and any committee subject thereto controlling apprenticeship or other training.

O. *Observable.* Able to be seen, heard, or otherwise perceived by a person other than the person performing the action.

P. *Race, sex, or ethnic group.* Any group of persons identifiable on the grounds of race, color, religion, sex, or national origin.

Q. *Selection procedure.* Any measure, combination of measures, or procedure used as a basis for any employment decision. Selection procedures include the full range of assessment techniques from traditional paper and pencil tests, performance tests, training programs, or probationary periods and physical, educational, and work experience requirements through informal or casual interviews and unscored application forms.

R. *Selection rate.* The proportion of applicants or candidates who are hired, promoted, or otherwise selected.

S. *Should.* The term "should" as used in these guidelines is intended to connote action which is necessary to achieve compliance with the guide-

APPENDIX C. Part 1607, Uniform Guidelines on Employee Selection Procedures (1978).

---

§ 1607.17

lines, while recognizing that there are circumstances where alternative courses of action are open to users.

T. *Skill.* A present, observable competence to perform a learned psychomoter act.

U. *Technical feasibility.* The existence of conditions permitting the conduct of meaningful criterion-related validity studies. These conditions include: (1) An adequate sample of persons available for the study to achieve findings of statistical significance; (2) having or being able to obtain a sufficient range of scores on the selection procedure and job performance measures to produce validity results which can be expected to be representative of the results if the ranges normally expected were utilized; and (3) having or being able to devise unbiased, reliable and relevant measures of job performance or other criteria of employee adequacy. See section 14B(2). With respect to investigation of possible unfairness, the same considerations are applicable to each group for which the study is made. See section 14B(8).

V. *Unfairness of selection procedure.* A condition in which members of one race, sex, or ethnic group characteristically obtain lower scores on a selection procedure than members of another group, and the differences are not reflected in differences in measures of job performance. See section 14B(7).

W. *User.* Any employer, labor organization, employment agency, or licensing or certification board, to the extent it may be covered by Federal equal employment opportunity law, which uses a selection procedure as a basis for any employment decision. Whenever an employer, labor organization, or employment agency is required by law to restrict recruitment for any occupation to those applicants who have met licensing or certification requirements, the licensing or certifying authority to the extent it may be covered by Federal equal employment opportunity law will be considered the user with respect to those licensing or certification requirements. Whenever a State employment agency or service does no more than administer or monitor a procedure as permitted by Department of Labor regulations, and

29 CFR Ch. XIV (7-1-89 Edition)

does so without making referrals or taking any other action on the basis of the results, the State employment agency will not be deemed to be a user.

X. *Validated in accord with these guidelines or properly validated.* A demonstration that one or more validity study or studies meeting the standards of these guidelines has been conducted, including investigation and, where appropriate, use of suitable alternative selection procedures as contemplated by section 3B, and has produced evidence of validity sufficient to warrant use of the procedure for the intended purpose under the standards of these guidelines.

Y. *Work behavior.* An activity performed to achieve the objectives of the job. Work behaviors involve observable (physical) components and unobservable (mental) components. A work behavior consists of the performance of one or more tasks. Knowledges, skills, and abilities are not behaviors, although they may be applied in work behaviors.

APPENDIX

§ 1607.17 Policy statement on affirmative action (see section 13B).

The Equal Employment Opportunity Coordinating Council was established by act of Congress in 1972, and charged with responsibility for developing and implementing agreements and policies designed, among other things, to eliminate conflict and inconsistency among the agencies of the Federal Government responsible for administering Federal law prohibiting discrimination on grounds of race, color, sex, religion, and national origin. This statement is issued as an initial response to the requests of a number of State and local officials for clarification of the Government's policies concerning the role of affirmative action in the overall equal employment opportunity program. While the Coordinating Council's adoption of this statement expresses only the views of the signatory agencies concerning this important subject, the principles set forth below should serve as policy guidance for other Federal agencies as well.

APPENDIX C.   Part 1607, Uniform Guidelines on Employee Selection Procedures (1978).

Equal Employment Opportunity Comm.

§ 1607.17

(1) Equal employment opportunity is the law of the land. In the public sector of our society this means that all persons, regardless of race, color, religion, sex, or national origin shall have equal access to positions in the public service limited only by their ability to do the job. There is ample evidence in all sectors of our society that such equal access frequently has been denied to members of certain groups because of their sex, racial, or ethnic characteristics. The remedy for such past and present discrimination is twofold.

On the one hand, vigorous enforcement of the laws against discrimination is essential. But equally, and perhaps even more important are affirmative, voluntary efforts on the part of public employers to assure that positions in the public service are genuinely and equally accessible to qualified persons, without regard to their sex, racial, or ethnic characteristics. Without such efforts equal employment opportunity is no more than a wish. The importance of voluntary affirmative action on the part of employers is underscored by title VII of the Civil Rights Act of 1964, Executive Order 11246, and related laws and regulations—all of which emphasize voluntary action to achieve equal employment opportunity.

As with most management objectives, a systematic plan based on sound organizational analysis and problem identification is crucial to the accomplishment of affirmative action objectives. For this reason, the Council urges all State and local governments to develop and implement results oriented affirmative action plans which deal with the problems so identified.

The following paragraphs are intended to assist State and local governments by illustrating the kinds of analyses and activities which may be appropriate for a public employer's voluntary affirmative action plan. This statement does not address remedies imposed after a finding of unlawful discrimination.

(2) Voluntary affirmative action to assure equal employment opportunity is appropriate at any stage of the employment process. The first step in the construction of any affirmative action plan should be an analysis of the employer's work force to determine whether precentages of sex, race, or ethnic groups in individual job classifications are substantially similar to the precentages of those groups available in the relevant job market who possess the basic job-related qualifications.

When substantial disparities are found through such analyses, each element of the overall selection process should be examined to determine which elements operate to exclude persons on the basis of sex, race, or ethnic group. Such elements include, but are not limited to, recruitment, testing, ranking certification, interview, recommendations for selection, hiring, promotion, etc. The examination of each element of the selection process should at a minimum include a determination of its validity in predicting job performance.

(3) When an employer has reason to believe that its selection procedures have the exclusionary effect described in paragraph 2 above, it should initiate affirmative steps to remedy the situation. Such steps, which in design and execution may be race, color, sex, or ethnic "conscious," include, but are not limited to, the following:

(a) The establishment of a long-term goal, and short-range, interim goals and timetables for the specific job classifications, all of which should take into account the availability of basically qualified persons in the relevant job market;

(b) A recruitment program designed to attract qualified members of the group in question;

(c) A systematic effort to organize work and redesign jobs in ways that provide opportunities for persons lacking "journeyman" level knowledge or skills to enter and, with appropriate training, to progress in a career field;

(d) Revamping selection instruments or procedures which have not yet been validated in order to reduce or eliminate exclusionary effects on particular groups in particular job classifications;

(e) The initiation of measures designed to assure that members of the affected group who are qualified to perform the job are included within the pool of persons from which the selecting official makes the selection;

235

APPENDIX C. Part 1607, Uniform Guidelines on Employee Selection Procedures (1978).

---

§ 1607.18

(f) A systematic effort to provide career advancement training, both classroom and on-the-job, to employees locked into dead end jobs; and

(g) The establishment of a system for regularly monitoring the effectiveness of the particular affirmative action program, and procedures for making timely adjustments in this program where effectiveness is not demonstrated.

(4) The goal of any affirmative action plan should be achievement of genuine equal employment opportunity for all qualified persons. Selection under such plans should be based upon the ability of the applicant(s) to do the work. Such plans should not require the selection of the unqualified, or the unneeded, nor should they require the selection of persons on the basis of race, color, sex, religion, or national origin. Moreover, while the Council believes that this statement should serve to assist State and local employers, as well as Federal agencies, it recognizes that affirmative action cannot be viewed as a standardized program which must be accomplished in the same way at all times in all places.

Accordingly, the Council has not attempted to set forth here either the minimum or maximum voluntary steps that employers may take to deal with their respective situations. Rather, the Council recognizes that under applicable authorities, State and local employers have flexibility to formulate affirmative action plans that are best suited to their particular situations. In this manner, the Council believes that affirmative action programs will best serve the goal of equal employment opportunity.

Respectfully submitted,

Harold R. Tyler, Jr.,
Deputy Attorney General and Chairman of the Equal Employment Coordinating Council.
Michael H. Moskow,
Under Secretary of Labor.
Ethel Bent Walsh,
Acting Chairman, Equal Employment Opportunity Commission.
Robert E. Hampton,
Chairman, Civil Service Commission.
Arthur E. Flemming,
Chairman, Commission on Civil Rights.

29 CFR Ch. XIV (7-1-89 Edition)

Because of its equal employment opportunity responsibilities under the State and Local Government Fiscal Assistance Act of 1972 (the revenue sharing act), the Department of Treasury was invited to participate in the formulation of this policy statement; and it concurs and joins in the adoption of this policy statement.

Done this 26th day of August 1976.

Richard Albrecht,
General Counsel,
Department of the Treasury.

§ 1607.18 Citations.

The official title of these guidelines is "Uniform Guidelines on Employee Selection Procedures (1978)". The Uniform Guidelines on Employee Selection Procedures (1978) are intended to establish a uniform Federal position in the area of prohibiting discrimination in employment practices on grounds of race, color, religion, sex, or national origin. These guidelines have been adopted by the Equal Employment Opportunity Commission, the Department of Labor, the Department of Justice, and the Civil Service Commission.

The official citation is:

"Section ——, Uniform Guidelines on Employee Selection Procedure (1978); 43 FR —— (August 25, 1978)."

The short form citation is:

"Section ——, U.G.E.S.P. (1978); 43 FR —— (August 25, 1978)."

When the guidelines are cited in connection with the activities of one of the issuing agencies, a specific citation to the regulations of that agency can be added at the end of the above citation. The specific additional citations are as follows:

Equal Employmeı Opportunity Commission
29 CFR Part 1607
Department of Labor
Office of Federal Contract Compliance Programs
41 CFR Part 60-3
Department of Justice
28 CFR 50.14
Civil Service Commission
5 CFR 300.103(c)

Normally when citing these guidelines, the section number immediately preceding the title of the guidelines

APPENDIX C.   Part 1607, Uniform Guidelines on Employee Selection Procedures (1978).

Equal Employment Opportunity Comm.   **§ 1608.1**

will be from these guidelines series 1–18. If a section number from the codification for an individual agency is needed it can also be added at the end of the agency citation. For example, section 6A of these guidelines could be cited for EEOC as follows: "Section 6A, Uniform Guidelines on Employee Selection Procedures (1978); 43 FR ——, (August 25, 1978); 29 CFR Part 1607, section 6A."

PART 1608—AFFIRMATIVE ACTION APPROPRIATE UNDER TITLE VII OF THE CIVIL RIGHTS ACT OF 1964, AS AMENDED

Sec.
1608.1   Statement of purpose.
1608.2   Written interpretation and opinion.
1608.3   Circumstances under which voluntary affirmative action is appropriate.
1608.4   Establishing affirmative action plans.
1608.5   Affirmative action compliance programs under Executive Order No. 11246, as amended.
1608.6   Affirmative action plans which are part of Commission conciliation or settlement agreements.
1608.7   Affirmative action plans or programs under State or local law.
1608.8   Adherence to court order.
1608.9   Reliance on directions of other government agencies.
1608.10   Standard of review.
1608.11   Limitations on the application of these guidelines.
1608.12   Equal employment opportunity plans adopted pursuant to section 717 of Title VII.

AUTHORITY: Sec. 713 the Civil Rights Act of 1964, as amended, 42 U.S.C. 2000e–12, 78 Stat. 265.

SOURCE: 44 FR 4422, Jan. 19, 1979, unless otherwise noted.

§ 1608.1   Statement of purpose.

(a) *Need for Guidelines.* Since the passage of Title VII in 1964, many employers, labor organizations, and other persons subject to Title VII have changed their employment practices and systems to improve employment opportunities for minorities and women, and this must continue. These changes have been undertaken either on the initiative of the employer, labor organization, or other person subject to Title VII, or as a result of conciliation efforts under Title VII, action

under Executive Order No. 11246, as amended, or under other Federal, state, or local laws, or litigation. Many decisions taken pursuant to affirmative action plans or programs have been race, sex, or national origin conscious in order to achieve the Congressional purpose of providing equal employment opportunity. Occasionally, these actions have been challenged as inconsistent with Title VII, because they took into account race, sex, or national origin. This is the so-called "reverse discrimination" claim. In such a situation, both the affirmative action undertaken to improve the conditions of minorities and women, and the objection to that action, are based upon the principles of Title VII. Any uncertainty as to the meaning and application of Title VII in such situations threatens the accomplishment of the clear Congressional intent to encourage voluntary affirmative action. The Commission believes that by the enactment of Title VII Congress did not intend to expose those who comply with the Act to charges that they are violating the very statute they are seeking to implement. Such a result would immobilize or reduce the efforts of many who would otherwise take action to improve the opportunities of minorities and women without litigation, thus frustrating the Congressional intent to encourage voluntary action and increasing the prospect of Title VII litigation. The Commission believes that it is now necessary to clarify and harmonize the principles of Title VII in order to achieve these Congressional objectives and protect those employers, labor organizations, and other persons who comply with the principles of Title VII.

(b) *Purposes of Title VII.* Congress enacted Title VII in order to improve the economic and social conditions of minorities and women by providing equality of opportunity in the work place. These conditions were part of a larger pattern of restriction, exclusion, discrimination, segregation, and inferior treatment of minorities and women in many areas of life.[2] The Legislative

---

[2] Congress has also addressed these conditions in other laws, including the Equal Pay
Continued

APPENDIX D. Illinois Collective Bargaining Bill.

ILLINOIS COLLECTIVE BARGAINING BILL

PUBLIC ACT 85-1032
(Senate Bill No. 1257))

An Act to amend Sections 3, 5 and 6 of the "Illinois Public Labor Relations Act", certified December 27, 1983, as amended.

Be it enacted by the People of the State of Illinois, represented in the General Assembly:

Section 1. Sections 3, 5 and 6 of the "Illinois Public Labor Relations Act", certified December 27, 1983, as amended, are amended to read as follows:

(Ch. 48, par. 1603)

Sec. 3. Definitions: As used in this Act, unless the context otherwise requires:

(a) "Board" or "Governing Board" means either the Illinois State Labor Relations Board or the Illinois Local Labor Relations Board.

(b) "Collective bargaining" means bargaining over terms and conditions of employment, including hours, wages and other conditions of employment, as detailed in Section 7 and which are not excluded by Section 4.

(c) "Confidential employee" means an employee, who in the regular course of his or her duties, assists and acts in a confidential capacity to persons who formulate, determine and effectuate management policies with regard to labor relations or who in the regular course of his or her duties has authorized access to information relating to the effectuation or review of the employer's collective bargaining policies.

APPENDIX D.   Illinois Collective Bargaining Bill.

(d) "Craft employees" means skilled journeymen, crafts persons, and their apprentices and helpers.

(e) "Essential services employees" shall mean those public employees performing functions so essential that the interruption or termination of such function will constitute a clear and present danger to the health and safety of the persons in the affected community.

(f) "Exclusive representative" except with respect to non-State fire fighters and paramedics employed by fire departments and fire protection districts, non-State peace officers and peace officers in the State Department of State Police, means the labor organization which has been designated by the Board as the representative of a majority of public employees in an appropriate bargaining unit in accordance with the procedures contained herein, or historically recognized by the State of Illinois or any political subdivision of the State prior to the effective date of this Act as the exclusive representative of the employees in an appropriate bargaining unit or, after the effective date of this Act recognized by an employer upon evidence, acceptable by the Board, that the labor organization has been designated as the exclusive representative by a majority of the employees in an appropriate bargaining unit.

With respect to non-State fire fighters and paramedics employed by fire departments and fire protection districts, non-State peace officers and peace officers in the State Department of State Police, "exclusive representative" means the labor organization which has been designated by the Board as the representative of a majority of peace officers or fire fighters in an appropriate bargaining unit in accordance with the procedures contained herein, or historically recognized by the State of Illinois or any political subdivision of the State prior to the effective date of this amendatory *Act* of 1985, as the exclusive representative by a majority of the peace officers or fire fighters in an appropriate bargaining unit or, after the effective date of this amendatory Act of 1985 recognized by an employer upon evidence, acceptable by the Board, that the labor organization has been designated as the exclusive representative by a majority of the peace officers or fire fighters in an appropriate bargaining unit.

(g) "Fair share agreement" means an agreement between the employer and an employee organization under which all or any of the employees in a collective bargaining unit are required to pay their proportionate share of the costs of the collective bargaining process, contract administration and pursuing matters affecting wages, hours and other conditions of employment, but not to exceed the amount of dues uniformly required of members. The amount certified by the exclusive representative shall not include any fees for contributions related to the election or support of any candidate for political office. Nothing herein shall preclude an employee from making voluntary political contributions in conjunction with his/her fair share payment.

(g-1) "Fire fighter" means, for the purposes of this Act only, any person who has been or is hereafter appointed to a fire department or fire protection district and sworn or commissioned to perform fire fighter duties or paramedic duties, except the following persons shall not be included: part-time fire fighters, auxiliary, reserve or voluntary fire

New matter indicated by italics - deletions by strikeout.

APPENDIX D. Illinois Collective Bargaining Bill.

PUBLIC ACT 85-1032

fighters, including paid on-call fire fighters, clerks and dispatchers or other civilian employees of a fire department or fire protection district who are not routinely expected to perform fire fighter duties, or elected officials.

(g-2) "General Assembly of the State of Illinois" means the legislative branch of the government of the State of Illinois, as provided for under Article IV of the Constitution of the State of Illinois, and includes but is not limited to the House of Representatives, the Senate, the Speaker of the House of Representatives, the Minority Leader of the House of Representatives, the President of the Senate, the Minority Leader of the Senate, the Joint Committee on Legislative Support Services and any legislative support services agency listed in the Legislative Commission Reorganization Act of 1984.

(h) "Governing body" means in the case of the State the State Labor Relations Board, the Director of the Department of Central Management Services, and the Director of the Department of Labor; the county board in the case of a county; the corporate authorities in the case of a municipality; and the appropriate body authorized to provide for expenditures of its funds in the case of any other unit of government.

(i) "Labor organization" means any organization in which public employees participate and which exists for the purpose, in whole or in part, of dealing with a public employer concerning wages, hours, and other terms and conditions of employment, including the settlement of grievances.

(j) "Managerial employee" means an individual who is engaged predominantly in executive and management functions and is charged with the responsibility of directing the effectuation of such management policies and practices.

(k) "Peace officer" means, for the purposes of this Act only, any persons who have been or are hereafter appointed to a police force, department or agency and sworn or commissioned to perform police duties, except the following persons shall not be included: part-time police officers, special police officers, auxiliary police as defined by Section 3-6-5 of the Illinois Municipal Code, night watchmen, "merchant police", temporary employees, traffic guards or wardens, civilian parking meter and parking facilities personnel or other individuals specially appointed to aid or direct traffic at or near schools or public functions or to aid in civil defense or disaster, parking enforcement employees who are not commissioned as peace officers and who are not armed and who are not routinely expected to effect arrests, parking lot attendants, clerks and dispatchers or other civilian employees of a police department who are not routinely expected to effect arrests, or elected officials.

(l) "Person" includes one or more individuals, labor organizations, public employees, associations, corporations, legal representatives, trustees, trustees in bankruptcy, receivers, or the State of Illinois or any political subdivision of the State or governing body, *but does not include the General Assembly of the State of Illinois or any individual employed by the General Assembly of the State of Illinois.*

(m) "Professional employee" means any employee engaged in work predominantly intellectual and varied in character

New matter indicated by italics - deletions by strikeout.

APPENDIX D.   Illinois Collective Bargaining Bill.

PUBLIC ACT 85-1032

rather than routine mental, manual, mechanical or physical work; involving the consistent exercise of discretion and adjustment in its performance; of such a character that the output produced or the result accomplished cannot be standardized in relation to a given period of time; and requiring advanced knowledge in a field of science or learning customarily acquired by a prolonged course of specialized intellectual instruction and study in an institution of higher learning or a hospital, as distinguished from a general academic education or from apprenticeship or from training in the performance of routine mental, manual or physical processes; or any employee who has completed the courses of specialized intellectual instruction and study prescribed above and is performing related work under the supervision of a professional person to qualify to become a professional employee as defined above.

(n) "Public employee" or "employee", for the purposes of this Act, means any individual employed by a public employer, including interns and residents at public hospitals, but excluding all of the following: *employees of the General Assembly of the State of Illinois;* elected officials; executive heads of a department; members of boards or commissions; employees of any agency, board or commission created by this statute; employees appointed to State positions of a temporary or emergency nature; all employees of school districts and higher education institutions; managerial employees; short-term employees; confidential employees; independent contractors; and supervisors except as provided in this Act.

Notwithstanding Section 9, subsection (c), nor any other provisions of this Act, all peace officers with the rank of sergeant or above in municipalities with more than 1,000,000 inhabitants shall be excluded from this Act.

(o) "Public employer" or "employer" means the State of Illinois; any political subdivision of the State, unit of local government or school district; authorities including departments, divisions, bureaus, boards, commissions or other agencies of the foregoing entities; and any person acting within the scope of his or her authority, express or implied, on behalf of such entities in dealing with its employees; provided, however, that the term "Public employer" or "employer" as used in this Act does not mean and shall not include *the General Assembly of the State of Illinois and* educational employers or employers as defined in the "Illinois Educational Labor Relations Act" enacted by the 83rd General Assembly as now or hereafter amended. County boards and county sheriffs shall be designated as joint or co-employers of county peace officers appointed under the authority of a county sheriff. Nothing herein shall be construed to prevent the State Board or the Local Board from determining that employers are joint or co-employers.

(p) "Security employee" means an employee who is responsible for the supervision and control of inmates at correctional facilities, and would also include other non-security employees in bargaining units having the majority of employees being responsible for the supervision and control of inmates at correctional facilities.

(q) "Short-term employee" is an employee who is employed for less that two consecutive calendar quarters during a calendar year and who does not have a reasonable assurance

New matter indicated by italics -- deletions by strikeout.

APPENDIX D. Illinois Collective Bargaining Bill.

PUBLIC ACT 85-1032

that he or she will be rehired by the same employer for the same service in a subsequent calendar year.

(r) "Supervisor" is an employee whose principal work is substantially different from that of his subordinates and who has authority, in the interest of the employer, to hire, transfer, suspend, lay off, recall, promote, discharge, direct, reward, or discipline employees, or to adjust their grievances, or to effectively recommend such action, if the exercise of such authority is not of a merely routine or clerical nature, but requires the consistent use of independent judgment. Except with respect to police employment, the term "supervisor" includes only those individuals who devote a preponderance of their employment time to exercising such authority State supervisors notwithstanding. In addition, in determining supervisory status in police employment, rank shall not be determinative. The Board shall consider, as evidence of bargaining unit inclusion or exclusion, the common law enforcement policies and relationships between police officer ranks and certification under applicable civil service law, ordinances, personnel codes or Division 2.1 of Article 10 of the Illinois Municipal Code, as amended from time to time, but these factors shall not be the sole or predominant factors considered by the Board in determining police supervisory status.

Notwithstanding the provisions of the above paragraph, in determining supervisory status in fire fighter employment, no fire fighter shall be excluded as a supervisor who has established representation rights under Section 9 of this Act. Further, in new fire fighter units, employees shall consist of fire fighters of the rank of company officer and below; provided, if a company officer otherwise qualifies as a supervisor pursuant to the above paragraph, he or she shall not be included in the fire fighter unit; provided further, if there is no rank between that of chief and the highest company officer, the employer may designate a position on each shift as a Shift Commander and the persons occupying such positions shall be supervisors. All other ranks above that of company officer shall be supervisors.

(s) (1) "Unit" means a class of jobs or positions which are held by employees whose collective interests may suitably be represented by a labor organization for collective bargaining. Except with respect to non-State fire fighters and paramedics employed by fire departments and fire protection districts, non-State peace officers and peace officers in the State Department of State Police, a bargaining unit determined by the Board shall not include both employees and supervisors, or supervisors only, except as provided in subsection (s)(2) below and except for bargaining units in existence on the effective date of this Act. With respect to non-State fire fighters and paramedics employed by fire departments and fire protection districts, non-State peace officers and peace officers in the State Department of State Police, a bargaining unit determined by the Board shall not include both supervisors and nonsupervisors, or supervisors only, except as provided in subsection (s) (2) below and except for bargaining units in existence on the effective date of this amendatory Act of 1985. A bargaining unit determined by the Board to contain peace officers shall contain no employees other than peace

New matter indicated by italics - deletions by strikeout.

APPENDIX D.   Illinois Collective Bargaining Bill.

PUBLIC ACT 85-1032

officers unless otherwise agreed to by the employer and the labor organization or labor organizations involved.

(2) Notwithstanding the exclusion of supervisors fro bargaining units as provided in subsection (s)(1), a publi employer may agree to permit its supervisory employees to form bargaining units and may bargain with such units. The Act shall apply in the event that the public employer chooses to bargain pursuant to this subsection.

(Ch. 48, par. 1605)

Sec. 5. Illinois Labor Relations Boards. (a) There is created the Illinois State Labor Relations Board ("State Board") which shall have jurisdiction over collective bargaining matters between employee organizations and the State of Illinois, *excluding the General Assembly of the State of Illinois,* between employee organizations and units of local government and school districts with a population not in excess of 1 million persons, and between employee organizations and the Regional Transportation Authority. The State Board shall consist of 3 members appointed by the Governor, with the advice and consent of the Senate. The Governor shall appoint to the State Board only persons who have had a minimum of 5 years of experience directly related to labor and employment relations in representing public employers, private employers or labor organizations; or teaching labor or employment relations; or administering executive orders or regulations applicable to labor or employment relations. At the time of his or her appointment, each member of the State Board shall be an Illinois resident. The Governor shall designate one member to serve as the Chairman of the State Board. The Chairman shall initially be appointed for a term of two years. The second member shall serve for a term of 3 years, and the third member shall serve a term of 4 years. Each subsequent member shall be appointed for a term of 4 years. Upon expiration of the term of office of any appointive member, that member shall continue to serve until a successor shall be appointed and qualified. In case of a vacancy, a successor shall be appointed to serve for the unexpired portion of the term. The terms of members shall commence on the 4th Monday in January of the year they are appointed except that if the Senate is not in session at the time the initial appointments are made, the Governor shall make temporary appointments in the same manner successors are appointed to fill vacancies. A temporary appointment shall remain in effect no longer than 20 calendar days after the commencement of the next Senate session.

(b) There is created the Illinois Local Labor Relations Board ("Local Board") which shall have jurisdiction over collective bargaining agreement matters between employee organizations and units of local government with a population in excess of 1 million persons, but excluding the Regional Transportation Authority. The Local Board shall consist of the Chairman of the State Board and two additional members, one appointed by the Mayor of the City of Chicago and one appointed by the President of the Cook County Board of Commissioners. Appointees to the Local Board must have had a minimum of 5 years of experience directly related to labor and employment relations in representing public employers, private employers or labor organizations; or teaching labor or employment relations; or administering executive orders or regulations applicable to labor or employment relations. Each

New matter indicated by italics - deletions by strikeout.

APPENDIX D.   Illinois Collective Bargaining Bill.

PUBLIC ACT 85-1032

member of the Local Board shall be an Illinois resident at the time of his or her appointment. The Chairman of the State Board shall serve as the Chairman of the Local Board. The member initially appointed by the President of the Cook County Board shall serve for a term of 3 years and the member appointed by the Mayor of the City of Chicago shall serve for a term of 4 years. Each subsequent member shall be appointed for a term of 4 years. Upon expiration of the term of office of any appointive member, the member shall continue to serve until a successor shall be appointed and qualified. In the case of a vacancy, a successor shall be appointed by the applicable appointive authority to serve for the unexpired portion of the term. The terms of members shall commence on the 4th Monday in January of the year they are appointed.

(c) Two members of each governing board shall at all times constitute a quorum. A vacancy on a governing board does not impair the right of the 2 remaining members to exercise all of the powers of that board. Each governing board shall adopt an official seal which shall be judicially noticed. The salary of the Chairman shall be $50,000 per year, or as set by the Compensation Review Board, whichever is greater, and that of the other members of the State Board and the Local Board shall be $45,000 per year, or as set by the Compensation Review Board, whichever is greater.

(d) No member shall hold any other public office or be employed as a labor or management representative by the State or any political subdivision of the State or of any department or agency thereof, or actively represent or act on behalf of an employer or an employee organization or an employer in labor relations matters. Any member of the State Board may be removed from office by the Governor for inefficiency, neglect of duty, misconduct or malfeasance in office, and for no other cause, and only upon notice and hearing. Any member of the Local Board may be removed from office by the applicable appointive authority for inefficiency, neglect of duty, misconduct or malfeasance in office, and for no other cause, and only upon notice and hearing.

(e) Each governing board at the end of every State fiscal year shall make a report in writing to the Governor and the General Assembly, stating in detail the work it has done in hearing and deciding cases and otherwise.

(f) In order to accomplish the objectives and carry out the duties prescribed by this Act, the governing boards or their authorized designees may hold elections to determine whether a labor organization has majority status; investigate and attempt to resolve or settle charges of unfair labor practices; hold hearings in order to carry out its functions; develop and effectuate appropriate impasse resolution procedures for purposes of resolving labor disputes; require the appearance of witnesses and the production of evidence on any matter under inquiry; and administer oaths and affirmations. The governing boards shall sign and report in full an opinion in every case which they decide.

(g) Each governing board may appoint or employ an executive director, attorneys, hearing officers, mediators, fact-finders, arbitrators, and such other employees as they deem necessary to perform their functions. The governing boards shall prescribe the duties and qualifications of such persons appointed and, subject to the annual appropriation,

New matter indicated by italics - deletions by strikeout.

APPENDIX D.   Illinois Collective Bargaining Bill.

PUBLIC ACT 85-1032

fix their compensation and provide for reimbursement of actual and necessary expenses incurred in the performance of their duties.

(h) Each governing board shall exercise general supervision over all attorneys which it employs and over the other persons employed to provide necessary support services for such attorneys. The governing boards shall have final authority in respect to complaints brought pursuant to this Act.

(i) The following rules and regulations shall be adopted by the governing boards meeting in joint session: (1) procedural rules and regulations which shall govern all Board proceedings; (2) procedures for election of exclusive bargaining representatives pursuant to Section 9, except for the determination of appropriate bargaining units; (3) appointment of counsel pursuant to subsection (k) of this Section.

(j) Rules and regulations may be adopted, amended or rescinded only upon a vote of four of the five members of the State Board and the Local Board meeting in joint session. The adoption, amendment or rescission of rules and regulations shall be in conformity with the requirements of the Illinois Administrative Procedure Act.

(k) The Governing Boards in joint session shall promulgate rules and regulations providing for the appointment of attorneys or other Board representatives to represent persons in unfair labor practice proceedings before a governing board. The regulations governing appointment shall require the applicant to demonstrate an inability to pay for or inability to otherwise provide for adequate representation before a governing board. Such rules must also provide that an attorney may not be appointed in cases which, in the opinion of a Board, are clearly without merit.

(l) The Chairman of the governing boards shall serve as Chairman of a joint session of the governing boards. Attendance of at least one member from each governing board, in addition to the Chairman, shall constitute a quorum at a joint session. The governing boards shall meet in joint session within 60 days of the effective date of this Act and at least annually thereafter.

(Ch. 48, par. 1606)

Sec. 6. Right to organize and bargain collectively; exclusive representation; and fair share arrangements. (a) Employees of the State and any political subdivision of the State, *excluding employees of the General Assembly of the State of Illinois*, have, and are protected in the exercise of, the right of self-organization, and may form, join or assist any labor organization, to bargain collectively through representatives of their own choosing on questions of wages, hours and other conditions of employment, not excluded by Section 4 of this Act, and to engage in other concerted activities not otherwise prohibited by law for the purposes of collective bargaining or other mutual aid or protection, free from interference, restraint or coercion. Employees also have, and are protected in the exercise of, the right to refrain from participating in any such concerted activities. Employees may be required, pursuant to the terms of a lawful fair share agreement, to pay a fee which shall be their proportionate share of the costs of the collective bargaining process, contract administration and pursuing matters

New matter indicated by italics - deletions by strikeout.

APPENDIX D.   Illinois Collective Bargaining Bill.

affecting wages, hours and other conditions of employment as defined in Section 3(g).

(b) Nothing in this Act prevents an employee from presenting a grievance to the employer and having the grievance heard and settled without the intervention of an employee organization; provided that the exclusive bargaining representative is afforded the opportunity to be present at such conference and that any settlement made shall not be inconsistent with the terms of any agreement in effect between the employer and the exclusive bargaining representative.

(c) A labor organization designated by the Board as the representative of the majority of public employees in an appropriate unit in accordance with the procedures herein or recognized by a public employer as the representative of the majority of public employees in an appropriate unit is the exclusive representative for the employees of such unit for the purpose of collective bargaining with respect to rates of pay, wages, hours and other conditions of employment not excluded by Section 4 of this Act.

(d) Labor organizations recognized by a public employer as the exclusive representative or so designated in accordance with the provisions of this Act are responsible for representing the interests of all public employees in the unit. Nothing herein shall be construed to limit an exclusive representative's right to exercise its discretion to refuse to process grievances of employees that are unmeritorious.

(e) When a collective bargaining agreement is entered into with an exclusive representative, it may include in the agreement a provision requiring employees covered by the agreement who are not members of the organization to pay their proportionate share of the costs of the collective bargaining process, contract administration and pursuing matters affecting wages, hours and conditions of employment, as defined in Section 3 (g), but not to exceed the amount of dues uniformly required of members. The organization shall certify to the employer the amount constituting each nonmember employee's proportionate share which shall not exceed dues uniformly required of members. In such case, the proportionate share payment in this Section shall be deducted by the employer from the earnings of the nonmember employees and paid to the employee organization.

(f) Only the exclusive representative may negotiate provisions in a collective bargaining agreement providing for the payroll deduction of labor organization dues, fair share payment, initiation fees and assessments. Except as provided in subsection (e) of this Section, any such deductions shall only be made upon an employee's written authorization, and continued until revoked in writing in the same manner or until the termination date of an applicable collective bargaining agreement. Such payments shall be paid to the exclusive representative.

(g) Agreements containing a fair share agreement must safeguard the right of nonassociation of employees based upon bona fide religious tenets or teachings of a church or religious body of which such employees are members. Such employees may be required to pay an amount equal to their fair share, determined under a lawful fair share agreement, to a nonreligious charitable organization mutually agreed

APPENDIX D.   Illinois Collective Bargaining Bill.

---

upon by the employees affected and the exclusive bargaining representative to which such employees would otherwise pay such service fee. If the affected employees and the bargaining representative are unable to reach an agreement on the matter, the Board may establish an approved list of charitable organizations to which such payments may be made.

Section 2. This amendatory Act of 1988 is intended to specify that employees of the General Assembly of the State of Illinois, including but not limited to employees of the Joint Committee on Legislative Support Services or any legislative support services agency listed in the Legislative Commission Reorganization Act of 1984, are excluded from the Illinois Public Labor Relations Act; that all rights provided for under the Illinois Public Labor Relations Act, including a right to file a petition under Section 9 of that Act, do not apply and were at no time applicable to such employees, notwithstanding the filing of any petition, or any other document or material, with the Illinois State Labor Relations Board, by or in behalf of any of such employees, and that the General Assembly of the State of Illinois is not subject to, and was at no time subject to, the jurisdiction of the Illinois State Labor Relations Board.

Section 3. This Act takes effect upon becoming a law.

Passed in the General Assembly June 30, 1988.

Approved July 1, 1988.

Effective July 1, 1988.

Index